Digital Contagions

Steve Jones
General Editor

Vol. 44

The Digital Formations series is part of the Peter Lang Media and Communication list.
Every volume is peer reviewed and meets
the highest quality standards for content and production.

PETER LANG
New York • Bern • Frankfurt • Berlin
Brussels • Vienna • Oxford • Warsaw

Jussi Parikka

Digital Contagions

A Media Archaeology
of Computer Viruses

SECOND EDITION

PETER LANG
New York • Bern • Frankfurt • Berlin
Brussels • Vienna • Oxford • Warsaw

Library of Congress Cataloging-in-Publication Data

Names: Parikka, Jussi, author.
Title: Digital contagions: a media archaeology of computer viruses / Jussi Parikka.
Description: Second edition | New York: Peter Lang, 2016.
Series: Digital formations; vol. 44 | ISSN 1526-3169
Includes bibliographical references and index.
Identifiers: LCCN 2016015060 | ISBN 978-1-4331-3232-2 (paperback: alk. paper)
ISBN 978-1-4539-1868-5 (ebook pdf) | ISBN 978-1-4331-3577-4 (epub)
ISBN 978-1-4331-3578-1 (mobi)
Subjects: LCSH: Computer security. | Computer viruses.
Computer networks—Security measures.
Classification: LCC QA76.9.A25 P376 2016 | DDC 005.8—dc23
LC record available at https://lccn.loc.gov/2016015060

Bibliographic information published by **Die Deutsche Nationalbibliothek.**
Die Deutsche Nationalbibliothek lists this publication in the "Deutsche
Nationalbibliografie"; detailed bibliographic data are available
on the Internet at http://dnb.d-nb.de/.

The paper in this book meets the guidelines for permanence and durability
of the Committee on Production Guidelines for Book Longevity
of the Council of Library Resources.

© 2016 Peter Lang Publishing, Inc., New York
29 Broadway, 18th floor, New York, NY 10006
www.peterlang.com

Printed in the United States of America

CONTENTS

ACKNOWLEDGMENTS

To make a book happen, a lot of things need to be in place: these range from institutions to funding and, importantly, to intellectual networks and friendships. This is a second revised edition of the book that came out in 2007, but I will extend many of the thanks across these 10 years. The book itself has changed in many ways; I have added text, and taken out some; I have edited and revised, fine-tuned, tweaked, and added some new sections, including the Afterword.

As for thank yous, I am grateful to the Finnish Cultural Foundation, Emil Aaltonen Foundation, Jenny & Antti Wihuri Foundation, and also to the TIESU-project, funded by the Research Program for Advanced Technology Policy (Proact), the Ministry of Trade and Industry, and the National Technology Agency (Tekes) for providing support for the initial research in 2003–2007. Institutionally, I want to thank my alma mater, Cultural History and also Digital Culture at the University of Turku (Finland). A major part of this work was written "in-transit," and I want to extend a thank you for their hospitality to the departments of Media Studies at the University of Amsterdam (Thomas Elsaesser) and the Berlin Humboldt University (Wolfgang Ernst). For granting the time and the possibility to do the editing, revisions, and additions, I thank my current institution, the University of Southampton (Winchester School of Art), for the support.

There are many individuals to thank. Hannu Salmi, Matthew Fuller, and Jukka Sihvonen gave continuously invaluable advice. Charlie Gere and Tiziana Terranova are to be commended for their input at a late stage of the work. Others who should not be forgotten include, in no particular order, Raine Koskimaa, Tony D. Sampson, Sakari Ollitervo, Pasi Väliaho, Matleena Kalajoki, Katve-Kaisa Kontturi, Ilona Hongisto, Milla Tiainen, Joss Hands, Teemu Taira, Henri Terho, Geert Lovink, Olli Pyyhtinen, Floris Paalman, Ryan Bishop, Ed D'Souza, Seb Franklin, Michael Goddard, Grant Bollmer, Yigit Soncul, Ebru Yetiskin, Olcay Öztürk, Burak Arikan, Joseph Nechvatal, Stefan Höltgen, Tero Karppi, Petri Paju, Petri Saarikoski, Tanja Sihvonen, Jaakko Suominen, Silja Laine, Maija Mäkikalli, Mikko Hyppönen, and the various people I interviewed for the book.

I am grateful to Sean Cubitt for his advice and friendship over the years and for writing the preface for this new edition. And a special thanks to Dr Jane Birkin for the help with the index and our conversations about media archaeology.

The people at Peter Lang were always very helpful. Mary Savigar planted the idea in my head about a new edition, and she deserves special thanks, as does Steve Jones, editor of the Digital Formations series.

***

Parts of this work have already been discussed in earlier texts, especially in the following:

"Denials of Service" in *No Software, Just Services*, edited by Irina Kaldrack and Martina Leeker. Lüneburg: meson press, 2015, 103–111.

"Digital Monsters, Binary Aliens—Computer Viruses, Capitalism and the Flow of Information." *Fibreculture*, issue 4, <http://journal.fibreculture.org/issue4/issue4_parikka.html>.

"The Universal Viral Machine—Bits, Parasites and the Media Ecology of Network Culture." *CTheory—An International Journal of Theory, Technology and Culture*, December 15, 2005, <http://www.ctheory.net/articles.aspx?id=500>.

"Viral Noise and the (Dis)Order of the Digital Culture." *M/C Journal of Media/Culture*, <http://journal.media-culture.org.au/0501/05-parikka.php>.

"Contagion and Repetition—On the Viral Logic of Network Culture." *Ephemera: Theory & Politics in Organization*, <http://www.ephemeraweb.org/>.

PREFACE

Sean Cubitt

There is a disturbing etymological puzzle underlying the title. "Contagion" appears to be a late fourteenth-century coinage, appearing in the wake of the Black Death in mediaeval French and Middle English, from the Latin roots "con," meaning "with," and "tangere," the active verb "to touch." The puzzle comes from another word we associate at least equally closely with electronic media, "contact." Here the root words are the same, with the only exception that "contact" comes from the passive form "tactum," "to be touched." Oddly, most people probably feel positive connotations about "contact," but negative connotations from "contagion." We have had six hundred years to develop these connotations, and yet there remains a nub of their origins: the contagious principle of something coming to touch us or to touch us together is more subjective than the principle of contact, where any two things could be brought together. The usefulness of the electrical contact as a major metaphor, dating back through early electrical experiments and familiar from the literature of the pioneering days of motoring and aviation, gives it both a certain objectivity and a sense of familiarity that we bring into the realm of communicative contact. Not so contagion, even though it is very close, at least etymologically.

The spark that leaps across the spark plug or the telegraphist's key has given us a metaphor of life since Mary Shelley's *Frankenstein*, and in that same moment opened up the contact to contagion, a reversal of perspective that reveals, as Parikka emphasizes, the contagion in every contact, the toxic active in every passive. "Something there is that doesn't love a wall," as Robert Frost observed. Something sees the structural forms on which communication depends as a barrier too many, a taxonomic frontier between orchard and pine, in Frost's poem, that might as well divide on any arbitrary or lethal imaginary line, or indeed sender from receiver, signal from channel, signal from noise. To put in touch is to infect, and so we put in place immunological barriers, which are not merely hygienic but apotropaic. The very structures we create to enable communication are themselves barriers to communication. Yet if we want to touch the world, we must be touched by it; and when we touch, the world presses back; and that mutual pressure, that mutual permeation, is communication, and involves us opening up, and therefore taking risks.

Where there is an etymological "touch," there are etymological fingers. The "digital" of digital technology derives from counting on our fingers, an action in which touching finger to finger enumerates the external world while also affirming reflexively the counting self and the counting body in an act that both unites and divides the counter as it unites and divides the counter and the counted, which now occur as tactile sensations as much as numbers abstracted from the welter of the world. To say such etymologies "derive" is to admit that it is *une dérive*, an errant word that has meandered away from its origin and taken on the connotations of its erring. As much as this wandering includes the fingerprints it has left and, as Parikka argues, implies the prints it might multiply into the future, the double touching of *Digital Contagions* implies a phenomenology, a bodily interaction with artefacts of the past that, as it multiplies sensations, multiplies the subjectivities they conjure into being. The more swiftly the digital operates, the closer it comes to prestidigitation.

Parikka invites us into an adventure in history and ideas about history through an archaeological method that has two major principles. On the one hand, it asserts the right of evidence to exist, whatever the tidal movements of societies, polities, economies, and cultures bearing on around it. It is not only that, since Hegel, the idea of history has implied its movement toward some goal, but that our most persuasive historians of left and right, from Giovanni Arrighi to Niall Ferguson, seek out from the storm of events some sense of coherence. The media archaeologist is bound to insist that even if the world is moved towards mechanisation or electrification, atomisation or flow, the individual instance of mediation has its own right to exist, whether it fits or not with the grander orchestrations of the times. In the fury and the mire of human and nonhuman life, history is an afterthought: a post hoc rationalisation. In the midst of things, *in medias res*, in the daily operations of media and mediation, there is no such teleology, only the battering of the need to communicate and the barriers that the very act of communication throws in its way.

Rather than the grand march of history, there is then only the ongoing cataclysm of events, that storm of wreckage Benjamin's angel witnesses piling up at its feet as it is blown backwards out of paradise. *Digital Contagions* traces that ongoing cataclysm as the very condition in and through which we construct as best we may the connections from which we might discover some mode of becoming human, and not only human. Parikka suggests a tactical, minor politics of life, not as it is, but, as he cites AI maven Chris Langton, "life-as-it-could-be," a life profoundly interconnected with technologies of mediation. Language, William Burroughs opined, is a virus: like a virus it has no aim but to replicate itself and needs to infect a host in order to do so, even if in the process, like a virus, it makes the host organism sicken. Our technologies of communication operate in much the same way, despite us, beyond us, with a life that includes and traverses but equally happily abandons us. At the same time, these contagions have radically enlightening side-effects, as it were, rational hallucinations we would otherwise never have been capable of, while they are not in themselves ultra-efficient, but mutated by their contacts, becoming internally noisy and changed, otherwise then themselves, so that their purity is always endangered. If media contaminate us, we contaminate them, and in that noisy mutuality we encounter each other in ever unpredictable communicative events, mutually implicated in a zigzag nomadism through time that constructs time itself in its conjoint wanderings.

Though there is in this book a fine history and archaeology of the computer virus, there is also a profound contamination of efficient models of communication in favour of codependent mediations between human and nonhuman agents that questions the very boundaries we have established between ourselves and our technological and natural others. Parikka offers us the alien as integral to any sense of self, the strange in every familiarity, the resistance of that which makes us social to the forms of the social that we have erected to control it. You will not read this book without being infected.

INTRODUCTION

The General Accident of Digital Network Culture

As usual, everything negative remains untold, yet it is, interestingly enough, always there, in an embryonic form. How is it possible to state that technologies are being developed, without any attempt being made at learning about the very specific accidents that go with them?[1]

—Paul Virilio (1999)

Any information system of sufficient complexity will inevitably become infected with viruses: viruses generated from within itself.[2]

—Neal Stephenson, *Snow Crash* (1992)

Disease and Technology

The history of media and technology is a history of accidents. Things break down almost as often as they actually do what they are supposed to do. We fantasize about machines of ultimate communication and functionality, but the reality is different and goes back to a variety of technologies of movement, communications, and transmission. The train introduced the train accident, with the boat came the boating accident, and inherent in several techniques of data storage, such as papyrus, paper, and film, is the always present possibility of the erasure of information.[3] Media are always embodied, and this embodiment is always related to the rather simple physics; things decay and rot; any communication medium is vulnerable to passing of time as much as the speed that might bring about a crash. One could, indeed, write a whole shadow history of technology through how it does not work; how it breaks down; how it frustrates and messes things up; how it disappoints and does not meet up with the expectations that are always rather sublime compared to the mundane everyday. Already the telegraph, the early network technology of the nineteenth century, was vulnerable to such problems as perceived in 1846 by Dr. Barbay, a semaphore enthusiast:

> No, the electric telegraph is not a sound invention. It will always be at the mercy of the slightest disruption, wild youths, drunkards, bums, etc. (…) The electric telegraph meets those destructive elements with only a few meters of wire over which supervision is impossible. A single man could, without being seen, cut the telegraph wires leading to Paris, and in twenty-four hours cut in ten different places the wires of the same line, without being arrested.[4]

As technological accidents have a history, so do diseases. Causes of diseases, which since the nineteenth century have been mainly recognized as harmful minuscule actors, infectious bacteria and viruses, affect the very basics of human societies. They accompany the so-called human world as the animals we choose to live with. And diseases are themselves conditioned by a variety of social mechanisms; the spatio-temporal occurrence of a disease, an outbreak, is always set in a field of definitions of causes, of sanitation measures, of security and other ways to control the territory. Diseases tell a story of society. Diseases are symptomatic of the ways cultures interact. They reveal paths of communication and commerce, of interaction and cultural hierarchies, which form the networks of a society: what affects what, who frequents whom and where, and so forth. Diseases *expose*.

The improvement of road networks from late antiquity exposed populations to a growing number of infectors. The Silk Road was such a network of goods as well as germs, from China to Europe and back. However, a major change occurred with urbanization, industrialization, and the new transmission channels of steam ships, railroads, and airplanes, which connected people and germs more efficiently than ever. The Black Death that infected Europe in the mid-fourteenth century was to a large extent an expression of the new paths of communication and transmission paved by the Mongol empire, as well as the new ship routes connecting the Mediterranean to the northern parts of Europe. In the nineteenth century, steam in the form of locomotives and transoceanic ships helped microorganisms to create a single, near-global disease pool.[5] Transmission and communication have always defined and transformed geopolitical boundaries, and any consideration of the global should be aware of the role germs play; geopolitics can be read through diseases and their paths. Ships are still in modern times the clandestine transport vehicles of diseases—whether the plague of psychoanalysis, as Freud quipped to Jung entering New York harbor, or the mythical figure of Count Dracula in Bram Stoker's novel of 1897.[6]

Transmission and communication come with a cost—an anxiety of established borders becoming all mixed up and trespassed. At the end of the twentieth century, another form of technological accident caused an immense amount of public anxiety. It seemed to combine these lineages of technological accidents and disease patterns and produce a truly novel situation. Computer viruses and worms, as the latest occurrences in the history of diseases, caused something that was referred to even as "hysteria"—the key sexed disease of the previous *fin de siècle*. Viruses have become a sign of the *fin de millennium*, indications of the uncontrolled threats of late modern technological mass society alongside a range of other threats, such as Chernobyl, AIDS, and Ebola. Digital viruses threaten to turn digital memory banks into "terminal gibberish."[7] As Wolfgang Schivelbusch notes, before industrialization, accidents seemed to refer to "coincidences" that attacked from the outside, usually in the form of natural catastrophes, such as storms and floods. With industrial machines, the accident became an internal problem as technologies seemed to potentially turn on themselves as a result of their own power.[8] The recent decades of global technological infrastructures have seen a range of technological accidents, perceived as risks to be minimized and managed, signified, and valorized in the (mass) media system (in the traditional definition of print media, television, and, for example, cinema). The utopia of the global village[9] and the vast number of accounts celebrating networks and cyberspaces as the key utopian (non)places of recent decades showed their flipsides to be a dystopia of global risks and accidents.

Digital Contagions is a story of accidents but also an analysis of the historical conditions that made it possible to conceive and program such an entity as a "computer virus" or a "digital worm." It is an attempt to write a media archaeology of computer and network accidents. As such, it asks: What are the material and incorporeal conditions of existence for such oxymoronic entities of the network age? Why does it make sense to talk of computer viruses, as if the computer and the network were alive and vulnerable to parasites—a

seeming force of nature but programmed by humans? *Digital Contagions* com-
plexifies the technological definition and understanding of computer viruses
through historical source work as well as theoretical arguments. It participates
in the past years of software studies discussions about algorithmic culture but
by way of a media archaeology of accidents.[10] Throughout the book there is a
very strong tendency to historicize, argue through historical sources, and use
history (in the sense of archaeology) as a method of situated knowledge: to
pinpoint strategies of knowledge as historical and contingent and to analyze
within a meshwork of perspectival positions that resist "categorical a priori
condition[s] of knowledge."[11]

Computer viruses become read as part of the global digital culture, although
through a specific source base that is mostly Anglo-American, consisting of
popular cultural discourse, computer texts aimed at the general public, computer science texts, and security discourse. Instead of offering an insight to
only the most recent events, I want to look at the early emergence of the
issue, in the midst of the era when computers started to become more widespread and the discussion concerning networks was emerging, that is, mostly

Figure 1. During the past twenty years, various software and art projects have addressed computer viruses as a curious aesthetic and media cultural phenomenon. One such example was the
Biennale.py net art virus from 2001, which was displayed on T-shirts and sold on CD-ROMs
($1,500 each). With the virus, computer code became a media performance. (Image reproduced
with the permission, credits: Eva and Franco Mattes, Biennale.py, 2001, Computer virus.)

the 1970s through to the 1990s. As I argue in this book, I see that the crucial issues, discussions, and positions concerning viruses and worms were already visible before the mid-1990s, which is why I want to underscore these earlier threads and lineages in this discourse network.[12] This means that I focus primarily on issues before the rise of the popular Internet in the mid-1990s, even if, as I argue below, it would be difficult to ignore the recent National Security Administration (NSA) revelations by Edward Snowden or the massive preparations by various national defense departments and industries for cyberwar.

Digital Contagions analyzes the media archaeology of this specific computer accident as a symptom of a more abstract cultural diagram. Computer viruses and worms and other related software are not, then, antithetical to digital communications but, as the book argues, at the very center of network culture. Neither is the digital virus solely an internal computer problem. It is a symptomatic part of security cultures before and after 9/11, with the emergence of digital culture, the worries of new social dilemmas, and networking as the key reference point in discussions of computer science. The virus is also an expression of the media ecology and the so-called biological diagram of the computer, where the biological sciences are actively interfaced with computer science, often with a special emphasis on bottom-up emergence.[13]

Methodologically, I am following Michel Foucault's ideas of (cultural) archaeology and genealogy.[14] I proceed in the same manner when understanding the primary question to be one of cultural mechanisms, or forces, that give birth to the myriad ways in which we program, discuss, debate, control, insulate, and police also software. The question is not so much what a computer virus is, but how it came to be what it is. This historical questioning requires that we focus on the conditions of a thing, not its essence.[15] In other words, what made computer viruses and like part of a computer problem, what gave rise to malicious software, and what other sorts of things does this general determination hide? What made computer viruses intelligible—in discourse and in practice— is a rather fundamental question that one could ask of many other formations of software too, especially the ones we take for granted. Hence, media archaeological excavation is committed to seeking the conditions of existence of cultural phenomena and the interplay between continuities and discontinuities. The theoretical underpinnings are always developed in a perspective, where temporality is seen as a polymorphous and overlapping layering, a coexistence of multiple temporal fields of longer and shorter durations.[16]

There are various stages to the emergence of self-reproducing programs, a theme that predates the issue of computer viruses. In the same manner as viruses can be said to be a possibility enabled by the computer architecture developed by John von Neumann,[17] they are a part of the network culture of the late twentieth century, sprouting during the early years of computing in the 1940s, taking a more familiar shape since the 1960s and 1970s as networking became a key paradigm for computing, and bursting into bloom during the 1980s and early 1990s with personal computers, the Internet, and the consumerization of digital culture. My main temporal emphasis is on the period between the von Neumann machines ideated around the end of the 1940s and start of the 1950s and the early years of the popular Internet in the 1990s. A story of networks is one of the Cold War, and similarly the story of software is one of changing security emphases, techniques, and containments. Software is a continuation of war by other means—but not merely war: it is also a story of software as part of emergence of the corporate culture based on digital communications, securitization of business transactions as well as the private sphere, and implementation of new ways of thinking about the computer as a hub of activity that indeed sometimes even fed part of discussions of artificial life.

I insist on talking about viruses and such as a form of a general accident of digital culture. But, surely, they are not merely accidents and not even accidental because they are programmed by people with specific intensions in mind and goals they want to reach? Indeed, there's more to the term "accident." An accident, as Paul Virilio writes, is not in this context intended to mean the opposite of absolute and necessary, as Aristotelian metaphysics has maintained. Instead, accidents are an inherent part of an entity. Accidents are internal to technologies: "Since the production of any 'substance' is simultaneously the production of *a typical accident*, breakdown or failure is less the deregulation of production than *the production of a specific failure, or even a partial or total destruction*."[18] For Virilio, the generality of the contemporary accident stems from its specific temporality. Key contemporary accidents, whether the 9/11 attacks on U.S. soil, the 1987 stock exchange crash, the Gulf wars since the 1990s, and the financial meltdown since 2008 are events that touch the whole globe, even if with differing effects. Such incidents of simultaneity and ubiquity are illustrative of the cybernetic networks of global scale that take over the spatial world of human perception.[19] Computer accidents share some similar features. Even if computer errors such as viruses can be argued to be just a *specific* form of technological accident, they reveal a whole bundle of issues having to do with security, accidents, and risk management embedded in issues of globalization, digitalization, and media culture. Yet, "general" does not mean "universal" in the sense that I would claim viruses and worms as the only accidents of network technologies. Instead, we have a bunch of faulty code, bugs, and spam that shows that the viral is merely one situated perspective on the issue. Bots and zombie machines are one further security threat that extends the discussion from viruses to other manners of losing control in networks. Perhaps the control was never really there anyway. As Finn Brunton demonstrates in his excellent book on spam,[20] bots are forms of software that do retain a relation to the human network of spammers and programmers, even if they automate a lot of labor involved. As anyone who is a frequent user of the Internet knows, it is not only for humans. The massive traffic of packets is one thing—one thing you are mostly unaware of, or as Wendy Chun reminds us,[21] we just don't know exactly what our computers are doing at a specific time, despite knowing some of the key theoretical points about them or even understanding programming. But another thing is the various forms of nonhuman agents that we sometimes treat as if humans, or sometimes they just steal that role. Bots do things for us, from floodbots that presented a form of excessive communication, which would have made the grounding figures of Dada proud, to the chat bots and zombie networks that redefine borders of inside and outside in computer culture. With the Internet of Things, a vast range of objects become vulnerable to such a loss of control, from the Jeep on the road to the household appliance[22] to the more geopolitically significant targets, such as gas pumps.[23]

Following Brunton, one could even say that issues such as bots relate to the bigger issue of how "what is available to our robots (computers, sensors, algorithms) is distinct from what's available to us, with our human brains."[24] Software triggers a plethora of issues, some of them even rather fundamentally ontologically and also operationally at the center of digital culture: What is perceivable? What is operational? What is automatable?

As the epigraph to this introduction by the fiction writer Neal Stephenson underlines, accidents can be understood as emergent phenomena on the level of socio-technological processes. Accidents are not external, but *hypertrophical* to the normalized functioning of a technological machine. Accidents do not merely break the rules of a system, but they actually use and bend them to their limit, exposing them along the way. Hence, it is not merely a question of malicious software[25] that is of interest here, but the wider sense in which patterns of virality, contagion, and containment are in operation in digital culture and articulated in relation to security of economic flows, to political issues, and to the representational as well as nonrepresentational materiality of digitality.

Cultural techniques are increasingly digital techniques, whether we are referring to labor done in offices or the huge growth of digital entertainment services or the infrastructure necessary to enable computer networking. Manuel Castells has divided the rise of digital network society into several distinct steps. For Castells, key components within this history of digital culture were the following: new technical paradigms, such as ARPANET (1969); integrated circuits (1971); personal computers (1974–1976); the software revolution, UNIX (1974); TCP/IP-protocols (1973–1978), which made the Internet technologically possible.[26] It is a short technological milestoning, but it provides an understanding of the material discourse networks with which cultural reality is intermingled. The material understanding of culture emphasizes that cultural meanings, articulations, perceptions, metaphors, statements, and discourses are not free-floating ideal signs and ideas; they are very deeply rooted in the information channels that make them possible. Meanings and significations happen always also in relation to material situations or *discourse networks*, which connect people, institutions, devices, and so on in a discursive and nondiscursive sphere.

The material characteristics remained immanent to incorporeal and abstract events on the socio-cultural and economic scales. The major crises of capitalism (1973–1975) and Soviet-led statism (1975–1980) coincided with the new technologies of digitality, a trend especially visible as information capitalism, which profited from the deregulation, liberalization, privatization, and globalization of this ascending world order, or "Empire" as Michael Hardt and Antonio Negri named it.[27] In *Empire* they argue that this turn toward information capitalism took place in the 1970s and at the end of the Vietnam War, after which transnational companies spread across the globe, and digital flexibility and information networks expressed the material basis of this new regime. In other words, globally infrastructured networks became the key vectors of power, wealth, and control as the material discourse networks supported by multinational computer business corporations. This infrastructuring spanned from hardware to operating systems and software. As they famously phrased it, "The network itself is the site of both production and circulation,"[28] hinting at the stakes in securing the uninterrupted working of the cross-national communications.

But it does not always take the work of cultural theory to recognize this. Sometimes these stories are told in the plain open and found in the archives. As *Scientific American* wrote in 1986, in the midst of the emerging digital boom and the coming age of the Internet:

This is an age of proliferating connections: among people, among machines, among silicon chips within a machine, among transistors on a silicon chip. Information is processed by networks of chips and communicated through much vaster networks of copper cables and glass fibers by electrons and photons. There are alternatives to such networks: people can travel to meet one another face to face, and they can process data themselves rather than having computers do the job for them. But in most cases these are poor alternatives compared with what it is now possible to accomplish through electronic and photonic connections. As a result functions once carried out by people are increasingly being carried out by systems of electronic and photonic materials.[29]

It is against the backdrop of such valorizations and evaluations that software and also viruses as well as worms emerged; as disruptions of the new era of the networked silicon chip; an accident of information that was often defined in a rather confusing way; as a fear of technological accident that could wipe out massive amounts of data necessary to sustain normal everyday life. The Millennium Bug scare was one feature in this story; uncontrollable, sometimes malicious code another one. Virus was the rupture in the digital dreams of communication, and a rupture in the symbolic framework of the everyday that could tear apart that e-mail, that storage device, that privacy of the mobile device with the multiple levels of personal secrets and corporate communications you carry with you.[30]

***

Digital Contagions consists of three main sections: (I) fear and security, (II) body, and (III) artificial life (ALife). Section I, "Fear Secured: From Bugs to Worms," engages with computer security discourses and practices, especially since the 1970s. Computer viruses appeared in the science fiction novels of the 1970s—for example, David Gerrold's *When HARLIE Was One* (1972) and John Brunner's *The Shockwave Rider* (1975)—but it was in 1983 that Fred Cohen, a computer scientist, engaged in experiments that marked the birth of a more sustained research into the computer science of viruses. Cohen understood the potentially malicious nature of these miniprograms, depicting them as forms of risk and danger, given the increasing reliance of institutions on computer infrastructure in the form of local area networks, plans for larger networks, software production, and so forth. The first chapter analyzes the technological, political, and economic tendencies in computer security, revealing how deeply the definitions of computer worms and viruses are embedded in issues of media, risk society, and (viral) capitalism.

Around 1985–1986, computer viruses reached the public debate for the first time and were from the onset described as "malicious miniprograms" and as threats to national security, international commerce, and the private user. The Pakistani Brain virus of 1986, Jerusalem of 1988, and Datacrime of 1989 were discussed widely in newspapers, but the 1988 Morris worm, or the "Internet worm," as it has also been called, truly alarmed the computing community and parts of the general public, especially in the U.S. It became a topic of TV news and newspaper headlines, and it was discussed for years. Viruses and worms were no longer just self-spreading programs with which to test the coming age of network society; they were also loaded with a plethora of meanings, connotations, and articulations drawn from discourses of disease and disease control, crime, and international politics. Hence, what was only the imagination of some science fiction writers in the mid-1970s gathered a new intensity some ten years later.[31] But fiction was much more than just a premediating shadow; it already articulated alternative insights to viral culture, acting as a sort of speculative design fiction of a computerized future world of nonhuman agents.[32]

In Section II, "Body: Biopolitics of Digital Systems," I give special attention to the virus culture since the 1980s and how a more generic sense of embodiment was mobilized as part of an understanding of security, insides, and outsides. "Viruses" and "virality" became central cultural figures in the sense that tuberculosis had been in the nineteenth century and cancer was in the 1970s.[33] Popular media culture became filled with parasites and viruses from the 1980s onward, pointing toward a new understanding of the openness of the body to its surroundings. The body became a possible vector of diseases that was also articulated together with information circulation. The virus and virality marked a state of liminality where the established borders of identity—whether biological or computational—became leaky. The human immunodeficiency virus (HIV) was at the center of numerous contested articulations concerning the actions, sexualities, gender, and ethnicities of human bodies; the computer virus (or the "computer AIDS," as it was often referred to) inhabited several similar fields of struggle, on which contests over "proper use of computing," "safe hex,"[34] "digital hygiene," and other key enunciations of what the software might operationally mean took place. Consequently, the second section addresses the discourses and practices of immunology, disease, healthy computing, and digital hygienics, particularly as they were expressed in the 1980s. Just as a judge pronouncing the word "guilty" transforms a person into a criminal, the various "pronouncements" of the heavily loaded term "virus," with all its associations, turns technological objects into malicious software, effecting incorporeal transformations.[35] This section, then, adds to the more technological and corporeal themes mapped in the first section, using as its key concept the incorporeal transformations of a material body (of software).

Section III, "Life: Viral Ecologies," expands the biological emphasis in order to ask questions about the media ecology of self-reproducing life in networks. Here I argue that technological evolution and the notion of self-spreading computer programs have much more widespread roots in the cultural history of modernity than the security-oriented notion a computer virus implies. Von Neumann's theories of cellular automata from the 1940s, Norbert Wiener's ideas of self-reproducing machines from the same age, the whole agenda of cybernetic automation of culture in the postwar era, the sciences of artificial life since the 1980s, and even the 1872 novel *Erewhon* by Samuel Butler all testify to this widespread cultural theme of technological life. In addition, by contributing a whole section of the book to artificial life, I want to emphasize the multiple contexts of computer viruses. Even though a major portion of the public discourse of computer worms and viruses has underlined the negative sides of these "malicious miniprograms" as products of criminals, vandals, and just badly informed youth, they actually have much more to say about technological culture. Hence, the key concepts or themes of the third section revolve around ecologies of networking, systems of complexity, and life as emergent relations and connections.

In the beginning of the 1990s, if not already earlier, the question of "beneficial computer viruses" emerged. The very same Fred Cohen who had in 1983 depicted viruses as potential threats to organized society reminded his readers of the positive possibilities these miniprograms have. Analyzing viruses in the contexts of nanotechnology, artificial life, and evolutionary software, he saw computer viruses not just as malicious and nasty pieces of program code.[36] In a similar vein, Mark Ludwig sparked a whole range of discussion and critique with his books on viruses and artificial life. He even included instructions for coding such programs.[37]

It is no wonder that ideas about "third nature" emerged around the same period. As McKenzie Wark proposed, perhaps the digital culture of the late twentieth century is to be understood as nature, a *third* nature that supplements the two previous ones. As industrialization changed the biological and chemical first nature into a product and a standing reserve for the accumulation of wealth in a society, so the third nature is a continuation of this process of translating nature into terms of information technology. "Second nature" was something conceptualized by Hegel, Marx, and Lukàcs; Wark's own analysis of the third nature of simulated digital culture offers a further vector to understand the layered ecologies. The telegraph began the process of bypassing the spatio-temporal coordinates of locality and sowing the seeds for a global network of virtual spaces, described metaphorically during the 1980s as "cyberspace" by several enthusiastic writers. With this new arena and nonplace of speed and *telesthesia* ("perception at a distance"), the speed and flow of information became the new earth, an artificial nature, a media sphere: "Second nature, which appears to us as the geography of cities and roads and harbours and wool stores is progressively overlaid with a third nature of information flows, creating an information landscape which almost entirely covers the old territories."[38] With the discovery of electromagnetism and the electric telegraph were detached from the bodies of messengers and seemed to inhabit a life of their own. Globalization was tied to this vector of information that was itself tied to the transport routes and infrastructures. Goods, money, and people circulate, but also garbage, crime, and disease.[39] This applies to the information nature of the third order as well: as AIDS has revealed the global patterns of disease in contemporary societies, so computer worms and viruses make visible the global tendencies of electrical nature that originated in the nineteenth century with the beginning of telecommunications, specifically the telegraph. The notion of "third nature" implies a multiplication of such hybrid objects in the spheres of telecommunications.[40] Viruses and worms are not only an issue of security, but also of the wider "turbulent space" of the Internet, "a space suitable to the spread of contagion and transversal propagation of movement (from computer viruses to ideas and affects),"[41] as Tiziana Terranova puts it.

Media Theory Meets Computer Technology: Definitions, Concepts, and Sources

On a technical layer, a digital virus is designed to attach a copy of itself to a host program. These have often been executable files (.exe or .com) but can also be found in data files, macroscripts, and, for example, the boot sector of a hard drive. The program is intimately tied to the infrastructures of storage and transmission of computer culture—something that has changed quite significantly over the decades. From transmission of floppy disks to hard drives to the ubiquitous wireless culture, we are dealing with alternative vectors of contagion that do not equal "touching" in the usual sense. Traditionally, computer viruses have also included a "trigger" and a "payload." This means, for example, that a virus in the age of discs might trigger after, say, 50 boots and then release its payload. These payloads varied: some old, classical viruses play a song, others format your hard disk, and some do nothing out of the ordinary. Some famous viruses have made letters fall off the screen one by one, imitated the "Yankee Doodle" tune, and printed insults. The viruses can be seen as a special form of the IF/THEN routine pair. The infection mechanism looks for infectable objects, and IF it finds them, THEN it infects them. The trigger can be set for a specific date, and IF it is reached, THEN the trigger is pulled.[42]

A virus attaches itself to other programs, but computer worms are more self-contained and do not need to be part of another program to propagate. Worms became a more central phenomenon in later years in network techniques of the World Wide Web, e-mail, and file sharing (although these techniques and worm programs date from the 1970s). Basically, and technically, viruses and worms are two different types of programs.[43] Often they are referred to via the generic terms "malware" or "malicious software." Malicious software, of course, includes a wide variety of different programs, such as Trojan horses in the form of spyware, botnets, loggers, and dialers. Several such programs are designed for commercial purposes. What is curious is that viruses spread across particularly homogeneous platforms with bad security features, which historically led to a lot of accusations concerning the Microsoft Windows operating system. The corporate image of the company probably enticed virus writers to target Windows, but the socio-technical characteristics are worth noting. The Windows operating system has become notorious for its security flaws, which seem recurrently to pile on top of each other with the massive penetration of this specific operating system across the world. In addition, compared with open source projects, which more efficiently employ user input in improving design flaws, the Microsoft model seemed rigid and inefficient.

It is important to note how fundamental these issues of definition are concerning the life of software. If the emphasis is placed on reproduction routines, virus- and worm-like programs cannot be said to be malicious by definition. Often it is taken for granted that computer viruses are malicious by nature and that their payload is always harmful. Yet, as several writers such as Fred Cohen have argued, virus-like programs can contain various types of payloads and perform several different routines in addition to their fundamental nature as semiautonomous and self-reproductive software.[44]

Digital Contagions can be characterized as cultural analysis that works with historical material and sources, which are introduced separately at the beginning of the bibliography.[45] Thinking is thinking *with* something, and for a media archaeologist, historical sources are material to think with.[46] Thus, as post-structuralist cultural theories of recent decades have instructed us, theories and empirical sources are deeply intertwined, and it makes no sense to return to questions that separate the thinking from the material world in which it is embedded. Already the empirical sources on viruses, namely, discourse and practices, include implicit premises and theories of what viruses are.[47] It is a matter neither of giving form to a corpus of sources nor of submitting oneself to the historical "facts," but of following the tendencies inherent in the sources. The methodological task is not merely to look for popular representations of viruses or to seek out the scientific truth of these technological products, but to look at the frames themselves—the where, why, and how these truths are produced: What are the technological, cultural, and historical frameworks or the discourse networks in which such positions function and interact? The function of media archaeology is to look at the immanent strategies producing reality.[48]

There is an ongoing tension, then, between underlining the emergent features of the phenomenon at hand (which is well illustrated in the epigraph by Stephenson) and analyzing the actors contributing to constructing the thematics of viruses and "malicious" software. Basically, this is an irresolvable tension, as I want to demonstrate that although different actors and actor-networks have been actively trying to pin down the meanings and uses of viruses, worms, and similar programs to serve their own ends, the phenomenon cannot be reduced to merely part of such strategies of signification and valorization. In other words, there is a constant danger of homeostatic biologism that would remain on an exclusively metaphorical level of analysis.[49]

A large proportion of the analysis in this book concerns U.S. society and its particular contexts of massive computerization since World War II, the atmosphere of Cold War fear and paranoia, and the context of global consumer capitalism since the 1970s. However, my perspective is not on national technological cultures but on cultures of global technology. The media technologies of modernization—from the telegraph to the digital networks of contemporary society—have engaged us in a deterritorialization of local cultures, a disembedding and a move toward what could be called a "culture of global flows."[50] As argued above, the digital culture of telecommunications is also a world of the third nature, which is not restricted to the spatio-temporal grids of human experience. It is post-phenomenological, untied to the world of human perception even if it might govern it. Global cultural practices thus demand a global perspective for cultural analysis, which does not, however, mean a universalization and decontextualization: it just demands that we rethink what we mean by situated knowledge in media ecologies that are transnational, software-based, and consist of multiple levels of agency that are not merely human.

The idea of "media ecology" has, of course, been used in various ways. Traditionally it emerged from the work of Marshall McLuhan, Lewis Mumford, Harold Innis, Walter Ong, and Jacques Ellul, even if the conservative work of Neil Postman has become a key inheritor of the term. As Michael Goddard describes Postman: "In both *Amusing Ourselves to Death* (1987) and the more recent *Technopoly* (1993), Postman adopts a form of populist technophobia that only seems to maintain from McLuhan his anecdotal style and love of metaphor and whose only antidote to the Behemoth of technological domination seems to be a quite conservative notion of pedagogy."[51] But media ecology cannot be reduced to Postman, and even the Toronto-based scholars of McLuhan and company had a richer notion of media. The radical advantage in their take was a strongly historical notion of media where perception became imbued in its material realm. With the Toronto school of media ecology, aesthetics came to be about not the object perceived but the spatio-temporal conditions, technological framing, and media distribution of ways of perception. The later European radical media ecology stems from the work of Matthew Fuller, which imports a range of alternative scholars into the discussion, including Kittler, Guattari, and N. Katherine Hayles. For Fuller, using the term "ecology" to describe media phenomena is justified as it indicates "the massive and dynamic interrelation of processes and objects, beings and things, patterns and matter."[52] As Goddard emphasizes, Fuller's way of handling media ecology pluralizes it and teases out the Guattarian potential to see it as a way to tap to the various ethico-aesthetic and politically significant experiments in media technological culture. It is a way to situate processes that are technologically abstract but concretely part of the political determination of our situation and subjectivity.

Media ecologies consist of concrete machinic assemblages and abstract machines. Technology is in such a perspective understood as an "assemblages" (*agencements* in French) of heterogeneous parts, consisting of organic and nonorganic, significatory as well as a-significatory entities, with differing durations and overlapping histories. Assemblages can perhaps be understood as concrete stabilizations on a machinic phylum of media ecology:

We will call an assemblage every constellation of singularities and traits deduced
from the flow—selected, organized, stratified—in such a way as to converge (…)
artificially or naturally. (…) Assemblages may group themselves into extremely vast
constellations constituting "cultures," or even ages. (…) We may distinguish in every
case a number of very different lines. Some of them, phylogenetic lines, travel long
distances between assemblages of various ages and culture (from the blowgun to the
cannon? From the prayer wheel to the propeller? From the pot to the motor?); others,
ontogenetic lines, are internal to one assemblage and link up its various elements, or
else cause something to pass (…) into another assemblage of different nature but of
the same culture or age (for example, the horseshoe which spread through agricul-
tural assemblages).[53]

This view on technology asserts that technology is "machinic" and based on
flows (although a machinic assemblage is never only technological).[54] Machinic assemblages help us to think of the world as intertwined; the "things"
connected (the linguistic concept of "virus" articulated to self-reproductive
software programs, for example) do not precede the connections.[55] And not
all machines are concrete or resemble what we think of as technological
machines. In this Deleuzian and Guattarian sense, some machines are more
abstract, yet as real as the concrete, even technological ones. Connections are
made across scales: biological terms are transported into technology, politics
intertwines with aesthetics, diseases spread across economics.

The phenomenon of computer worms and viruses is formed of various
machinations, concrete and abstract, that consist of technological, social,
psychological, and economic parts. In short, it is irreducible to one determining factor or territory that moves across the corporeal and the incorporeal;
the material and its various temporal articulations. The material, or corporeal, aspect has to be complemented by the *incorporeal* as conceptualized by
Deleuze and the new materialist tradition of thought, which insists matter
matters, is alive with life, and irreducible to the hylomorphic scheme of things
separated from their meanings. The material is immanently pierced by the
incorporeal and the discursive instead of a bifurcation of mind and matter.
Even though the corporeal reality of a computer virus might stay the same,
because it is a certain pattern of code that replicates, infects, and spreads, it
can be understood very differently. To use Claire Colebrook's example: "A
knife may cut a body, but when we call this event punishment we create a
whole new (incorporeal) world of morals, crimes, criminals, laws and judg-
ments."[56] This type of conception of language emphasizes pragmatics over
semantics, underlining the order-word nature of acts of language. Language
is not merely communication or about thinking but a force that materially

connects rhizomatically with its outside.[57] Material processes have their own duration that is not reducible to signification, but at the same time acts of order-words impose actual transformations in terms of categories, definitions, and events. Deleuze and Guattari refer to the incorporeal transformation of an airplane (the plane-body) into a prison-body in a hijacking situation, where the transformation is enacted by the "mass media act" as an order-word.[58] By way of different transformations, a computer virus has been turned, in various assemblages of enunciation (such as mass media acts), into malicious software, a security problem, but also a piece of net art, an artificial-life project or a potentially beneficial utility program. This logic also organizes my sections and chapters into the three themes of "security," "body," and "life," which all might sound general, vague, and abstract but actually pinpoint specific histories under those rubrics.

Eventualization

In reference to my title, *Digital Contagions*, "contagions" has a double role here: to present the contagions induced by computer worms and viruses, and to produce new types of contagions of thought within cultural theory and media history. Contagions are thus to be understood in the sense Michel Serres gives to parasites: parasites are not actually disconnections of communication, but thirds-excluded that guarantee the interconnectivity and movement of a system. Communication cannot go on without the element of the third-excluded mediator, of contagion, of even miscommunication at its center: communication is consists of both signals and noise, just as the classical communication theory of Shannon and Weaver taught.[59] Never just dismiss the proverbial or literal noise. The task is to engage the interference, not just as an engineering element to be reduced but as a key trait within the network societies of digital culture, a trace to be followed, a tendency to be thought with. Contagion is a jump cut, an open-ended system, an experiment.[60] What has to be noted early on, however, is how the theories and theoreticians used here are part of the same field as the phenomenon of computer viruses and the culture of virality (comprising, for the most part, continental theories of post-structuralism and radical difference of the 1960s to 1990s). Just as various ideas in computer science, cybernetics, and, for example, ecological thought were wired into the philosophies of Lacan, Derrida, Foucault, and Deleuze and Guattari, so their ideas concerning systems, aesthetics, and, for example, politics have had an impact on the digital (counter)culture in Europe and the United States since the 1980s.[61] Instead of being a problem, this has further enticed me to think with Deleuze and Guattari—their writings function as a form of nonlinear ecological system, relying on forces of variation that can act as a trigger of becomings, new modes of thought and action. Theories are not used as direct applications of an explanatory grid to a material but as ways of cultivation. They are different, more conceptual ways of articulating and mapping the contours of the viral ecology of late twentieth-century computer culture.

My general framework is to move in patterns and vectors outlined by Kittlerian material analysis but with the Deleuzian twist of embracing incorporealities and multiplicities. My theoretical references in this work should primarily be read in relation to this bipolar theoretical phasing between Kittler and Deleuze. Whereas Kittler brings in the technologization of Foucault and hence a necessary perspective on how to analyze material genealogies of technical media, Deleuze is important as a thinker of becomings. Their wedding in this work is obviously not the most frictionless one, but it can produce important ways to bring some Deleuzian movement into Kittler's way of analyzing discourse networks, which otherwise might tend to become too rigid. Whereas Deleuze (with Guattari) is important in creating the ethico-aesthetic agenda of the work, a sort of a minoritarian cultural memory if I may, Kittler is suitable for a historically oriented analysis and synthesis of discourse networks. Hence, the discourse network acts as a media ecology and a machinic phylum, consisting of incorporeal acts of ordering and corporeal movements of, say, hardwares, softwares, networks, people, and architectures. Kittler underscores that media in complex ways determine our situation and make possible what it is to state and think in a certain age; in contrast, Deleuze, with and without Guattari, tends to think in terms of movements and assemblages. Technologies are always part of social assemblages that select and employ them for particular uses and functions. Media technologies can be thought to occupy a certain phylum and virtual tendencies, but they are always situated as part of even larger and heterogeneous assemblages, which also helps us address issues of politics and agencies.[62] It is through *dispositifs* of media technological power that what exists and what is true become defined. Power, then, is the primary enactor of cultural techniques and functions as the filter through which cultural discourses and nondiscursive practices emerge.

Tracking and mapping multiplicities is a key focus of this work, and the task is reflected also at the methodological level. As noted above, this work is a meshwork of a number of elements, instead of being an *application* of any clear-cut theoretical idea or methodological guideline. In this task, I follow Foucault's general method, or ethos, of *eventualization*. In an interview published in 1980, Foucault outlined his views discussed in the earlier genealogical papers. An analysis and production of events aims to make visible singularities "at places where there is a temptation to invoke a historical constant, an immediate anthropological trait, or an obviousness that imposes uniformly on all."[63] For me, this produces an important impetus with which to break out from the hegemony of representation analysis. Analyzing representations can be defined as focusing on how cultural identities are reproduced (and resisted) in cultural discourses from mass media to everyday life. It is an attempt to focus on the productive power that moulds identities and produces cognitive and affective ways of being. Such an analysis can be seen as successful in its underlining of the dynamics of subject formation as part of representational grids, but recent years have also seen a critique of its insufficient approach toward the immanent materiality of culture.[64]

In a Deleuzian–Spinozian vein, media philosopher Luciana Parisi calls for new modalities of thought that would go one step beyond representational analyses to encompass a more material level of engagement. Representational cultural analysis ends easily, merely reproducing the same grid on which the entities are positioned. Critique risks solidifying the objects of the critique. According to Parisi, critical theories from semiotics to structuralism and post-structuralism do concentrate on determinants ("a semiotics of signification, bodies' positions in a structure, ideological overdeterminations"[65]) but are not able to take into account the material ethics of becoming. Thus, a focus on assemblages (Deleuze) or mixed semiotics (Guattari) articulates how signifying discourses and material a-semiotic encodings always act in pacts. Parisi's point, following Deleuze and Guattari, and Spinoza, is, then, that reality is not "exclusively constituted by significations, discourses and ideologies,"[66] and hence critical analysis of reality should methodologically focus not merely on reflections or representations of reality but also take reality itself as under construction.[67]

Following such ideas, *Digital Contagions* moves in the direction of thinking of the outside, the event as radically new, the unexpected—and not only mapping representational and symbolic orders and engaging in a politics of representation. As eventualization, this project challenges the assumed uniformity that surrounds this special class of software. Not merely malicious software made by juvenile vandals, but an inherent part of digital culture, computer worms, and viruses become much more interesting than only as security risks. Hence, the task is not only to reproduce the banal fact that viruses are represented as malicious but also to challenge this one-sided approach and to produce singularities that would open up novel fields of understanding. This attributes an active interpretive or, more accurately, connective role to the writer. As stated above, the writer connects, works with, materials to summon or conjure forth worlds that have been neglected, frozen. The analyst, or media archaeologist, eventualizes, which in Foucault's wake means "rediscovering the connections, encounters, supports, blockages, plays of forces, strategies, and so on, that at a given moment establish what subsequently counts as being self-evident, universal, and necessary."[68] Media archaeology should not only track the majoritarian understanding of the discourses and *dispositifs* of digital culture but also aim to follow the detours and experiments that remain virtual, yet real, in the shadows of the actuality of hegemonic understanding.

The accidental is not merely an object of research but points toward this method that has also a resonance with Deleuze's thought. In *Difference and Repetition*, he categorizes the questions "How much?" "How?" "In what cases?" and "Who?" as demands that restore multiplicity to ideas, and hence bypass the ethos focused on stable unmoving essences.[69] This can be understood as a Nietzschean questioning of genealogy, as further developed by Deleuze and Foucault, where thought and representations are revealed as posited in and of *violence*, power. This type of genealogical perspective on accidental ontology admits that any position is unstable, situated in relation to others, and devoid of eternity. No knowledge (*connaissance*) is outside the will-to-knowledge (*vouloir-savoir*), a realization that leads not to relativism but to admitting that knowledge is imbued in power and hence always a system that is more or less unstable.[70]

History and the archive as a structuring logic of history form an essential part of "what we are and what we are ceasing to be,"[71] acting as a form of depositary for possible actions and significations. Whereas the majoritarian central memory, or archaeological stratum, has so far devalued nomadic memories as secondary a-signifying practices, a Deleuzian ethos of memory emphasizes the constant need for deterritorialization of this central memory, but in a thoroughly affirmative manner. As Rosi Braidotti wonderfully writes, this is an "intensive, zigzagging, cyclical and messy type of remembering" that endures complexities, thus dislodging the established points of subjectivity from their places, opening up new sites and territories of acting and remembering.[72]

Braidotti also brings the force of imagination to the fore. Becoming minoritarian means engaging with the force of imagining "better futures." A nomadic memory of zigzag territorialization aims at actualizing "virtual possibilities which had been frozen in the image of the past."[73] Memory is conjoined with a creative imagination to bring forth a new, monstrous future of nomadic subjectivities that are resistant to the majoritarian modes of affecting, perceiving, thinking, and remembering. Historical analysis is also stretched toward the future. In general, cultural analysis is a matter of how to fold the outside, the event (*accidentum*), the unpredictable into effective and affective assemblages that make a difference—in other words, how to come up with a different future. As Grosz notes, this problematics is inherently tied to the question of time and to bringing forth such a form of duration that is not committed to continuous growth but to "division, bifurcation, dissociation" and difference.[74] This is a theoretically rewarding challenge and something that can also act as guidance to thinking about technology and the alternative genealogies that can inform both a fresh understanding of digital culture and also new methods for humanities. This is also the task of this book as well as the other two that form the so-called media ecology trilogy alongside this one: *Insect Media* and *A Geology of Media*. But first, viruses and software.

Notes

1. Virilio & Kittler 1999, 84.
2. Stephenson 1993, 371.
3. Schivelbusch 1977. Lundemo 2003.
4. Quoted in Sterling 1994, 12.
5. McNeill 1998, 170–178, passim. Vuorinen 2002. DeLanda 2003, 242.
6. Kittler 1997, 55.
7. Clark 1997, 79.
8. Schivelbusch 1977, 118–119.
9. McLuhan 1962.
10. A focus on accidents opens up a new perspective on media technologies. See, e.g., Virilio 1993, 212. On the cultural history of accidents, see also, e.g., Schivelbusch 1977. Trond Lundemo (2003, 25) has analyzed the ideas of uncontrollability and danger inherent in media technologies, demonstrating how "the decomposition of the machine and the erasure of memory," in particular, are key themes considering the age of digitality. Ontologically invisible digital technology reveals itself only in the event of breaking down, which gives accidents a special status in a cultural sense. Every media ecology or discourse network seems to have an accident of its own, and this work aims to highlight the position computer worms and viruses have in relation to the network culture of the late twentieth century. They *reveal* technology, and the power/knowledge relations that media are embedded in. These ideas stem originally from Heidegger's notions of the ontology of Being. See

Heidegger 1996, §16. Viruses and worms have been analyzed only partially and/or fleetingly from a cultural perspective, whereas technical and practical antivirus manuals and books have been abundant ever since 1988. For useful sources on the cultural contexts of computer worms and viruses in relation to the Internet, the AIDS phenomenon, the rise of the digital culture, and cyber risks, see Ross 1990; Lupton 1994; Saarikoski 2004, 360–377; Van Loon 2002a, 147–168; Sampson 2004, 2009, 2012; Galloway 2004, 176–184; Mayer & Weingart 2004a; Thacker 2005; Bardini 2006; O'Neil 2006. See also my articles Parikka 2005a, 2005b, 2005c, 2007; and Parikka & Sampson 2009.

11. Fuller 2005, 63.

12. John Johnston explains Friedrich Kittler's term "discourse network" to mark the archival condition of a particular age, or more accurately the potentials of inscription: "by a culture at a particular moment in time." Johnston continues: "The notion of the discourse network points to the fact that at any given cross-sectional moment in the life of a culture, only certain data (and no other) are selected, stored, processed, transmitted or calculated, all else being 'noise.' (…) In other words, on the basis of this particular selection of data not only perceptions, ideas, and concepts—all that is coded as meaningful in short—but also a system authorizing certain subjects as senders and others as receivers of discourse is instituted." Johnston 1997, 9–10. Cf. Kittler 1990, 1999. The term "discourse network" is thus not the best translation of *Aufchreibesystem*, "systems for writing down," for engraving or for recording. Kittler has attempted to broaden this perspective to encompass more technical information channels as part of the archival layer, or discourse networks. As Kittler puts it, even if all books are discourse networks, not all discourse networks are books: "Archeologies of the present must also take into account data storage, transmission, and calculation in technological media." Kittler 1990, 369. I use the concept of discourse throughout this work, but it should be read as stemming from a materialist understanding of discourse networks. Foucault underlines the need to see discourses and nondiscourses (material practices) as inherently intertwined. Discourses are immanent to, for example, habits, operations, spaces, and practices that produce the world—cultural techniques in the material sense. Discourses are about producing certain effects and affects, implying that the concept is not to be taken as solely textual. Deleuze insists that Foucault is not to be understood as an archaeologist of linguistic statements alone. Foucault's focus is on the relations of the visible and the sayable, which form the space of "the audiovisual archive." Historical *dispositif* consists of architectural, technological, and philosophical or conceptual elements. Deleuze 1998. See also Rodowick 2001, 49–54.

13. Cf. Terranova 2004, 98–100.

14. Compared to the earlier archaeological analyses, the genealogical ideas bring in an important emphasis on writing counterhistories. See Gutting 1989, 271. Several media archaeological theories are more accurately a combination of the genealogical and the archaeological. See, e.g., Zielinski 2006. I want to emphasize how the archaeological analysis of a priori conditioning of statements, objects, and processes (a certain form of Kittlerian view of discourse networks) should be tied intimately with a commitment to producing new genealogies. Here, as Foucault himself noted in his Berkeley lecture in 1983, genealogy becomes a mode of inquiry into how archaeological events condition the present, how the archaeological a priori continuously translates into our contemporary condition. Foucault 1994. Cf. Kittler 1990. Siegfried Zielinski (1999) positions

his archaeological quest in three intellectual traditions: (1) Raymond Williams's idea of culture as a way of life and technologies as cultural practices; (2) systems-theoretical approaches where technology is considered as unities of origination/production and use; (3) the metapsychological film theories of Jean-Louis Baudry, Jean-Louis Comolli, and Christian Metz, where the concept of apparatus is developed. On media archaeology, see also Huhtamo 1997, Elsaesser 2004, Huhtamo & Parikka 2011, and Parikka 2012.

15. See Deleuze 1990. In a manner reminiscent of Larry Grossberg's radical contextualism, I understand context not as the background of a study but as the essence of what a study tries to map, the "very conditions of possibility of something." See Grossberg 2000, 41. Context understood in this way draws from a Deleuzian–Nietzschean understanding of forces as the processes of differentiation that create the world. See Deleuze 1986.

16. This connects to the conceptualizations of time in cultural historical research promoted by, for instance, Fernand Braudel as well as the remediation thesis of Bolter and Grusin (2000). For instance, Braudel (1997, 205) notes how every actuality is composed of multiple durations and variable rhythms that coexist.

17. Cf. Longley 1994, 589–590.

18. Virilio 1993, 212. On Virilio and his notions of accidents, see Redhead 2004.

19. Scott Berinato: "Attack of the Bots." *Wired*, vol. 14 issue 11, November 2006, <http://www.wired.com/2006/11/botnet/>.

20. Brunton 2013.

21. Chun 2015.

22. See "Hackers Remotely Kill a Jeep on the Highway—With Me in It." July 21, 2015, *Wired*, <http://www.wired.com/2015/07/hackers-remotely-kill-jeep-highway/>.

23. "Iranian hackers broke into what they thought was a Chevron gas pump—but it was a honeypot." August 13, 2015, *Fusion*, <http://fusion.net/story/181527/security-honeypots-snare-hackers/>.

24. Brunton 2013, 112.

25. Malicious software can be defined generally as software that intentionally and without consent damages software or computer systems. It differs then from software bugs that are unintentional.

26. Castells 2001, 172. Cf. Campbell-Kelly & Aspray 1996, 283–300.

27. Castells 2001, 172–173. Hardt & Negri 2001. Castells refers also to the libertarian social movements of the 1960s and early 1970s in Europe and the United States as influential in this context.

28. Hardt & Negri 2001, 298. See also Hardt & Negri 2001, 32. Urry (2003, 9) emphasizes how global power should not be conceptualized as a substance of sorts, but an emergent complex process. The Empire should not, then, be understood as a hierarchy of power but as part of an emergent networked process that interconnects local issues with global vectors.

29. John S. Mayo, "Materials for Information and Communication." *Scientific American*, vol. 255, October 1986, 51.

30. The entanglement of media and catastrophe is, of course, not a novel theme, as exemplified, for example, by Mary Ann Doane (2006) in her analysis of the televised catastrophes that break the temporal and spatial habits of everyday life in a mediatized society.

31. See Gerrold 1975. Brunner 1976. Ryan 1985. Beeler 1973. Latva 2004.

32. See Parikka 2007.

33. See Sontag 2002.

34. "Hex" refers in computers to "hexadecimal," a specific way of marking the binary code in a base-16 system.

35. Cf. Deleuze & Guattari 1987, 66, 504. Wise 1997, 63. Following Wise's Deleuzian–Guattarian reading, technology is here seen as enacting corporeal materiality and being always entwined with the incorporeality of language (as the order-word). Slack & Wise 2002, 495.

36. Cohen 1994. See also Cohen 1991b.

37. See Ludwig 1993. Cf. Vesselin Bontchev: "Are 'Good' Computer Viruses Still a Bad Idea?" EICAR Conference Proceedings 1994, 25–47. Julian Dibbell: "Viruses Are Good for You." Wired, vol. 3, issue 2, February 1995.

38. Wark 1994, 120.

39. Sontag 2002, 177–178.

40. Cf. Latour 1993, 51–55.

41. Terranova 2004, 67. In more practical context, this essential of "parasitic computation" as part of the Internet infrastructure was articulated in 2001 by a bunch of scientists. Albert-László Barabási, Vincent W. Freeh, Hawoong Jeong, & Jay B. Brockman: "Parasitic Computing." Nature, vol. 412, August 30, 2001, 894–897.

42. See Harley, Slade, & Gattiker 2001, 87–88. Since February 2016, Archive.org has hosted the Malware Museum of primarily MS-DOS viruses and other examples from the 1980s and 1990s. They are emulated online and one can find examples of the different payloads of the viruses.

43. In this study, I use the term "virus" as a generic one, referring to "worms" only when required to emphasize something. This is also the general way these programs are discussed in popular media. See the Wikipedia entries on "computer virus" and "malicious software," <http://en.wikipedia.org/wiki/Main_Page>.

44. See Cohen 1991b, 1994. See also John F. Shoch & Jon A. Hupp: "The 'Worm' Programs—Early Experience with a Distributed Computation." Communications of the ACM, vol. 25, issue 3, March 1982, 172–180.

45. As Kittler (2001, 14–19) notes, cultural analysis, or Kulturwissenschaft, is in its modern form fundamentally cultural historical analysis.

46. As Wolfgang Ernst (2002) underlines, archives are not traces of a continuous past life; they are by nature fragmentary monuments embedded in media technological networks. The media archaeological task is, then, to write discontinuous links between such archival events. Archaeology does not write of things behind the archive, and it does not attempt to restore a way of life of human beings. Instead, it focuses on the arche, the technological conditions of existence, of culture.

47. On cultural analysis, see Bal 1999, 1, 12–14. See also Deleuze & Guattari 1987, 3–25. Walter Benjamin's concept of cultural history rests on a similar idea of historical materialism as a mode of thinking that proceeds with the past. Historical "objects" are thus no mere objects of thinking but participants in historical modes of thought. See Caygill 2004, 90–91, 94–95. Benjamin's stereoscopical historical research aims at combining the images of the past with the contemporary moment to create a critical constellation. It taps into tradition to find cracks that are to be transported as part of a creation of a novel

future. See Buck-Morss 1991, 289–292. This type of discontinuous view of history resonates with Foucauldian themes of archaeology.

48. Cf. Massumi 1992, 46.

49. Munster and Lovink (2005) argue "against biologism."

50. See Castells 1996. Cf. Beck 2002. Beck argues for a *cosmopolitan* agenda and theory of
    social research.

51. Goddard 2011.

52. Fuller 2005, 2.

53. Quoted in Delanda 1991, 140. Cf. Deleuze 1997b, 185–186.

54. Following Deleuze (1998, 39–40), machines are not solely technical machines but also
    social. The social machine that does not refer only to human societies—selects and
    assigns the technical elements used. In a Deleuzian–Guattarian ontology, the seemingly
    solid objects of technology, or of culture, such as identities, sexualities, gender, and insti-
    tutions, are only a consequence of a more underlying flux. The world is about connections
    between these flows, and in these connections seemingly solid objects form: technologies,
    humans, animals, cultural artifacts, and natural things. The solid objects are the molar
    entities of culture, whereas movement (as change) happens on a molecular level (Murphie
    & Potts 2003, 30–35; Deleuze & Guattari 1987). Flows do not emanate from individuals,
    but instead individuals are formed at the intercrossings of cultural flows, as slowing-downs
    of movements. Individuals are always part of synthetic (machinic) assemblages, which
    consist of a partial conjoining of heterogeneous flows. This Deleuzian–Guattarian view
    differs from the more structuralist (and Marxist) versions, where individuals are deter-
    mined by the structures. Individuals are not effects of an underlying power structure,
    whether economic, linguistic, or psychic, as some psychoanalytic accounts might sug-
    gest, but overdetermined sites of power and knowledge, not reducible to one type of
    power relationship. In other words, as Foucault reminds us, where there is power, there
    is also counterpower, implying the constant dynamics going on in cultural discourse net-
    works. Deleuze conceptualizes this as the primacy of lines of flight: a society is defined by
    the lines that escape the molar machinations, not the stable entities (Deleuze 1997b,
    188–189). In Foucault's terminology, the issue is about cultural techniques, where
    knowledge is in itself a technique for organizing, participating, and delineating the flows
    (Murphie & Potts 2003, 30).

55. Murphie & Potts 2003, 30–35.

56. Colebrook 2002, 119.

57. The materiality of the "object" of research is summoned by my understanding of how
    texts *function* as part of their surroundings. As a major component of my sources is writ-
    ten material, this would easily imply that the tracings I make are merely "symbolic," or
    semantic signs of *meaning* (signified). Nonetheless, the rhizomatic stance toward texts, as
    a supplement to representational analysis, feeds on Deleuze and Guattari's notions from
    the first chapter of A *Thousand Plateaus*, where they emphasize that texts are not to be
    (merely) interpreted, nor are they images of the world, but, more accurately, they *work*
    within the world. The linguistic model of the world is too restricted to account for the
    connecting of language "to the semantic and pragmatic contents of statements, to collec-
    tive assemblages of enunciation, to a whole micropolitics of the social field" (Deleuze &

Guattari 1987, 7). In cultural history, the reception of Foucault can be deciphered as the significant distinction. Whereas such Anglo-American writers as Peter Burke (2004, 76) see Foucault as part of the linguistic turn and as a thinker of the discursive, Roger Chartier (1997, 68–69), for example, has, rightly in my opinion, criticized this one-sided notion and highlighted the necessary articulation of the discursive with the nondiscursive. This is what Foucault clearly states in his *The Archaeology of Knowledge*. See Foucault 2002. I approach texts as machines of production, as creators of effects, affects, and thoughts that intertwine with nondiscursive planes of culture, and in this they are always multiplicities that cannot be reduced to their majoritarian, hegemonic uses and interpretations. There is always potential for some more, some new connection.

58. Deleuze & Guattari 1987, 80–81.
59. Shannon & Weaver 1949. See Serres 1982. Brown 2002. Kittler 1993, 168.
60. See Massumi 2002, 18–19.
61. Gere (2002) has noted how post-structuralism has contributed strongly to the same discourse and our understanding of digital culture. There has, since the 1960s, been a constant feedback between issues technological, theoretical, and cultural, which is why there is a constant strong resonance between issues of digital culture and, for example, certain strands of "French theory," such as that of Derrida or Deleuze and Guattari.
62. See Deleuze & Parnet 1996, 85. Cf. Kittler 1990. Also Matthew Fuller (2005, 60–62) notes that Kittler attenuates the political aspects of Foucault's discourse thinking.
63. Foucault 2000c, 226. This approach resonates with certain themes of media archaeological research where the focus has been on similar minoritarian tracings and analytics of becoming. Zielinski 2006.
64. See, e.g., DeLanda 1999. Grosz 2005, 44–46. Terranova 2004, 8–9, 35. Wiley 2005. Parikka & Tiainen 2006. Dolphjin & van der Tuin 2012. Deleuze and Spinoza contrast with the Kantian tradition of cultural analysis, which can in broad terms be characterized as critical analysis of conditions of knowledge. Kant's questioning for the conditions of knowledge that filter the world to us humans can be seen still as a dominant method of cultural analysis that sees the world as mediated by a priori categories (mental and cultural), which is why the world in itself is beyond our reach. (See Hallward 2006, 11–12.) The world is divided into spheres of the world-in-itself (*noumena*), the appearances and the subject, a division that has contributed to the representational emphasis of contemporary cultural analysis. In this mode of thought, the world is mediated by representations we have of it. Recent years of critique of correlationism have engaged with this dilemma, but it has also longer roots in feminist theory and post-structuralist philosophy. Elizabeth Grosz argues that the problem with representation-oriented cultural studies is that it restricts nature (and the material) to being the passive nonform that culture as an active force fabricates. Grosz argues that one should think of the material as the outside of the representational, as the event that *produces* the symbolic. Nature, the material, the event are the outside of the representational, the multiplicity that enables the emergence of a cultural order (Grosz 2005, 52, 220–221n4). In the Deleuzian–Spinozian approach to cultural reality, there is no primary division between noumena and appearances. Instead, reality is characterized by univocity. There is one voice for the world; all things are expressions of the same force of the world. The world is characterized by the fundamental immanence of processes and things, of relations traversing the whole. However, the

whole is not a uniform and determined essence, but a multiplicity, which leaves open the possibility of change, creation, and politics. In Deleuze's view, the world does not consist of differences between representations but more fundamentally of a differing at the heart of the nature–culture continuum: a force of differing that endows the material world with the potential to change, irrespective of representations "attached" to things and relations (Cf. Hallward 2006, 11–26.)

65. Parisi 2004b, 74.
66. Ibid., 75.
67. Ibid., 84.
68. Foucault 2000c, 226–227.
69. Deleuze 1994, 188. This stance can be attached to the division between majoritarian and minoritarian readings of culture and history. See Goodchild 1996, 54–55. On cultural analysis as experimental perturbations, see Massumi 1992, 68.
70. Foucault 2000e, 387.
71. Deleuze 1992, 164.
72. Braidotti 2001, 187.
73. Ibid., 188.
74. Grosz 1999. It would again be interesting to connect such themes to a Benjaminian ethos of critical historical analysis. See Buck-Morss 1991.

· I ·

FEAR SECURED

From Bugs to Worms

Society is becoming increasingly dependent on the accurate and timely distribution of information. As this dependency increases we become more vulnerable on the technology used to process and distribute information (…) This is particularly true for what are sometimes called infrastructural industries—banking, the telephone system, power generation and distribution, airline scheduling and maintenance, and securities and commodities exchanges. Such industries rely on computers and build much security into their systems so that they are reliable and dependable.[1]

— *Information Security Handbook* (1991)

—Do you remember the VIRUS program?
—Vaguely. Wasn't it some kind of computer disease or malfunction?
—Disease is closer. There was a science-fiction writer once who wrote a story about it—but the thing had been around a long time before that. It was a program that—well, you know what a virus is, don't you? It's pure DNA, a piece of renegade genetic information. It infects a normal cell and forces it to produce more viruses—viral DNA chains—instead of its normal protein. Well, the VIRUS program does the same thing.
—Huh?[2]

—David Gerrold: *When HARLIE Was One* (1972)

Prologue: On Order and Cleanliness

Is there anything more civilized than being clean? Tidied up, smart, without a stain or sign of aberrant smudge, without a sign of disorder and disease. It's where the cultural and the psychological seem to meet—or witness that they were never separate anyway. Sigmund Freud's text on cleanliness and culture from 1930, written in the midst of slowly developing European turbulence, remains an influential reference point for cultural theorists. In *Civilization and Its Discontents*, Freud writes:

> Dirtiness of any kind seems to us incompatible with civilization. We extend our demand for cleanliness to the human body too. We are astonished to learn of the objectionable smell which emanated from the *Roi Soleil* and we shake our heads on the Isola Bella when we are shown the tiny wash-basin in which Napoleon made his morning toilet. Indeed, we are not surprised by the idea of setting up the use of soap as an actual yardstick of civilization. The same is true of order. It, like cleanliness, applies solely to the works of man. But whereas cleanliness is not to be expected in nature, order, on the contrary, has been imitated from her.[3]

Cleanliness does not, of course, just come about, it has to be produced. It is a product of a wide range of cultural techniques[4] of cleaning that maintain the desired state, clean insides separated from the outsides; a state that is carefully managed where, actually, the process becomes as important to the "civilization" as the end product.

In digital culture, such an insight seems apt too. The notions of *digital* hygiene, orderly computing, and clean communication has appeared in the vocabulary of computer culture since the 1980s. Arguments for purity became deeply entwined in the politics of software and the post-Fordist capitalism of network culture.

The operations of order tap into a longer genealogy of modernization and modern computing, which has emphasized control and reliability.[5] Various types of accidents, deviations, errors, and mistakes stand out as anomalies. Computer viruses have not been mere "accidents of nature," but they are seen also as cunning forms of vandalism and terrorism: "Rather like Hitler's V1 'flying bomb,' no one knows when or where a computer virus will strike. They attack indiscriminately. Virus writers, whether or not they have targeted specific companies or individuals, must know that their programs, once unleashed, soon become *uncontrollable*."[6] The rhetorical production of the danger of viruses is a constant theme in the literature. With more nuance, several science fiction writers of the 1970s also mapped the issues of loss of control in new networks of communication, where actions are attributed not merely to human beings. David Gerrold's *When HARLIE Was One* (1972), John Brunner's *The Shockwave Rider* (1975), and Thomas J. Ryan's *The Adolescence of P-1* (1977) all played with the idea of self-perpetuating software programs that are not reducible to the physical or conceptual territories of computers as number-crunching machines.[7]

Computer security journals, books, and other publications had for years constructed an image of the computer virus as an unexpected danger: viruses defy the orderly calculations and operational control that the user should exert. According to one widely embraced view, computer security was to mean (1) confidentiality (the privacy of sensitive information), (2) integrity (authorized information and program exchange), and (3) availability (systems work promptly and allow access to authorized users).[8] In the mid-1980s computer security was defined in terms of access control and protection:

> Prevention of or protection against (a) access to information by unauthorized recipients or (b) intentional but unauthorized destruction or alteration of that information. Security may guard against both unintentional as well as deliberate attempts to access sensitive information, in various combinations according to circumstances. The concepts of security, integrity, and privacy are interlinked.[9]

Another key emphasis was to say that security and computer protection are based on *control, inspection,* and *integrity.* Inspection has meant locating security holes and known viruses, and integrity has meant methods for detecting unauthorized change in systems. As the third element, and perhaps in some ways the most crucial, control "has been the primary intent of the U.S. national standards on computer security."[10] As the key concept of computer security, it has meant controlling access to systems, as well as functions, resources, and the moving and sharing of data.

Computing emerges as a matter of trust and control of what happens in the computer, what the software, operating system, platform, as well as the user are doing in interaction. It's interesting to read against this aspired state of computing phenomena, such as viruses. A virus steals control and ruins "the trust that the user has in his/her machine, because it causes the user to lose his or her belief that she or he can control this machine," antivirus researcher Vesselin Bontchev noted in 1994.[11] Gradually during the past few decades trust has come to be debated in discussions of computer systems, and the Trusted Computing Group (in the wake of the Trusted Computing

Platform Alliance) has underlined the value of designing so-called trusted systems. For critics, this has meant the reduction of users' scope to have control over their computers and networks, which are increasingly defined already by system designers. This has been justified by security reasons and slightly recursive arguments that trusted (which does not equal trustworthy) systems are less vulnerable to malicious attacks than open systems.[12] Trust has become a key term—vague in its determination, yet constantly recursive—for the service transactions that are normalized as part of the user expectation of social media culture. Software and now platforms have to be trusted, something exposed in the numerous cases of platforms' security standards being exposed as inadequate.

James Beniger narrates the genealogy of control in his book *The Control Revolution* (1997). According to Beniger, the modern information society was born in the nineteenth century as part of the societal practices expressed by Max Weber as rationalization and bureaucratization. Both practices serve the objective of achieving control of the socio-economic complexity of modernity. Beniger analyzes technological solutions and formal models to provide control—for instance, the ideas of social programming and the machines of production, distribution, and data processing—from the Jacquard loom to the pre–World War II computing revolution.[13] Such modes of algorithmic processing automated complex patterns in coded form and produced seemingly reliable mechanisms for mass production. Trust and control were not mere ideal values of technological and management systems, but they had to be thought of as design features. Production information, that is, instructions or algorithms, became coded into "software" form, whether as early music rolls for pianos or models for automated looms, or later as census punch cards recording national population for statistical control purposes. Either way, the mode of production was controlled via coded operating instructions.

Controlling information gradually became an imperative in business and management environments. Capitalism and digital culture are historically based on the cultural techniques of abstraction, standardization, and mechanization, which were already part of the technological culture of the nineteenth century. Similarly, Turing's universal machine, one key model for the emergence of the modern computer, was above all a machine of ordering and translation, with which heterogeneous phenomena could be equated. This idea, concretized in typewriters, conveyer belts, assembly lines, calculators, and computers, served as the basis for both digital machines and capitalism. The concrete connection was the need to control increasingly complex production, circulation, and signs.

Rationality—as exemplified in Babbage's differential calculators, Taylor's ideas of work management, and cybernetics—was the image of thought incorporated in these machines.[14] In general, this might also be referred to as the abstract machine of control and order, actualized, for example, in the cybernetics of the post–World War II situation.

Cybernetics seems to fit some of this lineage of management-oriented technological control. Notions of control and order play a significant role in the archaeology of information-technological security, and these themes are especially visible in the thinking of Norbert Wiener, the pioneer of cybernetics. Wiener's cybernetics touched, most of all, on the question of understanding the world as a series of communication circuits and controlling them via successful feedback loops that maintain the homeostasis of a system. This theory relates closely to the problem of entropy, a notion in statistical mechanics from the nineteenth century: information was understood as a degree of organization; entropy translated as a degree of disorganization—not an absolute transcendent but a relational negative twin of organization.[15] Already Claude E. Shannon had transported the concept of entropy to information theory after World War II in his 1948 paper "A Mathematical Theory of Communication," where he described entropy in terms of randomness in a message system. Entropy was, then, introduced as a certain necessary component in communications intimately tied to the nonsemantic information value of a message.[16]

Wiener himself recognized cybernetics as part of the history started by G. W. Leibniz, and especially his dream of a universal language of mathematics. Following Aristotle's idea of the categorization of concepts, as well as the *ars combinatoria* plans of Ramon Llull and Athanius Kircher, Leibniz established a plan to decipher the grounding alphabetical system and conceptual basis on which the world rests. Leibniz's idea can be divided into three parts: (1) to create a handbook or an encyclopedia that would gather human knowledge in its entirety; (2) to select the most appropriate concepts and symbols to refer to this knowledge; and (3) to create a logic to handle these concepts, a mathematical tool (a calculus). For this task Leibniz planned his own *calculus ratiocinator*, the rational calculator that—more than being a machine—was a way of performing symbolic logic.[17] With it, numbers seemed to be doing the counting themselves, as suggested by the Greek etymology of the term "automata."[18]

The dream of an automated calculating machine is part of a media archaeology of computing in general. But it also hints at a rather fundamental question, too: In which way are numbers self-perpetuating, self-reproducing, and autonomous, outside the control of human programmers or at least formative of autonomous systems that are not merely the hardware formations, such as drones, but actually complex control loops that can cut out the human operator in some ways? Wouldn't programs or scripts like viruses represent a version of this automated number world? The automated self-moving machines of clocks, and even cinema in its own way, prescribed early versions of mechanistic movement, but what if, with computers and memory, a possibility of a programmed self-producing automata provided a further step on this path of Leibnizian imaginary?

For Wiener, Leibniz represented "the patron saint of cybernetics" because of his concepts of universal symbolism and calculus of reasoning.[19] The dream of achieving control through meticulous, discrete categorization led to more concrete techniques of design, manipulation, management, and engineering.[20] The *calculus ratiocinator* can be seen as a precursor to the information machines of the control revolution that Beniger analyzes. The early strand of cybernetics that was crystallized in the post–World War II Macy Conferences of the 1940s and 1950s underlined the themes of homeostasis and feedback. As Charlie Gere notes, this amounted to a view of "effective and efficient control and communication."[21] As part of the modern modulations of desire, cybernetics, systems theory, and information theory were all, in a way, theories of order and cleanliness.

Yet also noise has received its fair share of attention in writings about technology. The engineering problem of logical calculation and communication of signals without noise expands toward the more general cultural fields of power and articulation. The notion of noise has emerged as one key marker in contemporary theory literature relating to computer errors.[22] Noise has grown to refer to a bundle of terms, including undefinability, incoherence, incongruity, incompatibility, illogicality, irrationality, ambiguity, confusion, undecidability, ambivalence—all seen as tropes of "the other of order."[23] Metaphorics aside, for cyberneticists and early computer pioneers, noise represented a signal management issue.[24] Noise stands in as an indication of another sort of patterning that is constantly operationalized and through cultural techniques managed in relation to the insides and outsides of machines, programs, users, and illegitimate nonusers. Hence, it is interesting how the biopolitics of digital code translates certain expressions of sense into noise and simultaneously suppresses alternative logics of computer software.

But there is no denying that from early on in the 1980s, viruses have been conceived as a threat to any computer system, for (1) virus activity is deemed uncontrollable, because the actions of the virus program are outside the control of the user and the legitimate OS processes, and (2) viruses can behave indeterminately and unpredictably.[25] Viruses seem, then, to be in fundamental tension with the imaginary view of computers as controlled number crunchers optimized for a variety of tasks but always, at least dreamt to be, controlled. In terms of the mathematics that became important for early computer plans, Kurt Gödel had already proved the logical impossibility of a self-consistent machine, and dozens of works of fiction have similarly taught us (as if we did not know it) that machines do break down. Their operations are based and enabled by wider infrastructures, and even the most intelligent machines have breaking points—some more seemingly more psychological (like the troubled AI), some just dysfunctional. HAL 9000 breaks down in *2001: A Space Odyssey*, the computer-controlled robots "fall ill" in *Westworld*, the security mainframes threaten the whole world with their unpredictable functioning in *War Games*, and the computers in the famous TV series *Star Trek: Next Generation* are infected with a virus. Several similar audiovisual and textual examples of mechanical and digital machines failing their duties can be mentioned.[26] Instead of the usual stories of machines working, why not just write the history of things breaking down? In a slightly Tolstoyesque manner one can claim that the story of every perfectly functional machine is the same, but every broken and failed technology has its own story, its own particular interesting angle to the world. The methodology outlined in my introduction to this book was a suggestion for how to write such a nonlinear story of the disorderly, accidental, and contingent nature of technological culture. It's perhaps a story of noise, but one that is told as a ventriloquist of Michel Serres. Instead of antithetical relations, noise is already a folding within the system in the Serresian way of understanding the parasite. It is a question of the anomaly, of *anōmalos* as the uneven, the differing, the deviating, as well as the apocalyptic revealing of its own conditions of birth.

This emphasizes the conceptual space we should give to the error messages that reveal the networks of power that otherwise go unnoticed. The challenge is to draw a cartography that respects this multiple articulation of viruses and worms as a part of digital culture, deeply rooted in the *mathesis universalis* of the seventeenth century, yet constantly revived in the new contexts of the risk society and the nonlinear logic of complexity it adheres to. Hence, instead of mere resistance to noise, it is carefully managed, and noise-toleration and living with uncertainty becomes an essential part of the techniques of digital culture. Risk society understood through the language of cybernetics marked a step from controlling information to adjustment and toleration of uncertainty and risk. In short, the discourse of computer worms and viruses is in tension between elements that underline the need for top-down control, hygiene, and digital cleanliness and the forces that attract digital culture toward flexibility and self-organizing networks. This chapter is a mapping of the forces that want to define computer worms and viruses as malicious software, *a security problem*.

Security in the Mainframe Era: From Creepers to Core Wars

In the early phase of computing, viruses were neither an issue nor a security problem back in the age of the first mainframe computers—but bugs were. The first relay computers in the 1940s encountered strange problems that caused malfunctions. Upon closer inspection, the engineers found that little bugs had crawled between the relays. The operators of the Mark II Aiken Relay calculator found a moth inside the computer, and even reported it in the computer log as the "first actual case of [a] bug being found." Because the computers were used at nighttime, the bright, warm lights attracted different sorts of bugs. Debugging naturally meant removing the moths and other bugs from the relays.[27]

But, in fact, "bug" was a term already in use in industrial production at the end of the nineteenth century. An electricity production manual from 1896 makes an interesting reference in this case: "The term 'bug' is used to a limited extent to designate any fault or trouble in the connections or working of electric apparatus."[28] Similarly, the term "bug" was used for other types of communication failures with the telegraph and Morse code.

In later use, debugging is an interesting technique in computing, and the early programming ideas of viruses and worms can be dated back as far as the early debugging of programs of the 1950s and 1960s. A short review of the history of viral programs reveals the existence of these early self-reproductive programs as utility program loops. These self-replicating programs functioned according to instructions that made the programs copy themselves from one memory location to the next. This was intended to fill the memory space with a known value, consequently allowing it to be programmed with a new application.[29] Thus, the simple instruction "move (program counter) → Program counter + 1" seemed to mark the beginning of the era of the virus.[30]

The early ideas of recurring algorithms and other self-referential code also incorporate the basic tenets of viral programs. Michael Apter had conceptualized self-reproductive programs already in 1966 in his *Cybernetics and Development*. Using reproduction subroutines that were able to recycle the original instructions into the copy meant also taking into account that such growth subroutines would easily fill the whole memory space if they were not stopped manually via the keyboard.[31] Later, such program routines were also referred to as "forkbombs," a way of potentially crashing a UNIX or a Windows operating system with a little program that exponentially multiplies itself.

In another account, the first self-replicating programs were characteristically called "rabbits." The rabbit was a mainframe program routine that could potentially make thousands of copies of itself, which would jam the executable processes, preventing the normal functioning of the computer. David Ferbrache dates rabbit programs to the 1960s, giving an example from 1966 when some students wrote a script that "would invoke itself continually, generating large numbers of temporary files which would exhaust disk space."[32] Another recollection dates the rabbit program to 1974, when a programmer working at a large company wrote a program for IBM 360 computers called Rabbit. The program kept copying itself until the rabbit slowed down or "constipated" the computer.[33]

During the 1970s, another form of self-spreading program appeared on the U.S. computer scene. Originally it was a game called Animal, but the programmer, John Walker, modified it into a self-spreading and self-updating version called "Pervade." Walker's efficient program was able to spread and find older versions of the game and replace them with newer ones. It was thus a sort of a maintenance script. As it only replaced the old program, there was no fear of clogging the system. Pervade, however, encountered problems with other commands in some Univac systems. Walker recollects one incident in particular when the Pervade program interacted with a certain company's Univac system to produce problems in the daily running of programs. This was, however, considered at that time to be more amusing than dangerous. Walker's testimony is worth quoting at length:

> More than 20 years after ANIMAL was born and briefly thrived, it's hard to imagine that the first computer virus was viewed, in those days, not as a security threat but entirely with amusement. I was, at the time, very conscious of the threat a malicious program might have created and frequently, in discussions with other programmers and site managers, used ANIMAL as an example of an easily-exploited yet little-perceived vulnerability in a sophisticated operating system which its vendor

considered reasonably secure (and was, in fact, far more secure than typical present-day personal computer operating systems). I had hoped that ANIMAL would, in some small way, get people thinking about operating systems in which security was based on a formal model, as opposed to the chewing-gum and baling wire *ad hoc*, "find a hole and plug it" approach of the vast majority of systems, then and now.

In 1975, when most computers were isolated islands which communicated with one another primarily by exchanging magnetic tapes or card decks, with modem connections used mostly by remote terminals accessing a central computer, the risk posed by a malicious ANIMAL-like program was small and could have been easily contained. Today, as the Internet is knitting together all the computers of Earth into an intercommunicating and cooperative tapestry, the lessons of ANIMAL are more significant than ever.[34]

In later, networked systems, controlling the computing environment was even more demanding. New operating system and programming paradigms were developed since the 1960s and the 1970s onwards with increasing pace. The "complexity barrier" was discussed early on, along with emergent ideas for computer programs. This referred to finding learning patterns that could "evolve" from simple structural elements toward new semiautonomous patterns.[35] Since the 1970s, considerations of distributed programs were part of early discussions concerning worms. Each program was allocated its own niche in memory space, but from time to time the programs had problems maintaining these boundaries, resulting in operations on data or programs that belonged to different procedures. This caused random operations and damage and contributed to a development of the concept of "wormhole patterns." These were rogue programs that infiltrated other memory locations, and also other computers even![36]

Hence, the origins of self-reproductive software were not malicious in intent. In some contexts, such programs were described as an amusement. Writing self-reproducing programs with FORTRAN, the first programming language, was even considered to be a form of popular entertainment in early computer programming circles, an activity that was compared to playing video games.[37] In other words, such programs inhabited a very different status than nowadays. On the level of material code, such programs are deeply (although nonlinearly) connected across decades, with several routines and practices surviving from different contexts. Yet, when it comes to naming, rhetorics, and the incorporeal event where the programs are perceived, valorized, and signified, the difference is significant. This, of course, underlines the fact that media ecologies consist of articulations between corporealities and incorporealities: the temporal-material processes of virus programs are channeled as part of agendas of politics, national security, and economics. In addition, the situation was altogether different during the 1960s: self-reproductive software was an issue of experimental computer programmers and hackers, and the power to define the legitimacy of software was not restricted to security professionals, administrative personnel, and antivirus researchers, as it came to be at the end of the 1980s.

Computers were an inspirational part of the scientific community of the 1960s. This was so clearly visible in the enthusiasm with which they were received, especially in institutes such as the Massachusetts Institute of Technology (MIT). The military had been a key sponsor of various research facilities and inventions. Cybernetic research was used to model and simulate alternative scenarios for defense and offense, including postnuclear, but new automated and distributed systems were also of interest to the defense industry.[38] In addition to MIT and other university computer labs, interesting experiments were conducted at the AT&T Bell Laboratories. Some of them relate even to the media archaeology of worms and viruses. The game Darwin, created in 1961 by Robert Morris, M. Douglas McIllroy, and Victor Vyssotsky, is one of the experimental programs that can now be seen as precursors of modern-day computer viruses. The game was played on an IBM 7090 by programming an "organism" to conquer the core memory of the computer. The player with the better organism program would eventually wipe out others and inhabit their memory space. The player with the most cunning and adaptive program came out as the winner most of the time.[39] The programmers described the game in warlike terms, such as "a game of survival and (hopefully) evolution": "Each game continues until either time runs out or only one species remains. If the members of one species manage to destroy all members of all other species, the player who coded the surviving species wins."[40] The authors of the program referred to it occasionally as a "virus."

The idea of Darwin was developed later as "Core Wars," a 1980s adaptation of the original program. It was introduced in 1984 by A. K. Dewdney in his Computer Recreations section of Scientific American, describing the technical basics of such computer "attack" programs. Similar to Darwin, Core Wars was a program as efficient as possible in trying to kill other inhabitants of the memory space. The four main technical components of the game were (1) a memory array of 8,000 addresses, (2) an assembly language called Redcode, (3) an executive program called MARS (Memory Array Redcode Simulator), and (4) a set of contending battle programs.[41]

Even this program had its own afterlife. Artificial life researchers quickly adopted Core Wars after Christopher Langton invited Dewdney to introduce the game at the first (official) ALife conference in 1987. The scientists, led by Steen Rasmussen, remodeled Core Wars into a computational ecology where the focus was not on war among programs but on analyzing and synthesizing software interaction—artificial chemistry of sorts.[42]

The game programs were innovatively named into subcategories based on their behavior: Dwarf "is a very stupid but very dangerous program that works its way through the memory array bombarding every fifth address with a zero."[43] Dwarf itself did not move, unlike Gemini, which Dewdney described as an intelligent program: "The Gemini program has three main parts. Two data statements at the beginning serve as pointers: they indicate the next instruction to be copied and its destination. A loop in the middle of the program does the actual copying, moving each instruction in turn to an address 100 places beyond its current position."[44] Similar self-copying and spreading battle programs were Bigfoot and Juggernaut, modifications of the Gemini code.[45]

Experiments since the 1950s had demonstrated the technical feasibility of recursive code, interacting program types in computer memory, paving the way for interactions also outside one computer memory. They demonstrated the connected ecology of programs and scripts, and their relation to the limited resources of memory. Later, when the discussion consolidated, the similarities of Core Wars to the technical basics of computer virus code were so striking that Dewdney had to return to the Core Wars program twice, in 1985 and 1989, after the infamous Morris worm incident, emphasizing that Core Wars programs were not harmful, unlike *real* viruses.[46] Even if Core Wars might to some have resembled the "abundant examples of worms, viruses, and other software creatures living in every conceivable computer example," Dewdney's battle programs created with the Redcode programming language were, despite their militant rhetorics, harmless. No computer system was able to automatically execute programs created with that particular language, which also prevented Core Wars programs from spreading. Nevertheless, Dewdney listed a number of such militant viral programs that resembled the game.[47] Core Wars can perhaps be understood as one of the key models with which to grasp the idea of hostile programs. It also can be seen as working toward a neo-Darwinist understanding of computer culture, where natural selection, variation, and heredity are the key processes in the fight over limited resources.

Core Wars, and the other programs introduced above, illustrate the technological lineage, the ontogenetic lines, of the virus assemblage. These types of (semi)automatic programs seem to be characteristic of the media ecology of digital network culture, making it hard to reduce viruses and worms merely to malicious pieces of code and programming. In addition, the science fiction literature of the 1970s had already demonstrated how cybernetic ideas of self-reproducing and learning programs spread on the popular cultural level and also speculated with the wider sense in which semiautonomous programs might be the future of networks.[48]

But how did computer security operate before viruses? Against what sort of threats did the computer professionals (and to some extent the public, as addressed in newspapers and magazines, for example) prepare during the early years 1960–1980? I want to address three fears of such undesirable things that also shed light on the computer virus phenomenon: (1) computer errors and bugs, (2) surveillance and threats to privacy, and (3) physical dangers.

Until the 1970s computers were mostly professional tools—meaning that their use was restricted to computer professionals and certain institutions, such as banks, insurance, and airlines. The main applications included counting, registering, and controlling.[49] At the same time, automation was becoming the keyword of social change, where the idea was that computers would take over most routine tasks in society.[50] The current discussions in 2015 and 2016 are again returning to such discussions about automation and labor, with the threatening scenarios that emerging computer services and AI would present a further mass wave of unemployment.

In terms of the earlier security threats that are good to keep in mind considering our current culture too, one of the key computer fears had to do with programming errors and unintentional bugs. *Scientific American* wrote in 1980:

> The computer error has become legendary for its mindless disregard of plausibility and common sense. Most such errors can of course be traced to mistakes made by those who program or operate the computer; now and then, though the machine itself blunders. Parts fail or malfunction; extraneous signals are introduced into the circuitry; legitimate signals go unrecognized. Even if each component is highly reliable, the computer has so many parts that errors are not infrequent.[51]

Badly performing and programmed code might be an expression when evaluating the functionality of strings of code, and it was recognized as a sort of a serious computer problem early on. "Bad bits" became a problem in the 1980s with the mass production of commercial consumer software. Since the 1980s, bad bits have haunted not only office computers and software but also leisure products.

Second, during the 1970s the computer started to become more of a personal assistant for the first time. The potential user group grew from a limited number of computer experts to office employees, hobbyists, and, with the advent of the personal computer in the 1980s, children. This change was visible in the growing fears of surveillance and threats to privacy, key themes of digital culture since the 1970s.[52] Malicious technology, surveillance, and loss of privacy were themes that were also addressed in some films dealing with the computerization of culture, such as Jean-Luc Godard's *Alphaville* (1965) with its Orwellian connotations.[53] From the 1960s on, cybernetic automation was debated intensely in most Western countries, at least; for some, it was a promise of an optimized command-and-control system that spanned from leisure to work; for others, it represented the bypassing of the human being by machines.[54] The U.S. legal and political system had devoted itself to protecting its citizens against the powers of surveillance, but several technological advances, from the telegraph and the telephone to computers, had been eroding this "social value of the individual":

> Now, the contemporary era of electronics and computers has provided the final coup de grace to the technological premises on which the classical American law of privacy has been based. Micro-miniaturization, advanced circuitry, radar, the laser, television optics, and related developments have shifted the balance of power from those who seek to protect their conversations and actions against surveillance to those who have access to the new devices. What was once Orwell's science fiction is now current engineering. (…) Fears of manipulation and of penetration into the intimate spheres of autonomy through such techniques have made worried protests against "Big Brother" a growing response to such psychological surveillance.[55]

The fear of personal secrets getting into the wrong hands, which has been raised also in several computer virus incidents where viruses have spread through personal e-mails, has long genealogical roots. The various leaks of platforms from dating sites to gaming networks are part of a longer story having to do with trust, security, and platforms. However, as the quote above illustrates, individuality and personal security have been the foremost American values of the modern period, and this historical perspective provides a good understanding of the meanings and fears attributed to network computing. When computer systems were for the first time planned as "public utilities," with suggestions even of public "data bank grids," the threat to personal privacy was the first concern that the new data storage and retrieval systems raised.[56]

Third, the physical safety of machines was a vital security issue. Computers had to be protected against physical malfunctions as well as concrete attempts at intrusion. If computer viruses illustrate the new understanding of space that comes with the telecommunicatization of the world, then the computer security discourse until the 1970s and 1980s ran along more Euclidean lines. Computers were machines in a room, not virtually connected networks that communicate in an instant across the globe. Hence, there was another sort of a need that seemed more old-fashioned: to ensure the people operating the machines were trustworthy; to contain and control the people using computers. As noted in a computer security ad in *The Times* (1972): "The trend to centralization, confining data to a single physical location aggravates the consequences of fire, flood and technical failure. And simultaneously provides increasing opportunity for malicious damage, espionage and fraud."[57] In other words, when computers were "big cabinets locked away in a data-processing department,"[58] computer security was the task of keeping unwanted people out of such confined spaces.

White-collar crime and especially the growing amount of *computer abuse* were recognized as an alarming trend during the 1970s and beginning of the 1980s. The most urgent computer security problems had to do with data entry, with thefts or embezzlement by trusted employees, and also with pranks and sabotage. As noted at the end of the 1970s, a shift was taking place, however, from external security toward internal security problems. This meant "design flaws within the computer system itself."[59] In other words, bad bits again.

As already mentioned, computer security was not an entirely new field. Internal computer security had been the object of extensive research since the 1960s. It was described as a field that regulates "the operation of the computer system in four areas: access to stored objects such as files, flow of information from one stored object to another, inference of confidential values stored in statistical databases, and encryption of confidential data stored in files or transmitted on communications lines."[60] It was like the control of urban space but transposed into the architecture of the computer system: to know who and what is allowed to go where, when, and with what intent. The extensive security of spatial arrangements had to be supplemented with new techniques of intensive, non-Euclidean procedures that worked also on the program code level. This meant a media ecological turn where not only humans but automated objects and processes maintain security: the automated, digital program code as a gatekeeper, or as a security man—the pun that was visualized in *The Matrix* (1999), with the pastiche agents of the system roaming around in their dark suits.

The new security principles were established in the midst of changing computing practices. Computing was beginning to be more than a playground for experts; it was spreading itself to workplaces and homes and at the same time transforming itself from centralized computing procedures to networked, distributed, and decentralized notions of telecomputing. The third nature of telecommunication, to use McKenzie Wark's term, proved then to be an incentive for new types of threats. The new spatial and temporal arrangements that started with the telegraph in the late nineteenth century had grown their own problems. Information was threatened by the noise of bad bits and the virtual networks of *telesthesia* that worked also as vectors of a new class of crime.[61]

Attention was focused on securing where information flows, through which gates and passage points. As defined above, this meant limiting access to authorized personnel, controlling the flow of information to third parties, making sure that access to databanks is controlled, and securing communication lines against malicious attempts to disrupt and steal from the flow of confidential data. Viruses or digital worms were recognized as a plausible security threat only years after the earlier 1970s reports on computer crime. Yet, the expanded computer security discourse of the 1970s started to recognize the new security problems, which now included such virtual agents as viruses and worms.

One such area was fiction, where the idea of a virus had been articulated already in 1972 in David Gerrold's *When HARLIE Was One*:

> You have a computer with an auto-dial phone link. You put the VIRUS program into it and it starts dialing phone numbers at random until it connects to another computer with an auto-dial. The VIRUS program then *injects* itself into the new computer. Or rather, it reprograms the new computer with a VIRUS program of its own and erases itself from the first computer. The second machine then begins to dial phone numbers at random until it connects with a third machine.[62]

Instead of securing computers against physical intrusion by malevolent individuals and criminals, computer security started also to mean protection against malevolent computer programs. For instance, Trojan programs, which for many represent an early form of computer virus, have been discussed at least since the 1960s.

Trojan horses can be defined as programs that are not what they seem to be on the surface. Named after the Homeric legend of the Trojan horse, which allowed the Greeks to gain entry into Troy by smuggling soldiers within a wooden horse, the digital versions usually refer to shareware or freeware programs that contain malicious code or, for example, create a backdoor to the computer system.[63] Consequently, several commentators, especially in the 1980s, defined computer viruses as self-replicating Trojans, expressing the implications that I am trying to map.[64]

But what does it mean to think of computer programs as a security threat? That the humans are not the only thing to worry about, but also such "post-human" agents as programs? This shift in security priorities can be understood by noting how certain key concepts and practices of security shift place and territory, remediate[65] with the digitalization of culture. Gradually such terms as barriers, detection, surveillance, guards, protection, and observation were widely adopted within the context of computer security.[66] As the security discourse moved from emphasizing *physical* safety to securing the safety of *information patterns* it deterritorialized from practices based on human-to-human interaction to interactions between machines, programs, and the temporal, nonrepresentational processes of digital code. Computer networks had been a key theme in research and design, and networking was compared to the building of the new interstate highway system in the 1960s.[67] With such networks, security could no longer be achieved only through physical measures, such as controlling access to computing terminals. Computer networking made computers susceptible to "breaking in from a distance," with imperceptible "hidden programs" being the new destructive threat.[68] Interestingly, already in 1975, Brunner's *The Shockwave Rider* had introduced the computer virus (or the tapeworm traveling across communication lines) as a vector of control societies and the novel nonplaces of electric media systems. In addition, Ryan's *The Adolescence of P-1* addressed the issues of network security problems.[69]

In both official administrative and fictional texts, viruses and worms were understood as remote agents of computer network intruders, articulated as *prostheses* of the criminal mind, cracking passwords and tricking operating systems.[70] Computer viruses and the humans writing them were seen as interdependent: "The would-be perpetrator writes a program to do his dirty work for him. Although he must identify the weaknesses in the defense, it is the program that probes them remorselessly and at high speed, missing very little."[71] In a way, antivirus and security experts saw the security infoscape turning into a deterritorialized field of prosthetic technologies, originally conceived by humans but basically independent entities of a self-reproducing (third) nature—"electronic surrogates."

From the legislator's point of view, things were problematic. Computer crime and viruses were equated with wrongful entry into property or illegal intrusion, but the implantation of such an analogy in practice was more difficult. Laws against such vandalism and malicious harm were originally aimed at protecting clearly definable *physical* objects, such as houses from harm.[72] How was this type of legislation supposed to address the problem of crime where the criminal was several hundred or thousand miles away or even in a different country with different legislation? In other words, the concept of computer crime was, during the 1960s and 1970s (and still at the end of the 1980s, after several larger computer virus and worm outbreaks), hard to grasp. Security was usually designed to provide physical protection for data and equipment, but now access control and protection against manipulation were required at the level of software and network access.[73]

In general, this process expresses how the media ecology and information ecosystem was changing to one that would have to deal with new types of threats, such as worms, viruses, and Trojans. This also spurred new forms of expertise and clusters of governance at the level of program code: security specialists, government officials, and scientists working with such regimes of power and knowledge related to computing and networking. This represents the oft-quoted shift from Foucauldian societies of discipline working on anthropological bodies of men and women to the control routines that focus on codes and passwords and the intensive processes of cybernetic machines, as Deleuze notes.[74] Control focuses not only on the anthropomorphic bodies of humans but also increasingly on the technological bodies of network culture.

Among the most powerful expressions of this change was the rising trend toward connectivity. The linking of machines via local area networks and telephone lines served as one of the most important preconditions for the new security issues and later viruses. Or, to think about the issue the other way round, worms and viruses express the change in digital culture from number-crunching machine, such as the ENIAC, EDVAC, or Mark II Aiken Relay calculator, to networks such as ARPANET or Telenet and Tymnet and personal multimedia machines, such as the IBM PC, Amiga, or Atari. New technological lineages incorporated new types of social actions, including criminal ones. In other words, they offered new types of vectors for actions that were at times clearly illegal (such as fraud) but mostly in the gray area of law (such as hacking and system entry just for fun).

The change was gradual. Until the end of the 1960s, computing had meant basically batch processing: writing the program to punch cards and taking the instructions to the computer personnel, who then input the orders into the computer. The results were retrieved later as a pile of fan-fold paper. Time-sharing computers changed this and marked the first steps of interactive computing: users had direct access to the machine, which would be used by several others at the same time. Thus, a single computer's resources were at the disposal of several users at the same time via remote terminals.[75] For security specialists, time-sharing represented several issues. Sharing resources and software via networks or floppy disks meant continuous exposure to potential viral attacks.[76] The amount of potentially untrustable links had increased; issues of access became central, and monitoring usage because most important.

Networking was seen as the next step from time-sharing.[77] Leon Bagrit prophesized in the mid-1960s that the future of computing would be in personal computers that were connected to national computer grids for information retrieval.[78] Surprisingly, Bagrit was premediating the later cloud computing culture where information was not retrieved from nationally governed grids or data banks but from corporate server farms. Computer networks incorporated new types of software, too. In the early period of networking, networked programs, similar to viruses, also emerged. The first recorded real virus incident seems to have been the Creeper virus, which spread through the ARPANET network in 1970. Creeper was a utility program made to test the possibilities of network computing. Inspired by the first program, written by Bob Thomas, several programmers made similar virus-like programs.[79] For example, the Xerox Palo Alto Labs worked with worm-like utility programs, which will be addressed more fully in Section III. Interestingly, the same labs were developing new networked personal systems, such as the Xerox Gypsy and Star, that were to be key in the interactive local area networks of the future.[80]

ARPANET was a networking project that has been called the first interactive computer-to-computer network.[81] A usual narrative about its emergence emphasizes its defense function for Cold War communications: capacity for survival, flexibility, and high performance. ARPANET also attracted a lot of attention owing to its technical innovations, such as packet switching and other networking services, including e-mail. The ALOHAnet project from 1970 had already introduced itself as the world's first wireless packet-switched network—although it used a 9,600-baud radio messaging system. It had also introduced the Aloha LAN protocol, forerunner to later key networking protocols in its ability to wait for a suitable turn in relation to ongoing message transmissions.[82] Such network projects, often articulated in the defense industry, experimental research, and academic institutions, represented a living actualization of the aspirations and utopias of connectivity that digital culture now takes for granted.[83] In addition, the first commercial networks such as Telenet and Tymnet also provided a platform for new types of tele-actions that attracted the phone phreakers of the 1970s to try out the possibilities of hacking the system.[84]

It's important to realize that even some of the basic ARPANET network programs contained something like worm-like routines, blurring the distinction between what "normal" and "abnormal" might mean. Creeper was only one of the early virus and worm programs that were part of the new multimachine network architectures being tested in the 1970s. Actually, the origins of worm-like—and partly virus-like—programs lie in the needs of network computing in general. They are not anomalies in the simple sense of the word but part and parcel of the emergence of network systems. The ambiguity is part of the virus problem even today: essentially the same program can be defined as a utility program in one context and as a malware program in another.[85] Similarly, many basic utility programs have for years been virus-like, even though such programs often require the consent of the user to operate.[86]

To restate the point: on a corporeal and infrastructural level, viruses have been primarily a phenomenon of time-sharing, networking, and, broadly speaking, connectivity. As antivirus manuals warned, "increasing compatibility of computers and communication" also meant greater exposure to viruses that could spread even faster. The more users on the same network, the more viruses as well. The more homogeneous the ecosystem, the more vulnerable.[87] The modern-day problem seems to have begun in the 1970s with the increasing trend toward connectivity. The ARPANET project was started in the 1960s, and in 1974 the National Science Foundation emphasized in a similar, network-inspired spirit the need to create a "frontier environment which would offer advanced communication, collaboration, and the sharing of resources among geographically separated or isolated researchers."[88] Alas, although connectivity basically meant that people could share the computers, resources, and data, it also meant that all the connected users and machines became exposed to the malicious software on other machines. A whole web of trust and exposure emerges. Consequently, security became a *system* problem, which reflected the change of emphasis from single computing machines to interacting networks of computers. It was not the machines only but the networks that started to characterize the modern digital culture. At least from the 1960s on, computers (or televisions) interconnected via information networks were seen as the future mode of media culture.[89] Although industrial espionage, surveillance, and privacy were more acute security problems in the 1960s and 1970s, the true virus dilemma started during the latter part of the 1980s. Viruses were quickly connected as part of the history of computer crime, which was reflected in the use of similar terms to those used for previous security menaces. The incorporeal baptizing and morphing of these programs into malicious creatures was linked to the increasing importance software and network computing played in a post-Fordist culture. As networks and cybernetic machines started to grow into prime infrastructures of global capitalism from the 1970s on, the need to *control* such environments became a key concern.

The Shift in Safety: The 1980s

The self-spreading battle programs of Darwin seem somewhat removed from the viruses and worms that were identified as a security problem in the 1980s. Yet, as one of the programmers of Darwin stated in an interview, security and military issues were always present during the Cold War years and, for instance, the Korean War. Military issues and the Cold War created one context for the emergence of computers and computer science research in universities and labs. This was described as casting a veil of secrecy over computer development:

> The tangential relationship of this background to Darwin is that although in Darwin we were exploring what we regarded as a purely academic interest, we were well aware that technical advances can be put to use for destruction as well as for beneficial uses. I would guess, without clear recollection, that this understanding significantly influenced the precautions we took to avoid any results of our investigations with Darwin from being too widely known.[90]

Years later, the first "officially" recognized virus incidents occurred in the 1980s. Richard Skrenta's Elk Cloner virus, Joe Dellinger's virus family, and the Pakistani Brain virus were the first to be spotted and written about in newspapers and other media. In addition to being the first publicized computer viruses, they were part of the shift of security practices and discourses that occurred with the gradual "computerization" of society throughout the 1970s and 1980s. In this, the corporeal and the incorporeal intertwine. The increasing number of computers and computer users, new types of computing devices, such as floppy disks, and general ideas of network computing also contributed to the emerging viral phenomenon. These were the essential vectors for the spread of worms and viruses, and represent the material, the corporeal, part of the change. The material vectors were supplemented with the incorporeal transformation of self-reproducing programs into the category of malicious software and succinctly addressed as part of the world of crime, criminals, laws, vandalism, and so forth. This incorporeal event, which turned the focus toward jurisdiction, criminal law, and business issues, was an integral part of the standardization of software culture (objects, processes, definitions, etc.) since the 1980s and the creation of a media ecology based on mass-produced standard objects.[91]

The first virus-like programs copied themselves only in the memories of single computers, but with time-sharing and networking the programs spanned across machine boundaries. In general, it was warned that as a "mathematical fact," one cannot be entirely protected if sharing, transmission, and general access are allowed in a system. Flow restrictions were seen as difficult to implement in an atmosphere that since the 1970s had underlined the free flow of information.[92] The idea of connectivity, a desire of digital network culture right up to our contemporary social media culture, proved to be a security liability. Computer viruses were part of the system they operated in—underlining the fact that understanding the functioning of this system was the key to understanding the phenomenon of self-copying programs.[93] So although unauthorized system access and software piracy had been the main threats of this media technological system, the emphasis changed with the development of a new media ecosystem biased toward telecommunications and networking.[94] Later, during the 1990s, such ideas were developed in experimental software that emphasized evolution, mutation, and self-referentiality in the form of "floating code," which is not hardware-specific but designed for fluent network behavior across systems.[95] Such programs can be seen as new forms of optimizing behavior in complex and dynamic network environments, but in some instances they also brought forth new security and control problems.

In addition to technical control, the issue of security policy was raised, as was the more general question of what electronic interaction means. The threats to internal security via networks and malicious software created an atmosphere of distrust, reflected in Ken Thompson's important and frequently cited article "Reflections on Trusting Trust" from 1984. Thompson was the 1983 Turing award winner of the Association for Computer Machinery (ACM)—a prize that has been referred to as the "Nobel Prize within computer science." The message of his Turing award lecture was simple: every piece of code is potentially malicious if it does not originate from you yourself.[96] The problem of cybernetic culture turning into a mass media culture of networking was tied to the paranoid feeling of having to interact with potentially malicious code and untrustworthy people.

Thompson's statement of suspicion was like pointing out the urbanization of the computer world: the birth of network computing meant also being in frequent contact with more people, most of whom you do not know: so many strangers crammed close to you, close to your machine, or even their programs on your computer. What sociologists in the early part of the twentieth century addressed as problems of the modern city were now problems of modern computer architecture. Implicitly, Thompson posed the problem as follows: as long as self-reproducing programs are made by computer specialists, everything is fine, but when this knowledge ends up in the hands of a wider public, the key institutions of society face new threats. The legal system viewed instances of computer vandalism still as foreign, but Thompson was among the first to warn of the emerging new situation. According to him, the problem was the lack of general understanding of the security problems of digital culture:

> I have watched kids testifying before Congress. It is clear that they are completely unaware of the seriousness of their acts. There is obviously a cultural gap. The act of breaking into a computer system has to have the same social stigma as breaking into a neighbor's house. It should not matter that the neighbor's door is unlocked. The press must learn that misguided use of a computer is no more amazing than drunk driving of an automobile.[97]

So even "kids" were a potential security threat, and program code became malicious in a way that was earlier reserved for a much more physical damage—breaking and entering as well as drunk driving. The 1980s saw a rising number of computer crime and virus and worm incidents, which reflects also that such events were starting to be recognized by the legal system, the mass media, and the computer (security) community. Computer crime was beginning to be identified as a danger for societies increasingly dependent on electronic transactions.

Recent years have seen a significant discussion—and significant national investments—in cyber security with various cyber defense centers becoming operational from the U.S. to Canada to Europe to other parts of the world. But the issue of digital code and defense was identified and was part of discussions of international politics already earlier. The Cold War was again one relevant backdrop to these considerations. The need for more efficient encryption mechanisms was discussed in the face of national crime, and international espionage originating from the Eastern bloc was emphasized.[98] The communist countries served as an integral part of the Cold War–era "closed-world discourse," where issues of border control—in physical and information terms—were underlined. This, of course, changed after the turn of the decade of the 1990s with new globalized vectors for information, where computer viruses were no longer perhaps metaphorical communists, but increasingly, for instance, transnational terrorists.[99] Coming to 2010s, it also meant the blurring of boundaries between financially motivated crime, nongovernmental terrorism, and nation-based attacks, all of which had to be taken into account in discussing the cyber threats to critical national infrastructures in the past years.[100]

The United States had encountered hundreds of cases of computer crime and abuse already in the 1970s. However, the majority of cases probably went unreported. The increasing automation of society meant new forms of crimes (and jurisdiction concerning crimes) that focused on the seemingly nonmaterial aspects of property:

> As we enter the information age, business and white-collar crime is changing significantly. Valuable assets are increasingly represented by information, an intangible property, and its processing, transmission, and storage are rapidly becoming the targets of crime. Such crime includes fraud, theft, embezzlement, larceny, sabotage, espionage, extortion, and conspiracy.[101]

National and economic interests were central in the context of new security practices and discussion. References to international politics were frequent at the time of the Cold War. The "individualization" of the media sphere with personal computing in the 1980s changed certain emphases, but the basic arguments stayed the same: computer crime and malicious software constituted threats to organized society and the economy. The home became (once again, one might add) a central point of defense against the frightening world of media technologies. The user had to be educated, a theme that I will address in Section II.

Definitions of computer security can be read to reveal a lot about cultural dispositions, preferences, and values. Computer security was understood as

> that body of technology, techniques, procedures, and practices that provides the protective mechanism to assure the safety of both the systems themselves and the information within them, and limits access to such information solely to authorized users. *Computer security is of importance whether the information to be protected is personal in nature and therefore related to privacy concerns, whether it is defense in nature and therefore related to the security of the country, or whether it is sensitive in nature from a business point of view and therefore relevant to corporate well-being.*[102]

This definition reveals in its second sentence the key concerns of information culture, revealing the values implicit in computer security of the past decades: individual privacy (a key theme of the modern world and bourgeois subjectivity for the past 300 years, at least), national security (a key theme at least since the nineteenth century), and commercial security of international transactions (particularly emphasized since the 1980s). As the early capitalist societies of the mid-nineteenth century turned statistical mathematics and understanding of systems into insurance companies, probability management, and other tools for coping with insecurity and randomness, so the digital problems in unstable systems were tackled with territorializing definitions and policy management. Viruses became perceived as both a national threat and an international problem for information capitalism. Consequently, in the 1980s security became even more important a factor in the design of computer systems than ever before.[103] Although university computer labs emphasized openness and access to all users through to the beginning of the 1980s, the growth in hacking was about to change this stance.[104] In addition, the culture industry discussed security problems; for example, John Badham's movie *War Games* (1983) raised the possibility of a nuclear war launched by a computer error and a hacker.[105] Another key film, *Tron* (1982), introduced a hostile computer system that threatened not merely the ecosystem of the computer world but also the world outside its digital domain. In another context, in 1983 the U.S. national media brought "hacking" to the lips of the public with its reporting of the incidents of the "414 Gang" and then later in the 1980s with the case of the infamous Kevin Mitnick, later turned cyber security consultant.[106]

Computers had become part of society. They were not anymore solely used by a limited number of professionals in computing centers of the universities, state offices, banks, and insurance companies. They had penetrated the lives of small businesses and normal middle-class people. Computers started to mean not just number-crunching business applications or scientific tools but everyday media machines with leisure applications. Since the 1970s, microcomputing meant new perspectives to what computers could do. Many research centers, including Palo Alto PARC, were inventing what we now, retroactively, coin the "future of computing." Companies such as Texas Instruments saw the future of computing in home computers connected to telecommunications systems. Even if this was fully realized only in the 1990s, with the Internet and the easy-to-use browser, the computer was transformed into a versatile media player offering a real challenge to the hegemony of the television as the center of the household.[107]

However, with personal computing came also new types of problems, such as malicious software. The first much-reported computer virus, as mentioned above, was Elk Cloner, programmed in 1981–1982 by Richard Skrenta and intended to be only a harmless prank.[108] After 50 boots (according to some sources 30 boots), Cloner printed a "poem" on the computer screen:

Elk Cloner—the program with a personality
It will get on all your disks
It will infiltrate your chips
Yes it's Cloner!
It will stick to you like glue
It will modify ram too
Send in the Cloner!

Cloning and copying were presented as the key diagrammatic features of digital culture. Cloner was a boot-sector virus that intercepted certain command lines (DOS RUN, LOAD, BLOAD, and CATALOG). The virus remained resident in the system and infected every disk inserted to the floppy drive.[109] It was more of a harmless curiosity than a grave danger to the computer community. "I wrote it as a joke to see how far it would spread," says Skrenta. "But it's easy for a malicious mind to change or add a few lines and turn a harmless toy into a vicious tool."[110] Yet, the question was about not merely malicious people but the media ecology where viruses spread.[111] Nobody was looking for computer viruses back then, and the viruses themselves had trouble finding suitable vectors for spreading. For example, Elk Cloner was a boot-sector virus that spread only via floppy disks. The boot sector is a key part of data storage systems (from hard disks to floppies) that contain the vital booting information for the computer. The usual way for a virus to infect other machines was through the copying and exchange of disks—cultural habits that gained ground during the 1980s.

Also Apple II hosted viruses in the early 1980s. It had already succeeded in creating a friendly face for computing in general.[112] As Paul Ceruzzi notes, Apple II, introduced in 1977, had "excellent color graphics capabilities" and it was optimal for new "fast-action interactive games"; it was packed in an attractive plastic case, and through its name and other qualities was perceived as friendly and nontechnical. Of course, other examples illustrated the same point, for example the Commodore PET—who could imagine a computer with a kinder name? Thus, it is exactly in this context of "user-*friendly* personal computing" that worms, viruses, and other malicious programs were constructed as menaces of the information society: the wild viruses versus the tamed *pet* computers.

The history of personal computing with a friendly face begins in the 1960s. The PDP8 minicomputer was released in 1963, aimed especially at "educational users." The number of computer users and hobbyists increased throughout the 1970s, as reflected in the publication of the first home computing magazine, *Byte*, in 1975 and the opening of the first computer shop in Los Angeles the same year. Office applications such as word processing remained in the spotlight, but at the same time the designers kept the larger audience in mind.[113] There was more to computers, including entertainment. Games represented the new face of computing and the new computing audience; in general, applications marketed to children and youth, especially home computer entertainment, expressed this new trend as a revolution. "Probably the most important effect of these games, however, is that they have brought a form of the computer into millions of homes and convinced millions of people that it is both pleasant and easy to operate, what computer buffs call 'user friendly,'" reported *Time* in 1983.[114]

The focus on games but in general, the user-friendliness, was represented as a generational shift. It was well illustrated by the widely cited Apple Macintosh TV commercial from 1984, directed by Ridley Scott, which shows the new frontier of computing as revolutionary, personal, and playful in contrast to the gray standard image that IBM had risen to symbolize.[115] The new "dream machines" (as Ted Nelson described them in 1975) were supposed to act as catalysts of a new era of equality and innovation and the spreading of the hacker ethic. The imaginary of the computer underwent maybe not a revolution but at least a change between 1975 and 1985. A few years after, the aspirations of early pioneers were adopted as part of the marketing campaigns and industry visions of a new commercial network culture.

Such visions were in a key position to contain the fears surrounding computers. In addition to being nice and tame, the computer was also to be prestigious and reliable. *Time* magazine elected the computer the machine of the year for 1982. Hence it is no wonder that the computer industry predicted a gold rush of the digital age:

> There are 83 million U.S. homes with TV sets, 54 million white-collar workers, 26 million professionals, 4 million small businesses. Computer salesmen are hungrily eyeing every one of them. Estimates for the number of personal computers in use by the end of the century run as high as 80 million. Then there are all the auxiliary industries: desks to hold computers, luggage to carry them, cleansers to polish them. "The surface is barely scratched," says Ulric Weil, an analyst for Morgan Stanley.[116]

The same year, *Scientific American* described the revolution inherent in personal computing in a similarly striking way: "If the aircraft industry had evolved as spectacularly as the computer industry over the past 25 years, a Boeing 767 would cost $500 today, and it would circle the globe in 20 minutes on five gallons of fuel. Such performance would represent a rough analogue of the reduction in cost, the increase in speed of operation and the decrease in energy consumption of computers."[117] Computers were seen as the avant-garde of an ongoing "revolution," yet the revolution was constructed of numerous complex, interconnected parts. Enthusiasm was all around, predating the current glamour of Silicon Valley social media culture.

Computers were defined as machines for receiving, storing, manipulating, and communicating information. Different tasks involved hundreds of thousands or even millions of logical operations carried out using binary numbers. The machine was complex, but also increasingly available to the amateur users. It was practically impossible for the human intellect to follow this number of operations, which meant more or less trusting that the computer did what the user wanted it to do. Paradoxically, the fact that the computer automated several number-crunching functions on behalf of the user, which is often considered the advantage of computers, was also at the heart of the problem. A tiny piece of program code acting as a virus easily went unnoticed within the complex heart of automated computer operations.[118] Most of the computer events were anyway not really something that one knew about or necessarily understood.

Computers, after the "revolution" of the 1980s, were increasingly "plug-in" systems designed to suit the needs of people without professional understanding. In a sense, at the core of this turn is a new cultural perception and understanding of computers. The media theorist Norbert Bolz has emphasized the importance of this new cultural situation in a Marxist vein: modern perception informed by critical reason concerned itself with profundities, thus exposing and tearing "away the veil of appearances," whereas the contemporary situation is marked by an enchantment with the surface.[119] According to Bolz, the main function of modern user-friendly (computer) systems has been the concealment of the complex mechanisms of technical and cultural power inherent within such machines. Around 1980, structural complexity became functional simplicity, where the user submits to a "voluntary slavery." To paraphrase Bolz, technological objects demand the replacement of understanding with consent, where the graphical user interfaces (GUIs) are hiding the actual control logic of the machine. Friedrich Kittler has proposed similar arguments from a different point of view: the modern culture of operating systems is hiding the real mode of the computer. The user-friendly computer, even though it presents itself as a ubiquitous, interactive machine, is actually a hierarchical control machine that prescribes the possible user actions.[120]

The new commodity computers, such as the Apple II, were designed to be attractive to the eye. Until then, computers had been collections of screws and bolts; Apple designed these inside an attractive cover, making the computer an affiliate of the typewriter family. The processing units, circuits, and other hardwired bits and pieces were inside the cover, functioning autonomously, with the user having only limited power over the inside of the machine.[121]

In short, it is important to read the emergence of viruses against this backdrop of a change in computing design, habits, uses, and spread. The coming commonality of the machine was contributing to these issues, as a 1992 "management overview" concerning IBM PC machines running DOS operating systems reflected:

> Thus there is an enormous common platform by which a virus may spread and a far larger number of people with the knowledge to use or misuse these computers. The computers are comparatively cheap and thus readily affordable to amateur or deviant programmers. PCs running MS-DOS have no inbuilt security whatsoever; as soon as the machine is switched on it is wide open to investigation or attack. The IBM PC is a near-perfect platform for virus propagation.[122]

What were the reasons for this? First, mainly average users, not experts, used personal computers; this is what the whole computer revolution was about. People using mainframes were professionals who knew how to react when the computer started to act oddly.[123] Second, personal computers were designed for single users only, with limited security measures against any illegal access. However, computers were increasingly used for networking and file sharing, resulting in security and virus problems.[124] Third, mainframe computers had much more complex operating systems, but writing viruses for personal computers was not that hard. Even if an average user had little idea how the machine actually functioned, it was not an insurmountable problem for a student with knowledge of the basics of programming to write a self-replicating and spreading program.[125] Indeed, ever since "script-kiddies" have been a frequently quoted and widely despised form of computer user who has good copy-and-paste skills and not much programming knowledge. Concerning those who actually program, a large number of the early viruses were written in PC assembler language or in such high-level languages as C and Turbo Pascal.

The assembler language, closer to the machine language, made it easier to write boot-sector viruses and more compact programs. This was especially important before large hard drives and GUI systems, which usually in any case have the side effect of users neglecting virus-increased file length.[126]

All in all, the home user of a personal computer was in several respects destined to be on the defensive. As a Data-Fellows virus protection manual from the early 1990s pointed out, security in personal computers is such a big problem because the internal mechanisms of the computer are so vulnerable to infection. The manual argued that it is practically impossible to control a program once it is running. Thus, a program could basically destroy or at least corrupt data on the computer without the user knowing about it.[127] Viruses demonstrated that users were neither alone with nor in control of their computers and that malicious software taking over of the machine could interrupt users' standard routines (as it interrupts the call routines of an operating system).[128]

In short, maliciously minded hackers were not the only issue the user had to deal with; the whole computer system proved to be part of the problem. Computer architecture was so complex that the user was easily left feeling slightly lost. In this technical light, important issues contributing to the phenomenon of viruses were the new vehicles for transporting data introduced during the 1970s and 1980s: portable diskettes, or disks. First with disks, bulletin board systems, local area networks, and computer information services such as Compuserve and the Well, and later with Internet networking protocols, browsers, services, and platforms, the computer could connect with the outside world, downloading whatever what was wanted for pleasure or business—but also exposing oneself to vectors of disorder. At least that was the key narrative that was offered throughout the years.

At the beginning of the 1980s, the standard storage device of personal computers was the floppy disk made of Mylar plastic coated with magnetic material.[129] The disk was an important vehicle in promoting the arrival of computers among ordinary people. It was relatively fast, had both read and write abilities, and allowed "random access": a specific piece of data could be retrieved more easily than from a magnetic or paper tape, the earlier versions of mass storage.[130] It was not only storage, of course; the small, portable size was important as it eased the transport and exchange of data. But the operating systems had to be compatible, of course. The CP/M operating system, which facilitated the interaction of different computers, was soon replaced by the IBM MS-DOS system, resulting in "an almost unlimited pool of software" that programmers on another continent could develop for computers in other parts of the globe, but also allowing viruses to "spread across the scores of MS-DOS computers almost unstopped,"[131] as Ralf Bürger noted.

In other words, technical potential was crucial for digital contagions. Although, for example, the first PC virus, Brain, observed in 1986, used diskettes to spread, it became practically extinct when hard disks became more popular. Brain could use only the boot sectors of 360-kb floppy diskettes and was unable to infect the boot sector of a hard disk.[132] It did, however, spread successfully for several years, becoming perhaps the most widespread virus of the late 1980s. Even though it spread via diskettes, it did so practically worldwide: Brain started its life in Pakistan, but in no time crossed the Pacific, "spreading through the United States like a forest fire in a high wind."[133] According to one estimate, it infected 100,000 IBM PC disks in the United States alone.[134]

Some argue that the virus was meant as a warning to software pirates and that it spread only via illegal copying. The authors of the virus, Basit Farooq Alvi and Amjad Farooq Alvi, sold software applications and wanted perhaps to teach pirates a lesson. The body after all contained the message:

Welcome to the Dungeon
© 1986 Basit & Amjad (pvt) Ltd.
BRAIN COMPUTER SERVICES
730 Nizam Block Allama
Igbal Town
Lehore, Pakistan
Phone: 430791, 443248 2800530
Beware of this VIRUS
Contact us for vaccination[135]

But the authors later emphasized that it was written in order to test possible security flaws of the DOS-system as well as just to see how far such a program might spread. Brain, most active from 1986 until the end of the 1980s, was originally a relatively harmless virus. It exhibited interesting "stealth behavior" in that it could hide its presence from scanners. It infected the boot sector but was able to mimic a healthy boot process. It placed a part of itself in another section of the disk, which was marked as "bad" to prevent it from being used. The first version was harmless (and merely changed the disk name to © Brain). Later versions were more of a nuisance, causing real trouble for the computers infected. Brain spread worldwide within a few years.[136] Furthermore, in a curious version of ethnography of digital culture, the antivirus researcher Mikko Hyppönen traveled to Pakistan 25 years later, in 2011, and interviewed the original creators of the Brain virus![137]

Ever since the early viruses, pirate games had been among the main scapegoats. Manuals and other instructive articles listed illegally copied applications and games as central risks, because these disks had the biggest and widest circulation via different unverified channels.[138] The various instruction manuals worked as *prophylactic texts* and recommended as a key feature of "safe microcomputing" the avoidance of pirate programs and other suspiciously acquired applications. Often these protective measures were extended to pornographic material and other examples of leisure software. Games were often blamed.[139]

However, at least two objections can be raised. First, some computer security experts have acknowledged that the connection between viruses and software piracy was overstated. It has been accepted as a myth—but a useful myth in fighting piracy.[140] To create an atmosphere of fear over illegal products was useful. Second, commercial, legitimate software was also infected. Among the first Macintosh viruses was the peculiar Peace virus, which was programmed in 1987 and infected thousands of computers in 1988. The virus was basically benign, even ethical, as was the message it displayed: "Richard Brandow, publisher of the MacMag, and its entire staff would like to take this opportunity to convey their universal message of peace to all Macintosh users around the world."[141]

The virus spread to Aldus Corporation's main duplication facility, resulting in 10,000 copies of the Freehand program becoming infected. Thus, even though the virus was supposed to be peaceful, Brandow was some years later charged with malicious mischief by prosecutors in King County, Washington.[142] The incident demonstrated very early on that official software did not necessarily mean clean and trustworthy. This resonates well with Ken Thompson's point quoted above: in a postindustrial society based on mass communication and mass software, you can never be 100% sure of its origins and contents, or what it will do to your computer. Everyone knows this even from standardized legitimate software: code crashes, operating systems have issues, applications let you down frequently (just like when writing this chapter, my version of Microsoft Word kept on crashing mysteriously and often). But average users were forced to trust their computer software providers, even though *trusted* systems could not be equated to *trustworthy* systems.[143] Viruses such Peace or Concept, which spread on the Microsoft Windows '95 Software Compatibility Test, also demonstrated the potential dangers. Similarly, the AIDS Trojan incident of 1989 exemplified the problems of trusting otherwise convincing sources. A company called PC Cyborg shipped 10,000 Aids Information diskettes that actually included a hidden malicious program.[144]

Software seems to have become a major problem as it spread to lay users. Initially, the users themselves designed the programs and thus had the ability also to improve the software, but from the early 1980s on, computers were perceived as being "used by people who know no more about [their] inner workings than they do about the insides of their TV sets—and do not want to. They will depend entirely on the commercial programmers."[145]

There was a constant lack of good and reliable programs. Badly programmed software was not the only problem—software was also programmed to do bad things. This issue touched simultaneously the economic, political, and individual levels of society, as it was turned into an issue of risk and risk management. Although the first viral programs were made in computing laboratories by early hackers, one could no longer count on the same safety nets during the 1980s. Experts warned: software was no longer safe—it became a risk.

Fred Cohen and the Computer Virus Risk

Several of the early and mostly harmless viruses were modified over the years and sometimes equipped with malicious payloads. During the latter half of the 1980s, many computer programs were more than funny pranks or innocent tests. "Dangerous miniprograms" became an issue around the middle of the decade. Viruses were signaled as the new software demons that could turn the computer's memory into "a mass of confusion."[146] Lehigh University was hit in 1987 by a particularly calamitous program that infected the COMMAND. COM file, a crucial routine in DOS, and later also in Windows, that sets up the system during booting. The virus could perhaps have come up with no better part of a system to infect. In fact, the virus was so destructive that it damaged the infected machines *too* quickly—it ate out its own ecosystem. And consequently, it did not succeed in spreading beyond the university's computers. The virus received a lot of publicity, resulting in growing public awareness of computer viruses. It also led to the creation of the important Virus-L news group on Usenet, coordinated by Ken van Wyk, who was at the time working at the university.[147]

Another classic virus from the same year was Cascade, which made letters "fall" to the bottom of the screen. In a way, Cascade demonstrated the breaking down of the new digital era, as well as the digital ontology of writing: good-bye to the discrete human-readable Gutenberg Galaxy of letters; welcome the writing executed in code on screens. This machine code caused the visible surface layer of graphical user interfaces to crumble into pieces, underlining how language was no longer only about meanings and natural languages; it functioned increasingly as the binary machine code (and the program language intermediaries) that was more pragmatic and function oriented than semantic.[148] Viral code was rearranging not only the surface level of the computer screen but also the inner workings of the machine.

Soon the virus was also attracting explicit AIDS analogies: "It might do to computers what AIDS has done to sex."[149] Where AIDS had created a new culture of bodily anxiety and political paranoia, computer sex diseases were thought to create similar fears about communication and digital contact. The Datacrime virus was deemed one of the first so-called media viruses, attracting wide press and television coverage. Commentators noted that the activation day, Friday, October 13, 1989, fell near Columbus Day, probably why the media paid special attention to this program.[150] This demonstrates how viruses are parasitical in the wider sense: clinging not only to programs and operating systems but also to symbolically significant dates. The technical viruses also relied on the social routines and meanings.[151]

But not everyone even believed in the existence of such programs. Even after several reported virus outbreaks, many commentators declared that computer viruses were only an urban myth. For whatever reason, a lot of the security community seemed to be uninterested in computer viruses. One such commentator was Peter Norton, who later became known through one of the best-selling virus protection programs, Norton Antivirus.[152]

It was one particular computer pioneer who was central in bringing these miniprograms to the attention of the computer security community. Fred Cohen illustrated the risks of digital contagions by way of analytical insights to the computer science of viruses. From 1983 on, he warned of the dangers of computer viruses to organized society. Antivirus researchers and writers have, since the late 1980s, touted Cohen as the originator of virus awareness as a result of his work as a scientist (and also part of the information security industry from 1977). Cohen demonstrated the universality of risk and limitations in protection: practically any computer system was vulnerable to attack. Cohen's writings and tests proved that we have no universal foolproof way of determining whether a virus is present in a system.[153] Through Cohen we can also grasp the idea of viral risks as part of the risk society.

Cohen was working with viruses already in 1983, under the supervision of Professor Leonard Adleman at the University of Southern California. The school (now renamed the Viterbi School of Engineering) was then a hotbed of computer and network research. Adleman had previously been engaged with encryption analysis, and security research was obviously already on the agenda in the department. Later Adleman became one of the pioneers of DNA computing. In the 1970s, his student Cohen was occupied with designing protocols for voice, video, and data networks. Cohen's virus test results were publicized in a paper in 1984, and in 1986 in the dissertation "Computer Viruses." The texts—and Cohen's work in general—marked a new phase in digital culture demonstrating the characteristics of a risk culture. Cohen's frequently cited 1984 paper, "Computer Viruses—Theory and Experiments," showed that even if several potentially widespread threats to academia, business, and government had been recognized, policies for the prevention of viruses had not been considered.[154] Cohen came up with the widely recognized and accepted definition of a virus as "a sequence of symbols which, upon interpretation in a given environment, causes other sequences of symbols in that environment to be modified so as to contain (possibly evolved) viruses."[155] In this definition, "sequences of symbols" means computer programs and "environment" refers to computer systems; that is, viruses are programs that attach themselves to other programs and transform them into vectors for the further spread of the viral script.

More generally, it was not merely about of viral code but about the communication channels that form networks of computers. In fact, Cohen introduced a modified theory of Turing machines in the age of networking. Interpreting data was not restricted to the machine where the data was stored; theoretically, open-flow models made it technically feasible to teleoperate machines. The control of a machine did not, by definition, lie with the machine, but potentially with a telemachine or even in semiautonomous computer programs. Control was distributed.

As mentioned already above, software threats were already an issue in the 1960s and the 1970s (e.g., in Trojan horse programs), and people in computer security became gradually aware of the new dangers inherent in malicious miniprograms. However, Cohen was the one who—with Ken Thompson—pointed out that viruses, which had earlier been simply intriguing experiments in programming, would present a possible danger to information society. "Computer Viruses—Theory and Experiments" and Cohen's dissertation outline the following: (1) the definitions and the internal structure of virus programs, (2) the prevention and the cure for infected computers, and (3) the reasons viruses were such an effective and difficult problem for the security systems and policies of the 1980s.

According to Cohen, the problem with established security procedures was "transitivity."[156] In grammar, transitive verbs can be understood as connectors between subjects and objects, forming a circuit between them in a sentence. Transitive relations in general also form circuits, via relations of equality, set inclusion, divisibility, implication, and so on. For Cohen, transitivity had to do with the flow of information as part of the new focus on sharing and networking. Communication systems would have to work transitively. Even though isolationism would have provided perfect security against viruses and other network problems, it was not an option in a world becoming increasingly dependent on the flow of information.[157] Transitivity of information means that any information flow from A to B and from B to C implies also a link from A to C. Thus, it describes an open (but controlled, as with protocols) system of flows. The partition model was conceptualized as a basic limit to this flow, closing a system into subsets and restricting the free flow of information. Cohen cites the Bell-LaPadula security model (1973) and the Biba integrity model (1977) as policies that "partition systems into closed subsets under transitivity."[158] In Cohen's own words:

> In the Biba model, an integrity level is associated with all information. The strict integrity properties are the dual of the Bell-LaPadula properties; no user at a given integrity level can read an object of lower integrity or write an object of higher integrity. In Biba's original model, a distinction was made between read and execute access, but this cannot be enforced without restricting the generality of information interpretation since a high integrity program can write a low integrity object, make low integrity copies of itself, and then read low integrity input and produce low integrity output.[159]

Cohen demonstrated the vulnerabilities in existing security systems in a rather direct way. During 1983 and 1984, he conducted experiments on various computer systems that aimed to demonstrate the powers of virus programs. Essentially, viral programs were able to use the transitivity of systems to their advantage. This was a question that, for example, the programmers of the early Brain-virus in Pakistan were interested in: How do viral programs spread outside machines?

Cohen's own account of the first test sounds rather unglamorous in its description of the birth of the first "official" computer virus.

> On November 3, 1983, the first virus was conceived as an experiment at a weekly seminar on computer security. The concept was first introduced in this seminar by the author, and the name "virus" was thought of by Len Adleman. After 8 hours of

expert work on a heavily loaded VAX 11/750 system running Unix, the first virus was completed and ready for demonstration. Within a week, permission was obtained to perform experiments, and 5 experiments were performed. On November 10, the virus was demonstrated to the security seminar.[160]

The demonstrations did what they were supposed to do: they proved the real threat of viral penetration into most computer systems. In these simulated attacks, the virus acquired all system rights in under an hour; in one case it took only five minutes. According to Cohen, everyone was surprised, especially with how quickly it took over a system.[161] The program had proved its dangerous nature.

In fact, the virus tests were a little too efficient. After the amazing spreading capacity was perceived, and the potential dangers understood, the UNIX system administrators at the University of Southern California wanted to terminate testing. Several months of negotiation resulted in deadlock, leaving Cohen with an extremely important and fresh concept in his hands but without a system to test it on.[162] However, by 1984 Cohen was back to testing a Bell-LaPadula integrity system on a Univac 1108 computer.

Consider Cohen's words, where the virus is presented as an autonomous actor, as if alive:

> After 18 hours of connect time, the 1108 virus performed its first infection. A fairly complete set of user manuals, use of the system, and the assistance of a past user of the system were provided to assist in the experiment. After 26 hours of use, the virus was demonstrated to a group of about 10 people including administrators, programmers, and security officers. The virus demonstrated the ability to cross user boundaries and move from a given security level to a higher security level. Again it should be emphasized that no implementation flaws were involved in this activity, but rather that the Bell-LaPadula model allows this sort of activity to legitimately take place.[163]

Cohen discusses various types of viruses that exhibit different forms of behavior in varying environments. For example, the evolving virus was input with random code to produce Darwinian effects:

```
Program evolutionary-virus:=
{print random-variable-name, " = ", random variable name;
loop: if random-bit = 0 then
            {print random-operator, random-variable-name:
            goto loop:}
```

```
print semicolon:
}
Subroutine copy-virus-with-random-insertions:=
{loop: copy evolutionary-virus to virus till
            semicolon found;
    if random-bit = 1 then print-random-statement;
    if –end-of-input-file goto loop:
}
main-program:=
{copy –virus-with-random-insertions;
infect-executable:
if trigger-pulled do-damage:
goto next:}
next:}164
```

In practice, the idea of a virus with randomly inserted code was extremely unlikely to work. Computer programs are so unstable that there is always a very high chance that the program will not work with additional code. Hence, the artificial life prospects of this EV (evolutionary) program were still more imaginary than real. Of course, some years later, breeding programs in the form of genetic algorithms were incorporated as software tools into commercial projects. These provided a far more stable form of "evolution" as they were always oriented toward some specific task or a goal they were supposed to optimize.

Cohen's general aim was obviously to find models and procedures for secure computing—to maintain the flow of information in society that was increasingly focused on opening up things: opening up markets, deregulation, global communications, etc. For Cohen, the virus was not just a passive material, technological component but something active and spreading. In fact, Cohen suggests in his PhD dissertation that computer viruses express the fundamental properties of life: reproduction and evolution. Cohen's mathematical definition of life allows it to be regarded as a phenomenon that is not an attribute of a particular substance, but a form of connection:

> The essence of a life form is not simply the environment that supports life, nor simply a form which, given the proper environment, will live. The essence of a living system is in the coupling of form with environment. The environment is the context, and the form is the content. If we consider them together, we consider the nature of life.[165]

However, it should be noted that Cohen was not the only one drawing such analogies: one often neglected work is the thesis "Selbstreproduktion bei

Programmen auf dem Apple II-Rechner" by Jürgen Kraus, submitted at the University of Dortmund, Germany, in 1980, which was also an attempt to schematize principles of artificial life as similar to computer viruses.[166] The cultural representation of computer viruses and antivirus research seems to emphasize the Anglo-American world, neglecting the work done elsewhere. Nevertheless, self-reproductive software was emerging as a theme that cut across the whole machinic phylum (media ecology) of network culture. What is interesting is that Cohen seemed to touch on ideas of evolution as symbiosis rather than mere neo-Darwinist models of competition. I return to such discussions in Section III.

The viral life of digital code reads as part of the new conception of postindustrial society as a risk society. This discourse of risk had also, since the 1980s, become commonplace in contemporary digital culture. The changes in the use and management of computers alongside the erosion of centralized computing and the rise of personal computing have resonated with new security anxieties. Networking opened information channels between various parts of the world, but these channels also enabled the flow of contagious code and malicious software. Consequently, the fact that we are increasingly dependent on computers has become the greatest of our anxieties, as recognized by computer security professionals in the early 1990s. As the first epigraph to this section notes, the increasing dependence of society on information leads to new problems of reliability and communications vulnerability.[167] This new state of risk produced in its wake a new industry of risk management and digital security services.

Telecommunications and computers had, since the early 1970s, been perceived in the United States as a vital technological field for future improvements in education, public health, postal services, and the institutions of law and criminal justice. The 1970s were also the time when "information society" spread through various countries as a domestic strategic catchphrase. Soon it evolved into a neoliberal agenda. Around 1984–1985, the deregulation of financial markets and telecommunications took off in the United Kingdom and the United States. Doctrines of (seemingly) free competition, transnational markets, and privatization arose at the same time as the technological adjustments of high-speed networks, optoelectronics, and increases in memory capacity.[168] Computers were particularly important for industry and commerce, where computer risks started to equal business risks. New transnational networks seemed to bring new sources of wealth in the 1970s, but they also necessitated ensuring the infrastructure was safe and functional.

This meant recognizing and preparing for the new dangers owing to the massive interconnectedness of networks, a sort of risk society of complex systems where "[m]any believe the point has been reached where a failure within one key computer on a networked system could have repercussions which might impact a whole economy, for example, in a programmed securities trading or in the transfer of electronic funds out of one country and into another,"[169] as the *Information Security Handbook* wrote in 1991.

Digital security became an important topic for the business world. The issues in risk society led to a wide-ranging change of procedures, emphases, and discourses of computer security, which from the end of the 1980s increasingly emphasized risk *management*.[170] Because isolationism was unacceptable (especially businesswise), the computerized society had to tolerate a certain amount of insecurity and uncertainty in its communication networks. This was an expression of something inherent in a technological culture: the necessary by-product of communication was the possibility of miscommunication and communication accidents. Thus, even if I outlined the modern fear of noise and error at the beginning of this chapter, computerized culture since the 1980s has become more tolerant of noise, in a way. Noise and security problems became internalized with cultural practices and discourses under the heading of risk. Accidents are not just something that happens "out there"; they have become statistics, probabilities—things to be accounted for. Risks became part of everyday life when it was realized that the most efficient way of coping with them was to fold them in as a productive part of the consumer machinery. Hence, from a systems-oriented perspective, we might note how the issue was one of translation: How could the noise be translated as part of the network? How could the deterritorialized flows of self-reproductive programs be reterritorialized as part of the capitalist institutions?

Ulrich Beck, in his influential *Risikogesellschaft* (1986), described this as the birth of risk society, stating that modernity had moved from industrial production to risk production as well. Focusing on key accidents of the 1980s (Chernobyl, Bhopal, Exxon *Valdez*), the risk society thesis suggested that such risks were crucially different from the dangers of the industrial society of the nineteenth century. The new risks were spatially, temporally, and socially unbound and, thus, not causally determinable: responsibilities were no longer easily defined. Technological society produced risks and dangers that could never be entirely dealt with, but only minimized. In other words, the production of wealth was necessarily accompanied by a production of possible accidents and risks as the surplus of the system.[171]

At the turn of the millennium, Beck redefined his thesis with some new emphases. For Beck, risks mean not actual damage, but potential damage in the future. This creates a peculiar time-loop where the future appears to act on the present. This also relates to the much more recent conceptualization of premediation by Richard Grusin.[172] The linear continuity of time is broken, and a new type of interphase is created that fluctuates between the attractors of security and destruction.[173] I would like to pick out three themes from Beck's writing that I find particularly important considering the risks of computer viruses and worms.

First, risks are always part of the future tense—they are something projected, simulated, modeled. They are constructed via techniques of cultural perception and definition, which define also issues relevant for a political agenda. Who is in the position to make publicly valid risk statements? What types of phenomena are defined as risks? Who benefits from the fear that discourses of risks engender? In a web of similar questions, Joost Van Loon argues that risks are always constructed via visualization, signification, and valorization, all of which refer to processes of assigning risks a certain cultural place and meaning.[174] As analyzed in the next section, viruses work as part of a certain imaginary of a healthy body of digital society and are territorialized as diseases of such a body.

Second, as Van Loon and Beck argue, the media have a special place in the definition of contemporary risk culture: risks are mediated risks, defined and perceived via the technologies, discourses, and institutions of the media. Mediation refers here to virtuality in its philosophical sense: risks are virtual but not actual, potential but real. Risks are *becoming* real. Risks are media risks so that imaginary risks are on the same ontological playing field as what could be said to be "real" risks. Imaginary risks are also real on a certain level. Risks come in existence only through their mediatization, and this is always connected to a political agenda, which makes it worthwhile to analyze the a priori of such cultural perceptions of risk and accident.[175] Risks live in media representations and simulations; they are virtually real in various (scientific) scenarios and probabilities, news reports, (science) fiction stories, and so forth, all of which enjoy a considerable amount of cultural prestige in contemporary media culture. Again, Grusin's idea of premediation is relevant. Risks make good media events, and it is to a certain extent irrelevant whether the virtual risks ever actualize. Van Loon's analysis of the I Love You virus (1999) demonstrates the logic of media culture. The virus spread as an actual computer program via people's e-mails and information networks, but it attracted media attention and so spread as a media virus as well. The reproductive technological logic of the viral was duplicated in the media publicity logic that spread on the social bond of cyber risks:

> A simple example would be the "I Love You" computer virus which, apart from directly jamming network systems, also caused immense indirect problems as system operators and webspinners across the world had to generate warning messages and upgrade virus detection systems. This is an example of a risk that is able to reproduce itself not simply through failures of regulation and security, but exactly because of the risk-aversion ethos already put in place by the systems themselves. Once risks are able to work through successful risk-management systems and use them to proliferate themselves, that is, once they are not only able to act but also to anticipate and learn, we could speak of cyberrisks.[176]

A third theme of risk society, the blurring of boundaries between nature and culture, seems apt given that this is a book about *technological viruses*. The modern distinction between (passive) nature and (active) culture is not valid in a world defined by artificial and constructed mediations that continuously rest on corporeal and incorporeal events.[177] As Beck notes, natural phenomena such as ozone holes and pollution and diseases such as BSE are produced by humans and human activities. Paraphrasing Latour, Beck suggests that we live in a world of hybrids, made up of interconnections between heterogeneous phenomena interacting on an immanent plane. Thus, Beck sees risks as human-made hybrids that combine politics, ethics, mathematics, mass media, technologies, cultural definitions, and perceptions, which are all a real part of the construction of a society (or culture) of virtual risks.[178]

Hence, the flexible-risk society actually does not exclude dangers and risks but *includes* them in its onto-epistemology. Risk society is a society not of Wiener's cybernetics but of the second-order cybernetics that emerged in the 1960s, illustrated, for example, in the work of Humberto Maturana and Francisco Varela. Within cybernetics, the problem of solipsism was recognized early on. Reflexivity, the ability of a system to adjust itself via self-perception, was presented as an effective way of recursively making the system observe itself. Heinz von Forster suggested this solution in 1960, but Maturana and Varela went further, arguing that all systems and life in general are to be understood as *autopoietic* systems that maintain coherence against the flows of the outside. However, the boundaries between inside and outside are not fixed but constantly changing, as is the whole of the system. An organism—or, for example, a computer system—is actively engaged with the surrounding environment, as emphasized later by Varela in his concept of "enaction."[179]

Autopoietic machines work via organizational closure, where the system is open to flows of matter and energy from the environment (and vice versa) but maintains its organization. According to Maturana and Varela this was the key characteristic of living systems, whereas self-reproduction was argued by them to be part of an autopoietic system. Here self-reproduction continues the work of autopoiesis as a constant reformulation of the system—not a constant rebuilding of the same system but a creative reproduction.[180]

According to this idea, complex systems become stronger by becoming more tolerant. A rigid system that tries to cast out the parasite, the noise, the accident does not last as long as a system accustomed to the deviant. Hence, such systems understand the value of flexibility that was anyway becoming a key word for the late modern advanced capitalism of turn of the millennium.[181] Risk society understood through the language of cybernetics marks a step from controlling information to adjustment and tolerance of uncertainty and risk. Dangers are to be understood as risks to be perceived, signified, and valorized—as well as managed.

Cohen's work in the early 1980s marked a transition in the understanding of computer viruses as potential dangers of the information society. What Cohen emphasized was that viruses and similar malicious software programs were to be seen as threats to be studied: neglecting them would have been even a bigger risk. Cohen himself sees his research as the first serious published attempts to highlight these risks, whose dangerous nature was accentuated by the transitive nature of corruption: small amounts of code causing large-scale damage to computer systems and the people connected to these systems. His work was not, however, without controversy. To paraphrase Cohen, the security community found the work on computer viruses uninteresting and even offensive. Cohen himself was once accused of breaking into university computers.[182]

Despite the hostile first reactions, Cohen was later acknowledged as a key figure in the fight against viruses and as the one who recognized the universality of the virus risk. With the number of viruses "in the wild" rising phenomenally from the end of the 1980s onward, Cohen's work was seen as increasingly important milestone. As the threat was being recognized in the media, the first antivirus products appeared. Suddenly, around 1987–1988, there were probably dozens of programs aimed at finding and removing viruses and other intruders. Among the first were McAfee Viruscan, IBM Virscan, Turbo Anti-Virus, Flushot, Mace Vaccine, Vaccine, Aspirin, Datacure, Condom, and Virus Detective.[183] Even as the virus was floodlighted as a central threat to information capitalism, it spurred a whole new industry sector producing virus cures, scans, and security information. The increasing knowledge of computer worms, viruses, and other malware was quickly turned into practices that benefited the growing computer industry and digital culture.

Of course, the products often promised a lot while delivering less. For example, leaflets from the early 1990s promoting antivirus products promised "absolute protection," "ultimate prevention, detection and treatment," or simply the ability to detect "all viruses, known and unknown."[184] The discourse of risk was easily transformed into a business opportunity through the promise of a totally risk-free future. For cases of unsuccessful security, Lloyds of London offered virus insurance in 1989 after the Internet worm case, which caused a lot of worried voices to be raised among the public and in the media. The policy covered loss of telecommunications, market information services, and electricity supply; software and data faults; and virus attacks. At the same time, Control Risks Group Ltd. formed a new company called Control Risks Information Technology Ltd. (CRIT), specifically designed to battle computer crime, including espionage, fraud, malicious or illegal data modification, and denial or destruction of services. In the following years, virus insurance policies were discussed frequently.[185] As Byte magazine warned lay users in 1989: "Computer security is one of the safety features that you don't think about until it's too late. It's an insurance policy you hope you'll never need. While it would be nice to work where you don't need security, most of us never will."[186]

However, as critical commentators have noted, any programs that claimed to get rid of all viruses once and for all were "flat-out lying." Instead, as long as there were computers, there would be computer risks and viruses of some sort; computer viruses used normal computing functions and, thus, could affect any computer systems.[187] This is Neal Stephenson's insight in his novel Snow Crash: "Any information system of sufficient complexity will inevitably become infected with viruses: viruses generated from within itself."[188] Such a systems-theoretical point of view underlines the emergent processes in potentially any system complex enough: only closed systems can be "clean" and "organized," and one does not often come across such ideal systems.

The acceptance of risk led to a viral proliferation of manuals, handbooks, mailing lists, and newspaper articles, all aiming to give more information about viruses and protection. "Information" became the key word: people had to be educated to become better and more security-oriented users; policies to manage malware were to be implemented; potential loopholes were to be examined. "Threat-oriented risk analysis" became another key phrase, and everyone was to be on the alert.[189] But who was responsible for taking action? Who was to be aware of the situation? In addition to official national and international bodies in business and computing, the individual user was incorporated into a web of responsibility. She or he, whether using computers in the workplace or at home, was to be educated, which accurately illustrates several key points of information society capitalism. The potentially incompetent mass of users was part of the problem, integrated into the security checklist of this network ecology. In other words:

> Traditionally, computer security was someone else's problem, invariably performed by someone else on behalf of the user. Distributed Computing has removed the traditional support personnel from the scene and made the user perform all the management roles: system programmer, analyst, engineer, support group, recovery manager, capacity planner, security officer, and so forth. PC viruses brought the issue of technology and support for end users to the forefront. Now the user had to make sure they could recover and perform the security officer role on their system. Many failed, most did not know what to do, others chose to ignore the problem, many were unaware.[190]

In Section II, I will focus in more detail on the practices of safe hex (as a digital version of safe sex) and virus-free protection as the creation of a responsible user. Next, I will continue with the theme of risk perception within the media and the growth of public awareness (and anxiety). In short, if Fred Cohen's work marked the first stage and a certain singularity in computer risk perception using technical tools, the media channels and institutions were the next threshold, bringing viruses as part of a public debate. During the 1980s, computer viruses were not only technical viruses but also media viruses.

The Morris Worm: A Media Virus

According to computer security professionals, the first generation of computer viruses was programmed by a small bunch of computer enthusiasts with no intention to do serious harm: the first viruses merely flashed Christmas greetings and other screen effects. In Italy, the pioneer of "hacker art" Tommaso Tozzi designed a benign experimental virus in 1989 that displayed the word "Rebel!" on the computer monitor. It was most likely the first piece of software in Italy, and part of the wider scene of hacker art that was emerging.[191] At least in Europe, viruses were quickly moved to new contexts and uses in hacker experiments and technological arts, but also in other sorts of demonstrations. Often such tests actually had a positive side effect in exposing "the extreme weakness of PC security systems."[192] "Tactical accidents" were already part of the repertoire of early hackers in the 1960s and 1970s. System breaking and potentially also virus-like programs were used to discover flaws in time-sharing and network environments.[193]

However, there were also more alarming trends in computer sabotage. The Red Brigade leftist group, active in Italy since the end of the 1960s, threatened to hit the core of capitalist institutions by sabotaging government and organizational computers. In the United Kingdom, the Angry Brigade attacked a police computer in the early 1970s, and the U.S. leftist activists the Weather Underground worked actively toward similar goals. All of this told the story that computational infrastructure was perceived as the infrastructure of the capitalist society. Interestingly, John Brunner's *The Shockwave Rider* depicts virus-like tapeworm programs as hackers that scramble the codes of the power elite to produce dubious messages: "As of today, whatever you want to know, provided it's in the data-net, you can now know. In other words, *there are no more secrets.*"[194] The tapeworm that the main protagonist programs and releases consists of a code that forces computers "to release at any printout station any and all data in store whose publication may conduce to the enhanced well-being, whether physical, psychological or social, of the population of North America."[195] Computer viruses were imagined in this example as a form of Luddism of the network era. In some ways, in the age of continuous social media network hacks, Brunner's novel's words could not be more prescient.

Where such novels introduced alternative ideas of viruses, some computer clubs tried to see the problem in a wider perspective. The Chaos Computer Club (CCC), one of the most famous hacker clubs ever, issued a virus construction kit that enabled even users not familiar with the finer points of programming to make their own viruses, increasing the potential number of virus writers enormously. Yet, their interest was to write antivirus programs and look for ways to counter the rising number of malicious viruses.[196]

Hacker clubs were educationally important in developing a richer understanding of digital culture and the new cultural techniques of programming. They worked to dispel myths, as with the CCC's 1986 conference in Germany on computer viruses. The conference aimed to contextualize the new class of programs.[197] Computer viruses were part of a larger social issue concerning dependence on technology and the social conditions of programmers. A keynote address was given by Ralf Bürger, a programmer inspired by Fred Cohen's work. Bürger's mission was to educate people on computer viruses, which he tried to achieve by programming a virus of his own, Virdem, and handing out copies of the virus to conference participants. In 1987 Bürger also published *Das grosse Computervirenbuch.*[198]

By 1988, the risks of self-replicating software were widely acknowledged. In the July 1988 issue of *Byte* magazine, Jerry Pournelle gave a near-hostile account of viruses, which he represented as merely machine-wrecking nuisances, as dangerous as piracy and hackerism. Pournelle identified the Christmas message virus, the Lehigh virus, and the Israeli virus, even if he admitted to being unsure whether the last was a legend or not. According to Pournelle, viruses were stimulating an atmosphere of fear, where "many [bulletin board] sysops are getting scared enough to deny upload capabilities to new users."[199] Pournelle recommended fighting the fears—and viruses—with new vaccine programs, a dose of care, and by avoiding pirated software.

A couple of months later, *Time* magazine released its widely cited cover story "Invasion of the Data Snatchers." By providing animistic metaphors of intentionally malicious diseases, the article succeeded in capturing the attention of readers. As a protagonist the article used the fictitious persona of a Froma Joselow, a reporter who catches a computer virus:

> Joselow had been stricken by a pernicious virus. Not the kind that causes measles, mumps or the Shanghai flu, but a special strain of software virus, a small but deadly program that lurks in the darkest recesses of a computer waiting for an opportunity to spring to life.[200]

Viruses were depicted as information diseases reaching epidemic proportions. As the sexual revolution encouraged AIDS, it is hinted, so the open sharing of software exposed the body digital to novel diseases of communication. Similarly, as AIDS is seen as a disease syndrome eating humans—and society—from the inside, viruses are crumbling the information infrastructure, the pride of the country:

> Across the U.S., it is disrupting operations, destroying data, and raising disturbing questions about the vulnerability of information systems everywhere. Forty years after the dawn of the computer era, when society has become dependent on high-speed information processing for everything from corner cash machines to military-defense systems, the computer world is being threatened by an enemy from within.[201]

Using the voices of several commentators, experts, officials, and representatives, the article argues that "the worst is yet to come." Recounting the major incidents of recent years, it creates an atmosphere of digital risk, insecurity, and paranoia, which, in a way, are captured even in the title. The title is, of course, a reference to the 1956 cult film *The Invasion of the Body Snatchers*, directed by Don Siegel, which depicts a nice country town being infiltrated by aliens in the form of humans. The general theme of the movie is paranoia as to the invisibility of the creeping parasitical forces, and it has been seen as commenting on both the persecution of suspected communists by McCarthy in the 1950s and the paranoid logic of the McCarthy-led hunt itself. Even though the *Time* article hints at the dangers of hysteria, it probably only adds to the general atmosphere of insecurity—just as Pournelle's overkill warnings did. As Andrew Ross aptly noted, the article tapped into a specific American context of fears of national and individual bodily invasion. The discourse of computer culture, the rhetoric of AIDS, and the goals of the Defense Department are in full sync. According to Ross, U.S. political culture has its historical roots in the obsession with "hostile threats to bodily and technological immune systems."[202] As *The Invasion of the Body Snatchers* was positioned in the atmosphere of the 1950s, which emphasized the differences between us (U.S.) and them (the Soviet bloc), so these data snatchers were the 1980s equivalent. The aliens of the Siegel film were perhaps threats to the idea of American liberal freedom, and the allegory of viruses represented them as somewhat similar: they were threats to the basis of organized society, democracy, and civil rights. Of course, Siegel's film hints that the countermeasures against the aliens might prove at least as harmful as the original menace—an issue that was occasionally considered in the computer virus context as well.[203] The body digital and the power/knowledge apparatus producing it are discussed further in Section II.

Alas, much worse did come, at least according to some commentators, by the end of that same year. The Internet worm, also known as the Morris worm, forced several thousands of computers connected to the Internet to be shut down, hindering the normal functioning of the network. The incident generated a huge number of texts and commentaries when it was discussed on TV programs and in the news, and in newspapers, magazines, and journals. Whereas Fred Cohen was the one to wake up some parts of the computer security community, the 1988 worm was the one to shake up the popular consciousness in the United States. As John McAfee and Colin Haynes put it: "For the past fifteen years, computer security has been a dull field; suddenly, with the advent of viruses, it is making national headlines and the cover of *Time* magazine."[204] Of course, Hollywood productions with wide distribution played a key role in this revaluation. *War Games* included such hot topics of the Cold War as accidental nuclear strikes and hacking, and *Tron*, a Disney production from a year earlier, 1982, transported not only the protagonist but also the viewer inside the screen and the computer into a digital world where good and evil programs engaged in a battle reminiscent of the dualism of global politics. Several such films (alongside cyberpunk novels) gave a visual face to otherwise nonvisual information.[205] For most computer users, code was behind the facades of new, easy-to-use graphical operating systems that hid the code layer behind visual icons. And yet, program code was becoming highly visible in another sense: media visibility.

The Internet worm was the first real media virus, in a sense not alien to contemporary virus discourse: similar to risks of technological culture in general, computer risks are essentially produced, signified, and contextualized within the media. The creation of moral panics with the aid of the media is essential to the logic of risk society, and computer viruses function as media hybrids, assemblages of heterogeneous elements that are, however, articulated as consistent entities within the media. The assemblage works, then, in the mode of addition, $n + 1$: viral code + standard operating systems + distributed networks + media coverage + security concerns + Hollywood narratives + capitalist profit + international and national political agendas + HIV + …[206]

The worm was not the first network incident. I have mentioned the Creeper virus, which caused trouble at the beginning of the 1970s for the ARPANET network. ARPANET also collapsed on October 27, 1980, owing to a programming error that exemplified the problems in distributed systems. This particular incident was due to "an overly generous garbage-collection algorithm" that apparently constipated the network in a virus-like fashion. The problem was later defined as a software process running out of control, but it actually involved a larger set of interacting problems between software, hardware, and the ARPANET protocols.[207] In 1987 the dangers of network worms were proven. The Christmas Tree worm originated in West Germany and spread to the Bitnet network and from there to IBM's internal network, which it paralyzed on December 11.[208] A year later, the Morris worm did something that changed the way people thought and felt about viruses, worms, and computers ever since.

The 1988 worm incident can be understood as part of the history of the Internet. According to the historian Janet Abbate, the original builders of ARPANET "designed it to accommodate complexity, uncertainty, error and change,"[209] which are defining features of the network culture. Hence, worm and virus programs are not to be understood solely as anomalies of the computer environment but have a more fundamental role to play as an inherent part of distributed network computing. Worm programs demonstrated the potentials in distributed computing while at the same time involving the risk of "things getting out of hand" and the worm breaking loose.[210]

More specifically, it is worth giving an account of how this worm incident connected to the history of networking and how the media participated. First, then, what did Morris (Jr.), a Cornell university student, do? On a technical level, he programmed a worm that was supposed to propagate from one computer to another using the networks of the Internet. It used three techniques to penetrate security procedures: Sendmail, the Finger daemon (Fingerd), and password guessing. With the Sendmail e-mail program, the worm infiltrated a computer via a backdoor fault left in the application. With Fingerd, a UNIX system demon program, it caused a malfunction to get in, and in 5% of cases the worm got in by guessing the passwords of users. The worm, often mistakenly called a virus, was launched on November 2, 1988, at 5 p.m. It spread within a few days to thousands of university and state officials' machines, and even though it did not include any form of malicious payload, it apparently jammed several thousand computers. This, as one infected stakeholder commented, brought the network to its knees.[211] Consequently, online communications were shut down and e-mail messaging was denied.

The technical issues involved in self-reproductive programs and the problem of controlling their spread had been discussed in Apter's *Cybernetics and Development* (1966).[212] But now the issue was more widespread, part of the general culture of home and business computing. Even though some commentators have agreed that the release of the worm was an accidental event and that it was not intended to do harm, Morris was penalized for his actions. He was convicted in 1990 of violating the Computer Fraud and Abuse Act. His college punished him after a special commission found that even if Morris did not mean to do any serious harm, his act was "selfish and inconsiderate of the obvious effect it would have on countless individuals who had to devote substantial time to cleaning up the effects of the worm, as well as on those whose research and other work was interrupted or delayed."[213]

However, the emphasis should be placed not on the *particularity* of this one incident—or the person responsible—but on its *singularity*: on how this incident created a whole new cultural field that worried over digital contagions and feared digital demons that would "render our entire datasphere into terminal gibberish."[214] This singularity is due to the general media logic of virality and the views raised within the security community, which marked a new era in attitudes toward self-reproductive software. Paradoxically, as computer epidemics were increasingly monitored and controlled, the media-scape turned viral.

As Marc Guillaume notes, the abstract model of epidemics works on a certain logic of parasitism that need not have anything to do with disease per se, being more accurately about "circulation of objects, money, customs, or the propagation of affects and information."[215] This remark concerning the epidemic can be seen as characteristic of contemporary media culture: it works through circulation and parasitism, selective propagation, and intensification. The viral media is, then, to follow Guillaume, a machine of overexposure:

> By overexposing specific real or artificially constructed elements, the media instanta-neously causes a set of beliefs, fears and expectations to arise. The flow of rumours and representations is replaced by the remote-controlled polarization of opinions. Simply by exposing a few acts of terrorism or delinquency, the media engenders a flocculation of fear within the collective whole. The contagious sense of insecurity that results is merely a secondary phenomenon.[216]

In this sense, the media do not merely represent viral outbreaks but intensifies and incites, produces and infects. The media as a contagious mechanism of exposure are also viral to a large extent, and the pace of media is telling in this regard. The evening news reacted to the Morris case within hours. On November 3, the ABC evening news mentioned the incident. The next day, ABC returned to the subject, reporting the "worst case of computer 'virus.'" CBS and NBC were also alert. They introduced the basic facts of the spread of the virus and gathered comments from MIT, "virus hunter" John McAfee, a former Defense Department official, and even a colonel. It was clear that from the beginning the emphasis was placed on issues of national security, increas-ingly dependent on computer systems.[217]

Within a few days, on November 5, the media discovered that Robert Morris Jr. was the likely designer of the worm. His father was instantly drawn into the discussion and interviewed several times: he had worked with com-puter security issues for years and had codesigned the Darwin program. Morris Sr. stressed that the damage was not intended, but the U.S. Federal Bureau of Investigation (FBI) had already started looking into the case. The world of computers was no longer a world of computer *specialists* but something that touched the whole of society: "epi-demos: upon the people."[218] The impli-cation of this computerization or informationalization of society was that computer security, too, touched organized society as a whole, raising the corresponding fear: What if national computer systems fell into the hands of irresponsible people or some juvenile hackers?

Consequently, the hacker became one of the key conceptual actors of the digitalizing culture of the 1980s. Steven Levy's *Hackers* (1984) had depicted these computer pioneers as "heroes of the computer revolution" who were on a quest against software imperfections, inspired by a general desire to improve the world:

> Hackers believe that essential lessons can be learned about the systems—about the world—from taking things apart, seeing how they work, and using this knowledge to create new and even more interesting things. They resent any person, physical barrier, or law that tries to keep them from doing this.[219]

This idea included the message of free information and resistance to the authorities. However, "taking things apart" was transformed into a criminal activity, and in the public perception "hacker" became a synonym for a computer criminal. The ARPANET hackings (1985), the Wily Hacker incident (1986), which included international espionage, the NASA incident by the Chaos Computer Club (1987), and the Pentagon break-in (1987) introduced the figure of a criminal hacker who exploits the security vulnerabilities in national network computers.[220] The 1985 ARPANET case has also been seen as one of the catalysts for the 1986 Computer Fraud and Abuse Act: just before Senator Hughes announced that his committee was starting work on such a law, the hacking case had been all over the news headlines.[221]

The reactions to Morris and the worm were various, and it would be impossible to recount them all here. In 1990, Peter Neumann gave a comprehensive account of the feelings and comments:

> With regard to the Internet Worm, seldom has the computer community been so divided by one incident. In the final analysis, there seem to be fairly widespread moderate sentiments that the Worm was a badly conceived experiment and should have never been attempted, but that Robert Tappan Morris's sentence was essentially fair—neither meting out excessive punishment nor failing to provide a deterrent to would-be-emulators. But many diverse positions have also been expressed. On one side are thoughts that RTM should have received an extensive jail term, or perhaps should have been barred from the computer profession for life, or that companies willing to employ him should be boycotted. On the other side are thoughts that RTM became a sacrificial lamb to his country in demonstrating a diverse collection of flaws that have long cried out for greater recognition; or that he was an accidental whistle-blower whose most serious mistake was a programming error that enabled the Worm to replicate out of control *within* each penetrated system, contrary to what he had intended; or that the ARPANET was a sandbox anyway.[222]

The Morris worm pinpointed the technical flaws in existing computer networks, but the debated soon escalated to be about computer ethics. Computer crime and ethics had been discussed in relation to embezzlement and theft cases since the 1960s, but the 1980s situation represented something new.[223] According to several commentators, the hacker behind the worm had attacked the basis of an open society. The Morris worm incident, despite the huge volume of litera-ture on the technical details of the worm, was deemed a human problem. One of the participants in the discussion, Eugene Spafford, noted that the problem was due to the fast pace of the technological revolution. According to Spafford, although it had been totally acceptable in the 1960s that pioneering computer professionals were hacking and investigating computer systems, the situation had changed. Society, and increasingly also the business world, had become dependent on computing in general: "Many people's careers, property, and lives may be placed in jeopardy by acts of computer sabotage and mischief."[224]

Basically, the problem was not only what Morris did but where (and when) he did it. The Internet rose to be an infrastructure and symbol of com-puterization and information capitalism. As Ken Thompson warned in 1983, the computer world was no longer a playground for benevolent and eager enthusiasts but for all sorts of users who did not share the same value basis of computer community. In 1989, James H. Morris, a professor of computer science, gave a similar account of computerized society to those of Spafford, Thompson, and several other commentators:

> Along with the openness, diversity, and size come certain problems. People can bother you with junk mail, hackers can disrupt your computer systems with worms and viruses, people can get at information you would prefer to be private and even broadcast it if they choose. Like a big city, the academic networks are not under anyone's control. They carry any kind of communication without regard to its cor-rectness, tastefulness or legality.[225]

Such problems were the underbelly of an open architecture and adaptability of the Internet. It is worth noting that in 1989, after the worm incident, the same questions that dominate contemporary discussions of information net-works and the Internet were raised. Certain key perceptions that still circulate were raised in 1988: (1) viruses and worms are a threat to national security; (2) they are also a threat to international business; (3) the phenomenon was individualized and even "Oedipalized" so that the virus-creating individual was put at the center of the problem; the father–son dialectics of this partic-ular incident were brought to the forefront;[226] (4) the incident's implications were contained with a focus on the programmer as the origin of the problem.

The media perception was gradually followed by certain speech acts and the creation of practices that aimed to address the issue. I have pinpointed above the general discursive framework in which the worm was incorporeally baptized, but the incident also had practical repercussions. The raised awareness spurred new research centers, associations, publications, and other contagions. In December 1988, the Computer Emergency Response Team (CERT) was founded to battle the known threats to computers and computer networks. The federal government, and in particular the Department of Defense's Advanced Research Project Agency (DARPA), wanted to repair the so-called security gaps that UNIX machines had (as the Internet worm proved) and to educate users. The pedagogical aim became a general theme and catchphrase for years in computer security discourse.[227]

In the United Kingdom, the Computer Threat Research Association, with similar interests to CERT, was founded at the beginning of 1989. It was, however, unsuccessful and was quickly replaced with the British Computer Virus Research Centre (BCVRC). The new body was designed to collect and catalog computer viruses and analyze their structures to help combat the growing problem. It is worth noting that in Hamburg, the Virus Epidemic Center was already active in the summer of 1988, with the pioneering computer virus researcher Klaus Brunstein as its head. Its idea was also to test new viruses and produce so-called hygienic software programs to combat the digital infectors.[228]

The year 1990 saw the rise of a European Institute for Computer Antivirus Research (EICAR) as a nonprofit organization aiming to professionalize the fight against malware. It was founded "to support and coordinate the European efforts in the fields of research, control and fight against malicious computer program codes, especially of computer viruses and related security threats to automated systems as part of general computer and data security."[229] EICAR was designed to support the interests of researchers, governments, and also the corporate/commercial field and private users.

Jurisdictional matters came to dominate the attitude and actions concerning self-reproductive code. The 1986 Computer Fraud and Abuse Act was unanimously supported in the Senate, but the following years saw few convictions.[230] However, the FBI SunDevil operation at the turn of the decade and the Computer Fraud and Abuse Task Force founded in 1987 in Chicago were indications of this new atmosphere, which refused to tolerate "electronic vandalism." The busts and raids at the end of the 1980s and beginning of the 1990s demonstrated that hackers were no longer understood as eager computer enthusiasts—they were now treated as computer criminals. SunDevil culminated in a raid and the confiscation of 23,000 diskettes and 40 computers.[231] The cyberpunk author Bruce Sterling noted in his *The Hacker Crackdown* that the operation was not meant to be an attack on system intruders and hackers in the traditional sense but on credit card fraud and telephone code abuse. The operation carried political objectives and sent a message to the public and the hacker community: electronic crime would be dealt with by tough measures.[232]

In a way, these actions marked a certain professionalization of the field: computer viruses and worms were among the most contagious threats feared by digital culture, which spawned a huge number of papers, essays, books, institutions, and antivirus software programs. However, it was the antivirus field alone that professionalized: by the end of the 1980s and during the 1990s viruses were no longer simply toys for computer scientists and eager young hackers—such as Rich Skrenta—but part of a multimillion-dollar business of computer crime and crime prevention. Manuel DeLanda has made a similar point: as hackers used system crashing to expose flaws in computer systems, so their modern viral counterparts have become "a potential form of terrorism." Whereas previously the hacker ethic included the channeling of energy into mapping the potentials of the computer culture, after 1988 the horizons of hackers and organized computer crime had conjoined.[233] Of course, the change is not so clear-cut and much of interesting, artistic, experimental, and other code work with viruses has persisted. Yet, computer crime did increase: during the early 1990s viruses proliferated, with new clubs, organizations, and programs dedicated to manufacturing them. The media ecology or machinic phylum that spurred the self-replicating machines of von Neumann, Core Wars, Creeper, and other "benign" virus programs gave birth also to a number of viruses with the specific intent to cause havoc. This is the culture of "panic computing," the paranoid fear of contamination and disease that haunts the late twentieth-century network culture.[234]

Viruses and the Antidotes: Coming to the 1990s

The Morris worm incident touched primarily the UNIX environment. The UNIX operating system, created at the Bell Labs with the C programming language, had morphed into an open pedagogical platform. U.S. legislation did not allow the commercialization of the operating system, and universities could use it without charge. UNIX was pretty much written in the programming language C, and it was from the start optimized for various experimental tasks and reconfiguration. It was used for important research into new protocols, data structures, and architectures, and it played a key role in the development of network platforms from the late 1970s on. Every university could turn it into a utility it specifically needed: "flexibility" was the key word, while security was not an issue that was seen as that important. Instead, many kinds of programs could emerge as part of the environment. As Paul Ceruzzi points out, it was relatively easy to "write programs that acted like a virus, programs that could replicate themselves by producing executable code as output."[235] UNIX's university focus came with specific emphasis on the ease of file sharing. This increased the vulnerability of the system to viruses and malicious hackers. UNIX's weaknesses were visible in the Morris worm incident.

But for home use, different operating systems became the norm. IBM-compatible PCs, Macintosh desktops, Amigas, and Ataris represented a new wave of powerful home computers available to ordinary users. These systems also generated a corresponding number of problems. Relatively cheap prices made them available to a larger number of users and programmers, but, for example, PCs with the MS-DOS operating system had no form of inbuilt security. Also, the MS-DOS was then "a near-perfect platform for virus propagation."[236] Hence it is no wonder that around 1992, some 1,300 virus strains had been detected, and it was estimated that every month 38 new IBM PC viruses were created. The problem was about to explode. A table from a 2001 F-Secure white paper illustrates this explosion:

Virus type	Widespread	Replication media	Typical time needed to produce a new generation	Typical time to become widespread worldwide
Boot viruses	1988–1995	Diskettes	Weeks	>1 year
16-bit file viruses	1988–1995	Program files	Weeks	>1 year
Macroviruses	1995–	Document files	Days	1 month
E-mail worms	1999–	E-mail messages	Hours	24 h
Pure worms	2001–	TCP/IP connections	Minutes	Hours

Source: F-Secure white paper, 2001.

Boot viruses were relatively slow infectors, which could take more than a year to spread across the globe. However, as network connectivity and file sharing increased steadily during the 1980s and the early 1990s, this was visible in the rate of infections. Such even simple statistics demonstrate well the material infrastructures of globalization dependent on the increased network capacities of computing. In addition to being a phenomenon of spatial connections, globalization is a temporality, which reflects a time-based understanding of global flows. It took more than a year for a programmed script to become worldwide in the late 1980s, but with highly efficient worms using the TCP/IP protocol it takes only a few hours in the twenty-first century.

Even though the real network viruses, e-mail worms, and pure worms have been a phenomenon of recent years, widespread network infection became a discussion topic soon after the Morris worm incident. The latter half of the 1990s, approximately from 1995 to 2000, saw an actual revolution in viruses and worms, with a rising number of local area networks in companies, the Internet boom, and the increasing popularity of e-mailing. As the F-Secure paper notes, these technologies enabled new ways of communicating, but, at the same time, they opened up new channels of infection as well.[237] The key security threats of computer culture had been hacking, system breaking, and fraud, but now viruses and worms started to take to the stage. Viral activity shows mathematical patterns of epidemics that feed on themselves. This is where *demos*, the "people," referred no longer just to people in the human sense, but also to nonhuman actors, such as programs and operating systems.

Networks were imagined as key modes of operation of modernization at least from the nineteenth century on, as Armand Mattelart argues, referring to Saint-Simon's philosophy of networks as well as the ideas of "worldism" that saw underwater cable networks and universal post offices connecting the planet into one sphere.[238] Concerning the late twentieth century, Patrice Flichy argues that "communication" had been the central socio-technical utopia since the 1960s and that communication and community are the central media archaeological values still prevalent in today's Internet.[239] As shown above, communication became a vector of epidemic viral overflow, and during the 1990s a communications utopia was captured as part of the commercialization of the Internet in a way that placed "communication" and "community" among the key business concepts of the network economy (think of the Nokia-slogan "Connecting People").

Kevin Kelly expressed his admiration for the communicatory turn in *Wired*, the flag bearer of the new network economy:

> Information's critical rearrangement is the widespread, relentless act of connecting everything to everything else. We are now engaged in a grand scheme to augment, amplify, enhance, and extend the relationships and communications between all beings and all objects. That is why the Network Economy is a big deal.[240]

Kelly was one voice among many other apostles of network capitalism. Bill Gates foretold in 1995 how digital networking would revolutionize the business world via improvements in productivity through such technologies as web publishing, video conferencing, and e-mail: "Corporations will redesign their nervous systems to rely on the networks that reach every member of the organization and beyond into the world of suppliers, consultants and customers."[241] According to Gates, the Internet especially was to provide "friction-free capitalism" in a fashion articulated by institutional economics. To quote Gates: "We'll find ourselves in a new world of low-friction, low-overhead capitalism, in which market information will be plentiful and transaction costs low. It will be a shopper's heaven."[242] During the 1990s the hacker ethic ideals of liberation of the human mind were, with the commercial popularity of the Internet (from 1995), turned into aspirations of friction-free shopping.

Nicholas Negroponte offered a similar view of the future. According to Negroponte's frequently cited ideas, the world was changing from atoms to bits.[243] In the new world, businesses would be dependent on digital information that would become the key consumer product. In Negroponte's optimistic vision written from the elite university perspective, the future world of information would be a world of expressing one's selfhood and interacting with intelligent technological environments. To paraphrase *Being Digital*, the information highway will provide a global marketplace where people and machines interact, also without friction, in a wonderland of never-ending digital consumption.[244]

The idea of informational, networked capitalism stems from the 1960s and 1970s and the novel theories of postindustrial production. Peter Drucker released his *The Age of Discontinuity* (1969), Alvin Toffler his *Future Shock* (1970), and Daniel Bell his *The Coming of Post-Industrial Society* (1973), and all gave influential definitions of what the new economy would be like and what role information and networking would play in that rising society. Information was seen as the key that would unlock the new economy, and the shift to information technology was comparable to the prior move from agrarian society to industrial-based production mechanisms, as Jon Marshall summarizes it. In this, knowledge workers were beginning to be regarded as the "creative innovators or manipulators of symbols,"[245] who were also expected to handle protocols of worldwide action, flexibility, and noise tolerance.

Against this background, worms and viruses were (particularly since the end of the 1980s) understood as enemies of the new economy. In the informational circuits of corporate environments, viruses and other outside programs interrupted the "normal flow of operation," which, of course, took away from productive working hours: several hours to contact technical support, scan the machines, remove possible infections, and guarantee that no further machines were infected.[246]

In the EICAR conference of 1995, Urs Gattiker acknowledged the problem that viruses present for the information highway and for the opportunities of networking businesses on the Internet. Broken vehicles and unsafe drivers were crowding the information highway:

> For managers and policy makers alike the flourishing InfoBahn (information highway) is making it difficult to ensure a safe and natural progression of use of this technology. Everyone is anxious to capitalize on this new frontier. Growth has been incredibly rapid and those organizations who have not already established an InfoBahn presence may miss golden business opportunities. With the rapid computerization of information and data, however, protecting privacy and safety/security of data subjects and information systems becomes crucial while simultaneously maintaining the viability and accessibility of information. The freedom to acquire information will be facilitated by the hybridization of the telephone, television and the computer. Data collection will become easier with each evolution of technology. Data subjects will become information.[247]

In the U.S., the information highway and cyberspace were at the same time constructed as the new American dream. This was a politically and economically crucially important project of the 1990s, as expressed in the High Performance Computing Act of 1991.[248] The 1993 National Information Infrastucture program prepared by Al Gore launched the term "Information Superhighway," fueling the hype. In Europe, the 1994 Bangemann report "Europe and the Global Information Society" emphasized similar issues, and these two projects spurred several national strategies around the globe that aimed to benefit from the seemingly revolutionary flow of information (network) technologies.[249]

Capitalism was becoming *information* capitalism reliant on the handling and transmission of information. Production was increasingly tied to information networks, and information in itself, in the form of entertainment, news services, communication services, and so on, was the "end product" of production machinery.[250] As information became money, "computer viruses can make your bank sick," as *Bankers Monthly* wrote in 1988.[251] Furthermore, the security of the new networks was also securing the safety of the new places of transaction, investment, and shopping.

The increasing concern was also due to the sheer number of viruses, which was constantly on the rise. According to an F-Secure chart, the few PC viruses of 1986–1988 multiplied into 180 spotted in 1990, 2,450 in 1993, and 3,550 in 1995. In 2006 F-Secure estimated a number of 185,000 distinct computer viruses.[252] In the past years, instead of merely calculating viruses, the general amount of malware—some criminal, some government-sanctioned, as the NSA/Snowden leaks demonstrate—has dramatically further increased.

The annual Virus Bulletin conferences aimed to spread information and tackle the growing problem. In 1992, at the second international meeting, Fridrik Skulason summarized the situation at the beginning of the 1990s: more viruses, more anti-antiviruses, and more people writing viruses while cooperating more intensely—and still the problem was getting less media attention. Skulason pointed out that although new virus construction kits enabled even average users to write their own malicious software, these new viruses were badly written.[253] Virus writing became "popular," with allusions to the cyberpunk literature genre of the 1980s. This also turned into a prominent subculture, in the classical sense Dick Hebdige refers to: manifestations of *style* acted as a distinctive factor and a marker.[254] Virus writing was seen both as a practice and a style of cyberpunk cool, as the names of the virus-writing clans testify. Phalcon/Skism, Rabid, Younster Against McAfee (YAM), NuKE, Crazysoft, Demoralized Youth, and Funky Pack of Cyber Punks were among the most famous. One of the best-known virus writers called himself the Dark Avenger. Dark Avenger was the first to design virus *vaporware*, the Self Mutating Engine, in 1991. According to one estimate, it was able to produce 4 billion different forms of viruses. It was followed later that year by the Virus Creation Laboratory and the Phalcon/Skism Mass-Produced Code Generator.[255] This organizational phenomenon can be seen as partly overlapping the wider "script kiddies" problem, a term used for inexperienced young programmers or crackers who use premade script for vandalism without understanding much about the actual basics of such programs. The scene mushroomed with the popularization of the Internet in 1995.[256]

The number of viruses "in the wild" also spread more effectively. New virus clans shared information via bulletin board systems. In a way these can be understood as continuing the functions of the underground press. The magazines included PHRACK (from 1985 on), *Legion of Doom: Hackers Technical Journal*, *Phreakers/Hackers Underground Network*, and *The Activist Times*. Maybe the best known is *2600 The Hacker Quarterly*, published since 1984.[257] These magazines gathered together subcultures and interest communities keen on technology and hacking.

A new phenomenon was the selling of virus collections. Although some individuals and virus writers tried to earn an (illegal) buck that way, the U.S. government was also said to be involved. According to some sources, the Treasury Department ran a bulletin board where it was possible to download viral code. The bulletin board was closed down in 1993.[258] This was ironic given how often professionals within the field, as well as the media in general, emphasized the role of Eastern Europe and the former Iron Curtain countries in producing viruses. Viruses came from somewhere "out there." Of course, this picture was not altogether false—Bulgarian programmers, for example, were active in constructing viral programs.[259]

Again in 1994 the Virus Bulletin conference addressed the alarming rate of virus production. Vesselin Bontchev, an esteemed antivirus researcher, noted that the number of viruses was increasing and the quality of viruses was also better. Sure, there were lots and lots of viruses with sloppy code made by amateurs, but at the same time the new *polymorphous* viruses were making the job of virus scanners harder. Polymorphous viruses were, in a way, intelligent viruses: they changed their appearance each time they infected a new object. Virus-specific scanners were able to identify programs by unique viral signatures, a form of digital fingerprint. Polymorph viruses were, however, shapeshifters that encrypted the virus body differently with each infection.[260]

New programming techniques and construction kits encouraged new antivirus techniques. For example, heuristics and generic detection programs were techniques widely discussed in antivirus conferences and publications. These were "intelligent protective programs" to face the new and cunning viruses. Earlier antivirus software concentrated on identifying and removing already known viruses; the new programs were supposed to be able to determine from the general characteristics of a piece of code whether it was a virus. Heuristic programs were double-edged swords as they might also give false-positives and "identify" normal programs as viruses. This in general reflects the shifting boundaries and ambiguities between so-called *normal* computing and *abnormal* viral computing.[261] This is a core contextual issue in software criticism: Who defines what is software, what is legitimate software, and how it is used, where, by whom?[262] A good recent example of such a gray area of computing is the suggestion for "parasitic computing," which builds upon Internet communication protocols and taps into server processes that are idle. Different from breaking into a computer and from virus software, such processes share characteristics with cluster computing projects, such as the SETI program. Yet, even though it is not a security threat, parasitic computing could delay scheduled network processes.[263]

Generic identification relied on behavior monitoring and integrity checking, which meant searching for suspicious actions within the computer system. These activity monitors were able to detect new virus programs. Being memory-resident and preventive, these programs were supposed to act as blockers, preventing the execution of abnormal operations immediately when such was perceived. These intelligent programs also generated references to "artificial intelligence" and "artificial life" and the use of neural network models in computing.[264] These topics will be addressed in Section III.

As noted earlier, the first antivirus companies, and antivirus programs, were born around 1986–1987. In a way, this was paradoxical. Viruses were not a serious threat, more a peculiarity, a fact that caused antivirus vendors justification problems:

> By early 1988 a small but lucrative industry was specializing in securing computers from attacks by viruses. Computer specialists offered their services as security consultants or sold dedicated computer software designed to track down and kill viruses. By 1988, despite Brain and Lehigh, despite the two Macintosh viruses [Macmag and Scores] and a score of other isolated virus incidents, there was little real evidence of the oft-hyped unstoppable plague of computer bugs, but it is understandable that writers of anti-viral software and others in the new security industry should have exaggerated the threat. They were like burglar alarm salesmen without any burglars about. They had to emphasize the potential of viruses; they needed to convince customers and the press that a storm of viruses was gathering, to be unleashed on defenseless computer users in the next weeks or months, or in the coming year.[265]

The first antivirus programs included Ross Greenberg's Flu Shot and Data Physician by Digital Dispatch Inc. Others were Vaccine and Antidote.[266] One has to note that most of these early companies were small, independent entrepreneurs who sold their programs for a nominal price of $5 to $10. Some programs were even freeware or shareware. Dr. Solomon's Anti-Virus Toolkit at the end of 1988 was, however, among the more commercially established attempts to provide digital safety.[267]

Small or big, the companies emerged in the midst of the media panics about viruses. The 1988 *Time* feature on computer viruses was excellent in

creating an atmosphere of fear, but other examples can be cited. *Computers &*
Security wrote in its editorial in 1987 that "a computer virus can be deadly."
The editorial introduced a case where a computer virus had crashed a contin-
uous-process industry's computer system, "causing hundreds of thousands of
dollars of damage."[268] As usual in such examples, all companies mentioned are
anonymous, which makes it impossible to confirm the actual events. This type
of rhetoric fueled the new industry of computer security and antivirus companies, to paraphrase a *Computerworld* article. As the number of viruses and
worms grew, and as people became more conscious of the problem, the antivirus industry benefited. There was even continuous discussion of whether
viruses were a scam by antivirus companies to "prime their markets."[269]

Similar accusations have been numerous across the years. Rod Parkin presented "20 myths about viruses" in 1993, in which he included such claims
as "all viruses are destructive," "viruses are the most significant threat to businesses today," "all viruses are clever, sophisticated programs," "viruses are only
found in pirated software or games," "viruses only come from disreputable
sources or companies," and "virus researchers are all kind-hearted, reclusive
philanthropists." Parkin, representing the Midland Bank view, was in any case
propagating the notion that viruses are a real threat.[270]

At the 1994 and 1995 EICAR conferences, the criticism of antiviral companies and certain media preoccupations was even more intense. Ilkka Keso
compared antivirus vendors to arms dealers, who want to sell their products
by whatever means. Most antivirus tests were claimed by Keso to be "worth-
less" and even "purposefully misleading." Another paper attacked the "cult
of antivirus testing," claiming that a big part of the business is dishonest, too
involved in competition to produce trustworthy results, and that the whole
testing of products is still in its infancy: most of the antivirus software tests
were claimed to be misleading.[271]

Some of the criticism was rather apt, considering that some parts of the
industry were getting used to employing strong metaphors and rhetoric. Ross
Greenberg, for example, warned against the threat of viruses in *Byte* (1989),
noting that the problem increases as more computers are networked. Millions of dollars had already been lost, and there was more to come, which is
why Greenberg advised readers to "protect your microcomputers, use common
sense and as many preventive measures you can. Don't be fooled into thinking
you can beat the threat."[272] This warning and advice to buy antivirus software
should be read against the background that Greenberg was then the owner
and CEO of Software Concepts Design; that is, he was in the industry himself.

The evaluation of software and digital culture was carried out from a business perspective, which had been an increasingly strong trend since the 1980s.

Similar issues were expressed even more intensely in commercial adver-tisements. Companies secured the usefulness of their antivirus programs by articulating future threats of viruses that would multiply exponentially:

> PCs are threatened by a growing virus problem. In the last few years the number of PC viruses has grown from less than one hundred to over two thousand. Systems are continually being attacked by newly emerging viruses. Although the files on these computers can sometimes be repaired after an attack, the computers may not be pre-pared for further attacks. *The only defense* against the threat of further infections is the installation of a virus protection program containing a memory-resident monitor.[273]

Although the brochure referred to more or less generally agreed details on the growing number of viruses, the idea that this antivirus program was the *only solution* is dubious. A similar tone is used in the brochure for the Thunder-BYTE PC Immunizer, which presents worst-case scenarios similar to a disas-ter movie, with human lives in jeopardy, companies crashing, and files being erased and disks being formatted—all as a result of computer viruses![274]

A concrete example of the media hype surrounding malicious programs was the Michelangelo virus incident in 1992. Although several previous viruses had been in the media spotlight, causing exaggerated reactions, Michelangelo crys-tallized several key themes of the viral and antiviral phenomenon of the 1990s. The virus was very beneficial for the antivirus companies. The viral spread across media circuits started well before Michelangelo activated. One commen-tator, part of the antivirus business, estimated that some 5 million computers would be hit and destroyed on March 6, the birthday of the artist Michelan-gelo. As the *Wall Street Journal* wrote on the day the virus was activated: "The world will find out today whether Michelangelo is a genuine plague or just a digital common cold. But already Michelangelo-mania qualifies as the greatest high-tech hysteria to grip the nation since the Skylab fell out of the sky in 1979."[275] Michelangelo—like viruses and worms in general—became a symbol for technological failure complementing the centrality of earlier accidents such as satellites. Even though only 5,000 to 10,000 machines became infected and unoperational, the hype and the fear were enormous. Thus, as an apt example, the Michelangelo virus scare was fought with special "Michelangelo Limited Edition" scanners to detect the virus.

Commentators did already then wonder whether the incident was exag-gerated, and whether the antiviral software producers had in fact released the virus. Others found positive aspects in the hype, emphasizing that this form of media attention raised the security consciousness of companies and individuals and that it was precisely this forewarning that caused the failure of the virus.[276]

In any event, the virus incident illustrated how deeply viruses and the antivirus business were connected. In other words, viruses were not just disruptors of the flows of information money; they were also captured as a part of it. This idea stems from a conception of capitalism as an apparatus of capture, a machine of appropriation. Buying antivirus products meant buying off fear, which increasingly served as an essential element of consumer capitalism, something that was, of course, already part of the industrial capitalism of the nineteenth century, expressed through so-called future management in the form of insurance products that objectified risks and security into sold products.[277] This feedback loop, a reterritorialization of the deterritorialized flows of self-reproductive code, is illustrative of the idea of *viral capitalism*—another key element in the media ecology of viruses (consisting of viral information technology, viral media, and viral organization of capitalism). This anxiety was captured as part of the capitalist machinery of production.

Viral Capitalism and the Security Services

Many themes in computer security and software culture seem to hint of a peculiar trend. If such security problems did not exist, it would be as beneficial to invent different forms of accidents to keep the industry going. This idea that "if it's not broken, break it" provides, then, an interesting way to approach the functioning of so-called information capitalism. The glamorization of risks in venture capital culture of digital corporations is one example of this, but it might be said to apply also for security software and services. Of course, similar trends occurred in the cultural history of diseases long before computer viruses. As Nancy Tomes notes in her history of germs in America, the fear of microbes was, from the 1880s onward, turned into a lucrative business, with special goods and services designed for hygiene. This meant, for example, "safeguards against the dangers of sewer gas and polluted water, such as special toilet attachments and household water filters,"[278] and on to antiseptic floor coverings and wall paint as well as sanitary dish drainers and fly traps.

Dangers and risks facilitate the development of a long tail of products for the consumer market, which aims to provide tools for controlling the uncertainties and anxieties of everyday life.[279] The previous themes discussed can be synthesized under the notion of viral capitalism, which stems from an idea of capitalism as capable of continuous modulation and heterogenesis. The "object" virus actually stems from the abstract machinery of virality guiding processes and interactions on various cultural levels, such as software. Technology is merely an index of this immanent logic that spreads across scales of culture (from aesthetics to capitalism, from media to politics).[280] The virus as a software object is an index of the (capitalist) drive toward virality as a mode of operation based on contagion, mutation, and colonization of various networks.

The power of capitalism resides in its capability to appropriate the outside as a part of itself. In a sense, capitalism incorporates the ability to subsume heterogenesis as part of its production machinery. In its functioning, capitalism is an abstract machine of invention that also reproduces itself all the time, refusing to tie itself to any transcendent point (even though the actual workings of capital do constantly stop at some intervals of profit-oriented points, such as companies, corporations, and monopolies).[281]

Philosopher Brian Massumi argues that in information-age capitalism, the circulation of things replaces mere production as the key dynamic principle of surplus value. This amounts to a change also in the commodity's status where it becomes a self-organizing and living entity—a form of self-reproductive object: "The commodity has become a form of capital with its own motor of exchange (fashion, style, 'self-improvement') and cycle of realization (image accumulation/image shedding …). Its value is now defined more by the desire it arouses than by the amount of labor that goes into it."[282] The commodity acts by way of propagation of circulation, infecting and creating new circuits.

Such analyses of capitalism became rather central since the late 1990s. In *Empire*, Michael Hardt and Antonio Negri argue that we live in a world not only of despotic imperial regimes but of a global body of capitalism that catalyzes the continuing processual nature of informational culture. Capitalism and Empire are more accurately axiomatic than transcendent. For Hardt and Negri, the capitalist axiomatic works through an ontology of relationships, which is "a set of equations and relationships that determines and combines variables and coefficients immediately and equally across various terrains without reference to prior and fixed definitions or terms. The primary characteristic of such an axiomatic is that relations are prior to their terms."[283] Hence, there is no transcendent justification for the existence of the capitalist "laws" or "principles"; they are the ground on which the self-organizing functioning of the system is positioned. As a form of organization, capitalism presupposes nothing but itself as a logic of relations and a power of renewing itself. For Hardt and Negri, the Empire is not reducible to a particular substance only but relates to the abstract but effective logic of capture and transformation.

Luciana Parisi has made important remarks concerning the basis of information capitalism and the problems with Hardt and Negri's account. According to Parisi, the Empire becomes too easily a transcendent apparatus of power opposed to the creative virtualities of the multitude, which leads to a dualism of death and life, organic and inorganic. Instead, she proposes an endosymbiotic conception of capitalism, where it "exposes a machinic composition of molecular bodies involving continual and differential degrees of variation between bodies that capture and bodies that are captured."[284] Hence, she proposes an ongoing nonlinear symbiosis instead of a dualism. Capitalism, despite functioning as an apparatus of capture, does not proceed in a rigid manner of linear capture but proliferates differences in its wake. As Massumi writes, the rationality of neoliberalism works through a type of pragmatics, not perhaps so much through grounding principles or normative laws. Its cultivation of the metastable systems of markets and affects resides in its focus not on truth but on how the future (the unknown) can be managed on the basis of the data of the past (statistics). What matters is how to keep things running.[285]

Parisi pays attention to the novel forms capitalism takes in societies of control. Instead of clinging to molar formations and operating as exclusions of, for instance, spatial form, control modulation attaches to the differential moment that moves between states.[286] Parisi's stance approaches what I call viral capitalism in her take on seeing (bio)information capitalism as not interested in homeostasis and balance but in cultivating a "metastable equilibrium of parallel networks of communication incorporating all variables of communication."[287] In other words, it clings to the intervals and the emerging web of relationships. Parisi offers, then, a more accurate view of the working of contemporary capitalism than Hardt and Negri, in that her take, the idea of symbiosis, is more fully developed and multifarious.

What Parisi accentuates is that capitalism should be seen as an intertwining of such various tendencies that create a "complex environment of heterogeneous forces of production, populations of institutions, markets, corporations and bureaucratic agencies."[288] Capitalism is not a self-identical machine that only reproduces a stable preexisting body; it is not a closed system, but part of a wider ecology open to a "microphysical environment."[289]

Flexible global capitalism lives at the heart of the antivirus discourse, as Stefan Helmreich notes.[290] Computers and antivirus protection are modeled on discourses that emphasize adaptation, flexibility, agility, and adjustability.[291] These features have been emphasized since the early 1990s, with the introduction of polymorphous viruses, which are able to create numerous variations of themselves, rendering them potentially invisible to traditional virus scanners. What is interesting is how this tension between morphing viruses and antivirus discourse developed into an information commodity spiral.

Whereas "normal" viruses were identified by a specific code string, the polymorph code could produce variations as a sort of a camouflage operation. The self-encrypting procedure introduced random bytes into the code so that the overall "appearance" of the program was constantly changing. With early self-encrypting programs this was more rigid, as they included a small piece of decryption code at the beginning of the program that easily gave away the whole virus. Later, the sophisticated polymorphs were harder but not impossible to discover. The production of such disguising code was automated with special polymorphic engines that worked to add random code to viruses: a difference engine of sorts. This procedure, however, left a stamp of the engine on the virus that again made it easier to identify. In any case, the camouflaging did not alter the actual functioning of the parasitic code and the potential payloads.[292] Normal scanners had constant trouble pinpointing viral code, which led to the use of heuristic scanners, as mentioned above. The most interesting part is how this ontology of relations between morphing viruses and the development of continuously more intelligent antivirus programs resonated in another scale as part of the abstract machine of capitalism. The morphing power of capitalism was able to tap directly into this creative tension between new viruses and ever-renewing protection programs.

One elaboration of the abstract machine of viral capitalism is found in Deleuze's idea of how every social machine finds it equivalent in its technical machines: thermodynamic machines for the nineteenth century, cybernetic machines for the late twentieth century.[293] Yet, whereas Deleuze sees viruses as a threat to the cybernetic machine, we must complexify this scheme. Building on the work in software studies and media ecology,[294] we can claim that viruses as cybernetic objects and processes resonate with the social machine of the early twenty-first century. The term "ecology" does not refer here to naturalizing the functioning of a capitalist logic of profit and commodification (even though naturalizing its functioning has been a key tactic capitalism has used to justify its existence). Instead, media ecological and ecosophical analysis is attuned to exposing the complexities of matter and politics that characterize capitalist logic.

Indeed, what if we could extend this further to encompass the idea of services? Indeed, as recent years in software culture and digital economy have shown, the issue of viral capitalism, or the all-inclusive logic of digital services can turn into a complex ecology that does not merely divide software and actions into legal/illegal, but engages with some fundamental business models too. To address a recent example, consider the possibility of denial of service as a service itself. As writers such as Finn Brunton have explained, DoS, or distributed denial-of-service (DDoS), attacks using botnets are a feature of the history of malicious software.[295] Worms such as Mydoom (2004) and many others have become milestones in this alternative history of the Internet service economy read through its underbelly. However, the various cultural techniques of actually denying a service are even more abundant, including smurfing and fraggling as ways to enforce bandwidth consumption, ICMP echo request/reply pinging, and even by sending single malicious packets, such as the Invite of Death attacks using the Internet Telephony Protocol (VoIP). Such techniques relate to the protocological nature of the Internet[296] but also open up as specific ways of emphasizing the issue of service over software. Through a DoS perspective one starts to understand how even such "anomalies" or "dangers" as zombie networks of bots are part and parcel in the formation of the service relations of Internet platforms. A thousand captured machines pinging your favorite games service network is the call of the half-dead slowing down your bandwidth.

Denials-of-service offer a further addition to considering slowness as a service. One can even buy this slowing down as a service by way of hiring suitable hacker groups,[297] just like one can acquire services like the "neighborhood watch" of distributed webmasters, data management, and distributed clouds to ensure the accessibility of your site even for individuals or small groups/companies.[298] What's noteworthy in the context of this section and the history of security in software is that security services extend from mere protection against malicious software to encompass visitor management, content distribution across servers, and traffic optimization.

As an example of the curious twists of the discourse of service and denial-of-service in Internet culture, the end of 2014 provided an additional example of the inclusive powers of the service economy. During the Christmas holidays in 2014, on Boxing Day, the hacker group Lizard Squad claimed responsibility for a denial-of-service attack on the Sony PlayStation and Xbox networks. In the middle of the post-Christmas gaming, the attack brought down the networks, making headlines as the hacking incidents had done earlier in December.

In a manner that provides an added twist to the issues of digital economy of (in)security, the Lizard Squad situation was resolved by a very surprising mediator: Kim Dotcom, the controversial founder of Megaupload, the Mega storage/sharing service and a vocal Internet rights and freedoms activist. According to his testimony, the hackers were offered vouchers for premium Mega Lifetime accounts in exchange for ending the attack and promising never to do it again. The situation was resolved with both sides releasing Twitter statements.

Lizard Squad (@lizardmafia) commented in a very satisfied tone:

> "Thanks @ Kim Dotcom for the vouchers—you're the reason we stopped the attacks. @ Mega Privacy is an awesome service."

> The happy tone was echoed by Kim Dotcom on Twitter: "Xbox Live and PSN services coming back. Many regions fully restored. Full recovery imminent. Enjoy your gaming holidays. You're welcome:-)"

> Later on the same day, 26/12/2014, "Remember … Lizard Squad only gets the benefit of free Mega premium accounts if they don't attack Xbox Live & PSN again. #Thatsthedeal."

> This did not, however, stop Lizardsquad from offering their services as a separate DDoS-tool called the LizardStresser that one could hire for internet attack needs: "LizardStresser's highest level of attack promises 30,000 seconds—just over eight hours—for $129.99 a month or $500 for 'lifetime' usage."[299]

Besides DDoS as a service, the case of the Mega storage/sharing platform is also a curious commentary on the Internet economy. As part of the new vanguard of Internet hero sort of politics of individual cult-producing freedom fighters (alongside, for example, Julian Assange), Kim Dotcom's politics (also accused of piracy) has turned to quoting the Universal Declaration of Human Rights on the home page of the storage/sharing platform Mega, branded as "The Privacy Company: No one shall be subjected to arbitrary interference with his privacy, family, home or correspondence. Everyone has the right to the protection of law against such interference."[300] Storage and privacy become part and parcel of their business, or more specifically, as specified in Mega's Terms of Service:

> Our service includes UCE [user controlled encryption]. You should keep your encryption keys safe and confidential and not release them to anyone unless you wish them to have access to your data. If you lose or misplace your encryption keys, you will lose access to your data. We strongly urge you to use robust anti-virus and firewall protection.[301]

Significantly, as hacking and related techniques have been adopted as part of the discourse of network politics over the past years, it can also refer to a service-oriented "politics" or "diplomacy" that counters denials-of-service with access to service. Kim Dotcom's offer (#thatsthedeal) counters the hacker actions by a Christmas gift of free encrypted storage vouchers ensuring access to gaming network services for millions of users.

What's more, issues such as antivirus software become part of a bigger debate and bundle having to do with encryption of data communications. This is another sort of a shift over the past years in security discourse, not only because of identified criminal activities only but also because of such cases as the NSA and Government Communications Headquarters (GCHQ) controversial surveillance activities revealed by Edward Snowden. Such events, revelations, and discussions with massive implications across issues of Internet management have also raised the perspective as to how much archaeology of networking is precisely about security and surveillance from the early days onwards.[302]

In the topic of viral capitalism also opens up a bigger issue: To what extent has security become one of the defining profitable services that has gained economic and political value in the post–9/11 global Internet culture, even if, as we have seen above, it has longer roots as part of the emergence of digital culture over the decades? Can the idea of infection and contagion be seen, actually, to define the wider abstract logic of informational capitalism and its corporate services too?

"Like a missionary or a vampire, capital touches what is foreign and makes it proper,"[303] write Hardt and Negri. And we might add that similar to a virus that inserts its own jump routine at the beginning of an infected program to ride along its functioning, capital rides on the powers of the virtual, taps into them, modulates such contagious routines. Digital culture under capitalism seems a really effective mechanism able to convert the specific accidents as part of the circulation and the monetarized flows. The noise of the network machine is folded back (reterritorialized) into its circuits defining the society of control and security.

The next section concentrates on the body politic of digital network culture: What aesthetico-political implications does the viral express, and what forms of (in)corporeal and tactical meanings did the technologized media culture of the 1980s create for this specific class of software? What types of objects and processes are allowed to flower and what mischief is weeded out? The cultural history of digital diseases is not restricted to technical computer architecture, but also touches the biopolitics of digital life, the *epi-demos* of digital platforms, software, and systems.

Notes

1. Shain 1994, 4.
2. Gerrold 1975, 175.
3. Freud 1995, 739.
4. On cultural techniques, see Siegert 2015. See also Winthrop-Young, Parikka, & Iurascu 2013.
5. On control and freedom in computing, see Chun 2006.
6. Editorial, *Virus Bulletin*, July 1989, 2.
7. See Gerrold 1975. Brunner 1976. Ryan 1985. These novels are analyzed in Parikka 2007.
8. Shain 1994, 5.
9. *Oxford Dictionary of Computing* 1986, 335.
10. Peter V. Radatti: "Computer Viruses in Heterogeneous Unix Networks." *Virus Bulletin Conference Proceedings*, September 1995, iv.
11. Vesselin Bontchev: "Are 'Good' Computer Viruses Still a Bad Idea?" *EICAR Conference Proceedings* 1994, 31.
12. See, e.g., the Wikipedia page for trusted computing, <http://en.wikipedia.org/wiki/Trusted_computing>.
13. Beniger 1997.
14. Gere 2002, 19–40.
15. Wiener 1961, 11.
16. See Shannon & Weaver 1949.
17. Davis 2000, 3–20. See also Pividal 1999.
18. Künzel & Bexte 1993, 113.
19. Wiener 1961, 12.
20. Bauman 1995, 7. Friedrich Kittler (1996) emphasizes that Leibniz came up with an "economy of signs" that had a big impact on communications media, first with Morse code and later with digital communications media.
21. Gere 2002, 121. N. Katherine Hayles (1999, 103) argues how the notions in statistical mechanics and information theory took on elements of a moral theory as well. Entropy functioned as a moral evil for Wiener, and communication—between humans or machines—was conceptualized as a battle against noise. Since then, control perspectives have been incorporated into various scales as part of the personal computer systems. See Suominen 2003, 227, passim. Cf. Salmi 2006. Moreover, so-called trusted computing has worked toward another hierarchization of computer systems.
22. See, e.g., Nunes 2010. See also Parikka & Sampson 2009.
23. Bauman 1995, 7.
24. Kittler 1993a, 242.
25. Pavel Lamacka: "Harmless and Useful Viruses Can Hardly Exist." *Virus Bulletin Conference Proceedings* 1995, 195.
26. See Lundemo 2003.
27. Naval Historical Center, "The First Computer Bug." <https://commons.wikimedia.org/wiki/File:H96566k.jpg>. Järvinen 1991, 189.

28. See the "bug" page on the website of the Institute for Computational Engineering and Sciences, University of Texas at Austin. <http://archive.is/http://users.ices.utexas.edu/~organism/bug.html>.

29. Slade 1992.

30. Kevin Driscoll: "The Common Code Virus." *The Risks Digest*, vol. 6, issue 48, March 1988, <http://catless.ncl.ac.uk/Risks/> (accessed November 20, 2015). Driscoll also describes the symptoms of this piece of code: "It had the effect of copying itself to the next memory location, which was then executed. (…) At the top of memory, the Program Counter rolled over to zero. Thus, in a matter of milliseconds, the entire memory contained just copies of this instruction (no memory protection in those days). This had an interesting symptom on the control panel. The normal random-like pattern of the address lights became the distinct binary counter pattern. Because every memory cell was overwritten by this process, it left no clues about its origin."

31. Apter 1966, 94.

32. Ferbrache 1992, 5.

33. "Two Old Viruses." *The Risks Digest*, vol. 6, issue 53, March 1988, <http://catless.ncl.ac.uk/Risks/>. A similar observation dates to 1973, which shows that several programmers thought about the same ideas. See "Old Viruses." *The Risks Digest*, vol. 6, issue 54, April 1988, <http://catless.ncl.ac.uk/Risks/>. Other examples are "bacteria"—programs that have been listed as one of the oldest forms of programmed threats. A bacterium is another name for a rabbit program. It does not explicitly damage any files, and its only purpose is to reproduce exponentially. This, however, might have such serious consequences as taking up all the processor capacity, memory, or disk space, and consequently preventing the normal use of the computer. Thomas R. Peltier: "The Virus Threat." *Computer Fraud & Security Bulletin*, June 1993, 15.

34. John Walker: "The Animal Episode." 1996 (1985), <http://www.fourmilab.to/documents/univac/animal.html>. The link includes listings for the Animal and Pervade programs, as well as parts of a 1985 letter to *Scientific American* describing the program. See also Ferbrache 1992, 6. Cf. "Virus Precursor: Animal." *The Risks Digest*, vol. 6, issue 52, March 29, 1988, <http://catless.ncl.ac.uk/Risks/>.

35. See, e.g., Terry Winograd: "Breaking the Complexity Barrier Again." *SIGPLAN Proceedings of the 1973 Meeting on Programming Languages and Information Retrieval* 1974.

36. Slade 1992.

37. Ken Thompson: "Reflections of Trusting Trust." *Communications of the ACM*, vol. 27, August 1984, 761.

38. Gere 2002, 61.

39. A. K. Dewdney: "In the Game Called Core War Hostile Programs Engage in a Battle of Bits." *Scientific American*, vol. 250, May 1984, 19. Ross 1990. Hafner & Markoff 1991, 263–264. Robert Morris was the father of Robert Morris Jr., the creator of the 1988 Internet worm analyzed below.

40. "Darwin, A Game of Survival of the Fittest among Programs." A letter by V. Vissotsky et al. to C.A. Land, 1971, transcribed and online at <http://www.cs.dartmouth.edu/~doug/darwin.pdf>.

41. A. K. Dewdney: "In the Game Called Core War Hostile Programs Engage in a Battle of Bits." *Scientific American*, vol. 250, May 1984, 15.
42. Johnston 2007.
43. A. K. Dewdney: "In the Game Called Core War Hostile Programs Engage in a Battle of Bits." *Scientific American*, vol. 250, May 1984, 16.
44. Ibid., 18.
45. Ibid. See also Lundell 1989, 25–26. K. Cohen 1994, 4–7.
46. Dewdney referred to a spy thriller, *Softwar: La Guerre Douce* (1984), in which the Soviet Union buys a supercomputer from the West for weather-forecasting purposes. The computer is loaded with a "software bomb" that "proceeds to subvert and destroy every piece of software it can find in the Soviet network." The novel does not depict, however, self-reproducing software but simply a version of a Trojan attack and a logic bomb. A. K. Dewdney: "A Core War Bestiary of Viruses, Worms and Other Threats to Computer Memories." *Scientific American*, vol. 252, March 1985, 14. See Breton & Beneich 1984.
47. In 1989 Dewdney emphasized that his Core Wars programs had no direct connection to the booming number of virus infections. Again stating that Core Wars programs were not hostile to programs outside the game, he referred to real computer viruses as acts of vandalism. Comparisons between his programs and these vandal programs were often, according to Dewdney, misconceptions cultured by journalists and the media in general. The misconceptions were not, however, hard to understand given the amount of fear and panic hostile computer viruses had created since the years of Core Wars and Dewdney's first column on the game in 1984. See "Of Worms, Viruses and Core War." *Scientific American*, vol. 260, March 1989.
48. See Parikka 2007.
49. Cultural historian Jaakko Suominen has named the era from roughly 1958 to 1973 as a time of "automation and integration," referring to the central trends in computing. According to Suominen, the general metaphors for technology were the automatic factory, the reactor, and the spaceship. Only computing professionals had firsthand experience of computers, and media representations constructed the main popular imagery. The primary applications and uses for computers were calculation, registration, control, prediction, and surveillance, and the problems experienced were intuitively connected: Will the machine replace the human? Do computers make mistakes? See Suominen 2003, 227. Cf. Saarikoski 2004, 411.
50. See Bagrit 1965.
51. "Bad Bits." *Scientific American*, vol. 242, February 1980, 63.
52. See Lance Hoffman: "Computers and Privacy: A Survey." *Computing Surveys*, vol. 1, 2, June 1969. Cf. Ceruzzi 1998, 118–121. Privacy concerns were, however, part of the TV culture of the 1960s. Sconce 2000, 144–147.
53. In addition to films, the news featured such emerging threats. The *NBC Evening News* on July 31, 1973, included a story under the headline "1984 Threat" describing the dangers inherent in the contemporary mass record-keeping boom in banks, loan companies, and census bureaus. Vanderbilt News Archive, <http://tvnews.vanderbilt.edu/>.
54. Bagrit 1965.

55. Alan F. Westin: "Legal Safeguards to Insure Privacy in a Computer Society." *Communications of the* ACM, vol. 10, issue 9, September 1967, 534. In 1988, Roger Clarke defined "dataveillance" as "the systematic use of personal data systems in the investigation or monitoring of the actions or communications of one or more persons." See "Information Technology and Dataveillance." *Communications of the* ACM, vol. 31, issue 5, May 1988, 499.

56. See Lance Hoffman: "Computers and Privacy: A Survey." *Computing Surveys*, vol. 1, issue 2, June 1969.

57. "We Solve the One Problem No Computer Can." *The Times*, February 24, 1972, 23.

58. "How the Human Factor Bugs Security." *The Times*, September 10, 1985, 22.

59. Dorothy E. Denning & Peter J. Denning: "Data Security." *Computer Surveys*, vol. 11, issue 3, September 1979, 227–228. See also Parker 1976. Bell and La Padula (1976) do, however, discuss computer sabotage in such terms as could include malicious programs as well. For an online collection of relevant security papers from the 1970s, see "History of Computer Security," <http://csrc.nist.gov/publications/history/index.html>.

60. Dorothy E. Denning & Peter J. Denning: "Data Security." *Computer Surveys*, vol. 11, issue 3, September 1979, 229.

61. See Wark 1994, 120.

62. Gerrold 1975, 175.

63. Harley, Slade, & Gattiker 2001, 663.

64. See, e.g., Fites, Johnston, & Kratz 1989. Trojan programs themselves had been active computer security problems since the 1960s. Denning 1991b, 288–289.

65. On remediation, see Bolter & Grusin 1999.

66. R. Stockton Gaines & Norman Z. Shapiro: "Some Security Principles and Their Application to Computer Security." ACM *SIGOPS Operating Systems Review*, vol. 12 issue 3, July 1978.

67. Mosco 2004, 137–138. Cf. Hardt & Negri 2000, 297–300.

68. McAfee & Haynes 1989, 15.

69. See Deleuze 1990, 240–247. Brunner 1976. Ryan 1985.

70. Denning 1991a, iii.

71. Maurice Wilkes: "Computer Security in the Business World." *Communications of the* ACM, vol. 33, issue 4, April 1990, 399.

72. Samuelson 1991, 482.

73. "However, the security experts of both government and private sector organizations with the biggest, most carefully guarded systems have failed to produce fully effective defensive measures to protect their systems against sabotage, infiltration, and virus infection. A major factor is that computer security must move away from its traditional role of providing only physical protection for data and equipment. This issue is causing great confusion among security professionals, who have been used to dealing in access controls and the protection of data from theft or overt manipulation by hostile people." McAfee & Haynes 1989, 14.

74. Deleuze 1990, 240–247. On control, see also Franklin 2015.

75. Ceruzzi 1998, 77–78, 154–155. Not everyone agreed that the future of computers was about time-sharing and networking. For example, Andrew Booth stressed that ideas of time-sharing involve "nothing new" under the sun. "The Future of Automatic Digital Computers." *Communications of the* ACM, vol. 3, issue 6, June 1960, 339.

76. Lundell 1989, 39. Lundell also quotes Fred Cohen: "But in order for systems to allow sharing, there must be some information flow. It is therefore my major conclusion that the goals of sharing in a general-purpose, multilevel security system may be in such direct opposition to the goals of viral security as to make their reconciliation and coexistence impossible." See also Fites, Johnston, & Kratz 1989, 35.

77. Robert Kahn: "Networks for Advanced Computing." *Scientific American*, vol. 257, October 1987, 128.

78. Bagrit 1965, 33.

79. John F. Shoch & Jon A. Hupp: "The 'Worm' Programs—Early Experience with a Distributed Computation." *Communications of the* ACM, vol. 25, issue 3, March 1982, 179. Hafner & Markoff 1991, 280. Lundell 1989, 21. According to Lundell, the Creeper was a virus that got away, and a special Reaper program was designed to clean the network of Creeper programs.

80. See Hiltzik 1999, 209–210. Cf. Jeff Johnson et al.: "The Xerox Star: A Retrospective." *IEEE Computer*, September 1989, 11–29.

81. Robert Kahn: "Networks for Advanced Computing." *Scientific American*, vol. 257, October 1987.

82. See the Wikipedia page about ALOHAnet, <http://en.wikipedia.org/wiki/ALOHAnet>.

83. On ARPANET, see Abbate 2000. Flichy 2001. Packet switching means that information is not sent in a continuous stream, but in small parts, packets, that do not necessarily have to follow the same paths to reach the receiver. This leads to a more efficient utilization of network capacity at least when it comes to most traffic.

84. See Hafner & Markoff 1991, 34–35, 110–111. Also Digital Equipment's (DEC's) corporate network Easynet was the target of hacker attacks. In Europe, computer networks tended to be more government-controlled throughout the 1980s. According to Hafner and Markoff, "Multics was one of the first time-sharing systems that paid real attention to security as an explicit design goal." Hafner and Markoff 1991, 265.

85. Cf. Harley, Slade, & Gattiker 2001, 189. In *Viruses Revealed!* they emphasize that even if the Shoch–Hupp worm was a reproductive worm, it did not have security-breaking intentions, nor did it try to hide itself. Ibid., 21. Often, antivirus researchers stress that even benevolent viruses are harmful as they tie up computing resources (memory), making it unavailable to the normal operations of the system. Cf. Fuller 2003, 131–132.

86. Spafford 1997, 263.

87. Fites, Johnston, & Kratz 1989, 5.

88. Quoted in Briggs & Burke 2002, 308–309, 21. The Computer Science Research Network (CSNET) was founded in 1979. The first key players in networking plans, especially in the United States, were universities and research institutes.

89. Bagrit 1965, 33. R. Stockton Gaines & Norman Z. Shapiro: "Some Security Principles and Their Application to Computer Security." ACM *SIGOPS Operating Systems Review*, vol. 12 issue 3, July 1978, 19–28. See also Halbach 1998.

90. Victor Vyssotsky, e-mail to author, June 2, 2005.

91. See Bürger 1988, 255–256. Fuller (2005, 93–96) sees standard objects in terms of continuous "ideally isolated systems" (A. N. Whitehead) that are designed as stable and ready for composition. Standard objects go through standards, handlers, testers, and so forth to

enter a larger state of potential systematic connections, whether we are talking of freight containers or network objects.

92. "Virus on All Things Considered." *The Risks Digest*, February 8, 1988, <http://catless.ncl. ac.uk/Risks/>. Cohen 1986, 83–95.

93. "Of Worms, Viruses and Core War." *Scientific American*, vol. 260, March 1989, 90.

94. See Lundell 1989, 41. See also Parker 1991a. The earlier forms of technological crime included phone phreaking in the 1970s.

95. See Trogemann 2005.

96. Ken Thompson: "Reflections on Trusting Trust." *Communications of the* ACM, vol. 27, issue 8, August 1984, 763. See also Ferbrache 1992, 9. Thompson was also one of the main designers of the UNIX system. Hafner & Markoff 1991, 267.

97. Ken Thompson: "Reflections on Trusting Trust." *Communications of the* ACM, vol. 27, issue 8, August 1984, 763.

98. Vanderbilt News Archive. "Computer Crime." *CBS Evening News*, March 3, 1983.

99. Cf. Galloway 2004, 178.

100. See, e.g., Gordon W. Snow: "Statement Before the Senate Judiciary Committee, Subcommittee on Crime and Terrorism," Washington, D.C., April 12, 2011, FBI Cyber Division, https://www.fbi.gov/news/testimony/cybersecurity-responding-to-the-threat-of-cyber-crime-and-terrorism.

101. Donn B. Parker & Susan H. Nycum: "Computer Crime." *Communications of the* ACM, vol. 27, issue 4, April 1984, 313. See also Dorothy Denning & Peter Denning: "Data Security." *Computing Surveys*, vol. 11, issue 3, September 1979. These themes were, of course, not altogether new, as a computer security advertisement from *The Times* illustrates. It emphasizes the changes in security brought about by the increasing number of remote processing systems. *The Times*, February 24, 1972. A letter to the editor of *The Times* in 1974 makes the same point: "The fact is that these [computer] systems have developed significantly in scope over the years and vast files of information can now be handled; furthermore access to the information may now be obtained through remote terminals and central processors frequently cope nowadays with several programmes at one time." *The Times*, September 17, 1974, 20.

102. Willis H. Ware: "Information Systems Security and Privacy." *Communications of the* ACM, vol. 27, issue 4, April 1984, 315 (my italics).

103. Maurice Wilkes: "Computer Security in the Business World." *Communications of the* ACM, vol. 33, issue 4, April 1990. See also Levy 1985, 417–418.

104. Hafner & Markoff 1991, 68.

105. As Doug McIlroy, one of the originators of the Darwin program remembers, 1983 was a crucial year: "In 1982, Vyssotsky, by then a fairly high executive managed to divert an investigation into 'inappropriate' use of company computers into a study of corporate computer security. That was the year of the movie *War Games*, which can be taken as the start of general awareness of security as a major computing concern." Doug McIlroy, e-mail to author, April 25, 2005.

106. Peter Denning: "Moral Clarity in the Computer Age." *Communications of the* ACM, vol. 26, issue 10, October 1983, 709–710. Denning 1991a, 441–443. "The 414 Gang." *Computer Fraud & Security Bulletin*, vol. 6, issue 1, November 1983. In addition to the United States, Germany had an active hacking scene in the early 1980s. Clough & Mungo 1992,

164–165. On Kevin Mitnick, see, e.g., Hafner & Markoff 1991, 15–137. In general, security specialists commenting on the hacker image argued that the attitude of the press was too tolerant, leading to a romanticized view of hacking as innocent computer breaking by enthusiastic teenagers. These professionals themselves were already warning about the future risks in system breaking and hacking. On Mitnick's current trade as consultant, visit his company site: <https://www.mitnicksecurity.com/>.

107. Haddon 1993, 129. See also Briggs & Burke 2002, 286–287. Suominen 2003.

108. "Elk Cloner," <http://www.skrenta.com/cloner/>. "A Threat from Malicious Software." *Time*, November 4, 1985. However, the *Oxford Dictionary of Computing* from 1986 (2nd ed.), e.g., includes neither "virus" nor "worm" as an entry.

109. Ferbrache 1992, 8–9. "Two Viruses." *The Risks Digest*, vol. 6, issue 71, April 26, 1988.

110. "A Threat from Malicious Software." *Time*, November 4, 1985.

111. "RE: Prize for Most Useful Computer Virus." *The Risks Digest*, vol. 12, issue 30, September 11, 1991. The viruses were written by Joe Dellinger as personal experiments. The virus did, however, spread via a game called Congo. See also Ferbrache 1992, 8–9. Ferbrache documents a third virus from the beginning of the decade. Apparently it did not have a name, and it was written for research purposes in 1980.

112. Ceruzzi 1998, 264.

113. Briggs & Burke 2002, 286–288. Suominen 2003, 227.

114. "Machine of the Year. The Computer Moves In." *Time*, January 3, 1983. On the history of home computing in Finland in the 1980s and early 1990s, see Saarikoski 2004.

115. Briggs & Burke 2002, 323–324.

116. "Machine of the Year: The Computer Moves In." *Time*, January 3, 1983.

117. Hoo-min D. Toong and Amar Gupta: "Personal Computers." *Scientific American*, vol. 247, December 1982, 89.

118. According to *Virus Bulletin*, "background operation" is a term applied to programs that run in multitask environments over which the user has no direct control. *Virus Bulletin* 1993, 327.

119. Bolz 1998. As Wendy Chun (2006, 3–4) aptly notes, even though the user is left with the illusion that "your computer sends and receives data at your request," networked computers are actually in continuous connection with each other via the Ethernet technology.

120. Kittler 1993a. Cf. Fuller 2003.

121. See the description of the Apple II machine in Levy 1985, 263–264.

122. "Computer Viruses—A Management Overview." *Virus Bulletin Conference Proceedings* 1992, v. Harley, Slade, and Gattiker (2001, 129) emphasize the same point: user-friendly programs and operating systems hide information from the user, for the system is more complex in its programming.

123. Lundell 1989, 36.

124. Spafford, Heaphy, & Ferbrache 1991, 319

125. See Lundell 1989, 36. McAfee & Haynes 1989, 3, 9.

126. Harley, Slade, & Gattiker 2001, 85–86.

127. Data-Fellows, F-Prot, *Käsikirja*, n.d., 43.

128. Several computer virus–activation routines seemed to take advantage of this upper hand they had over average users in almost a bullying tone. The Casino virus (1991) forced

the user to gamble in a jackpot game. The stakes were the contents of the hard drive. Another example is the YAM.Math virus (1993), which denied execution of a program unless the user could give correct answers to addition and subtraction questions. These viruses—or, more accurately, these virus *payloads* triggered by activation routines—can be understood as expressing the uncontrollability, and even helplessness, that a user might experience with a computer or a computer virus.

129. "Personal Computers." *Scientific American*, vol. 247, December 1982, 92. Cassette players remained the most frequently used mass storage tool for several personal computers for a long time. Only in the late 1980s with, e.g., the Amiga 500 did disks become more popular in homes.

130. Ceruzzi 1998, 236–237.

131. Bürger 1988, 256.

132. Steve R. White, Jeffrey O. Kephart and David M. Chess: "Computer Viruses—A Global Perspective." *International Virus Bulletin Conference Proceedings* 1995,173. See also "Brain Virus Remembered." *The Risks Digest*, vol. 6, issue 75, May 1, 1988, <http://catless.ncl. ac.uk/Risks/>. The Stoned virus can be used as a similar example. Around 1989, 5.25-inch diskettes were the standard, and Stoned could spread only using that platform. With the proliferation of 3.5-inch diskettes, Stoned began slowly to disappear. White, Kephart, & Chess 1995, 173. Several similar examples could be given, but this is enough to support my point: computer viruses and similar digital programs are inherently tied to certain socio-technological platforms. The 1980s was more or less an era of personal computing and the start of a networking era that was truly realized at the beginning of the 1990s and the so-called Internet era.

133. Lundell 1989, 45. It was first found on university computers, which is quite natural: universities were key nodes in diskette sharing.

134. Ibid,

135. Highland 1991b, 302.

136. Harley, Slade, & Gattiker 2001, 25, 337, 338. Slade 1992. Highland 1991a. See also "Brain Virus Shows Up in Hong Kong." *The Risks Digest*, vol. 7, issue 66, October 18, 1988, <http://catless.ncl.ac.uk/Risks/>. The spreading of Brain was slow. Even though the first reports came in 1986, it was still thought to be a new virus in 1988. This illustrates the low media coverage viruses received before 1988. See "New Virus Reported." *The Risks Digest*, vol. 6, issue 52, March 31, 1988. See also Re: © Brain Virus in Risks Digest 6.52. *The Risks Digest*, vol. 6, issue 55, April 5, 1988, <http://catless.ncl.ac.uk/Risks/>. Also the Apple Macintosh, Commodore Amiga, and Atari ST had their viruses from early on. In 1987, nVIR was found in West Germany, having the honor of being the first Mac virus. One version of it also included a peculiar payload: it used the MacinTalk program to reproduce the words "Don't Panic!" Atari's Pirate Trap and Amiga's SCA viruses also appeared in 1987, the latter becoming infamous for its supposedly ironic message: "Something wonderful has happened Your AMIGA is alive!!!" Ferbrache 1992, 12. The variation across different nations and computing cultures should not be neglected: whereas PC viruses were at the center of media focus in the United States, Finland was more concerned with Amiga viruses. The SCA virus spread to Finland via importers and illegal pirate games. Saarikoski 2004, 363–364. "Outo tauti Amigassa." *Mikrobitti*

11, 1987. "Amigan virus jatkaa riehumistaan!" Mikrobitti 2, 1988. "Amigan virukset." *Mikrobitti* 4, 1988. "Onko Amigasi käynyt vieraissa?" *C–lehti* 3, 1989.

137. "Searching for the first PC Virus in Pakistan." F-Secure company website, <https://campaigns.f-secure.com/brain/>.

138. Data-Fellows, F-Prot, *Käsikirja* n.d., 44. See also Saarikoski 2004, 363. Ross 1990. "Data Viruses, Trojan Horses and Logic Bombs—How to Treat Them?" *Computer Fraud & Security Bulletin*, vol. 10, issue 6, 1988.

139. Ibid., 56. David Aubrey-Jones: "Diskettes: Risk and Security." *EICAR Conference Proceedings* 1994, 131. See Helmreich 2000a. See also "'The Itch Syndrome.'" *Virus Bulletin*, October 1989. Some commentators saw not only pirate games but *all* games as part of the problem: "Unfamiliarity with the culture of the PC can (…) present problems. The ease of access and widespread use of PCs (many people own one at home) encourages the exchange and swapping of software (especially games) and experience. This is completely in contrast to the bureaucratic, centralized and heavily controlled culture of centralized computing. The capabilities of many modern PCs easily outstrip mainframe computers of a few years ago and the sense of power accorded to end-users may lead to almost fanatical extremes." Jean Hitchings: "Human Dimension of Computer Viruses." *Virus Bulletin Conference Proceedings* 1995, 26. On the history of the software industry, see Campbell-Kelly 2004. Campbell-Kelly, however, neglects virus and antivirus programs.

140. Harley, Slade, & Gattiker 2001, 341. See also Cohen 1991a, 389.

141. *Virus Bulletin* 1993, 26. See also "Computer Virus Spreads to Commercial Software." *InfoWorld*, March 21, 1988.

142. *Virus Bulletin* 1993, 27.

143. See Ken Thompson: "Reflections of Trusting Trust." *Communications of the* ACM, vol. 27, issue 8, August 1984, 761–763. Mark Day refers to this in the Risks Digest Forum in 1985: "On viruses, etc.: it is certainly the case that you only want software which is written by people you trust (and ENTIRELY by people you trust—see Ken Thompson's Turing Award Lecture for a further discussion of this). But is that different from needing to have bookkeepers and treasurers that you trust in order to avoid embezzlement? If bankers and national security types don't take steps to ensure that they have good software, then they certainly have a problem, but not a hopeless one. There have been previous proposals to have independent 'software certification agencies' to ensure software quality, but I don't know if they would really be able to solve this problem." "Viruses and Worms." *The Risks Digest*, vol. 1, issue 28, December 9, 1985.

144. Harvey, Slade, & Gattiker 2001, 355. A few years later the person responsible for the Trojan was sentenced in an Italian court.

145. "Machine of the Year: The Computer Moves In." *Time*, January 3, 1983.

146. "A Threat from Malicious Software." *Time*, November 4, 1985. Similarly, the Arf Arf Got You Trojan program received some media attention in 1985. *The Computer Fraud & Security Bulletin* told the story of a director at CBS who caught the program from a public Family Ledger bulletin board. In advice repeated ever since, commercial users were alerted to the new danger they were in: "The dangers to the commercial user are obvious. Operators of commercial systems should be instructed not to access bulletin boards from company equipment and under no circumstances should they even think of copying across public

domain software." "Not Arf and Worm Programs." *Computer Fraud & Security Bulletin*, vol. 8, issue 1, November 1985, 11. See also "The Insidious Infection." *Infosystems*, vol. 32, issue 5, May 1985. The warnings were backed up by several virus reports during the following years.

147. Alan Solomon: "A Brief History of Viruses." *EICAR Conference Proceedings* 1994, 118. Slade 1992. Harvey, Slade, & Gattiker 2001, 346–347. Other 1987–1988 viruses included Stoned and Jerusalem. Originating from the University of Wellington, New Zealand, the Stoned virus (1987) became the most widespread virus on the MS-DOS operating system. New versions of the virus were found around the world for several years after the first version. It became famous for its reference to the effects of the drug cannabis, printing "Your PC Is Now Stoned" to screen. Stoned operated as a cunning virus that overwrote the master boot record (MBR) and stored the original MBR to another place on the disk. F-Prot *Päivitystiedote*, vol. 2, issue 4, June 1992. See also Alan Solomon: "A Brief History of Viruses." *EICAR Conference Proceedings* 1994, 118. Slade 1992. Harley, Slade, & Gattiker 2001, 603. The Jerusalem virus, also known as the PLO virus and the Israeli Time Bomb, was supposed to activate on May 13, 1988, the fortieth anniversary of the state of Israel—hence the reference to the PLO and the idea that the virus was a political act. It was discovered at the Hebrew University by Yisrael Radai, who worked at the university computer center. Actually the virus was the fourth part of a virus family called sURIV, and it originally contained a bug that caused the virus to reinfect repeatedly the same .exe files. Owing to this, the activation in 1988 was largely ineffective. It basically constipated itself. "An Israeli Virus." *The Risks Digest*, vol. 6, issue 6, January 1988. "Another PC Virus." *The Risks Digest*, vol. 6, issue 25, January 1988. Lundell 1989, 163.

148. Trond Lundemo (2003) analyzes the Cascade virus as a "physical objectivation of the word and letter, in a truly Mallarmean understanding of language," commenting on the changing nature of writing. Harley, Slade, & Gattiker 2001, 26.

149. "The Virus Reaches Israel." *The Risks Digest*, vol. 6, issue 12/January 1988.

150. Harley, Slade, & Gattiker 2001, 30. "Friendly Advice … [Datacrime]." *The Risks Digest*, vol. 9, issue 32, October 1989, <http://catless.ncl.ac.uk/Risks/>.

151. See Guillaume 1987.

152. Harley, Slade, & Gattiker 2001, 29. Fred Cohen, e-mail to author, November 4, 2003. According to a 1988 survey, computer security in general had a low priority in UK companies; at least one in four had no security policies at all. "Computer Security a 'Low Priority in UK Companies,' Survey Reveals." *Computer Fraud & Security Bulletin*, vol. 10, issue 8, 1988, 12–14. The virus hunters John McAfee and Colin Haynes have offered a view on why it was so hard to admit that such a problem as a "digital virus" could exist. They argue that it is the *uncanniness* of the idea that causes the most problems—comprehending the notion of a digital disease is a cognitive problem: "Another danger stemming from human attitudes toward the virus problem is the natural tendency to downplay an issue that is so difficult to comprehend. Furthermore, if there is a temporary lull in the publicity surrounding viral outbreaks, we risk becoming complacent about the dangers of infection. We are dealing with a piece of computer software that has no morals, no thought processes that can be anticipated. It has been created by a human being, whose motivations can be investigated once known; however, once let loose, the

virus inexorably pursues a single purpose—to seek computing environments in which it can reproduce itself as extensively as possible. The infection and replication processes are now happening automatically." McAfee & Haynes 1989, 16.

153. "Although monitoring and analytical programs have a place in the antiviral pantheon, this fact means that they, and, in fact, all other antiviral software, can never give 100% guaranteed protection. Without this early work, it is likely that some toilers in the antiviral vineyards would still be pursuing that elusive grail." Slade 1992.

154. Cohen 1984.

155. Cohen 1986, 1.

156. Fred Cohen, e-mail to author, November 4, 2003.

157. See Cohen 1986, 84. "Clearly, if there is no sharing, there can be no dissemination of information across subject boundaries, and a virus cannot spread outside a single subject."

158. Ibid., 85.

159. Cohen 1984.

160. Cohen 1986, 204.

161. Ibid., 207.

162. Ibid., 208–209. The fear of information falling into the "wrong hands" was a continuous concern. Apparently, one conference on computer security and viruses in 1988 was originally canceled because the U.S. Department of Commerce thought the subject was too sensitive for open discussion. The conference was reorganized in 1989—in Canada. "First International Conference on Secure Information Systems." The Risks Digest, vol. 6, issue 53, March 31, 1988.

163. Cohen 1986, 211.

164. Ibid., 177.

165. Ibid., 222. At the same time David Jefferson, an artificial life researcher, was active at the University of Southern California, providing Cohen with his support. Levy 1992, 254, 315.

166. von Gravenreuth 1995, 15.

167. Shain 1994, 4.

168. Mattelart 2003, 109, 115–116.

169. Shain 1994, 4.

170. See, e.g., Anderson & Shain 1994.

171. Beck 1986, 1988. Whereas accidents are actualized events, risks are to be seen as temporal expectations. Risks are probabilities and express the novel conceptions of time modernization has brought with it—a future that is uncertain, but potentially remedied with (e.g., political) action. See Reith 2004. Nigel Clark (1997) offers an interesting and affirmative perspective on remediations of nature in the context of risk society in his text "Panic Ecology. Nature in the Age of Superconductivity."

172. Grusin 2010.

173. Beck 2000, 213.

174. Van Loon 2002b.

175. Actualized virus incidents, such as the Morris worm, are part of the logic of the virtual in that through media channels they are transformed into expectations, predictions, and thresholds: How about the next incident? When will it occur? Will it prove to be even more disastrous? What preventive actions should be taken? As Van Loon notes, politics

filters risks from hazards. Material facts (whether concerning the existence of HIV or the computer virus) are translated into vocabularies of politics and statistics where "risks imply a specific form of knowledge of causal relationships between particular conditions, specific actions (decisions) and possible consequences." Van Loon 2000, 166. See also Van Loon 2002b. Biologization is seen as having an important role within computer virus discourse. Some commentators have warned against the "medicalization" that blurs the causal fact that humans make malicious software: "Viruses, worms, Trojan horses, pest programs, and logic bombs are extremely dangerous forms of computer and networks contaminants. They represent a serious threat to the viability of computer usage in an increasingly fragile world. Describing them using biological analogies is deceptive, however, since computer viruses are man-made and theoretically can be cured by convincing people of the seriousness of their use." Parker 1991b, 521.

176. Ibid., 159. See also Van Loon 2000.
177. However, the question is not one of a virtual reality, as cyber theorists often articulate this media cultural situation, but concerns the metaphysical notion of the reality of the virtual—where reality in every case (not merely in the media culture of the late twentieth century) is virtual. See Žižek 2004, 3–4.
178. Beck 2000, 221. Latour 1993. On virtuality, see also Deleuze & Parnet 1996, 179–185.
179. Hayles 1999, 131–159. See also Maturana & Varela 1980.
180. Heylighen & Joslyn 2001, 11.
181. Serres 1982, 68. Martin 1994, xvii.
182. Fred Cohen, e-mail to author, November 4, 2003. Harley, Slade, & Gattiker 2001, 24. See also "The Legend—Fred Cohen." Alive, vol. 1, issue 1. Archived at <http://vxheaven.org/vx.php?fid=1060>.
183. Järvinen 1990, 146–189. Fites, Johnston, & Kratz 1989, 133–145.
184. C:Cure Virus Buster leaflet. Virex for the PC leaflet. Vaccine Antivirus system for DOS leaflet. All undated. Thank you to Mikko Hyppönen, from his personal archives at F-Secure.
185. "Virus Insurance from Lloyds of London" and "Control Risks Forms New Computer Security Company." Computer Fraud & Security Bulletin, vol. 11. issue 4, 1989. "Insuring Computer Virus." The Computer Law & Security Report, vol. 6, issue 4, 1990. See also "The Computer Virus—A Threat under Control or a Warning of Things to Come?" The Computer Law & Security Report, vol. 5, issue 6, 1990.
186. "Security." Byte, June 1989, 254.
187. Harley, Slade, & Gattiker 2001, 284–285.
188. Stephenson 1993, 371.
189. On risk management issues, see Harley, Slade, & Gattiker 2001, 172–300.
190. Mark Drew: "Distributed Computing—Business Risk or Risking the Business." EICAR Conference Proceedings 1994, 93. Drew continues: "The issue is also a personal issue, every individual is responsible and accountable and this is a key message that must be conveyed to staff, associates, partners, agents, suppliers, and collaborators." However, as Dorothy Denning highlighted in the end of the 1970s, each user was to be responsible for his or her safety in network environments. See "Secure Personal Computing in an Insecure Network." Communications of the ACM, vol. 22, issue 8, August 1979, 476–482.

191. Tozzi 1991. See his webpage for information about the Rebel, coded in 1980s with the help from Andrea Ricci and exhibited in the 1990s: <http://www.tommasotozzi.it/>.

192. "The Computer Virus—A Threat under Control or a Warning of Things to Come?" *Computer Law & Security Report*, vol. 5, issue 6, 1990, 8.

193. Reijo Sulonen, interview with author, November 23, 2005.

194. Brunner 1976, 248.

195. Ibid., 249.

196. Bernd Fix, e-mail to author, November 7, 2005.

197. Ibid.

198. Clough & Mungo 1992, 80–82. Bürger 1988. The same year, 1987, the Vienna virus was found. Clough and Mungo describe this virus as raising much interest, being "certainly the hottest thing seen in 1987." Cf. Alan Solomon: "A Brief History of Viruses." *EICAR Conference Proceedings* 1994, 117.

199. "Dr. Pournelle vs. The Virus." *Byte*, July 1988, 199.

200. "Invasion of the Data Snatchers!" *Time*, September 26, 1988, 40.

201. Ibid., 41.

202. Ross 1990. This theme is continued in the next chapter. On *The Invasion of the Body Snatchers*, see, e.g., Ahonen 1999. Hardin 1997.

203. See John Markoff: "Computer Virus Cure May Be Worse than Disease." *New York Times*, October 7, 1989.

204. McAfee & Haynes 1989, 15. Cf. "The Kid Put Us Out of Action." *Time*, November 14, 1988. Earlier in 1988, *Time* discussed an older virus, Brain, programmed in Pakistan. It was also a cover story. See "You Must Be Punished." *Time*, September 26, 1988.

205. See Chun 2006, 177.

206. Cf. Van Loon 2002b, 179. Harley, Slade, and Gattiker note that the Morris worm was probably the first mention people heard of such software programs: "News stories about the event appeared in the general media, and, for many years afterward, no news story about viruses failed to mention the Internet worm, regardless of the fact that it used technologies radically different from the other, more common, viruses." Harley, Slade, & Gattiker 2001, 29. On the intimate relationship between television and catastrophes, see Doane 2006.

207. Neumann 1991, 539. Eric C. Rosen: "Vulnerabilities of Network Control Protocols: An Example." *ACM SIGCOMM Computer Communication Review*, vol. 11, issue 3, July 1981.

208. "The Christmas Virus [End of the Season?]." *The Risks Digest*, vol. 6, issue 1, January 2, 1987. *Survivor's Guide to Computer Viruses* 1993, 28–29.

209. Abbate 2000, 219. The tension between open architecture and security demands has been noted by Severo Ornstein: "The primary purpose of the Internet is to foster the sharing of information, ideas, programs, data, etc., among its thousands of users. In designing any shared computer system, there is an inherent tension between demands for security and the desire for easy exchange of information. Unlike vital military, business, and financial networks, the Internet design has been deliberately biased toward increased capability, at the known and accepted cost of some loss in security." Ornstein 1991, 519. Although the Internet worm started the era of virus paranoia, it is part of a longer history

of the Internet. This is also because Robert T. Morris was the son of Robert Morris, who had been a pioneer in the computer security and design community. Morris Sr. had even participated in the original work on the Core Wars game, a precursor of viruses!

210. "The 'Worm' Programs—Early Experience with a Distributed Computation." *Communications of the* ACM, vol. 25, issue 3, March 1982, 172–180.

211. Jon Rochlis & Mark Eichin: "With Microscope and Tweezers: The Worm from MIT's Perspective." *Communications of the* ACM. vol. 32, issue 6, June 1989, 692. Lundell 1989, 8–9. Harley, Slade, & Gattiker 2001, 347–352.

212. Apter 1966, 94.

213. Ted Eisenberg et al.: "The Cornell Commission: On Morris and the Worm." *Communications of the* ACM, vol. 32, issue 6, January 1989, 709. Harley, Slade, & Gattiker 2001, 351. Lundell 1989, 8–18. "Student Convicted on U.S. Computer Tampering Charge." *Wall Street Journal*, January 23, 1990. "Student Indicted on Charge Linked to Computer Virus." *Wall Street Journal*, July 27, 1989.

214. Clark 1997, 79.

215. Guillaume 1987, 60.

216. Ibid., 64.

217. Vanderbilt News Archive Abstracts, <http://tvnews.vanderbilt.edu/>.

218. Guillaume 1987, 59.

219. Levy 1985, 40.

220. On these incidents, see Clifford Stoll: "Stalking the Wily Hacker." *Communications of the* ACM, vol. 31, issue 5, May 1988, 484–497. Klaus Brunnstein: "Computer Espionage: 3 'Wily Hackers' Arrested." *The Risks Digest*, vol. 8, issue 35, March 2, 1989, <http://catless.ncl.ac.uk/Risks/>. Jon Jacky: "Yet Another 'Hackers Break Milnet' Story, Some Interesting Twists." *The Risks Digest*, vol. 5, issue 40, September 28, 1987, <http://catless.ncl.ac.uk/Risks/>. Morris was even named as "the ultimate hacker." See Harold Joseph Higland: "The Arpanet Virus Attack." *Computer Fraud & Security Bulletin*, vol. 11, issue 5, 1989. See also Hafner & Markoff 1991, where they discuss Kevin Mitnick, the Wily Hacker incident, and Robert Morris Jr. Hackers are also discussed in Section II.

221. Tuomi 1987, 134. See also "A bill to amend title 18, United States Code, to provide additional penalties for fraud and related activities in connection with access devices and computers, and for other purposes," 1986, <http://thomas.loc.gov/cgi-bin/bdquery/z?d099:HR04718:@@@L=2=m>. For the underground point of view, the reader might want to see the Computer Underground Digest archive from 1990 (<http://www.textfiles.com/magazines/CUD/>) and the Dutch *Hack-Tic* archive from 1989 (<http://www.hack-tic.nl/index.html>).

222. Peter Neumann: "Inside Risks: Insecurity about Security?" *Communications of the* ACM, vol. 33, issue 8, August 1990, 170. On discussion and comments concerning the worm, see vol. 32, issue 6 (June 1989) of the *Communications of the* ACM. See also Bryan Kocher: "A Hygiene Lesson." *Communications of the* ACM, vol. 32, issue 1, January 1989, 3, 6. Peter Denning: "Sending a Signal." *Communications of the* ACM, vol. 33, issue 8, August 1990, 486–488. Lundell 1989, 1–18. See also the *Risks Digest*, especially vols. 7–9, for an extensive discussion of and reactions to the incident. From vol. 7, issue 69 on, the archives offer an interesting, almost real-time account of the worm incident. See, e.g.,

"Virus on the Arpanet—Milnet." *The Risks Digest*, vol. 7, issue 69, November 3, 1988, <http://catless.ncl.ac.uk/Risks/>. *The Computer Law and Security Report* saw that the prosecution of Morris would send the right message to the hacker community. The report recognized hacking as a growing international problem. "Virus Hits Major U.S. Computer Network." *Computer Law & Security Report*, vol. 4, issue 5, 1989. In general, see Hafner & Markoff 1991, 253–346.

223. On early computer crime, see Parker 1976.

224. Eugene Spafford, "Crisis and Aftermath." *Communications of the ACM*, vol. 32, issue 6, June 1989, 686.

225. James H. Morris: "Our Global City." *Communications of the ACM*, vol. 32, issue 6, June 1989, 448–450.

226. Cf. Van Loon 2002b, 161–162.

227. "Computer Emergency Response Team (CERT)." *The Risks Digest*, vol. 8, issue 14, January 24, 1989, <http://catless.ncl.ac.uk/Risks/>. Ferbrache 1992, s.19. Scherlis et al. 1991. On ethical discussions at the end of the 1980s, see Denning 1991a, 505–511.

228. Ferbrache 1992, 23. Cf. Longley 1994, 620–621. On the Hamburg Research Center, see *Risks Digest*, vol. 6, issue 83, May 1988, <http://catless.ncl.ac.uk/Risks/>

229. <http://www.eicar.org/9-0-Constitution.html>. It is also worth noting the founding of the *Virus Bulletin* journal, which is still active in the field: <http://www.virusbtn.com/>.

230. In Britain, the Computer Misuse Act of 1990 made malicious virus writing illegal. The first conviction was in 1995, when Chris Pile (the Black Baron) was found guilty of hacking and planting viruses. See "British Man Pleads Guilty on Malicious Virus Writing." *Computer Underground Digest*, vol. 7, issue 43, May 28, 1995, <http://www.textfiles.com/magazines/CUD/cud0743.txt>.

231. Ferbrache 1992, 28. On the 1986 Computer Fraud and Abuse Act, see U.S. Code Collection, title 18, part 1, chapter 47, section 1001, <http://www4.law.cornell.edu/uscode/18/1001.html>.

232. Sterling 1994, 153–165. For hacker discussions of the operation and related issues, see Computer Underground Digest archives: <http://www.computer-underground-digest.org/>.

233. DeLanda 1991, 227–228. One must, however, note that the computer underground participated in restricting the spread of malicious viruses. See "Z-modem Virus Alert." *Computer Underground Digest*, vol. 2, issue 19, December 31, 1990.

234. Lupton 1994.

235. Ceruzzi 1998, 284. Mackenzie 206, 85. Also the Digital Equipment Corporation's internal network, Easynet, dating from 1984, was built to support simplicity, uniformity, and ease of use, making it susceptible to hacker attacks. See Hafner & Markoff 1991, 111.

236. Edward Wilding: "Computer Viruses—A Management Overview." *Virus Bulletin Conference Proceedings* 1992, v.

237. F-Secure white paper 2001. Concerns about e-mail communication had already been raised in 1984. See Willis Ware: "Information Systems Security and Privacy." *Communications of the ACM*, vol. 27, issue 4, April 1984, 315–321.

238. Mattelart 2003, 40–43.

239. Flichy 2001.

240. Kevin Kelly: "New Rules for the New Economy." *Wired*, vol. 5, issue 9, September 1997, <http://www.wired.com/wired/archive/5.09/newrules.html>. *Scientific American* wrote in 1986 of this turn within information society: "The triumph of the integrated circuit has been paralleled by the spread of networking at a higher level. In the not very distant past telecommunication was something that took place only between two people. Now the owner of a personal computer can draw information from data bases around the country, and computers communicate directly with one another without human involvement. The information explosion has triggered a communications explosion." John S. Mayo: "Materials for Information and Communication." *Scientific American*, vol. 255, October 1986, 52.

241. Gates 1996, 153.

242. Ibid., 181.

243. Negroponte 1995.

244. This is what Manuel Castells refers to as the "faceless capitalist collective, made up of financial flows operated by electronic networks." Castells 1996, 474.

245. Marshall 2003.

246. Dmitry O. Gryaznow: "Scanners of the Year 2000: Heuristics." *EICAR Conference Proceedings* 1995, T-7.

247. Urs E. Gattiker: "The Information Highway: Opportunities and Challenges for Organizations." *EICAR Conference Proceedings* 1995, P1-14.

248. See <http://assembler.law.cornell.edu/usc-cgi/get_external.cgi?type=pubL&target=102-194>. Cf. <http://www.pff.org/issues-pubs/futureinsights/fi1.2magnacarta.html>.

249. For info on the NII, see <http://clinton1.nara.gov/White_House/EOP/OVP/html/nii1.html>. The Bangemann Report can be found on the web: <http://ec.europa.eu/archives/ISPO/infosoc/backg/bangeman.html>.

250. Hardt & Negri 2000, 298.

251. Beth Ellyn Rosenthal: "Computer Viruses Can Make Your Bank Sick." *Bankers Monthly*, October 1988, 55–58.

252. F-Secure, The Number of PC Viruses 1986–2006 Chart, 2006.

253. Fridrik Skulason: "Virus Trends." *Virus Bulletin Conference Proceedings* 1992, i. See also Edward Wilding: "Computer Viruses—A Management Overview." *Virus Bulletin Conference Proceedings* 1992, v–xiii.

254. See Hebdige 1985.

255. Alan Solomon: "A Brief History of Viruses." *EICAR Conference Proceedings* 1994, 125. Solomon: "The Computer Virus Underground." *Virus Bulletin Conference Proceedings* 1994, 1–10. See also Clough & Mungo 1992.

256. I am grateful to Matthew Fuller for pointing this out. See also the Wikipedia page at <http://en.wikipedia.org/wiki/Script_kiddie>.

257. Clough & Mungo 1992, 58–59. See also the 2600 website at <http://www.2600.com/>.

258. Ibid. Todor Todorov's Virus Exchange bulletin board was one of the first well-known systems distributing viruses. See Vesselin Bontchev: "Future Trends in Virus Writing." *Virus Bulletin Conference Proceedings* 1994, 78. F-Prot also reported several Finnish bulletin board systems spreading viruses. See, e.g., F-Prot, *Päivitystiedote*, vol. 2, issue 4, June

1992. For a detailed account on virus construction kits, see F-Prot, *Päivitystiedote*, vol. 2, issue 7, January 1993.

259. Pavel Baudis: "Viruses behind the ex-Iron Curtain." *Virus Bulletin Conference Proceedings* 1994, 157–164. Clough & Mungo 1992, 106–135. Cf. David S. Bennahum: "Heart of Darkness." *Wired*, vol. 5, issue 11, November 1997, <http://www.wired.com/wired/archive/5.11/heartof.html>. Eastern European viruses included Yankee Doodle and Cascade. It is worth noting that several of these viruses, written in the early 1990s, in the midst of political turmoil, were in a way also nationalist and political. For example, in Bohemia the 17th November 1989 virus included a message: "Viruses against political extremes, for freedom and parliamentary democracy."

260. Vesselin Bontchev: "Future Trends in Virus Writing." *Virus Bulletin Conference Proceedings* 1994, 70. Harley, Slade, & Gattiker 2001, 129–131. See also Steve Gibson: "Polymorphic Viruses Escape Detection but Get Our Attention." *Infoworld*, April 20, 1992.

261. Cf. Sampson 2004.

262. On software criticism, see Fuller 2003.

263. Albert-László Barabási, Vincent W. Freeh, Hawoong Jeong, & Jay B. Brockman: "Parasitic Computing." *Nature*, vol. 412, August 30, 2001, 894–897.

264. Harley, Slade, & Gattiker 2001, 152–153. Glenn Coates & David Leigh: "Virus Detection—'The Brainy Way.'" *Virus Bulletin Conference Proceedings* 1995, 211–216. Richard Zwienenberg: "Heuristic Scanners: Artificial Intelligence?" *Virus Bulletin Conference Proceedings* 1995, 203–210. David J. Stang: "Computer Viruses and Artificial Intelligence." *Virus Bulletin Conference Proceedings* 1995, 235–246. See also Frans Veldman: "Combating Viruses Heuristically." *Virus Bulletin Conference Proceedings* 1993, 67–75. On the interconnections of viruses and antivirus programmers, see Frans Veldman: "Virus Writing Is High-Tech War." *EICAR Conference Proceedings* 1994, 151–156.

265. Clough & Mungo 1992, 90.

266. Ibid. Harold Highland: "Data Physician—A Virus Protection Program." *Computers & Security*, vol. 6, issue 1, February 1987, 73–79

267. Alan Solomon: "A Brief History of Viruses." *EICAR Conference Proceedings* 1994, 119–120. Cf. "Good Virus Protection Comes Cheap, Test Shows." *Network World*, October 21, 1991. For a review of Anti-Virus Toolkit, see *Byte*, July 1989, 88IS-3.

268. Editorial, *Computers & Security*, vol. 6, issue 1, February 1987, 1–3.

269. Michael Alexander: "Health Insurance for Computers." *Computerworld*, April 23, 1990. Aki Korhonen: "Jenkkilä." *Mikrobitti*, vol. 1, 1991.

270. Rod Parkin: "Is Anti-Virus Software Really Necessary?" *Virus Bulletin Conference Proceedings* 1993, 57–65. Cf. "Computer Virus Cure May Be Worse than Disease." *New York Times*, October 7, 1989.

271. Ilkka Keso: "View from Large Corporation: Anti-Virus Tests" and "Cloaked Business." *EICAR Conference Proceedings* 1994, supplementary papers. Kari Laine: "The Cult of Anti-Virus Testing." *EICAR Conference Proceedings* 1994, 65–87. Cf. Sara Gordon: "Why Computer Viruses Are Not—and Never Were—a Problem." *EICAR Conference Proceedings* 1994, 167–182.

272. Ross M. Greenberg: "Know Thy Viral Enemy." *Byte*, June 1989, 280. Cf. "Editorial. Crying 'Wolf!'" *Virus Bulletin*, September 1990. *Virus Bulletin* takes a critical stance on

this exaggeration of the virus phenomenon. This illustrates that one should not see the industry as corrupt and one-sided. For example, *Virus Bulletin* (at least the volumes for 1989–1995) tries to avoid discussions that are too rhetorical and ideological, focusing more on technical details.

273. Brochure for VIREX antivirus program from the early 1990s. (my italics)

274. ThunderBYTE PC Immunizer brochure from the early 1990s. Electronic Systems and Special Services (ESsaSS). An Information Security brochure from Computer Security Engineers (CSE) offered a central narrative of the security dilemma in information society with personal computing: "Traditionally, *Materials, Capital* and *People* have been considered the three means of production. However, it is now clear that *Information* must be added to this troika. Without its information intact, no corporation, private or public, is able to survive in modern society. Maybe for a few hours, a few days or even a few weeks, but certainly not for any longer period of time. Despite this fact, most managers regard information as a commodity, which is just there to be used as required. They do not generally consider security threats to their information base." The ad continues by referring to "statistical information" that has shown the dangers in malware for companies: "95% of companies hit by a computer calamity no longer exists 5 years after the incident, whereas only about 80% of these companies would be expected to be out of business after 5 years anyway. Thus, in about 15% of the cases, the computer calamity can be said to be the decisive factor causing the business to close." Such examples can be contrasted to an F-Prot antivirus software brochure from the early 1990s that uses more neutral language and a down-to-earth approach.

275. Michael W. Miller: "High-Tech Hysteria Grips U.S.; Skylab? No, Michelangelo." *Wall Street Journal* (Eastern Edition), March 6, 1992. Cf. "Ding! Whrrrrrrrrrrr. Crash!" *Time*, March 16, 1992. "Virus Barely Causes Sniffle in Computers." *New York Times*, March 7, 1992. See also Alan Solomon: "A Brief History of Viruses." *EICAR Conference Proceedings* 1994, 126.

276. Bernard P. Zajac: "The Michelangelo Virus—Was It a Failure?" *Computer Law & Security Report*, vol. 8, issue 3, 1992. See also the discussions and reports at Risk Forum, <http://catless.ncl.ac.uk/php/risks/search.php>. The virus also made TV news headlines. The virus was discussed before and after the activation date on the NBC and CBS evening news programs. See <http://tvnews.vanderbilt.edu/>.

277. Massumi 1993, 12.

278. Tomes 1998, 11.

279. See Murphie & Potts 2003, 186–187, 190–191. See also Bauman 1993, 204–205. See a hacker's point of view on the virus: "Viruses—Facts and Myths." *Computer Underground Digest*, vol. 4, issue 49, October 7, 1992. Cf. "Re: CuD 4.49—Viruses—Facts and Myths (1)." Computer Underground Digest, October 25, 1992, <http://www.soci.niu.edu/~cudigest/>.

280. Ansell-Pearson 1997, 145–147.

281. Deleuze & Guattari 1983, 223–250; 1987, 20. See also Goodchild 1996, 97–98. DeLanda 1998.

282. Massumi 1992, 200.

283. Hardt & Negri 2000, 326–327.

284. Parisi 2004a, 144.
285. Massumi 2005.
286. Parisi 2004a, 134.
287. Ibid.
288. Ibid., 140.
289. Ibid.
290. Helmreich 2000a. The antivirus researchers noted the possibilities in business models based on updating: "When new viruses are discovered, anti-virus software is updated to deal with them on a cycle of weeks or months. Anti-virus vendors generally offer monthly updates, and in a typical corporate environment new updates are installed every one to six months. Because it takes a typical new virus many months, or even a few years, to become widespread, this is reasonable. The recent rise of macroviruses, which can become widespread in just a few months, has put some downward pressure on these time-scales, but not changed their general magnitude. It is still feasible to deal with new viruses through a largely manual process: a customer finding a new virus sends it in to a vendor, the vendor analyses it by hand and returns detection and repair information to the customer, and other customers get the information over the next months, in their regular updates." David Chess: "The Future of Viruses on the Internet." *Virus Bulletin Conference Proceedings* 1997, archived at <http://vxheaven.org/lib/adc02.html>.
291. See Martin 1994.
292. Harley, Slade, & Gattiker 2001, 129–131. Ludwig 1993, 47. In a more experimental fashion, Mark Ludwig tried to create a polymorphing virus with "genetic memory" that could help it evolve more efficient variations. The Darwinian Genetic Mutation Engine was supposed to experiment and remember the successful variations, which would be passed on to later versions of a normal DOS virus. See Ludwig 1993.
293. Deleuze 1990, 244.
294. See Fuller 2003, 2005. See also Chun 2006. Mackenzie 2006. Brunton 2013.
295. Brunton 2013.
296. Galloway 2004.
297. Brunton 2013. Stuart Dredge, "Lizardsquad now helping anyone copy its PlayStation and Xbox attacks." *The Guardian*, December 31, 2014, <http://www.theguardian.com/technology/2014/dec/31/lizard-squad-ddos-service-playstation-xbox-lizardstresser>.
298. See, e.g., https://www.cloudflare.com.
299. Dredge: "Lizardsquad now helping anyone copy its PlayStation and Xbox attacks."
300. Mega the Privacy Company webpage, <https://mega.co.nz/#info>.
301. Mega, <https://mega.co.nz/#terms>.
302. See Sprenger 2015 on Internet politics and infrastructures.
303. Hardt & Negri 2000, 226.

· II ·

BODY

Biopolitics of Digital Systems

Rigorously speaking, there is never silence. The white noise is always there. If health is defined by silence, health does not exist. Health remains the couple message-noise. Systems work because they do not work. Nonfunctioning remains essential for functioning. And that can be formalized. Given two stations and a channel. They exchange messages. If the relation succeeds, if it is perfect, optimum, and immediate, it disappears as a relation. If it is there, if it exists, that means that it failed. It is only mediation. Relation is nonrelation. And that is what the parasite is. The channel carries the flow, but it cannot disappear as a channel, and it brakes (breaks) the flow, more or less. But perfect, successful, optimum communication no longer includes any mediation. And the canal disappears into immediacy. There would be no spaces of transformation anywhere. There are channels, and thus there must be noise.[1]

—Michel Serres (1980)

Disease is politics, and always has been, whether it was syphilis in the old days, and even herpes.[2]

—David Cronenberg

Prologue: How Are Bodies Formed?

The previous section was focused on what happens to practices and definitions of security in network culture. The understanding of security changed, software became a more central part of computing culture, and the operations of how software is defined across media, the legal system, the industry, and various users became different. The purpose of Section I was to show how computer viruses became perceived as they are most often perceived: as malicious software, as well as operational part of viral capitalism that also extends to the incorporation of a variety of (security and insecurity) services as its monetarized body. The genealogy of digital worms and viruses led us to the projects of the early pioneers in the 1950s and 1960s at the Bell Labs, MIT, and other research facilities, especially in the U.S. As computers and networking became more central to national and international infrastructures and the finance world, viruses and worms were incorporeally transformed into menaces of the information society. They were no longer merely innocent and fascinating, almost-alive programs but started to represent a danger to society at large. The new security standards of digital culture tried to weed out the experimentality of the hacker mentality that also spawned software such as self-reproducing programs. Of course, virus writing did also become a form of vandalism, with no other intent than to cause havoc. Still, we can dig deeper into the political and economic connections that the discourses and practices of computer diseases exemplify. Although I touched mainly on the issue of the viral logic of the capitalist abstract machine and the assemblage of the viral object, such metastable system qualities could be seen as also characterizing, for example, themes of post-Fordist labor practices, where self-organization, the emphasis on communication and interaction, and free movement of the workforce are key modes of operation.[3] Also deliberately left for later discussion were the rich implications of the terms themselves: computer *virus* and *worm*. As we know, these are concepts that have become familiar through biology, where, for example, the virus has a history of its own. Related to the Latin word for a slimy, repulsive substance, poison, but also virility, viruses entered modern medicine and hygiene during the eighteenth and nineteenth centuries as minuscule, submicroscopic, infectious agents. "Virus" was actually at first only used to denote an X factor, the unknown cause. As a result of advances in the technologies of microscopes, filtering, and analysis, viruses were gradually identified as parasites of living organisms that themselves occupied a curious twilight zone between life and death with their singular structure of a protein cover over nucleic acid (genetic material).[4] Viruses became key objects for twentieth-century biochemistry and genetics research, and they were informational before they became integrated into computer culture discourse.

Computer viruses are often explained *as if* they were biological viruses. If biological viruses are thought of as submicroscopic actors that can multiply only via living host cells, without a metabolism of their own and consisting of a "pure information" core of DNA or RNA, then digital viruses are often explained through this field.[5] Computer viruses become conceptually secondary to biological viruses. They are placed in a spatial grid of representation where their characteristics are metaphorically transported from the discourse of biology.[6]

To talk of computer viruses mobilizes a whole field of references to biology and nature. CPUs are referred to as brains; system networks are environments; computers get infected and sick; and these diseases are countered with vaccines. Consequently, as the perception of biological viruses has never been "innocent," outside the power/knowledge relations of society, technological viruses are perceived, valorized, and signified similarly in complex fields of culture. Technological objects are embedded in such assemblages where the technological machines are part of social assemblages—synthetic compositions of heterogeneous flows, symbiotic by nature.[7] Here, the fact that the technology and design of digital culture has "borrowed" from biology (and vice versa) does not fall entirely under the notion of "metaphorics" but can be approached also as a more fundamental becoming biological of digital culture identified by Tiziana Terranova as part of the politics of network culture: technics of nature, biological computation, and the wider vocabulary of emergence that started to infect information culture since the 1990s.[8] This theme, analyzed in more detail in the next section, is part of the material assemblages of digitality. For example, the intensive qualities of software (how it functions, acts, and reacts in relation to other software, operation systems, and protocols) are not reducible to discourses but present materially specific technical effects and affects as well. Using biologically attuned models and modes of analysis (such as ecology) does not have to be seen as succumbing to easy-going metaphorics. Instead, as the early designers of digital culture themselves thought, nature and biology have presented complex ways of seeing objects, couplings, and processes that were already transported as part of the new models of digitality. This does not mean that technology is biological and evolves naturally. Quite the contrary. We have to be aware of the historical nature of this coupling of biology and computation, of new models of emergent intelligence and networking, of the forms of software that do not escape a political economy even if they seem to refer to scientific models that are closely aligned with learning from nature. Providing a critical genealogy of this situation is important.

To talk of viruses is to talk of embodiment, but not merely involving human bodies. Computer software has raised the question as to what could be the electronic embodiment of computer culture, and where is materiality placed in this picture? For sure, addressing viruses, one has to take into account the wider political history of the viral—both as a metaphor and as operationalized tool of exclusion and stigma. This section is thus dedicated to investigating the various bodily metamorphoses in viral culture. It's a sort of an obvious route to take: computer viruses appeared to the popular consciousness around the same time as AIDS and HIV. As in the AIDS discourse, the connotations, articulations, and contexts of digital contagions have political, gendered, and sexualized implications and consequences, with disease and health acting not just as medical concepts but also as a structuration of the power of digital culture. As "life" and the living body became crucial components of the fields of power and knowledge during the nineteenth century, in a similar vein the digital body and "computer life" became objects of keen societal interest in the latter half of the twentieth century.[9] It also was insufficient to talk of the body merely as a general category, or of life as something of a universal. Instead, through viral and disease markers, bodies got marked, divided into goods and bads, operationalized, contained, gendered; the gay body, the female body, the infecting body, the unstable body—a variety of pejorative uses of the term in the midst of a wider discursive production of different models of embodiment in the social field that included technologies of computing and networks. To talk of the care of the biological self extended to operations that tried to address the pedagogy of the technological subject as part of the society of control.

But where to start the discussion of the body? What is a body?—a question that seems too obvious but already over the decades of feminist theory complexified, too. An important first step is to acknowledge that a body is not something that is necessarily human. Bodies exist across a multiplicity of scales. To quote Deleuze: "What is the body? We do not define it by saying that it is a field of forces, a nutrient medium fought over by a plurality of forces. For, in fact, there is no medium, no field of forces or battle. There is no quantity of reality, all reality is a quantity of force."[10] In a Nietzschean vein, cultural analysis is "lowered" to the level of forces that produce the visibility of bodies. Any body whatsoever—and body is always also already qualified—is constituted within a field of forces that refers to physical as much as social, conceptual terms. Bodies are not merely visible and intact molar bodies but also molecular becomings that emphasize this affective, minoritarian nature, which, for example, Rosi Braidotti builds her concept of the body on. I also want to insist that it is the task of an archaeological analysis to excavate such constellations of forces that define and operationalize bodies but also show their nonlinear and open-ended nature.[11]

For Deleuze and Spinoza, bodies are defined not by the class or genus they inhabit (chemical, biological, geographical, social, political, technological, etc.) but by the compositions they form with other bodies and the relations of motion and rest. This ethological view of the world suggests that everything forms on a plane of immanence and is thus capable of affecting others on the same plane. Of course, such foldings and connections have always been highly regulated. Paths between the insides and outsides of the body are part of the power architectures of a culture, of maintaining cultural hierarchies, based on inscriptions of "health." Naturally, disturbances are consequently understood through images of disease, of dangerous mixings, of leaking bodies, as in sickness or the mystified menstrual cycle of the female sex.[12] The biological body and the body politic are in an intimate isomorphic relationship with each other, revealing how the epidemia "works on the social bond; it may reinforce, transform or undo it."[13]

Embodiment can be approached through specific genealogies of the body politic and its media ecology, from the city and the state to the architectures of computation. The imagery of the body politic was tied to a *longue durée* of the social order of the state as a body. The ruler is the head, merchants the stomach, soldiers the executing organs (hands), and peasants the feet. The analogies were used by philosophers such as Plato to differentiate between a healthy *polis* and a "feverish" one. Later, in medieval times, the figure of the body politic became mobilized to evoke unity: the world is a hierarchical whole, similar to an organism with its governing head. Whether the empire or the religious *corpus mysticum et politicum* of the papal Church, order equaled hierarchy, which equaled health of the body. For instance, in John of Salisbury's *Policraticus* (1159), the head is the prince, the heart equals the senate, and the soul is analogous to the clergy. In a similar manner, the body politic analogy worked in matters material, such as the organization of the city. This interfacing of the body and the city acted as a power apparatus for channeling bodies into proper Christians, and for those who were considered barely human, such as Jews.[14]

Later the body politic was appropriated as an integral part of the *corpus* in early modernity, with, for example, the theories of sovereignty and state of early modernity. With Leviathan we have a new formation (yet a continuation of the Christian body politic) where the (standard male) individual body is part of the body politic. Leviathan was no longer, however, the expression of transcendent religious unity, but an artificial body, established through contract.[15] The idea of an organic and unified body was used continuously through a mobilization of health and disease. Referring to the natural state of a body in contrast to disease and sickness proved to be a strong and strategically useful image even after the religious connotations had vanished. In Leviathan, were perhaps the figures of sickness, part of the artificial man of the state (*civitas*), now seen not as metaphysical evils but as dissonances that have to be taken care of, managed, and channeled into health? Is sickness of the body as a management problem that harks back to issues of security?[16]

The practical task with the image of body politic was to establish unity (and weed out multiplicity, translated as disease). With modern technological media and transnational political networks, this situation has further complicated. Whereas early modernity functioned through the city, the state, and the body politic that guaranteed order alongside such lines, the poststate era of networks has been obliged to find alternatives to this form of ordering. Even Foucault turned to issues of security in his later lectures, emphasizing security not merely as disciplinary containment but also as ensuring controlled circulation of the things (diseases, etc.).[17] But coming to technical networks, whether the later social media platforms and Internet infrastructures, or the earlier versions of networking since the 1960s, the issue is not merely of biological diseases or human bodies. Also important are the bodies and biopolitics of the biochemical and the molecular (genes, bacteria, viruses) and nonhuman actors (objects and processes in digital network ecology, such as software). This can be also thought of as the move from disciplinary societies to societies of control, but also of security. Whereas discipline functioned through the distribution of bodies in space—the biopower of the body politic of cities and states—the control society focuses increasingly on algorithmic codes and passwords and the modulation of cybernetic patterns.[18] What we have with network societies and the third nature of telecommunications is a new mode of digital biopower that operates on "the massive and dynamic interrelation of processes and objects, beings and things, patterns and matter"[19] that form the contemporary media ecology.

Since the discoveries of William Harvey in the early seventeenth century concerning blood circulation, movement and circulation have been general standards also for a healthy body and a flourishing city. As Richard Sennett notes, Harvey's discoveries were soon translated into discourses and designs of public spaces and urban media ecology where free movement equaled health.

A healthy body in a healthy society was understood through the paradigm of flow.[20] Hence, the biopolitics of bodies acted through the medium of the city, and even though the focus has slowly moved toward underlining the healthy flow of networks, the logic seems to remediate earlier examples. The age of technical networks as key organizational models can be seen emerging at the end of nineteenth century, and hence the rise of network capitalism dates much further back than the age of computers. As Schivelbusch notes, the new vectors of movement represented by the railroads, steamships, and the telegraph enabled new sorts of flow of things and messages, where circulation (of people, goods, and information) was to guarantee a balanced social situation. A commentator from 1895 emphasized the importance of roads, railways, and waterways as "the arteries through which this blood is conducted, while telegraphs and telephones may be compared to the nerves which feel out and determine the course of that circulation, which is a condition of national prosperity."[21] The regulatory ideal of a healthy body works also in the age of computational networks, where obstacles to the flow of information are seen as instances of disease and imbalance in a manner that resonates with the early articulations between the biology of blood circulation, rising capitalist economic theories, and city planning.

Recent years have seen a heightened interest in the topic of terrorists moving in the pathways of such global networks both on a macro physical level (transport, territorial claims, etc.) and on the micro levels of digital communication (social media platforms, software-enabled cybercrime). Such complex systems of global scale have made the problem of identification of malicious flows difficult, which has further emphasized the need to find effective control mechanisms to filter the circulatory systems. Good examples are the Snowden leaks about the massive and controversial NSA and Government Communications Headquarters (GCHQ) surveillance programs, which themselves have been identified as security problems. Whereas in the more or less binary Cold War global system the enemy was more easily located and spatialized, the multifarious nature of the network society finds its enemies within itself, dispersed, heterogeneously distributed. This expresses the biopolitics of the digital body, where the pathogenic networks are countermeasured with network organization and software.[22] Paranoia is not merely a narrative theme reserved for Pynchon novels but an increasingly effective part of the regulatory surveillance mechanisms of the enemy within.

This section is again interested in formations. In other words, my argument concerns the *formation*, the *emergence* of bodies, the production of the body digital and the computer (network) as the central diagram or abstract machine of network culture. What types of forces define the borders and thresholds of this digital body? What is produced as normality, what as abnormality? What sort of cultural techniques define the insides and outsides of the computational architecture? How is disease differentiated from health? In other words, what would be a better way to approach health than through the breakdown of this presumed unity? In this sense, the concept of the body is close to the definition of an assemblage; health is a process and a network, as Andrew Goffey elaborates, referring to Deleuze.[23] Power aims to seal off this processuality and to form hierarchies and stable nodes that connect the flow of lines, yet networks gain their force only from the connections they establish. In this sense, understanding immunities is vital: Do we conceptualize the self and immunity as a field of military operations, or do we try to move in the direction of networks as flexible systems of adaptation?

Diagrams of Contagion

Viruses have been understood since the nineteenth century as foreign elements invading otherwise integral bodies. They are the Other, the abject, the ever so slightly difficult element that exists outside identity. Or as Joost Van Loon puts it: "Viruses make us ill because they are replicating themselves; like waste, they are virulent abjects of modernity."[24] They are what could be called a floating signifier, too—they have been a marker of disease, ideologically unwanted and the system anomaly. The novel *The Adolescence of P-1* portrays viruses as something comparable to "communists" and "cancer"—all three symptoms of the anomalous and the point where the biological, the political, and the technological seem to coalesce. First it was the Russians, then the viruses that had to be kept out: "If Simpson had any idea that he had Russians in his computer, he'd scream."[25]

Luca Lampo from the net art group *[epidemiC]* emphasizes the importance of this construction of the anomalous and connects it to a mental history of fear of the other:

> We feel that "The Virus" is the "stranger," the "other," in our machine, a sort of digital sans papier—uncontrollable diversity. Once Hollywood, like Empire, finished killing "Indians" and the "Soviet Russians," the Hollywood propaganda machine had to build other anti-Empire monsters to keep alive the social imaginary of 2001: aliens, meteors, epidemic (…) so many monsters. Now the "virus" equals damage, it is easier to sell the idea of a "full spectrum" anti-virus product that would "kill them all," with

no distinctions. Instead, our work says that there are many types of viruses: good, evil, entertaining, boring, elegant, political, furious, beautiful, and very beautiful. "There are no good viruses," anti-virus producers say.[26]

The virus—both as a concept and an assemblage—has been a complex mesh of overlapping meanings and pejorative uses. It's far from a neutral term and is often used for particular purposes. But how did it become meaningful to speak of not only biological virality? A brief answer would suggest via language—just as HIV spread from being a medical term to being a general cultural entity. HIV infects cultural categories: "AIDS is a disease, an industry, a career, a universal signifier that invites us to share a concern over our being in the world, and even invites us to condemn the evil that has brought it into our world."[27] Of course, it was already much before AIDS that diseases and catastrophes could be said to have been a contagious media phenomena. Similar to rumors. A good early example is the 1755 Lisbon earthquake, the first worldwide (at least Europe-wide) media event that horrified people in images and in words. For decades it was recounted in numerous pamphlets and letters, such as the letter that was turned into a public media story and reprinted in various countries: "An Account of the late dreadful earthquake and fire, which destroyed the city of Lisbon, the metropolis of Portugal: In a letter from a merchant resident there, to his friend in England."[28]

Diseases and catastrophes are not merely linguistic representations but, more fundamentally, *events*.[29] The event of AIDS, the event of a computer virus infection synthesizes into a machinic assemblage and includes various types of flows from incorporeal acts of judgment ("You are sick! What did you do to deserve this? Practice safe hex as a digital version of safe sex!") to corporeal movements and interactions of bodies (whether animal fluids or the electronic world of code). Another way to describe the issue is to talk of the incorporeal act with which the technological machinations, bits of code that self-reproduce are named "viruses"—an event that summons a plethora of cultural and historical stratifications. As a judge might have the power with an incorporeal act to transform an innocent person into a guilty one,[30] so the media, computer scientists, and security specialists are among the key groups that have "pronounced" the malicious nature of these programs, turning them into menaces to, and diseases of, organized society.

In her essay "Illness as Metaphor" (1978), Susan Sontag demonstrates the power of articulations. Language exists as a powerful set of active interventions in the world that incite and suggest, channel and contain. Tuberculosis and cancer, to take two central diseases of the last centuries, are perceived and signified not as mere clinical constructs but as more complex machinations. Tuberculosis, along with hysteria, was articulated together with Romantic ideals of feminine subjects, suffering but idealized bodies. Tuberculosis was an artistic disease, taking over the lungs, the part of the human body most associated with the nearly immaterial ether of creativity. It was also an illness of the poor—"of thin garments, thin bodies, unheated rooms, poor hygiene, inadequate food."[31] In contrast, cancer was something low, degrading, and middle class, usually striking the "lower parts" of the body: colon, bladder, rectum, breasts cervix, prostate, testicles. What Sontag has succeeded in demonstrating is the synthetic, machinic nature of diseases (to transform the issue into Deleuzian vocabulary): diseases are assemblages, heterogeneous articulations of bodily metamorphoses (viruses and bacteria acting on the molecular level), societal reactions (disease control, medications, hospitals, various other institutions, border control), and order-words (seeing language primarily as ordering and commanding, instead of communicating). Diseases are a mobilization, a synthesis of a whole arsenal of cultural institutions, metaphors, articulations, and references.

In "AIDS and Its Metaphors" (1989), Sontag addresses computer viruses. Analyzing the rise of "virus culture" during the 1980s, Sontag notes how information also seems to have been exposed to viral diseases. Sontag illustrates how these notions are metaphors drawn from virology that "reinforce the sense of omnipresence of AIDS."[32] Computer culture draws from biology, and viral infections in general are increasingly depicted in the language of computers. Both discourses present a malicious actor, the virus, as taking over the host cell or program in order to make more replicas of itself.[33]

The post–World War II years were marked by new cures against infectious diseases, with antibiotics, in particular, as the game-changing medicine. This created an atmosphere of contagion-free health, prosperity, and confidence about the future, which, of course, was much needed in most countries after the turmoil of the war.[34] In the United States, the Surgeon General announced that contagious diseases were a thing of the past and that they represented no severe threat in the future.[35] Yet, since the 1970s and especially the 1980s, we have faced a threat in the form of new viruses (and drug-resistant strains of disease) as the almost seasonal recurring theme that defines not only attitudes towards health but also the geopolitical body politic, borders, and more.

Viruses became a contagious danger both in biological and in symbolical terms. "It is a modern plague: the first great pandemic of the second half of the twentieth century. The flat, clinical-sounding name given to the disease

by epidemiologists—acquired immune deficiency syndrome—has been short-
ened to the chilling acronym AIDS,"[36] wrote *Scientific American* in 1987. Just
as nuclear war was the central fear of the Cold War era, so the biological
nonface of a virus became the central driver of anxiety in the years just before
and especially after the fall of communism and the binary setting of world
order. A perfect disease of the network society: a virus. The fear of atomic
apocalypse turned into a seemingly postideological world of biological danger.
This change is accurately evident in Terry Gilliam's remake of Chris Marker's movie *La Jetée* (1962). Whereas Marker's experimental audiovisual essay
from the middle of the Cold War depicted a world of postnuclear apocalypse,
Gilliam's *Twelve Monkeys* (1995) focused on the danger of viral bioterror—a
theme that has evolved into a continuously repeated general warning, not
least as a result of the fear of international terrorism since 9/11.[37] Yet, as
Eugene Thacker argues, such intertwinings of the viral and the network are
diagrammatic, where "the diagram provides a cross-section, a transversal (similar to the transverse cross-sections used on frozen cadavers in digital anat-
omy). Diagrams cut across separate organs and organ systems, they cut across
institutions, governments, social classes, technical paradigms, and cultural
forms."[38] Diagrams are thus seen in terms of abstract machines, which do not
represent any particular world but are formative of reality by way of distributing singularities and organization. They are immanently placed on the social
field and pilot concrete social machines. In other terms, diagrams can be seen
as the presentation of power (*pouvoir*) in a formation, where forces are taken
in their Spinozan manner as capacities to affect and be affected.[39] Here, the
concept of diagrams can help us to understand how concrete machinations,
such as in medicine or technology or network security, are intertwined on
a level of abstract machines, diagrammatically and immanently linked on a
social field. Diagrams select elements and assemblages and make them spread
and resonate over their original contexts of birth.

Viruses were analyzed as cultural symbols already in the midst of the
viral culture. These earlier analyses addressed their subject mostly under the
rubric of metaphorics in the manner of the "linguistic turn" of cultural theory in the 1980s. Some of the analyses provided interesting insights, however. For instance, Jeffrey Weinstock writes about the paranoia of contagion
in his article "Virus Culture" (1997). According to Weinstock, notions of
infection, contagion, and viruses (biological, digital, and metaphorical) have
become symptomatic of Western media culture, especially American society.
Alongside AIDS discourse, he addresses computer viruses and the cyberpunk

literature genre of the 1980s as presenting new constellations of the natural and technological. William Gibson's 1984 best-selling novel *Neuromancer*, in particular, introduced the theme of the virus. Yet, Weinstock argues, the issue of the viral should be *evaluated* as a functional element of society and politics. Viruses work through contagion of paranoia, the expected infection that creates "an aura of fear." The virus is transformed from microorganisms into an infection on the macroscopic level of society, where the disease is fought via isolation, splintering, and blaming.[40] Viral culture works through the contagion of affect.

Hence, as Weinstock and Sontag write, and Tony Sampson connects as part of social theory of contagion, virus culture not only is about biological viruses, or even computer viruses. It also concerns a whole cultural condition, affecting fictional and factual accounts of inside and outside, of boundaries and crossings. In addition to biological bodies, HIV spreads in digital games, computer programs, and media representations. As noted in the previous section, virality diagrams media technologies according to its own logic of contagion where viruses are not merely the represented object of media but a description of the how media works. In a more journalistic vein, Douglas Rushkoff's best-seller *Media Virus!* from the mid-1990s introduced the idea of how the media and popular culture in general act virally, transmitting messages that "attach" to people, invert habits of thought, and reproduce themselves. An example of such a viral media object in Rushkoff's sense could be the AIDS computer game, created by a Japanese software firm at the beginning of the 1990s. The game is an AIDS simulation, from the moment of infection to death.[41] "AIDS" designates not just a certain disease, or immunodeficiency syndrome, but also a strong cultural symbol, adopted in various contexts, deterritorializing and reterritorializing across a range of cultural phenomena, not least owing to the media technological logic of network digitality based on the ease of copying and transmitting information. In a way, the virus shows in its logic of reproduction the very basic elements that we find structuring computing and digital culture, that is, reproduction (copy) and transmission (communication).

Although the first AIDS cases in the United States date back approximately to the beginning of the 1980s, HIV as a cause of the syndrome was discovered around 1983 and has been discussed widely since 1984.[42] This did not stop the one-sided argument, namely, that it was mostly a problem of homosexuals, drug addicts, and other "marginal elements."[43] With such articulations and imaginations the virus became a symbol of terror, spreading through the intimate touch of bodily fluids. It was repeatedly claimed that the virus and the immunodeficiency syndrome were mostly something that homosexuals and drug addicts had to deal with. Anal sex and needle sharing were the causes for the infection of society.[44] Of course, it was very hard for the popular media to top the statements by such people as Jesse Helms, Norman Podhoretz, Pat Buchanan, and, for example, Jerry Falwell, who became famous for his "analysis" that "AIDS is God's judgment on a society that does not live by His rules."[45]

The Times speculated in 1985 in the United Kingdom that in the best case "the AIDS figures will fall significantly when the susceptible pool of promiscuous homosexuals has been used up through death or mutation of lifestyle."[46] However, a few years later the emphasis was different. Slowly it was realized that this particular virus could not be thought of as affecting solely the marginalized groups of homosexuals, drug addicts, or Haitians (as the cliché was); rather, "the toughest virus of all"[47] was spreading to society at large:

> In a moral sense any disease that affects some people affects all people. Yet it has been possible for mainstream members of industrial societies to feel safely (even smugly) distant from the groups that have been the main victims of AIDS: male homosexuals, intravenous-drug abusers, Haitians, some black Africans and hemophiliacs. That security blanket has been now stripped away. Three major health authorities assert that AIDS is everyone's problem.[48]

HIV proves to be an interesting case, as it can be seen as an epidemic in nonscalar networks. As the sciences of complexity have argued in recent years, the question is a mathematical one: homosexuals merely exhibited a vastly connected subculture where a parasite could easily spread at an enormous pace owing to the high interconnectedness and intensive sex life of certain key hubs. As it was then claimed, the question was one not of sexual orientation (and God's punishment) but of vectors of social interaction that could be also modeled mathematically. Everything boils down to a problematics of vectors where a node has enough connecting links for a parasite to take advantage of the network, whether social or technological. According to scientists of complexity, all viral phenomena can be described as exhibiting an uneven topological formation where only a few links connect to a wide array of other links and consequently act as hubs of a new form of epidemic. As network theories have during recent years argued, epidemics have also an abstract form; from sex habits and viral vectors of HIV to computer viruses and viral marketing, all act under similar formal patterns of reproduction.[49]

Here, neither mathematics nor biology is removed from politics. My point with these examples is to recall the interconnected (and in a broad sense political) issues inherent in diseases. When Sontag writes that with epidemics of large proportions demands "are made to subject people to 'tests,' to isolate the ill and those suspected of being ill or of transmitting illness, and to erect barriers against the real or imaginary contamination of foreigners,"[50] I read this as illustrating a key cultural historical trait. Efforts to isolate the agents of the disease as well as the affected individuals and groups mean actions on the level of the body politic also, emphasizing that the issue is not only meta-morphic but also isomorphic (or diagrammatic). With articulations concerning divisions between the healthy and the diseased, the boundaries between desired and undesired actions, between promoted and forbidden ways of being are created.[51]

HIV was not the only issue, but it was often perceived as the perfect crystallization of the viral diagram, where several cultural traits of AIDS infection were transported into other situations. The virus became a vector of change, expressing the novel bodily ontologies of not only biological entities but also of technological, media, and cinematic ones. The trope of the disastrous killer virus originates from 1960s fiction. Alistair MacLean's *The Satan Bug* (1962) used the theme of techno-scientific viruses in its plot, and Michael Crichton's novel *The Andromeda Strain* (made into a film in 1971) can be seen as one of the key examples in the history of virus culture. The successful sci-fi thriller depicted a virus-like agent arriving on earth from outer space aboard a U.S. army satellite.[52] In the novel, the virus wipes out a small village and demonstrates its lethalness. The story is as much about the virus as it is about the scientific apparatus mobilized to make sense of it. The virus is revealed to be an alien life form and not just an anomaly: even if it is deadly from the human perspective, it can be a symptom of life in a different horizon. The novel also questions the autonomy of the human body: even if one tries to clean out all bacteria, dirt, and waste from the body, still there is no clean and pure core within the body and the self. The human creates dirt from itself and is in constant contact with a "dirty" outside, making us inherently connected to our surroundings.

Such articulations were at least partially a consequence of the heightened visibility and significance of virology from the 1950s onwards. Early twentieth-century virology bore the stamp of conflicting views and definitions, but the field found a consensus after World War II. Hence the 1950s saw the founding of such key journals as *Advances in Virus Research* (1953), *Virology*

(1955), *Voprosy Virusologii* (1956), *Acta Virologica* (1957), *Progress in Medical Virology* (1958), and *Perspectives in Virology* (1959), without forgetting the key textbook by Salvador Luria, *General Virology*, from the early 1950s.[53] In addition, Luria, Max Delbrück, and Alfred D. Hershey were awarded the Nobel Prize in 1969 for their work on viruses, which presented these actors not merely as foreign intruders but as similar units to genes. They proposed thinking of viruses, too, as "bits of heredity in search of a chromosome."[54] Soon viruses as a cultural topic were quick to spread across Western media culture.

Technological and media viruses appeared approximately at the same time as the killer viruses from space. In this vein I also consider David Cronenberg's films cultural symptoms that deal with the virality of late twentieth-century culture. Where Mark Seltzer in his *Bodies and Machines* provided an inspiring account of the human–technology assemblage of the nineteenth century, and Tim Armstrong highlighted the complex intertwinings of the subject with early twentieth-century modernism in his *Modernism, Technology and the Body: A Cultural History*, Cronenberg presents a powerful cinematic diagram of the body and the machine of the postindustrial media era.[55] Embodiment is a continuous theme in his work, which, particularly from the 1980s on, resonated with the cultural fear of viruses that cross insides and outsides and open up the biological body and the somatic body politic.[56] His earlier work in the 1970s was occupied with strange infectious diseases and mass hysteria that spreads like a virus—underlining how the incorporeal is intimately tied to material vectors of infection. In *Scanners* (1981), thinking becomes a projectile that proceeds via the telephone network in an aggressive manner. Infrastructures become weaponized.

Yet, with Cronenberg, the viral condition is not privileged as part of distributed networks or computers. Broadcast media, too, can act virally and infect. In *Videodrome* (1983), the male protagonist, Max Renn (James Woods), involves himself in a play of S/M fantasies and hallucinations, enacted by a video channel that programs people's brains. The television screen and the signals it emits penetrate the viewer's body. The self becomes an other—not anymore on the couch of a psychoanalyst but on the couch before the television. Although it would be possible to analyze Cronenberg's film as expressing certain themes of the mental history of technological fear, especially the fear of the impact of television, it can also be seen as part of the virus culture of the 1980s: the (male) self is opened up and his bodily boundaries and sense of identity are truly put into question via this encounter with technological forces of televisual transmission, expressed nicely in the evil Professor

O'Blivion's (Jack Creley) McLuhanian line: "The television screen is the ret-
ina of the mind's eye. Therefore the television screen is part of the physical
structure of the brain." The body has been infected with elements outside
its (presumed) boundaries, and increasingly these elements are technological
and audiovisual. Contagious media. This is part of the viral condition that
dismantles erected boundaries between nature, technology, and Man.[57]

Among filmmakers, Cronenberg was not alone in his viral condition;
one can cite the complex bodily infections and transformations in films such
as George Romero's *Crazies* (1973), the *Alien* series (first part 1979), *Species*
and *Outbreak* (both 1995), all part of a cultural motif that has been repeated
in recent years. According to Jerry Aline Flieger, this refrain of viral culture sums up as a symptom of the "fragility of the human self" that is open
to new technologies—the body is punctured with foreign forces.[58] The
viral invasion marks posthumanism after the figure of the cyborg: the body
is not punctured by visible media technologies trespassing on the human
body but by swarming forces of subliminal nature to which the human body
is merely a secondary carrier, a host, not the focal point. Further developments of critical posthuman include for example Rosi Braidotti's feminist
theory.[59]

A whole panorama of 1980s science fiction works illustrate the vulnerability of the body and stable identity in the age of cybernetics. In Greg Bear's
Blood Music (1985), a genetic research project ends up on the wrong tracks,
unleashing an intelligent new life form that threatens to soften the whole
globe into jelly-like substance. These intelligent germs take over the human
body, transforming it from the inside out:

> Something is happening inside me. They talk to each other with proteins and nucleic
> acids, through the fluids, through membranes. They tailor something—viruses,
> maybe—to carry long messages or personality traits or biologic, Plasmidlike struc-
> tures. That makes sense. Those are some of the ways I programmed them. Maybe
> that's what your machine calls infection—all the new information in my blood.[60]

In *Blood Music*, the human is transformed into an information entity, with
viruses taking over, invading this "soft machine."[61] Similar themes are played
out in Octavia Butler's *Clay's Ark* (1984), where in a manner reminiscent of
The Andromeda Strain a spaceship imports a viral life form from outer space
that acts as an invading parasite for human and animal hosts.[62] In addition, two
novels from the beginning of the 1990s deepen the ties between the computer
and the body, namely, Pat Cadigan's *Synners* (1991) and Neal Stephenson's

Snow Crash (1992). Both novels also deal explicitly with computer viruses infecting human bodies through the mediation of cyberspace. In this manner they can be considered key novels of the computerized technoscape of recent decades, alongside William Gibson's canonized work, such as *Neuromancer* (1984). As Gibson and cyberpunk problematized the dichotomy of (organic) nature versus (artificial) technology, Cadigan and Stephenson illustrate the same theme with viruses. For them, both computer and biological viruses are about information. A computer virus moving in the cyberspace of digitality is able to infect a human being connected to the machine, which reinforces the common ground these entities seem to have in a cybernetic culture: the naturality of the artificial and the artificiality of the natural becomes a theme that speaks to this situation of the contagion as a social force. In *Synners*, the virus causes strokes: "If it gets into the system and finds someone hooked in with the interface, it'll get them, too. You got that? A *contagious stroke*, a fucking *virus*, are you with me yet?"[63] In a similar fashion, in *Snow Crash* a "digital metavirus, in binary code, that can infect computers, or hackers, via the optic nerve"[64] causes havoc in a near-future, mass-mediated computer society based on the universality of digital network media.

What these narratives present is a central theme of technological culture, that is, the fusion of body and machine, of nature and technology. If we understand science fiction scenarios as "public stages or arenas to negotiate technical innovation and identity politics,"[65] we can see how sci-fi mobilized various evaluations of this cultural sensibility. Viruses interface humans, technologies, and natures. From a cultural historical perspective this, of course, is no surprise: the biological and the technological have always been intertwined.[66] More specifically, humans and machines found a common ground with the computer and systems theory projects of the 1950s and 1960s, well analyzed by N. Katherine Hayles.[67]

In this context we must not forget the idea of cultural virality introduced with the discourse of the meme in the 1970s. Originating in Richard Dawkins's *The Selfish Gene* (1976), memes have been understood as "cultural genes" and self-propagating viral ideas that Susan Blackmore explicitly associated with computer viruses. In general, the computer and the Internet are fertile ecosystems for meme groups, as Blackmore argues, even though she emphasizes that the issue is not about technologies but about reproduction:

> All this talk of viruses makes me wonder just why we call some pieces of computer code a virus and others a computer program. Intrinsically, they are both just lines of code, bits of information or instructions. The word is, of course, taken directly by

analogy from biological viruses and probably based on the same intuitions about the way these bits of code spread. The answer is not so much to do with the harm they do—indeed some really do very little—but to do with their function. They have none apart from their own replication.[68]

Thus, recent decades have seen a number of cultural strata inhabited by viruses, which underscores the centrality of this vector of trespassing bodies. In memetics, viruses are conceived as informational objects, a translation that problematically forgets their material ontology. Yet, reading the various expressions, it is interesting how various (several of them contradictory) expressions of the viral seem to contribute to a viral diagram of network culture that feeds on the notion of information as immaterial organization. Such an understanding, like in memetics, is far from sufficient explanation but has to itself relate to the wider cultural theme of the diagram of virality: that virality and contagion become seen as explanations of the social. As noted, one solution would be to understand this viral and bacterial colonization of the technological as a *metaphorization* of culture with viruses; another would be to use the idea of an abstract machine piloting this virality—a diagram as Thacker has expressed it.[69]

The Order-Word of AIDS

Viruses were depicted in words and images, represented in various amusing ways even. This cultural imaginary of viral invasion of healthy cells was in a wonderful way visualized in the educational cartoon series from the 1980s, *Il était une fois la vie* (1986), which represented viruses and other nuisances as mean-looking and evil-spirited hooligans.[70] Viruses are, of course, entangled in language too, but linguistic formations are entangled in the material reality. Steven F. Kruger points out in his *AIDS Narratives* how language has a special place as a technique of contextualization: "Viral infection of cells is generally understood in terms of the linguistic metaphor: as the introduction into a host of parasitic genetic information capable of using the cellular apparatus of transcription and translation to further the expression of its own genome, directing the synthesis of new viral nucleic acids and proteins, and hence new viruses."[71]

But it is not just that viruses are language; as part of the Cold War–era contemporary arts and literature, it was suggested that language itself is also a virus. William S. Burroughs originally introduced the idea of the life of language as a proliferating self-copying machine destined to populate the world with pieces of itself. Burroughs writes in his characteristic style:

> My general theory since 1971 has been that the Word is literally a virus, and that it has not been recognized as such because it has achieved a state of relatively stable symbiosis with its human host; that is to say, the Word Virus (the Other Half) has established itself so firmly as an accepted part of the human organism that it can now sneer at gangster viruses like smallpox and turn them in to the Pasteur Institute. But the Word clearly bears the single identifying feature of virus: it is an organism with no internal function other than to replicate itself.[72]

Issues of literature were in tune with the scientific understanding of the world. With the general "textualization" or "informationalization" of the world during the latter half of the twentieth century, computer science and the sciences of life overlap: everything is regarded as a code. The human body is seen as coded (with DNA), and computer viruses are coded actors of the digital world. Kruger argues that computer *viruses* are not just a case of a metaphor being applied afterward to such programs but that they have from the beginning been designed to imitate biological viruses. Both need hosts, both are parasites by nature, and both aim to self-replicate, "though they depend on the function ('execution') of the 'host' programs they have infected in order to 'replicate.'"[73]

Another approach to this would similarly take seriously the idea of the world as based on language—but language not as (merely) signifying but as *ordering*. In other words, what does it imply, in the light of Deleuze and Guattari's notion of language as an order-word, that we think of computer code as language? The pragmatics of language emphasize that it does not primarily operate as communication; it does not mediate in the transparent sense. Language has effects on the corporeal world, which makes it occultist by nature. Language enacts, effects, and affects, and does this not merely as a result of its semantic powers, but as an a-signifying machine of order-words.[74]

Language is already tied to its outside, the world, and the power relations operating in and between assemblages. Language is no autonomous sphere with only internal laws, but a rhizome operating within the world. In this way, all acts of language are acts of power: attempts to draw territories, define borders, impose operations. Order-words are assemblages of enunciation that mobilize and transform bodies and hence create new affects (actions and passions) for them.[75] The description seems to apply especially well to computer code, which exhibits this occult quality of doing what it says in the form of executing sentences. Code expresses immanently the affects it comprises. Of course, this "expression" (or "execution" of commands) is always done in relation to its surroundings, which in technical terms include an operating system. Yet, there is a specifically interesting quality in computer language resulting from its nonrepresentational status. It does not "mean"; it functions and enacts changes, subjugating meaning to pragmatics.

Affects are capacities for creating and receiving action—being part of larger assemblages. Of course, we have variations and we have minor linguistic practices that aim to stutter the majoritarian languages. For example, fictions of computer viruses from the 1970s and the 1980s have created novel openings that do not merely territorialize the viral function into a criminal act or a security problem. Fiction can hence act as a deterritorializing machine that triggers becomings, new modes of subjectivity functioning on the molecular level.[76]

But, then, how do the crossings of biological and computer bodies and viruses concretely express themselves? What types of biological concepts does the computer discourse of the 1980s promote? This can be approached as an analysis of *topoi* (sing. *topos*). Topoi are "commonplace motives 'floating' within cultural traditions and simultaneously forming their storehouses of discursive formulas"[77] that can be used consciously in propaganda or persuasion or merely passively remediated in media cultural discourse, as Erkki Huhtamo defines them. The term is taken from the Latinist scholar Ernst Curtius and transported into the media archaeological toolbox of methods. Media archaeological topos research focuses on how certain key discursive structures are used recursively in various historical contexts with novel articulations and for alternative functions. I am here conjoining the idea of language as pragmatics and order-words (commanding and channeling, not meaning) with the idea of topoi as historically recurring order-words that are used in various historical contexts. It is specifically due to their historical recurrence that certain modes of ordering gain cultural plausibility and hence act as (seemingly) convincing modes of argumentation. The articulations work through the spatialization and metaphorization of phenomena to a certain grid of meanings—a specific way in which topoi are used as order-words. A multiplicity inherent in any cultural "object" is stratified according to changing modes of order-words, of which allegorization and metaphorization are examples.

McAfee and Haynes offer one such key topos of viruses infecting the "nervous system of the computer":

A virus may attach itself to other software programs and hide in them. Or it may infiltrate the computer's operating system—the programming that acts as the computer's nervous system. The operating system regulates the flow of information and instructions to the central processing unit (the CPU), which is the equivalent of the brain. All computer operating systems—for example, MS-DOS, PC-DOS, UNIX, and others—are vulnerable, some more than others.[78]

This way of referring to computers as organisms and CPUs as brains stems from the 1950s. Here the computer is seen as directly analogous to a biological organism. Nervous systems are equivalent to operating systems, a peculiar analogy, considering that most operating systems are software marketed for a certain price and in other ways connected to the capitalist economy. MS-DOS, PC-DOS, and UNIX represent the healthy backbone of the computer body, vulnerable to outside diseases. However, one has to note, to the credit of McAfee and Haynes, that they do also fight the virus hysteria when claiming that not every virus is harmful and that there are a number of different types of programs that are viral by nature and that can even be "used in positive ways to make software more versatile."[79]

There is, however, a more lurking danger inherent in networks, McAfee and Haynes warn. It is not enough to rule out the obvious dangers, such as malicious hackers, for the new diseases are more cunning than that. Infections are described as "intelligent agents" that are able to fool the user into trusting them: "The same precepts currently associated with the AIDS virus apply to computing—when you insert an unknown diskette or download from a network, you expose yourself to a long chain of potentially infectious contacts."[80] The issues of trust persist as a key trope in current computer culture too, exemplary in the various social engineering that goes into spamming ("Dear Sir, I need an investment partner" and many other narrativizations that we receive mostly in our spam folders) and other sorts of cultural practices of networked fraud.

But the issue also presents an interesting perspective on the history of computer crime. As discussed in the previous section, computer security and crime control went through a major change during the 1970s and 1980s. Computer security was no longer concentrated on controlling only the physical facilities where machines were actually placed; it had to work on the networks the computers were attached to. Networking itself created new types of threats. Phone phreakers, hackers, and electronic crime such as fraud and embezzlement were on the security agenda long before worms and viruses were deemed malicious. With hackers (gradually also presumed dangerous to network society) the identification of culpability was still possible: they were, after all, people, often marginalized as anxious teens that committed such acts. But software programs causing problems was a different case: Could one say that the programs were doing the crimes? Or were the programmers responsible, as was most often emphasized? But it is exactly in the midst of the virus fear of 1980s that an idea of programs as an inhuman force became articulated. Even McAfee and Haynes testify to this: "Programs with a will to destroy—an unseen inhuman enemy without motivation—comprise an alien concept that is difficult for those who are not knowledgeable about computer theory to accept as reality."[81]

The computer virus discourse did label and point out certain vectors of risk, malpractices, unethical acts, and suspicious groups that were placed in the spotlight.[82] The so-called Israeli (or Jerusalem) virus of 1987 employed the power of the AIDS discourse to point out the reckless from the careful: "It might do to computers what AIDS has done to sex," said Bushinsky. "The current free flow of information will stop. Everyone will be very careful who they come into contact with and with whom they share their information."[83] Peter Denning made the connection explicit with his explanation of the link between AIDS and the computer virus. Both are described as a parasitic retrovirus that uses other cells to self-reproduce and incorporate "itself into the genetic material of the cell that it attacks, causing the cell to alter its function; the reproductive processes of the cell spawn new copies of the retrovirus."[84]

In another, overlapping topos the blame was put on the individual. Computers do not have lives of their own; people create viruses, and the problem is thus a human–social phenomenon. This leads to *the user* being under the microscope, with an emphasis on the issues of proper and improper computing. At the same time, the emphasis was put on illegitimate uses of software code and criminal ways of computing, and virus writers and hackers were placed under special scrutiny. But also the average user, and her ways of connecting to the world of computers and networks, gradually became an issue of national and global interest: using pirate programs, connecting to suspicious bulletin board systems, visiting porn sites, and being careless and imprudent in her way of computing are things that put the body of the computer at risk. With the use of the AIDS threat, several, occasionally far-fetched, analogies were mobilized as part of the fight against malicious viruses, worms, and other threats lurking within digital networks. The politics of affect features as a major part of the security of software culture. We will return to the practices of proper and improper computing a bit later.

Programs were often directly named with AIDS references. In the early 1980s a virus-like program carried the name Cyberaids, probably the first of its type. Later came several similar cases. Sontag reports that the 1987 Lehigh virus was also called PC AIDS, while in France the term *le sida informatique*, information AIDS, was in use early on.[85] The computer "virus" with a reference to AIDS that gained the most popular attention was actually not a virus but a Trojan horse—a fact that did not stop allusions being made to HIV and computer viruses. The AIDS Information Diskette was mailed to tens of thousands of medical, commercial, and state organizations in Europe, Africa, and the United States, and was supposed to include facts on AIDS. Instead it infected several computers and included a blackmail demand for 200 British pounds to clean the system.[86] Later, the man responsible for this incident, a zoologist called Joseph Popp, was arrested and put into psychiatric care.

So, my point, before going into a deeper and more thorough analysis of bodily issues of digital virality, is that in the several virus incidents that have occurred over the years, especially since the mid-1980s, the HIV and general virus connection has been (at least) twofold. On a linguistic level, viruses have been used as political tools, order-words, and topoi that divide between what is proper computing and what is banned. At the same time, they are part of an a-signifying field of a socio-technological media ecology, which lives on liminality, self-reproduction, complexity, and distributed networks. In this light, Andrew Ross is right when he points out that media commentary has fueled the virus scare and media panic by using the rhetoric of AIDS with moral statements that draw on a general "paranoid style of American political culture."[87] For Ross these computer programs and the representations they produce tell the narratives of hacker subculture, the history of computer technology, the notion of ethics in computing, and the role of media in contemporary society.[88] In addition, I want to make the point that not everything is *human*–social and not everything is reducible to representational analysis. *Meaning* is not the only issue crucial to this media ecology of networking. Under, or between, these social representations operate other fields of a-signifying material. The material elements also participate in intensive differentiation and mixed semiotics where these materials (for example, software and the computer environment) are actively part of the politics of digital culture. In addition, software can be understood as an affective modality in that it intensely participates in various constellations from technology to politics. Furthermore, the issues of anxiety and politics of affect are as crucial in this understanding of the assemblage of the virus. This could be referred to even as a media affect-fear-blur, which is a mode of collective perception and *the monetarized accident form* that does not work on a well-argued rational basis but on the vagueness of the phenomenon, as Massumi notes. This is the low-level fear that saturates the media assemblages of capitalism.[89] Viruses are also produced through a variety of media machinations, including that of the face.

Excursus: Faciality

It's compulsory. Everything needs to have a face of its own. Faces everywhere: white, black, male, female, young, old, for every identity. Identities everywhere—there is no lack of identity, but an abundance.

As Deleuze and Guattari write in *A Thousand Plateaus*, subjectification works through assigning faces to anonymous preindividual flows. Faciality is a marker system that places lines on a grid, makes them interact, gives them names and positions in a field of society: it's also an address system. Faciality works as an abstract machine that assigns both the background (the white wall) and the position (the black hole) that are to subsume all the flows passing through a culture.[90] From a societal point of view, you need a face, an address, an account to exist. Not restricted to media culture, but powerfully captured as part of its power structures, faces are what capitalism needs, as Philip Goodchild writes:

> Oedipalized representation operates by giving people faces; a person is recorded on the socius and participates in society according to the appearance which he or she is given, and by which he or she is recognized. Capitalist culture is largely concerned with the investment of desire in the production, recording, and consumption of faces. The capitalist subject wishes to produce a face of his or her own, to be recognized and acclaimed; films, television, newspapers, and magazines operate less as 'media' than as machines for the production and recording of faces.[91]

Even though we are dealing here with decidedly very faceless flows of digital codes (subrepresentational, temporal), they are continuously coded to have a face.[92] Viruses, too, have faces. Virus scanners have since the late 1980s tried to identify viruses based for example on their code signatures:

```
C:\> VIRSCAN c:
© Copyright IBM Corporation 1989, 1990
Virus Scanner Version 1.41
Starting virus scan on Sat Apr 07 22:51:45 1990
Scanning system memory for dangerous and/or well hidden resident viruses
Found signature in (C:\PROG\TARKIN.EXE) at offset 12650 (316AH)
```

8ED0BC000750B8C50050CBFC062E8C0631002E8C0639002E8C063D002E
   8C0641
008CC0
This file may be infected with the 1813 (Jerusalem) virus.
(Continuing Scan)[93]

Although virus code was fundamentally trying to stay invisible by, for example, hiding itself at the beginning or end of "normal" code, viral programs
were soon visible on another scale of media. Incorporeal acts of signification
assigned them their specific *meaning* as malicious software, marking them
a place in the symbolic order of digital culture. Visual media intensified
this act. The Morris worm became known through its connection with the
face/name system—Robert Morris Jr. Similarly, recent viruses such as the
Netsky and Sasser worms have to a large extent been visually perceived
events.[94] The programs were written by a German teenager who wanted
merely respect and fame; he did end up being a celebrity on a small scale,
interviewed in various publications, although his Netsky worm made it to
television before he did.[95] Yet it was the teenager Sven J. who truly gave a
face to the algorithmic processes of Netsky and another young man who got
his face in *Time* magazine for the Melissa virus—David Smith, "No John
Dillinger."[96] To these we should not forget to add the maker of the I Love
You virus, identified as the 23-year-old student from Manila Onel de Guz-
man. One curious example is the female virus writer Gigabyte, who wrote
her Sharpei worm with Microsoft's C# programming language apparently to
teach a feminist lesson: women can code and they can code well. According to the 17-year-old Belgian, virus writers are not merely pimple-faced
teenage boys, not just the faces constantly repeated and circulated in media
representations.[97]

The nonvisual nature of the algorithmic worm patterns was always an
issue when it came to presenting them on mass media. The Morris worm was
dissected in true scientific style with "microscopes and tweezers" at the MIT
laboratories. Yet, for the press, this proved to be a disappointment at first:

> The media was uniformly disappointed that the virus did nothing remotely visual.
> Several reporters also seemed pained that we were not moments away from World
> War III, or that there were not large numbers of companies and banks hooked up to
> "MIT's network" who were going to be really upset when Monday rolled around.[98]

This did not prevent the virus from being visualized in symbolic terms, usually in cartoon style. The images often used easily recognizable elements from

popular fiction, such as crime stories or science fiction. In addition, the whole Morris worm situation included "cinematic" elements in itself:

> At 4:22 a.m., once upon hearing of the virus going after yet another host in a "new" manner, Rochlis remarked "This really feels like the movie *Aliens*. So where's Sigourney Weaver?" Seeing the virus reach out to infect other machines seemed quite scary and beyond our control.[99]

Such articulations, or topoi, of viral incidents and "digital Godzillas" have been repeated ever since, depicting "killer viruses" that attack the protagonists (usually male heroes) who defend the innocent lay users—who are frequently gendered and sexualized with rhetorics of rape and other images of vulnerability.[100] The Morris worm incident became a paradigm that has been followed ever since: with new viruses we have the television talk shows and news reports, the security professionals assessing the threat, and so on. In addition to being a security threat to the Windows operating systems in particular, worms and viruses are increasingly becoming media incidents that spread with the aid of audiovisions and texts. This is, of course, a near-banal statement, as the antivirus researchers themselves emphasize: even people who do not use computers are familiar with the concept of the computer virus through Hollywood movies such as *Pulse* (2006), *Independence Day* (1995), *Hackers* (1995).[101] The faceless computing processes animating the expressive machines of the cybernetic era also have a visual nature, although the microscopes of digital virology were not able to dig into the actual contents of code within the computers, which forced them to adapt other, indirect techniques of visualization.

Faces talk of viruses and security. They instruct and guide, vocalize what needs to be sensed. If we follow Trond Lundemo's argument, the algorithmic accident needs somebody to give them a voice, to remediate them:

> The separate regimes of manual, electric and cybernetic machines have different ways of breaking down. Their malfunction may be hidden, sudden or gradual. The physical presence and the visibility of the film strip in cinema is contrasted by the invisibility of the digital code. The hidden erasure in the computer must for this reason be represented visually. The many different symptoms of the computer virus are such ways of visualisation, and a field that in itself deserves a comprehensive historiography. "I love you," "California," "Win a Holiday"—in a subject line of an e-mail, these messages are associated with a disaster.[102]

This is how accidentality and its ambiguous nature as chance and necessity are controlled and assigned a place in the grid of understanding. This is a very

Figure 2. The F-Secure virus hunter Mikko Hyppönen in a CNBC Interview. Virus researchers also have been made into media figures.

Source: Mikko Hyppönen press photos, <http://mikko.hypponen.com/photos/>. Used with permission.

practical solution to the problem of lines of flight of deterritorializing mini-programs—a way to territorialize them and create a milieu where they can be grasped. Knowledge works through "the combinations of visible and articulable that are unique to each stratum or historical formulation."[103]

Digital Immunology

Faciality is one mode of capture among others. The meaning of the previous short excursus was to demonstrate how program code and scripts are continuously remediated as visual media on television, in cartoons, and in other graphic design forms. In addition, the construction and maintaining of the territory of a healthy, integral body of society has been intimately tied to the medical discourses of each age, especially during modernization (as medicalization). In her innovative analysis of the cultural-medical landscape of the

late twentieth-century United States, Emily Martin argues how flexibility and
the notion of an adjustable immune system work as central cultural symptoms.
Martin analyzes different ideas of the immune system and the body, ranging
from the body as a police state and warlike scenarios to a softer version where
the bodies of the self are fluid and in constant interaction with the environment. Martin connects these figures to a more general cultural trend of flexibility, an index of advanced capitalism. The new idea of an agile self, capable
of responding to the various changes and pressures the environment produces,
serves as "an ideal model of being in the world" and a sort of template "for
ideal forms of conducting business or making products."[104] Martin offers an
insightful analysis of the so-called postdisciplinary societies of control, which
is in resonance with Deleuze's ideas of the phenomenon. Martin sees immune
systems thinking as a move from the rigid Fordist system of organization based
on constraining and "immobilization of the body" toward a flexible system of
differentiation. Yet, such a figuration of "agile, dancing, flexible" bodies is also
subject to forms of containment that work more subtly via a temporal and
moving modulation, not spatialization and containment. Such bodies of the
post-Fordist order "cannot stop moving, they cannot grow stiff and rigid, or
they will fall off the 'tightrope' of life and die."[105]

To paraphrase Andrew Goffey, the key ideas of Sir Frank MacFarlane
Burnett in the 1940s and 1950s established immunology as the "science of
self–nonself discrimination." In the second part of the twentieth century, in
particular, immunological thinking was occupied with "the nature of biological identity and the mechanisms of organic integrity." This is part of the biopolitical agenda, having to do with "the nature, maintenance and protection
of populations: a delegation of the health of the body to a set of autonomous
biological mechanisms, an interiorization of a social and political problematic parallel to the interiorization of the social repression of desire traced out
by Gilles Deleuze and Felix Guattari in their *Anti-Oedipus*."[106] Such a rigid
self–nonself model of immunology can also be understood as weaponized
models based on the defense of territory. Even in the context of networks
and connectivity, it builds on closed territories and access controls that can
be implemented in different ways. This also reveals how "nature" and "biological truths" are tactically used: biological concepts can be used to highlight a phenomenon as a "matter of fact" that abides by law-like behavior. For
example, neoliberal capitalism can be naturalized and biologized as a form of
self-organization, which builds on pseudoscientific trust in self-balancing and
self-correcting behavior of systems. Of course, as many accounts have shown,

the various rhetorics and market emphasis and deregulation that characterize neoliberalism are not about laissez-faire, but instead are products of mar-
ket-geared orientation and incentivization by the state.[107] In contrast to such
uses of biology, my take on media ecologies wants to denaturalize the ecologies
of network culture: ecologies are not natural but historical, changing, and also
in the future open to variations and further potentials.

I want to further continue discussing the virus discourse of the 1980s and
1990s and analyze the articulations of "technological public health," "digital
disease control," and the figures of immunity that go along with issues of security. Of course, one has to note the variety of ways the image of the pristine
body of the computer is contrasted with ideals of the healthy computer. The
computer as a (presumably) rational machine offered, at least until the end of
the 1980s, a perfect fantasy object for the clean body, as Christine Boyer notes:
"The computer seems to be our age's clean, innocent machine, promising a
synthetic world born from mathematics in a pure state, not yet tainted by the
dark disciplinary devices of our all-too-human making."[108] The clean body of
modernization found its imaginary ideal in the computer organism. Just as the
body biologic (and politic) was, from the end of the nineteenth century, the
object of constant attacks by minuscule viruses and bacteria, so the computer
soon had its own share of dirt. In some rhetorical cases, public health and
hygiene are the central reference points; in other cases more direct references
to AIDS are used. Some articulations see the split between the healthy body
of a computer and the infectious virus as uncrossable; others see the border as
more flexible. Whatever the case, immunological references within computing discourses and practices bring forth powerful mechanisms of naturalization
that are used to draw the borders between healthy and unhealthy processes of
computing.[109] Naturalization works here as a strategy of stratification, where
fluid lines of flight are captured into condensations. Stratification works as
a screening: by producing repetitive action, habits, and cycles, a territory is
formed. Easily, strata might turn to present themselves as transcendent: God,
State, Nature, Self.[110]

The notion of malicious agents of disease and the need to maintain strict
borders between inside and outside are central tenets when discussing computer viruses. This pertains especially to the 1980s, the early years of computer
worm and virus outbreaks. Viruses and worms are seen as clandestine silent
infiltrators trying to find ways to alter the healthy operations of a system.[111]

In the early 1970s, the novel *When HARLIE Was One* (1972) fantasized a
virus program that strikingly resembled its biological counterpart in that both

were unhealthy pieces of vandal renegade code. In the novel, virus programs are described as "renegade genetic information," just like biological viruses of pure DNA. Both infect *normal* cells and *force* them to produce more viruses, as the novel narrates.[112] Just after the publication of the novel, in 1973, the movie *Westworld*, written and directed by Michael Crichton, used a similar idea of a computer disease. A computer-controlled robot entertainment world starts to malfunction and threatens the safety of the human visitors. The extremely complex robot figures are explained as having been built autonomously by other computers, which makes their operational principles too hard to grasp for the human designers. "Getting sick" is the term used to refer to program breakdowns of high-complexity systems.[113]

The figure of the city provided a recurring topos. Bryan Kocher, the ACM President in 1989, addressed the need for a "hygiene lesson" taught by the then-recent Morris worm incident:

> Just as in human society, hygiene is critical to preventing the spread of disease in computer systems. Preventing disease requires setting and maintaining high standards of sanitation throughout society, from simple personal precautions (like washing your hands and not letting anyone know your password), to large investments (like water and sewage treatment plants or reliably tested and certified secure systems).[114]

Computer security became conflated with discourses of hygiene, arguing that the parallels between digital viruses and sexually transmitted diseases "are painfully obvious." Kocher continues that computer diseases are, like biological diseases such as cholera, tied to specific contexts in which they flourish. Consequently, hygiene measures are needed to ensure the safety of the polis.

In the same year, James Morris writes of "our global city," with all the positive and negative aspects of a modern metropolis. This exemplifies the idea I proposed at the start of this section: the practices and discourses of previous media ecologies, namely the city, are constantly remediated in these novel contexts of network culture. As in the Middle Ages, the computerized version of the city faces the need for sanitation systems and other solutions to help address the growing side effects. "The global city" needed digital sanitation services:

> Along with the openness, diversity, and size come certain problems. People can bother you with junk mail, hackers can disrupt your computer systems with worms and viruses, people can get at information you would prefer to be private and even broadcast it if they choose. Like a big city, the academic networks are not under anyone's control. They carry any kind of communication without regard to its correctness, tastefulness, or legality.[115]

Morris is not so drastic in his demands for countermeasures, but he emphasizes that one must find the middle path between the total anarchic openness (of the Usenets) and hierarchically controlled data networks.

In many ways this was the liberal ideal of computing: regulated but still exhibiting symbolic values of freedom. Health meant autonomy, part of the imaginary of computer culture. As Helmreich notes, "Computers are imagined as pristine, autonomous entities that exist prior to their embedding in networks—an idea that echoes the liberal conception of society as made up of individuals who exist prior to the society of which they are a part, an ideology deeply written into U.S. political culture."[116]

Bodies are mobilized and defined through the use of notions such as immunity, individual integrity, and the hostile outside. According to Emily Martin, interest in the immune system dates from the early 1970s, even if traces of the trope are found even earlier. Martin refers to a 1970s TV program *The Immortal* in which a hero is equipped with a special supercharged immune system. A decade later, AIDS as a disease of the immune system had an obvious impact on the centrality of notions of immunity and the border of self and other. Martin notes how the immune system became understood as a maintainer of this boundary, "often accompanied by a conception of the non-self world as foreign and hostile."[117] Dysfunctions of the autoimmune system were consequently described in terms of a civil war.[118] As Lily E. Kay notes, John von Neumann conceptualized systems of self-reproduction in rather militarized terms. Such automata were fighting for scarce resources, engaging in a competition for *Lebensraum*.[119] Both the biological organism and the computer "body" have in recent decades been wrapped in a discourse of battle, defenders, and combatants.

Gibson's *Neuromancer's* (1984) world of computing is a paradigmatic example of how the life of computers and cyberspace was pictured in the 1980s and 1990s. The novel's cyberspace is a battlefield for jacked-in hackers, artificial intelligence programs, attack viruses, and defensive countermeasure programs called ICE (intrusion countermeasure electronics). *Neuromancer* provides an imagery of communications technology as weaponized: "Case triggered his second program. A carefully engineered virus attacked the code fabric screening primary custodial commands for the subbasement that housed the Sense/Net research materials."[120]

Neuromancer offered the digital culture of the 1980s a wide array of impactful concepts and metaphors that played an important part in the symbolical design and signification of the new technologies of the personal computer and network society.[121] Viruses were part of this scene. As Paul Saffo notes, John Brunner's *Shockwave Rider* (1975) inspired a bunch of hackers, including the Internet worm programmer Robert T. Morris Jr., but it was the dark neon-lit figures of digital urbanity, speed, and cyberspace of Gibson who attracted a whole generation of wannabe cyberpunks to write viruses and hack systems. Is there a whole new generation of computer kids "learning their code of ethics from Gibson's novels"? was the worried question. Saffo writes: "Unambiguously illegal and harmful acts of computer piracy such as those alleged against David Mitnick (arrested after a long and aggressive penetration of DEC's computers) would fit right into the *Neuromancer* story line."[122] Interestingly, some software pioneers have also hinted at the connection between early virus-like programs such as Darwin and the Cold War atmosphere of the 1950s and 1960s.[123]

In 1988, the Morris worm was described as an attacker and invader bringing computers and institutions "to their knees," and the computer scientists at MIT were brave figures of hardworking defensive troops, who with little or no sleep persisted in a continuous battle, "attacking the virus."[124] In another context, the same Internet worm was described in similar terms, presenting the virus as a furious monster breaking in, as in a scene from a monster movie:

> The program kept pounding at Berkeley's electronic doors. Worse, when Lapsley tried to control the break-in attempts, he found that they came faster than he could kill them. And by this point, Berkeley machines being attacked were slowing down as the demonic intruder devoured more and more computer processing time. They were being overwhelmed. Computers started to crash or become catatonic. They would just sit there stalled, accepting no input. And even though the workstations were programmed to start running again automatically after crashing, as soon as they were up and running they were invaded again. The university was under attack by a computer virus.[125]

The topos of war is also used in *Virus! The Secret World of Computer Invaders That Breed and Destroy* (1989). To paraphrase the writer, Allan Lundell, military models have provided the reference points for most computer security systems. For example, password access can be described as analogous to a fence or a wall separating the inside from the outside.[126] Of course, what has to be noted is that electronic warfare, the information bomb, is not a mere metaphor but refers to the actual ways war is being transformed with digital computers. War *is* to a large extent about softwar(e), where network technologies have to a great extent been the product of military funding, and the programs of network technologies are potential vectors of disruption, interruption, sabotage, and scrambling.[127] Current focus on cyber security is merely an extension of Cold War research into new technologies and the networked opportunities of action at a distance.

As for defense, digital immunology systems were developed in the early 1990s in various research centers in the United States. Stephanie Forrest (University of New Mexico) was one of the pioneers, alongside Jeffrey Kephart (IBM Thomas J. Watson Research Center, New York). For Forrest, the immunological model and the biologically inspired design were natural consequences of "the uncontrolled, dynamic, and open environments in which computers currently operate."[128] This biologization of computer security functioned as a symbiotic coevolution where the increasingly nonhierarchical computer operations and user procedures were infected with similar sounding problems—which in their turn were "controlled" only via subtle and complex models of immune systems. Nancy Forbes outlines the main issue of such a systematic yet flexible defense mechanism as having to find lasting definitions for the self as separate from the nonself (the white wall and the black holes). Protection systems are filters for intruders and they function via detection, prevention, and elimination. Such systems are endowed with a memory, or an archive, for remembering previous attacks or infections and potentially for recognizing new ones.[129]

Forrest's ideas of a digital immune system protecting the "self" of the computer are well summarized in *Communications of the ACM* in an article titled "Computer Immunology." The key text offers a range of definitions and concepts that resonate with the general cultural understanding of the immune system. For the writers, the immune system works as a layer of protection against "dangerous foreign pathogens, including bacteria, viruses, parasites, and toxins."[130] As in biological organisms, the immune system acts as a form of filter that kills hostile invaders, and in computer networks similar multi-layered protection systems could detect and eliminate foreign particles and thus protect the integrity of the system. Hence, the immune system inhabits a liminal status between the system and its outside. This is further emphasized by autoimmune diseases (such as AIDS), where this assumed protective membrane turns on the host organism or system. In addition, as Forbes argues, *digital immune system breakdown* has to be accounted for in the same way as lymphocytes attacking an organism's own cells.

In many of the instances, computer immune system is proposed to be based on the distinction between "self" and "other." In computers, the biological "self" of internal cells and molecules is seen as "short sequences of system calls executed by privileged processes in a network operating system."[131] These processes are the *healthy signature* of the normal computer self, in contrast to the "abnormal anomalies" of intruders and viruses trying to capture the processes (system interruptions). The individuality of the computer is maintained with a database of normal procedures that a computer can process without the need to suspect an infiltration of unhealthy code.[132] Interestingly, in 1995 IBM produced an "automated immune system" available commercially. This was in connection with IBM's multimillion-dollar research project that the company claimed "will lead to an automated immune system for computers patterned on biological processes."[133] Of course, on another level one could claim that the aspirations for trusted computing of the Trusted Computing Group (of the biggest corporate hardware and software manufacturers) work in such a direction of immunizing the computer platform against dubious programs, but also against user control.

"Immunization" has also been used to refer to certain types of antivirus software and checksum procedures (the latter check for alterations in software before running it). In essence, this procedure also relies on an archival principle of comparing the program at hand with an archived, presumably healthy version and judging by this comparison whether the code is uninfected. This form of immunization, however, produced a huge number of problems in the ordinary execution of programs.[134] Such examples demonstrate well how the issue is far from metaphorical and engages more accurately with the importance of material definitions of digital bodies, their detection, filtering, and channeling: a border control mechanism of network systems.

Lundell's *Virus! The Secret World of Computer Invaders That Breed and Destroy* addresses software adaptation, flexibility, and resilience. Vaccinations are explained as "small stresses to the body that prepare it to deal with greater stresses."[135] For computers, system-resident auditing software is proposed as an allegory. But there seem to be also additional parallels in terms such as "antigens," "free radicals," "inflammation," and "fever," as well as "white cells." These are understood by Lundell as "traveling internal checker programs":

> Basically a decentralized defense from within, white blood cells and macrophages travel through our veins and arteries looking for "unauthorized" visitors. In computers, roving "checker programs" could travel paths leading to all important parts of a system, disabling unauthorized or unrecognized programs, peripherals, terminals, and the like. These checker programs could refer to a log of authorized production program changes to determine whether a certain code should be permitted to execute or even whether it should be system-resident. In this way, unauthorized programs hidden within authorized programs (like viruses and Trojan horses) could be detected.[136]

Basically, what Lundell proposes is quite similar to the idea presented in the 1997 *Communications of the* ACM article on computer immunology. Both describe a process of immunity programs that are based on a database, or a log of authorized normal processes allowed to run. Programs without such clearance are to be treated as invaders and stopped. This is password control: instead of physical borders and spaces of confinement controlling movement, we have numerical access points that either grant access to a piece of information or reject it.[137]

In addition, this question of control is tied to archives as databases of authorized processes. In a conceptual way, AIDS is an archival danger—the possibility of erasure of the archives that define what is self and what is other, an erasure of memory. Similarly, erasure of computer memory threatens such distinctions. An erasure of memory would mean a complete program malfunction within the most important control components of a system:

> In our model of the computer immune system, for example, the virulence of a virus can crash its host or hosts very quickly. An attack on the computer's immune system could occur if a white blood cell checker program attacked other checker programs, should its integrity be infiltrated by a virus. The system could also crash should antibody-related destroyer programs attack legitimate processes, or if a control infinitely recursively called itself.[138]

Lundell emphasizes the decentralized nature of this self, although he refers to classical notions of "intruders"—"us and them." In general, Lundell proposes a holistic approach to the computer world, in which a single body is always part of a larger whole, "where we in relation to the planet are like viruses in relation to our bodies."[139] Lundell's proposition of security and the immune system ordered as flexible, holistic entities resonates with Martin's analysis of the immune discourse in the era of advanced capitalism. Abstract processes also express themselves in corporeal cultural objects.

However, providing a solid definition of a self in a networked environment remained a continuous issue. In contrast to the binary models, holistic flexibility proposed a softer form of memory and self, acknowledging the primacy of change: "There are many legitimate changes to self, like new users and new programs, and many paths of intrusion, and the periphery of a networked computer is less clearly defined than the periphery of an individual animal. Firewalls attempt to construct such a periphery, often with limited success."[140] This is basically the same problem that Fred Cohen was already engaged with in the 1980s, namely, how to reconcile the need to restrict the paths of sharing and transitivity flow that are part and parcel of the vectors for spreading viruses with not succumbing to isolationism;[141] how to keep the "body of the network" open but at the same time restrict unwelcome elements from entering the flows of information.

The critique of a too-simplistic understanding of immunology stemmed already from the work of an early key name in the history of science, Ludwig Fleck, and his book *Entwicklung einer wissenschaftlichen Tatsache: Einführung in die Lehre vom Denkstil und Denkkollektiv* (1935). For Fleck, an investigator of syphilis, the idea of infectious disease was

> based on the notion of the organism as a closed unit and of the hostile causative agents invading it. The causative agent produces a bad effect (*attack*). The organism responds with a reaction (*defense*). This results in a conflict, which is taken to be the essence of disease. The whole of immunology is permeated with such primitive images of war. The idea originated in the myth of disease-causing demons that attack man.[142]

Fleck argued that the presupposition of organisms as self-contained and completely autonomous units was inadequate. In fact, organisms are in constant interaction with their environments. With this emphasis, Fleck was already close to much later second-order cybernetics and systems theory, which underline the interaction of an organism with its surroundings. For these approaches, the defining point of a living system is located not in any specific instance or substance but in the ambient point of connection between an inside and an outside. This is a circular organization of negative feedback that functions to maintain a sensitive balance. The interesting part in their autopoietic theory of systems is its focus on processuality: unities are based on relationships that maintain nodes. Unities exist because of continuous processes of self-reproduction. This implies also a move beyond subject–object relations and toward systems as events and processes. Relations between organisms and their environment are primary.[143] In another register this could also be called Spinozan immunology, based on affects and interactions of bodies on an immanent plane.

The outside was already folded with the inside:

> It is very doubtful whether an invasion in the old sense is possible, involving as it does an interference by completely foreign organisms in natural conditions. A completely foreign organism could find no receptors capable of reaction and thus could not generate a biological process. It is therefore better to speak of a complicated revolution within the complex life unit than of an invasion of it.[144]

Fleck's ideas are interesting because they tried to steer away from binary models of self–other toward more complex ideas of systems. This is fruitful also in the analysis of conceptualizations of computer systems: instead of seeing viral code as deviant aberration from normal computing, it actually meshes with the operations of computer systems as an interesting variation on themes of network computing. This is why too rigid accounts of the computer self are unsuitable for a realistic consideration of computer security and software culture. This has led computer scientists to emphasize that computer immune systems have to be dynamically formed. Even though such systems have been thought to rely on distinguishing self from anomalies, the definition of anomalous behavior has been a difficult task. Databases of normal behavior (measured by allowed system calls) have to be continuously open to redefinition, and no scanning procedure is completely safe. Hence, instead of seeing the computer as clearly defined by its borders (whatever they might be), some computer scientists have pointed out the need for multilayered protection, distributed detection (no one central database and control of anomalies), and open-ended detection of "previously unseen foreign material."[145] This highlights how the border of the computer (as drawn by discourses of the immune system) is not a natural, clear-cut entity but is continuously under construction and negotiation.

As Donna Haraway reminds us, bodies are not transcendently existing autonomous natural entities but are actively created in symbolic, technical, and political fields. The self is not a preexisting identity to which an immune system is assigned; our understanding of the self is prescribed in relation to the scientific understandings and valorizations of the immune system. Within discourses of the immune system, bodies and boundaries are drawn with the aid of concepts of the normal and the pathological. The immune system is a program of territorialization that actively *assigns* elements to classes of self and other. It places and identifies objects on the scale of familiar or foreign, being more an active apparatus of selection than a merely passive surface of recognition.[146]

In immune system discourse this means that those elements represented as foreign to the self of an immune protection layer cannot be totally foreign after all. The immune system uses the same language to identify the elements that approach it; in a way, it "sees" them or "mirrors" them internally.[147] In other words, the outside is constantly *folded* within the inside, an idea that problematizes the strict separation of inside and outside. This is a model based not on representation but on an active creation of a territory (which is always in a potential state of becoming, of de- and reterritorialization).

The question is a rather fundamental one: Who, and in what types of networks of power and knowledge, defines what is normal functioning of a computer and what is a disease? The genealogy of incorporeal events becomes again a relevant way to consider software culture. A temporal perspective on individuation reminds us how crucial it is to step out of the rigid self–non-self model of immunology into a more flexible understanding of connectivity on complex enough notions that acknowledge the processuality behind formations of identity of systems.[148] The aim is to avoid dualistic accounts and underscore the complex nature of this assemblage or, in general, this media ecology where relations are perhaps endosymbiotic—various types of actors from bacteria to humans and technology constituting "a heterogeneous biosphere of evolution."[149]

Interestingly, such approaches were also introduced in the computer design context. Terry Winograd and Fernando Flores's *Understanding Computers and Cognition* from the 1980s introduced important new ideas concerning, first, the embodied boundaries of computer systems and, second, postrepresentational approaches to understanding the interactions of such systems. In the wake of Heideggerian notions of technology, they underlined the issue of breakdowns as key technological features. Heidegger argued in *Sein und Zeit* at the end of the 1920s how breakdowns, accidents, provide a fundamental ontological point regarding tools.[150] Winograd and Flores translated this insight to computer systems discourse and design. Breakdowns are interrupted moments of "habitual, standard, comfortable 'being-in-the-world.'"[151] Heidegger's example of the broken-down hammer becomes an example for a wider ontological principle and a statement concerning design and technology. Of course, computers are not hammers, even though both should be defined not by their object-nature but by the processes and networks they engage in (assemblages, as Deleuze and Guattari would say). Winograd and Flores note how computers are actually networks of equipment that demand the cooperation of various parts from human arms and hands to keyboards, screens, and devices, not forgetting all the internal processes of the machine. Only a breakdown in some relationship in this web reveals the complexity of the machine working under our noses.[152] Computer design could, then, take into account such potentials for accidents and incorporate them affirmatively into systems. This emphasis on computer design provided an interesting account where accidents were integrated into computer systems planning, and where computer systems were not mere pristine bodies but interacting and intertwining bodies of a symbiotic kind. This focus on breakdowns leads to an understanding of the interconnected nature of computers as assemblages, where accidents are internal to the functioning of the machine—an ontology of failures constitutes their mode of being-in-the-world.

The Care of the Self: Responsible Computing

The media ecology of networking has included various stages and processes of purification. The discourse of digital immunology has consisted of practices, concepts, and metamorphoses where certain computer operations were defined as normal and healthy and others went through the incorporeal transformation to being labeled the *pathogens* of the computer world. Viruses are most often christened as malicious software, whereas "crawlers," "spiders," and sometimes also "bots" are considered legitimate background processes.[153] Another good example are port scanners that can be used to map network traffic and scan for potential security holes. Yet, they are also perceived as illegitimate tools for hackers searching for potential entry points to systems. This tension was made visible in Knowbotic Research's Minds of Concern project that allowed the scanning of activists' sites. The project was withdrawn from the New York Museum of Modern Art owing to its twilighting between legitimate (security) use and illegitimate scanning.[154]

In a very apt way, Wendy Chun has called the networked computing culture as "based on the leak"—not merely the intentional political leak but that computers themselves leak data constantly through their networked being without us knowing exactly what is going on inside the computer.[155]

The references to digital hygiene have also worked as ways to contain images of the leaky computer culture, or somehow make it seem more of a controlled demarcation between health and disease. Computer hygiene has included of a range of practices, demands, advice, and precautions that have been directed at tackling the ever-growing problem of "digital cholera," "computer AIDS," or one of the other disease references mobilized in particular cases. Protective computer programs were one obvious solution, which has been analyzed above in several contexts. But the notion of the user and her way of interacting with the computer also became an important practice. Computer security included backing-up, distrusting strangers, and a range of other procedures that seemed mundane but were part of a general preparation of the user to be the safe link in the networking chain: "The best defense against this contemporary threat is user awareness and safe computing habits,"[156] and with echoes of the collective responsibility: "We must all help in keeping each other 'virus free.'"[157]

Personal computers were only on their way to conquering the offices and homes of the Western world during the 1980s. The idea of using computers in everyday life was new. Whereas earlier computer use had been the privilege of a few people in universities, banks, and insurance companies, now they were marketed as essential tools for everyone, from children to adults. Earlier, the television set had received similar attention, and the entrance of the TV into living rooms was also buffered with careful advice on how the viewer should behave.

The term "computer literacy" was applied in various ways and contexts. The idea was that computing was revolutionizing not just the basics of work but also the very symbolic structure of society. "Knowledge work" with computers represented a new form of labor that did not simply follow earlier forms of production. Knowledge workers did not represent a uniform class, nor did labor with computers have to be bound by nationality. Instead, "the language" of computers enabled new forms of productive action that were not "work" according to the old standards of the industrial era but yet represented the core of the knowledge economy and its thrust toward communication, cultural and social knowledge, and what has been referred to as, for example, "immaterial labor."[158]

Just as the earlier national movements for literacy aimed to make the whole population into responsible citizens through the use of literature, something that Kittler analyzed in his *Discourse Networks 1800/1900*,[159] so computer literacy was proposed to be the next step in civilizing oneself to become a proper citizen of digital society. Pioneers such as Alan Kay paid special attention to this aspect of literacy that implicitly was in this way integrated as part of the industry rhetorics and business planning:

> What then is computer literacy? It is not learning to manipulate a word processor, a spreadsheet or a modern user interface; those are paper-and-pencil skills. Computer literacy is not even learning to program. That can always be learned, in ways no more uplifting than learning grammar instead of writing. Computer literacy is a contact with the activity of computing deep enough to make the computational equivalent of reading and writing fluent and enjoyable. As in all the arts, a romance with the material must be well under way. If we value the lifelong learning of arts and letters as a springboard for personal and societal growth, should any less effort be spent to make computing a part of our lives?[160]

In Britain in the context of publicly funded initiatives, the BBC sponsored a Computer Literacy Project with a television program encouraging people to engage with computers. Similar projects spread during the 1980s in other European countries.[161]

In some cases, computer education was to teach about the dangers of the computer world too. As users were taught proper computing, the issue of the improper or even illegal use of computers came also to the fore. Earlier computer cultures of mainframes during the 1950s–1970s were hierarchical in the sense that only a few assigned people had access to computing facilities. The culture of personal computing changed this situation. Computing became dehierarchized, noncentralized, and distributed, something that one could do on one's own without any mediating authorities: the dream of interactive personal computing. This, of course, was the main reason the counterculture became interested in computers: no more passive operators of mainframes but active users of personalized machines of expression and production.[162] The idealized business vision of the 1980s was that everyone was supposed to become an individual media producer equipped with her own personal computer. One has only to recollect Timothy Leary's enthusiastic accounts of computers as instances of personal freedom. In 1984, Leary wrote how the "intoxicating power of interactive software is that it eliminates dependence on the enormous bureaucracy of knowledge professionals that flourished in the industrial age."[163] However peculiar Leary's public image might have been, his statements were in many ways in sync with the general utopia of digital culture. Counterculture was good business culture, with Leary even featured on an Autodesk commercial promo in the 1980s.[164]

But some were quick to point out that freedoms were to be accompanied by the new *responsibility* the user was expected to practice. For example, in business contexts, individuals were held responsible and accountable for all of their actions, a message that was to "be conveyed to staff, associates, partners, agents, suppliers, and collaborators."[165] To paraphrase a commentator from 1986, even if computer data were much less sensitive to disclosure, they were more sensitive to being modified. The new media technologies of digitality demanded a new form of attention in the business environment:

> So it is important that management spell out for the users what all of its expectations
> are. It is important that those expectations include the responsibility on the part of
> all the users *to report to management anything strange that they may observe in the expected
> behavior, use, or content of the system.* Any variances from those expectations should
> be reported.[166]

The individual was subjected to a wide range of guiding, advice, and demands that were to make her into a proper user of the computer, a responsible citizen (later *netizen*) of the emerging digital polis. The consuming individual became important to maintaining the civilized behavior and the normal functioning of the corporation. But computers and the flow of information were no longer restricted to big organizations with their centralized computing facilities but became an issue of the individual user and the household. The new responsibility of the user was expressed in an advertisement in *Byte* magazine's January 1985 issue. The picture shows an anonymous person, a female, in front of a computer monitor. Her eyes are framed out of the picture, and the text says, "She's temporary. The damage is permanent," hinting that users are the ones making mistakes, not technology. "It can happen to you—because a leading cause of data loss is human error. If you employ people and computers, you're vulnerable." The human being is the weak link in the human–computer symbiosis planned already by Joseph Licklider in 1960. He noted the same thing: even if the nerve channels of human beings have many parallel levels, basically we humans are "noisy, narrow-band devices" who are a lot slower and less accurate than computing machineries.[167] Humans were not to be trusted in a culture of digitality, which was "becoming increasingly dependent on the accurate and timely distribution of information."[168]

Figure 3. "She's temporary. The damage is permanent." (*Byte*, January 1985. Used with permission, © Byte.)

A similar point is made in an earlier advertisement from *Scientific American* in 1981. This refers to computer crimes, picturing a police line-up with three middle-aged, formally dressed men (clearly referring to businesspersons) and an IBM computer. The text says, "The computer didn't do it," which, again, underlines human agency. The ad promises that IBM continues its search for new safeguards and security measures, while outlining the whole theme of risk society: "True, there's probably no such thing as total security. But with proper precautions computers can be more than just safe places to keep information. They may well be the safest."

Figure 4. "The computer didn't do it." (*Scientific American*, September 1981. Used with permission, © IBM Corporate Archives.)

These are 1980s examples of a "care of the self" that has acted as a key technique of subjectification in Western cultural history. For Michel Foucault, this notion means the techniques with which the individual made herself into a self-governing subject. Care for the self refers to a range of norms, practices, regulations, and recommendations through which the subject made herself a genuine subject. It can be understood as placing oneself in relation to oneself, meaning a range of actions and thoughts through which one regulates one's being.[169] In early modern secularizing Europe, health became one of the key responsibilities of the individual body, where simultaneously this paradigm of the self was turned into an issue of society: a healthy individual body contributes to a healthy society in the biopower thought of the seventeenth century, as Sennett analyzes.[170]

The idea that germs cause disease (an idea we owe to Louis Pasteur and Robert Koch, among others) was by 1900 turned as part of a bundle of techniques of hygiene and disease prevention that were to function through individual and collective responsibility. As the historian Nancy Tomes writes, the "golden era" of the American public health movement introduced such practices as municipal sewerage systems, water purification, garbage collection, and food inspection. Similarly, the campaigns taught the individual body that "microscopic living particles were the agents of contagion, that sick bodies shed germs into the environment, and that disease spread by seemingly innocuous behaviors such as coughing, sneezing and spitting, sharing common drinking cups, or failing to wash hands,"[171] which were all to be battled with techniques of hygiene and purity (or "civilization," as Freud explained it). Of course, whereas the early bacterial anxiety was very much concerned with the home (and the female/mother as responsible for the household), the digital bug anxiety focused on the home computer and the virtual tele-environment of communications it was entangled with.

Such practices of care are part of the governance of individuals. Human actions were to be assigned into assemblies of practical rationalities and functionalities that were useful in the nexus of state-corporations. These technologies of the self or "self-steering mechanisms" were powerful tools in enforcing certain ways of life—public and private—to control the mass of society. They can also be understood as cultural techniques comprising acts of reading, memory, writing, and numeracy, none of which is an expression of an inherent human capability but instead an end result of a long and meticulous process of rehearsal and pedagogical attention.[172]

So, when a professional in computer science and computer crime lists in 1991 that computer security includes "increased awareness and motivation training for new computer users and for the population of future computer users, teaching them to be cautious, for example, to avoid putting untrusted software into their computers as they would avoid putting tainted food into their bodies,"[173] this is also to build proper subject and work as subjectification (*assujetissement*), a key component of societal life. Who would want to distribute digital diseases that originate from dubious sources and in the process become labeled as a virus distributor, a vector of infection? "Just like with biological viruses, subject behavior has a significant effect on the probability of infection. By altering the habits of users and examining how most virus infections occur, it is possible to educate staff on the risk which their different actions carry, and thus minimise the risk of virus infection."[174]

Similar advice was abundant, given out in antivirus guidebooks, popular news articles, and even scientific accounts of computing. It demonstrated how digital culture was a paradoxical intertwining of the utmost optimism of a digital networked future in a postindustrial world of leisure and self-improvement and fear and anxiety of surveillance, computer accidents and data loss. The idea was to *educate* users into following the rules of proper behavior. In other words, perhaps fear and anxiety were functional within this atmosphere of digital optimism. For what was essential was that a range of countermeasures was on offer to fight the dark side of digitality. The user was not left on her own, even if it was constantly emphasized by authorities and experts in computing that users should also carry responsibility. The issue was discussed at the end of the 1970s in the context of computing in insecure networks, where every user was presumed to be responsible for her own security, achieved through her own actions and care.[175] This was managed through techniques of soft power—power through attraction rather than coercion, an elemental way that control works in contemporary network societies.[176] For example, "health" and "security" were such vague attractors that provided much of the wanted effects and acted as efficient order-words. In general, such governance was entwined with the assembling of the Western information society from the early 1980s on.

There is an interesting paradox in the computer (security) discourse of the 1980s. Personal computers were supposed to be "about freedom and simplicity, not bureaucracy," just as mainframes with their access controls, passwords, and authorizations were not.[177] Yet, security was simultaneously touted as indispensable. On the one hand, we have all those voices that embrace the new liberties of nonhierarchical computing; on the other hand, these articulations emphasize the need to "be clean," to keep a constant eye on the behavior of the system. In other words, there was a security machine operating at the heart of the liberal discourse that demanded that users fulfill their responsibilities as key nodes in the digital networked economy and prescribed constant self-control and self-supervision to ensure the functioning of the system.[178] To be accurate, the paranoid machine was not an Orwellian big brother of surveillance from above; it started to function as a sensitive piloting, controlling, and guiding of desire. Self-improvement and control, governance, becoming a digital subject.

Addressing home users, *Byte* advised in 1988 to "be secure, not sorry." According to the story, there are three types of people causing trouble with computers: those who are intent on harming other people, those who are careless, and those who have not been trained properly. Although accidents and system failures are an obvious cause of computer problems, it is fundamentally the user who is at the center of the issue.[179] Contributing to the discourse of the responsible user, another *Byte* story instructed the user to keep her PC healthy.[180] Even though the focus was on such physical threats as dust, excessive heat and cold, and power-line surges and spikes, the overall rhetoric of the story emphasized the computer as something that the user is in an intimate relationship with and that needs constant maintenance and care to function properly. It is as if the personal computer, where the emphasis is on the word *personal*, was something almost part of our living bodies, needing constant attention.[181]

Software, too, required care. Jerry Pournelle advised in *Byte* in 1988 that users should keep an eye on where they get their computer programs, hinting that there is no such thing as free software: "If you don't put strange programs in your system, you can't get strange results. That 'free' copy of a program you got from a bulletin board may be more costly than you think. You're not even safe getting pirated software from a friend; even if there have been no signs of infection, some virus programs don't wake up for a long time."[182] These are typical warnings where unsuspecting users are cautioned of the dangers of reckless network use. Bulletin board systems, the first incarnations of the network society to come, were seen in a similar light to websites in the 1990s as potential sources of virus infection. Guidebooks listed the ABCs for avoiding viruses and conducting "safe hex." "Do not copy programs," "do not bring program disks from home to work," "do not boot your computer from an unknown disk," "check all disks before using them," "check all downloaded software before using it"—these and a range of similar recommendations were used to guide the user to proper PC habits.[183] The preferred option was to identify the potential infiltrator *before* it crept into your computer and, if this failed, at least identify the infector before it activated its routines. After possible infections, users were often advised to *quarantine* potentially infected systems and avoid contact via networks, disk sharing, and e-mail to other systems and users.[184]

After the Israeli/Jerusalem virus incident of 1988, experts raised the issue of *decency in computing*, which was presented as analogous to sexual decency: "The computer community is grateful for stopping the process of unauthorized copying of software that reached incredible use lately. Exactly like AIDS, that generated the safe sex phenomenon, the computerized virus is about to generate the phenomenon of decent use only of software."[185] Such order-words were addressed to the general public, yet they worked within the antivirus community as well. The mission of the *Virus Bulletin* journal, for instance, was to provide the user with safety tips and information on viruses.[186] In the Virus Bulletin conference of 1992, user education was underscored. Three main principles were given: (1) do not take risks; (2) if you pass on software or data, make sure it is not infected; (3) if you receive some software or data, protect yourself by checking it.[187] Even if no reference to biological sexual diseases was intended, the constant discussion of AIDS, HIV, safe sex, and personal responsibilities in intimate contacts was implicitly the backdrop against which virality was discussed. A management overview from the same year (1992) recognizes similar problems and brings the issues of education and risk management to the fore. What are introduced are "hygiene rules" for computers. Free software and shareware programs downloaded with modems from bulletin boards are labeled as high-risk software. Importantly, as measures aimed to normalize the corporate production of digital culture, hygiene is implied to be the same thing as commercial computer programs that are actually bought, not acquired for free.[188]

Viruses and worms draw the line between healthy capitalist consumer products and software programs distributed as shareware or even freeware. The idea goes something like this: products that go through quality assurance procedures acquire in the process extra costs that are transferred to the consumer. Thus, the product might be similar to one that is available for free or for a low price, but buying one from "a reputable manufacturer" guarantees the product's cleanliness. In other words, cleanliness and hygiene are what the consumer pays for. Trust has a cost. This demonstrates how consumer products succeed in their role as "anxiety relievers." Such measures of corporate digital product culture involved producing fear complemented and reinforced by the products to contain the issue. The desire to consume as a way to fight fear and anxiety is at the very heart of digital culture and, in our case, the discourse of such digital contagions as worms and viruses against the backdrop of viral capitalism.

In addition, backups, PC audits, regular checks for viruses, personal responsibility for reporting viruses, avoiding ignorance and arrogance, and increased security awareness are staged as steps toward a safer computing culture. What's interesting is that this governance was focused on both concrete actions of the users and their attitudes towards software and security. "People are the biggest problem" was the constant theme of computer security from the time lay users started using computers. This referred to the "the computer didn't do it" theme mentioned above. It was also acknowledged that computer viruses are similar to biological viruses (especially venereally transmitted ones), at least in one respect. Both cause shame and embarrassment: "An individual who suspects from the behavior of his PC that a virus is present may well have a guilty conscience. If so, he or she may try to clean up that PC before anyone else notices, and may fail to tell anyone that other PCs could be infected."[189] As most viruses were thought to spread through using or copying pirated software or otherwise illegal software (porn files, for example), an infection would imply that illegal or at least embarrassing actions had taken place. Years later, in 2001, similar ideas were used in emphasizing the ambiguous status of computer viruses as invasions of intimacy: "Even when the virus involved is not particularly dangerous and can be removed easily, victims still feel a sense of invasion and discomfort at having been attacked by an unknown assailant. 'I wish I could get my hands on that guy who did this to me,' is a common cry. This fact is important: even viruses which do nothing more than spread are seen as dangerous and intrusive."[190]

This was also referred to as the "itch syndrome." People with diseases have been stigmatized throughout history, and computer users with diseases received similar responses. It worked according to the assumption that individuals are responsible for their own bodies and thus for their own diseases, making diseased people victims because of their own actions or just being. Often, people with AIDS or cancer are blamed for being sick just because of their own weakness, low self-esteem, or whatever self-inflicted reason. Cancer, more specifically, has been articulated as a disease of the repressed (a disease of the middle classes), who do not seem to find a proper way to express their inner feelings and drives.[191] As Sontag notes, before the nineteenth century, disease was often seen as a dire consequence of bad behavior and lack of morals, but the modern view of medicine changed this. However, the focus on the individual intensified. Disease was no longer punishment but a form of self-expression, a symptom of repressed character: "Passion moves inward, striking and blighting the deepest cellular recesses."[192]

The itch syndrome was at first especially prevalent in the business environment. Going public about computer problems might have bad consequences for the public image and reliability of any business. Viruses, or other forms of computer problems, were seen primarily as embarrassing.[193] This veil of secrecy multiplied the growing problem: few wanted to go public with their computer virus problems. This, in general, represented one of the biggest problems in computer security research: When a large proportion of the virus outbreaks in computers go unnoticed and unreported, how can one monitor the rate of the incidents? As Sarah Gordon noted in 1994, the "it's not me" syndrome resulted in a failure to report virus and worm incidents and other problems with software. The virus, as a sign of disease, was stigmatizing.[194]

Of course, some antivirus researchers were anxious that people would not regard viruses as filthy diseases:

> Users will get a lot more relaxed about viruses. We've long since passed the stage where a virus is regarded as a loathsome disease, to be kept secret. But we're increasingly seeing people who regard a virus on their system with about the same degree of casualness as a bit of fluff on their jacket. Sure, they'll wipe it off, but there's no real need to worry about it happening again. This is perhaps a bit too relaxed attitude, but what can you expect if a user keeps on getting hit by viruses, and nothing terrible ever seems to result.[195]

Such articulations demonstrate how "computer hygiene" as a media ecological theme involves not only technical instructions, innocent recommendations for users, or even allegories of biology, but a whole assemblage of corporeal and incorporeal countermeasures connected to power/knowledge relationships in society. Security policies and risk assessments are part and parcel of this ongoing process of defining the approved uses of computers. The similarities of computer virus warnings with messages from the U.S. surgeon general are striking: "Practice digital hygiene yourself. Don't exchange programs with anyone whose computer habits are not up to your own standards. Refuse to use software if the manufacturer's seal has been broken!"[196] There was even a discussion concerning the need for "Centers for Computer Disease Control" in 1988.[197]

Destructive and unlicensed software has been consistently defined and outlined as an "undesirable" risk—a category that often includes games and pornography, too. Hence, risk-reduction security policies were introduced at the end of the 1980s to keep the users of digital culture on the right track. Often written in the form of a checklist,[198] these instructions were aimed at "domesticating" users into the order of commercial computing. This was accentuated in the 1990s with the discourse of information highways, which associated the connections of the new digital culture with the older road

networks of previous industrial culture.[199] In the culture of automobile trans-
portation, driving conduct was an essential part of the functioning of the
system. No drunk driving, no speeding, no irresponsible behavior, because
these might result in casualties and risking of the whole network's safe flow.
Information highways were controlled with restrictions, recommendations,
norms, and other forms of order-words that channeled behavior. But who
were the drunk drivers and the irresponsible vandals of these nascent digital
networks?

The Psyche of the Virus Writer: Irresponsible Vandalism?

The final part of this section analyzes the other side of these hygiene measures
of digital culture. During the 1980s and early 1990s, a special focus was placed
on the importance of the individual user as a node in the flow of information.
But in addition to the legitimate users, the other side, the supposed malicious
outlaws who created viruses and showed disrespect for the common values
of digital utopia, were under the proverbial microscope. Here I want to show
how the writers and distributors of viruses were stratified as part of a field of
digital security that ranged from psychological categorizations to pejorative
references to international Cold War politics. The virus writer became an
abject body.

This stigmatizing categorization proves to be another recurring topos in
the media archaeological sense. The late nineteenth-century media technologies were described as value-neutral with their use, the human intentions,
the determining factor whether they became a power for good or evil. Take
wireless in the United States, for example. You had the robber barons who
were seen as corrupt men taking advantage of technology for their own ends,
but you also had the inventor heroes, the romantic self-made men such as
Samuel Morse, Thomas Edison, and Alexander Graham Bell, who took technology into good hands.[200] The same scenario was repeated with computer
technologies: computers and software were frequently seen as neutral, whereas
it was the people inventing, applying, and using the media that blew life into
the machines.

The problem with psychological accounts has been their highly reduc-
tionist nature in their focus on the individual, atomistic aspects of culture.
Of course, this is not an accidental feature. Modern power individualizes and

turns into cultural assemblages issues of the individual. Crime is a good example of such mechanisms. As Foucault suggested, crime was transformed during the nineteenth century into an expression of the state of mind of the criminal, implying the need to cure the criminal of his or her deviant, sick psychical state and lead him or her back into the approved practices of culture. Thus, practices of confession and inspection became ways to probe the individual, even deep probe, as with various psychological and psychoanalytic methods. There was an assumed layer of operational truth behind the façade: of a madman, of a psychically sick person, of a criminal, of a sexual "pervert," and so on. The confessional mechanism had its origins, according to Foucault, in the Middle Ages, but the juridico-medical apparatuses of power and knowledge of the twentieth century took full advantage of it. The confessions and truths were disconnected from the religious themes of sin, redemption, and universal truth and localized to a more secular plane of controlling the body, the psyche, and social life of the individual.[201] The operationalized psychologization assumes the self-identical individual, the indivisible, to be the atomic base unit of society. Society is implicitly taken to be made up of a conglomeration of these individuals, some naturally healthy, others gone wrong and in need of correction. Such views were of course rather specific in certain neoliberal political discourses since the 1980s, especially in the United Kingdom and the U.S.

Virus writers and malicious hackers were translated into psychological categories, states of mind (gone awry). Instead of seeing these as representations of hackers and virus writers, I analyze these imagings as orderings that connect to the issues of fear production analyzed in the previous chapter. As noted above, viruses were perceived, valorized, and signified in various techno-capitalist-media assemblages, which reduced their multiplicity to that of malicious software. Similarly, the wide subculture of hacking (and virus writing) has been reduced and stabilized as part of a general category of "vandalism." The issue has been objectified via the media assemblage, in particular, with its production of images of the actors of digital culture.[202] We can analyze this again as the working of the abstract machine of facialization. The antivirus security industry was also eager to amplify such articulations:

> Every virus writer that I have met has admitted to the *cowardly* and *craven* nature of their activities. It somehow reflects upon all of us that *human nature can sink so low* as to transfer some of its own baser instincts for destruction into an environment which is arguably the most thrilling development since the invention of the wheel.

(…) The dedicated virus writer may therefore become *obsessive* and shun any other activities which may take him away from his obsession. This lack of social interaction makes them withdrawn and uncommunicative as well as leading to a general tendency to *social inadequacy*.[203]

Thus, it seems that the descriptions of disease within the body of the computer are extended to the people related to underground programming subcultures and practices—as either coders or distributors. The disease of the computer is seen as emanating from a (mentally) sick person. As socio-technical phenomena, computer viruses are articulated as an effect of a more fundamental level of psychology, where, as computer security professionals write, "the history of computer virus programs is a small part of the history of people's attempts to do undesirable things with computers."[204]

Or, as in another case, virus writers are seen as men who cannot find anything more interesting to do and who do not even seem to enjoy girls[205]—a deviation from heteronormativity. Perhaps there are indeed possibilities to embrace the viral as a queer machine? In recent media arts, writer-artists such as Zach Blas have actually developed this idea much further as an interest into viral aesthetics and queer technologies.[206]

But the various pejorative, victimizing, or just purely criminalizing terms were the mainstream of discussions about virus culture.[207] The Lehigh virus of 1987 was described as having been developed by "someone with 'a very, very sick mind.'"[208] *The Computer Virus Crisis* book (1989) calls these people psychotic vandals and terrorists, while also acknowledging that one might be enticed to spread viruses for the pure intellectual challenge.[209] The negative aspects of these people are highlighted visually with an image of a dubious-looking older man handing diskettes with worms to a young boy. The reference to pedophilic "candy-men" is obvious, again sexualizing the distribution of diseased software, but a striking resemblance is that the person is pictured looking like Fidel Castro, even with a cigar hanging from his lips! This articulation turns out to be a more general fear of communist infiltration when reinforced other rhetorics around that time, including John McAfee and Colin Haynes's evaluation that "computer viruses give the Soviets, or any other potentially hostile power, a whole new approach to defense."[210] One must remember that at the end of the 1980s, the Soviet threat was still prevalent from the U.S. perspective, despite the "glasnost" politics of Mikhail Gorbachev since 1985. So, a pedophile-communist virus writer was perhaps the most hair-raising digital threat one could think of!

Figure 5. The image was originally a poster distributed at a security conference in 1986 held by the National Computer Security Center.

Source: Fites, Johnston, & Kratz 1989: *The Computer Virus Crisis!*, page 80, "Never Accept Gifts from a Stranger." Used with permission.

After the Cold War, tensions had subsided and other types of imaginaries of threats became the reference point for motivations. By the end of the 1990s, virus writers became terrorists:

> Virus writing is evil and cannot be justified in any circumstances. It follows that prosecution of virus writers is something which should be universally accepted as appropriate action. Virus writing needs to be recognized as a criminal act by international

conventions and virus writers should always be subject to extradition. *Just like murderers and terrorists*, virus writers should find no escape across national boundaries.[211]

As terrorists, communists, and pedophiles, virus writers were the "dark side of network culture." They were depicted as frustrated, vengeful maniacs destined to hurt people. Virus writers might have a "grudge against big business, the government, or against computing community establishment as a whole."[212]

There was a range of different ways to underline the psychopathologies of virus writing. Although McAfee and Haynes do see variations within the concept of hackers and hacking, the "bad" sides are described with overkill metaphors and concepts and implications of (mental) disorder. Digital disease equals mental disease, the implication goes. One has to note that this anxiety about digitality depriving people of a healthy social life was not a topic within the virus discourse alone. The developing digital culture of the 1980s was in general anxious about the people connected to these machines that proved to be addictive and emotionally binding—something very different from the traditional view of computers as rational machines. Computer and video games, for example, were recurrently seen as addictive nuisances of this growing cultural field.[213]

Hence, it is a striking fact that since the 1980s, both people engaged with computers and drug addicts have been labeled under the rubric "users."[214] As addictive stuff, computer culture spurred anxieties. In this light, computer worms and viruses have not been the only digital problems the media has channeled. Perhaps viruses and worms were not so much exceptional instances of fear of computers but a metonym of digital culture in general, referring to the fears and worries over the increasing, almost parasitic, presence of these new media technologies in everyday life? As Deborah Lupton has argued, computers were ambiguous cultural products alternating between seduction, a potential for "sensuous pleasure," and a threat of invasion and contamination.[215] And, of course, earlier youth cultural phenomena, such as rock music in the 1950s and 1960s, had experienced similar overreactions and media panics, suggesting that such discourses were not merely about the new media technologies (whether the audio technologies that spread rock music or the computers and viruses or television) but also about the youth that had to be protected. Also, media panics can be analyzed as recurring media archaeological figures that are attached to the emergence of new media. Yet, in addition, the archaeology of hackers spans from the early wireless amateurs of the beginning of the twentieth century, when such boy tinkerers became paradigmatic celebrated subjects of new technology. These boys represented the "rise of the boy inventor-hero as a popular cultural archetype,"[216] as Susan Douglas writes in her history of American broadcasting. Such heroes were described in terms that made them reminiscent of prankish fiction boy protagonists such as Tom Swift, which eased the anxiety around the possible misuses of communication technology: boys will be boys.[217]

However, boys were not just boys, but part of a multiplicity of cultural flows. The bigger and more interesting question was always about the cultural techniques formative of gendered subject positions as well as the various material assemblages in which rhetorics was mobilized. "Boys" or "vandals" writing worms cannot just be reduced to their all-too-human psyches. They must be seen as interlocked in a media ecological field much larger than themselves. Viruses, worms, virus writers, hackers, and other actors are expressive of the media ecology, which enables and conditions them. Digital technologies, the discursive networks of the desire for network programming and self-spreading software, the long genealogy of the Western conception of security, the linguistic order-words of health and disease, and so forth—all these accompany the whole phenomenon.

But in popular media, it was always easier to adopt the more straightforward way that focuses on the individuals involved. "Punish virus spreaders," an angry letter in *Byte* (1989) demanded at a time when the public anxiety over malicious software was growing strong:

> How long will it be before a virus infects a computer system at a hospital, a police department, or a military installation? (...) Viruses and other forms of computer tampering are not just a threat to the free flow of information. (...) They have the potential to inflict enormous harm, and the people who are responsible for them should be subject to criminal prosecution. They are engaging in malicious destruction of property as surely as if they had walked into someone's office and tossed a match into a file cabinet. It's only a matter of time before something much more serious happens as a result of their antics.[218]

One question that emerges is how this relates to the even more discussed figure of the hacker. The original profile of the hacker was far from malicious, but it had to do with the ethics of computing. Publications such as Steven Levy's *Hackers* were probably in a key position of producing the image of hackers and hacking as expressions of the hacker ethic. These people working at MIT in the 1960s or tinkering as hobbyists on the West Coast during the 1970s were perceived by Levy to be idealistic and exemplary figurations of a spirit of freedom and liberating powers of computing. Computing had a huge part to play

in counterculture.[219] Levy's narrated version of the hacker ethic consisted of
a number of slogans:

1. Access to computers—and anything which might teach you something
   about the way the world works—should be unlimited and total.
2. All information should be free.
3. Mistrust authority—Promote decentralization.
4. Hackers should be judged by their hacking, not bogus criteria such as
   degrees, age, race, or position.
5. You can create art and beauty on a computer.
6. Computers can change your life for the better.[220]

With the emphasis on such descriptions, Levy constructed his narrative of
hackers as open-minded tinkerers and *bricoleurs* who have the one sole aim
of finding the ultimate hack. Computers and programming were pictured as
ends in themselves, as well as positive addictions and expressions of a life
committed to improving the technological society. As Levy writes, for these
pioneer hackers the aim was to make systems work better and at the same time
to resist corporate bureaucratic forces, symbolized by IBM. Dysfunctional and
irrational systems were a challenge to any ambitious hacker.[221] Taking things
apart to inspect the workings of a system was part and parcel of the definition
of a hacker, and this was done without malicious intent. This does not con-
tradict the fact that "intentional system crashes" were part of the repertoire
of hackers at MIT:

> The faith that the ITS (Incompatible Timesharing System) had in users was best
> shown in its handling of the problem of intentional system crashes. Formerly, a
> hacker rite of passage would be breaking into a time-sharing system and causing such
> digital mayhem—maybe by overwhelming the registers with looping calculations—
> that the system would "crash." Go completely dead. After a while a hacker would
> grow out of that destructive mode, but it happened often enough to be a considerable
> problem for people who had to work on the system. The more safeguards the system
> had against this, the bigger the challenge would be for some random hacker to bring
> the thing to its knees.[222]

Is the germ of viral vandalism already present in these explorations of innovative computer wizards of the counterculture of the 1960s and 1970s?[223] Most
clearly not, but increasingly experimental hacking was seen as an index of
vandalism. Various types of recurring code, self-reproductive programs, and
parasitic routines were outlawed. Of course, such tactics have been kept alive

in net art, where the forkbomb script is one such example that closely touches on the earlier phenomenon of illegal code. The routine consists of a simple program that copies itself endlessly to constipate the system (much like the rabbit routine decades earlier). Alex McLean's version of the program won the software art prize at the Transmediale festival in Berlin in 2002, and the hacker-artist Jaromil wrote his own piece for UNIX systems, consisting of only 13 characters: ":(){: | :& };:"[224]

Hackers were moved from being at the core of computerization to the outskirts of the digital utopia. They were increasingly depicted as unlawful system breakers, as the computer game Hacker from the mid-1980s suggested. Activision's Hacker advertised itself with the slogan: "Makes you feel like you've unlocked someone else's computer system!" The game was judged to be "socially irresponsible," which demonstrated the transformed understanding of the term.[225] Such individuals as Kevin Mitnick, Craig Neidorf, and Robert Morris Jr. became recurring names signaling the anonymous dangers lurking in the networks. Similar to how Melissa, Nimda, I Love You, and other viruses and worms named the danger of connection at the end of the 1990s and beginning of the twenty-first century, hackers' proper names were the digital outlaws that represented a threat to the otherwise normalizing digital culture of the 1980s. In more recent years, the focus has often been on whistleblowers or then copyright infringement crimes, as with the debate around the controversial character of Kim Dotcom.

Helen Nissenbaum provides an enlightening account of the ontology of cyberspace and the changing meanings of hackers in recent decades. According to Nissenbaum, the earlier hacker ideals, a hacker ethic, were, of course, cherished throughout the 1980s and 1990s by writers such as John Perry Barlow, Howard Rheingold, and Nicholas Negroponte, all of whom celebrated the Internet as the new frontier of "great freedoms and liberty." Their views were adapted as part of the capitalist mythology of the superhighway of digital networks, illustrated in the United States by Al Gore's visions.[226] This normalized version of the hacker ethic did not, then, prove to be a threat to, but only a fulfillment of, the neoliberal use of ideas of freedom and connectivity.

But hacker demonization also served specific government and business interests. It was deemed necessary to "control the definition of normalcy in the new world order of computer-mediated action and transaction; the good citizen is everything that the hacker is not."[227] In addition, to paraphrase Nissenbaum, the fear of hackers provided excellent support for further expenditures on security, vigilance, and punishment, consequently illustrating exactly the same pattern as with viruses some years later. As I argued in the previous section, the fear of viruses was turned into a digital business that allowed people to "buy off digital fear" with antivirus software and other consumer products.

Nissenbaum refers also to Andrew Ross's insights into how AIDS is part and parcel of the discourse of digital fear. Also Ross argues that AIDS was used as a powerful tool to spawn fear and anxiety, or even hysteria, among the growing digital population. Hacker counterculture was linked to sickness and disease. The pejorative references to computer AIDS, the need for "hygiene lessons," and sick software were extended to a certain social group, the hackers. So whereas such writers as Hugo Cornwall in his *Hacker's Handbook* offered a view of hackers as merely harmless pranksters, the officials were engaging in overkill actions, exemplified by the FBI's Operation Sundevil of the early 1990s.

What Ross, writing in 1991, in the midst of the hacker and virus hysteria (as he names it), emphasizes is that the virus crisis had, of course, increased sales of antivirus software while also exposing the weak points in computer and Internet systems. In addition, the notion of the paranoid machine emerges again:

> Virus-conscious fear and loathing have clearly fed into the paranoid climate of privatization that increasingly defines social identities in the new post-Fordist order. The result—a psychosocial closing of the ranks around fortified private spheres—runs directly counter to the ethic that we might think of as residing at the architectural heart of information technology. In its basic assembly structure, information technology involves processing, copying, replication, and simulation, and therefore does not recognize the concept of private information property. What is now under threat is the rationality of shareware culture, ushered in as the achievement of the hacker counterculture that pioneered the personal computer revolution in the early 1970s against the grain of corporate planning.[228]

Hence, this privatization of the digital sphere was in many ways contrary to the hacker values that had been cultivated since the 1950s and 1960s, first in computer laboratories in universities, then in network cultures. Of course, this imaginary of the Internet[229] did not disappear altogether. It was incorporated into the productive machinery of digital capitalism, which really came to life in the 1990s with the popular Internet. But many of the visions of freeware and shareware cultures, as well as open-source software, were marginalized, and the pejorative descriptions of hackers as adolescent criminals, digital vandals, and computer outlaws functioned to support this shift of cultural emphasis. Of course, coming to 2010s, there has been a wider adoption of the value of "open" even to an extent that corporate capitalism has started to embrace it as part of the business models and capturing of commons as well as the affective value in hackerism, even down to business school rhetorics benevolent towards it.

But for a long time, values of open, free, and hackers were not seen as compatible with the perceived need to standardize digital culture. With the "maturing of software production," controlled production teams and professionally managed distribution chains guaranteed the positions of larger companies such as Microsoft. The standardized software houses were legitimized as the "right" producers of digital culture, whereas various alternative actors and distribution mechanisms were marked as secondary in the eyes of the user majority. Whereas the pioneer programmers of computer labs and university research facilities in the 1950s–1970s saw software as a branch of scientific knowledge, the 1980s commercial industry of personal computers soon turned its back on these original ideas of free ownership of code. Software became shielded by copyright jurisdiction. The idea of software as *consumer ware* actualized on a mass scale during the 1980s, when it became desirable to own software and to make money through selling it in large quantities, or, more precisely, selling the right to use software. From then on, software was *licensed* for use.[230]

The issues were not only internal to the society, however. In addition, international references to the Cold War period and terrorism were frequently used. In this sense, it is only natural that perhaps the greatest imagined threat to the body politic of U.S. society in the twentieth century, communism and the Eastern bloc, is intertwined in the discursive field of digital threats:

> As the sources of viruses multiply—from pirate boards, construction sets, manic Thai programmers, Russian and Bulgarian computer freaks—access becomes much simpler. In the future everyone will be able to plant a virus on his "worst enemy": disgruntled employees, industrial saboteurs, blackmailers, electronic vandals. We may no longer be able to trust technology. A computer program could, without warning, become an uncontrollable force, triggered by a date, an event or a timer.[231]

The danger from behind the Iron Curtain remained, even though the Cold War gradually moved to the sidelines. The face of communism changed into fears of terrorism and anarchism, "an uncontrollable force" without any rational motives. The so-called ideological division between East and West collapsed, but the fear of "Russians and Bulgarians" remained in the form of viruses. This represented a battle against the threatening digital diseases of computer networks—postideological micropolitics of a sort.[232]

Possibly the most frequently discussed issue was not a single virus but a person: Dark Avenger from Bulgaria. He was responsible for a number of harmful viruses as well as the infamous Self-Mutating Engine, which made viruses polymorphous, that is, harder to detect with traditional scanners.[233] Dark Avenger was known in antivirus circles, but he was elevated to an almost mythical position in 1997 by the *Wired* magazine story "Heart of Darkness," a reference to Joseph Conrad's 1902 novel. In Conrad's text, the narration takes us to Africa, the heart of darkness of colonial powers of the nineteenth century. *Wired* took the reader to the "heart of darkness" of digital culture, the "ground zero of the global epidemic"—Eastern Europe.

The virus and its creator acted as figures of evil software. The code of the Dark Avenger virus attached to .com and .exe files, activating its payload of hard disk erasure every sixteenth boot. The code included also a signature, which assigned the credits to Dark Avenger, city of Sofia, 1988–1989:

> The computer, self-destructing, would eventually crash, some precious part of its operating system missing, smothered under Dark Avenger's relentless output. Programs passed along in schools, offices, homes—from one disk to the next they carried the infection along, and in 1991, an international epidemic was diagnosed. One-hundred sixty documented Bulgarian viruses existed in the wild, and an estimated 10 percent of all infections in the United States came from Bulgaria, most commonly from the Dark Avenger. Dataquest polled 600 large North American companies and Federal agencies early that year, and reported that 9 percent had experienced computer virus outbreaks. Nine months later, it found the number had risen to 63 percent. Anecdotal stories, of companies losing millions in sales and productivity due to virus attacks, became commonplace. The press seized upon the threat. The war drums of fear beat first in Europe, closer to the epicenter. Papers carried lurid pieces describing the havoc it wreaked. The tattoo was quickly amplified in the U.S. "Bulgarians Linked to Computer Virus," read a headline in *The New York Times*.[234]

It was not all projection but there were concrete contexts behind Bulgarian virus production. In the 1970s, the Eastern bloc advocated copying Western, mainly American, computers instead of continuing their own development projects. This was accentuated after 1985 with an emphasis on "total computer literacy"; computer courses became obligatory in school curricula. Thus, as the schools received their clones of Apple and PC computers and the students were taught high-tech programming skills, a sort of a digital intelligentsia was born in the Eastern bloc, including Bulgaria. However, as *Wired* reported, people did not find a sufficient number of things to do with computers:

In the late '80s, students in Bulgaria had access to more computers than their peers in any other Eastern European country. They did what young people do when they first meet machines—they played, they explored, they programmed. The Bulgarians were busy building a digital culture of their own, feasting off the fruits of Marxism-Leninism. And then, one forbidden fruit came to be known. In 1988, the Bulgarian computer-hobbyist magazine, *Computer for You*, founded in 1985, translated a German article about viruses into Bulgarian. It was a simple article, just an introduction to computer viruses. But it helped spread the idea. Several months later, the first pernicious homespun code appeared.[235]

In Soviet Russia, the situation was similar: plenty of programmers with no possibilities to channel their energies. The society was not computerized, far from it, which spawned a digital underground of experienced but frustrated programmers.[236] The situation seems to have been essentially similar in other European countries, such as Czechoslovakia. Computerization around the change of the decade (1989–1990) brought computers into the country, which was followed by an increase in various types of programs, including viruses. In Czechoslovakia, political viruses were frequent during the changes occurring in the early 1990s.[237]

With the breakup of the Soviet Union, a new type of security threat was created. Instead of the in some ways more stable or predictable Cold War system between two main blocks, public anxiety was turned toward subnational anarchic elements, global crime, terrorists—and malicious software as part of the other security threats. The virus was the stranger and the other in this machine producing Western anxieties, as artist Luca Lampo suggested: Soviet Russians and other monsters were replaced in the Hollywood machine with new enemies, such as aliens, meteors, and epidemics.[238] The new non-governmental post–Cold War threats provided fuel for entertainment productions, security agencies, and demands for increased funds in national and international security. These are not merely unfounded representations and prejudices; recent years have seen malicious software playing an ever-growing role in international crime and terrorism. For example, bots as a class of autonomous software programs are seen as a recurring key threat to the Internet; they can collect passwords and other important personal information, participate in automated fraud by deceiving per-click revenue streams, and act as powerful denial-of-service weapon swarms that aim at, for example, "extortion and taking out rival businesses."[239] The whole issue of botnets is in itself interesting as something of a dark side of parallel computing, very large amounts of data traffic, and infection routines; it's also something of an interesting challenge to thinking about flows of data and individuality of machines as an illusory feature when it comes down to current and emerging forms of networking. It's no communist utopia, but all is shared, computer culture is leaky, as Wendy Chun puts it.[240]

It is in any case clear that there is much more going on in the network ecology than just human passions. Tiziana Terranova has even suggested that networks are not merely the passive background of human politics and organization but also an active participant in themselves.[241] The network is in itself a dynamic space, an emergent phenomenon, that manifests its presence in terms of such "anomalies" as viruses, worms, and hackers. Yet, the anomalies are very much part of the political constitution of the politics of network culture.

However, if this section has placed a great deal of emphasis on the incorporeal articulations of bodies politic, digital, and biological, several scientists and writers have been convinced that the connection between biology and computers is profound. This can be thought of as expressing a form of contagious ecology of software that characterizes the genealogy of network dynamics. In other words, a constant theme since the beginning of the 1990s, with roots in the media archaeology of technology as an autonomous living force, has been the idea of computer worms and viruses as a form of life, not just devastation and destruction. In this vein, a key yet often neglected context of computer viruses is as part of the cultural history of artificial life.[242] The next section moves deeper into discussing the biological paradigm of computing[243] to ask the question of how life is sustained and controlled in the context of digital culture. This also sharpens the focus on the biopolitics of digital life as one of emergence, distributed computing processes and simulated ecologies where also parasites and viruses might have their own place and function.

Notes

1. Serres 1982, 78–79.
2. Lukas Barr: "Long Live the New Flesh. An Interview with David Cronenberg." <http://industrycentral.net/director_interviews/DC01.HTM>.
3. See Terranova 2004.
4. Magner 2002, 290–293.
5. For definitions, see, e.g., the *Oxford English Dictionary*.
6. On the representational and the spatial grid, cf. Terranova 2004, 8–9, 35.
7. Deleuze & Parnet 1996, 84–85. Cf. Parisi 2004b. See also Parikka 2005c.
8. Terranova 2004.
9. On biopower in the nineteenth century, see Foucault 2000a. On control societies, see Deleuze 1990, 240–247. Galloway 2004. Franklin 2015.
10. Deleuze 1986, 39–40. Cf. Olkowski 1999, 44–47.

11. Goodchild 1996, 28–30. Deleuze 1986, 1–8. Foucault 2002.
12. Turner 2003.
13. Guillaume 1987, 59.
14. Sennett 1994, 23–24, 156.
15. Agamben 1998, 125. Elizabeth Grosz (1995, 106–107) points out how the figure of the body politic is coded in masculine form and maintains a standard nature–culture division.
16. On security, see Foucault 2007.
17. Ibid.
18. Deleuze 1990, 240–247. Cf. Mayer & Weingart 2004b, 28–30.
19. Fuller 2005, 2. On cities and the media ecology of cyberspace, see Boyer 1996.
20. Sennett 1994, 255–261.
21. Quoted in Marvin 1988, 141. Schivelbusch 1977, 171–174.
22. Thacker 2004. Cf. Bardini 2006.
23. Goffey 2003, 1.
24. Van Loon 2002b, 123.
25. Ryan 1985, 147.
26. Lampo 2002.
27. Van Loon 2002b, 141.
28. Quoted in Salmi 1995, 199.
29. Colwell 1996.
30. Cf. Deleuze & Guattari 1987, 66, 504. Wise 1997, 63.
31. Sontag 2002, 15.
32. Ibid., 155.
33. Ross 1991, 77.
34. See Tomes 1998, xi–xiv.
35. Ibid., 17.
36. Robert Gallo: "The AIDS Virus." *Scientific American*, vol. 256, January 1987, 39.
37. I am grateful to Malte Hagener for pointing out this example. See also Grusin 2010 on premediation of risks and security after 9/11.
38. Thacker 2005.
39. Sasso & Villani 2003, 107–113. In addition, in diagrams there is also the potential for lines of flight, deterritorializations, which act as singularities of resistance that can open up diagrams toward the outside.
40. Weinstock 1997.
41. Rushkoff 1996. R. Rivas: "The AIDS game." *World Press Review*, vol. 9, 1993.
42. See, e.g., "Double Agent." *Scientific American*, vol. 251, July 1984. "AIDS: In the Blood." *Scientific American*, vol. 251, September 1984. "AIDS Update." *Scientific American*, vol. 252, April 1985. "Knowing the Face of the Enemy." *Time*, April 30, 1984.
43. Jeffrey Laurence: "The Immune System in AIDS." *Scientific American*, vol. 253, December 1985, 70. See also Duncan Fallowell: "AIDS Is Here." *The Times*, July 27, 1983, which illustrates certain first reactions and representations of AIDS.
44. Similar sorts of prejudices against the poor, immigrants, and people of other ethnicities than white were already part of the early twentieth-century discourse of the germ contagion. Tomes 1998, 11.
45. Sontag 2002, 147.

46. Duncan Fallowell: "AIDS: The Facts, the Fears, the Future." *The Times*, March 6, 1985. The article discusses heterosexual AIDS, but sees it only as an African problem: "In America the number of AIDS cases among heterosexuals unassociated with any of the risk categories is nil—as it is in Britain." See also Patton 2002, 129–130.

47. "The Toughest Virus of All." *Time*, November 3, 1986.

48. "The AIDS Pandemic." *Scientific American*, vol. 256, January 1987.

49. Barabási 2003, 123–142.

50. Sontag 2002, 166.

51. See Patton 2002, x. Kruger 1996, 42–61.

52. Crichton 1998. Actually, one of the early theories for AIDS, too, was that it came from outer space on a meteorite or a returning space ship! See Fallowell: "AIDS Is Here." For an analysis of killer virus novels as emblematic of the bodily crisis in late capitalism, see Dougherty 2001.

53. Van Helvoort 1996, 142.

54. "50, 100 & 150 Years Ago." *Scientific American*, April 2005, 18. Quoted in Bardini 2006, note 6. See also, e.g., "Reconstruction of a Virus in Laboratory Opens the Question: What Is Life?" *New York Times*, October 30, 1955. "Mutation Agent Held Clue to Life." *New York Times*, January 26, 1960. Yet, in a way, this virus culture is part of the scientific landscape of the nineteenth century and its notion of the germ theory, which supposes that diseases are caused by microorganisms. As Laura Otis (1999, 7) shows in her inspiring analysis in *Membranes*, this theory was also part of the masculine and imperialist assemblage of the century, resonating with socio-political themes of colonialism. The outside, with its bacteria and other dangerous entities, was to be fenced out to maintain the pristine individual body, analogous to the body politic of the Western white colonialist powers. The cultural fear of penetration (a very masculine fear) has long roots in the nineteenth century, which has led to two persisting cultural prejudices, to paraphrase Otis: first, the tendency to think of female sexuality as "passive penetrability" and, second, to value the intactness of the hymen—where its rupture means the fall into "the realm of the passive, the penetrated, and the impure."

55. Seltzer 1992. Armstrong 1998.

56. See John Protevi's (2001, 101) analysis of AIDS, where the virus becomes an invader that without respect renegotiates the borders of the outside and the inside and the frail wall of fold that separates them: "Body is seen as an interiority encased by a protective barrier, a frontier. According to the oppositional cultural imaginary, the ideally seamless mucuous membrane walls are in fact fragile, prone to tiny invisible tears, opening the inside to an outside that should stay outside. The response to this factual degeneration from ideal separation is to police the borders of the somatic body politic. The messages we all know by now: separate inside and outside. Avoid mixing the famous bodily fluids. The truth about AIDS is a liminology, a discourse on borders: keep your fluids to yourself! Don't bring foreign blood inside!"

57. See Bukatman 1993, 78–93. Concerning *Videodrome*, Rosi Braidotti writes aptly, "What makes *Videodrome* a classic is that it addresses the issue of the physicality and the corresponding malleability of the male body, while it also shows to what extent the body is constructed, thus striking an anti-humanist note." Braidotti 2002, 249. Braidotti notes

that this becoming is at the same time very conventional, only repeating several sexist and even humiliating images of women.

58. Flieger 2003, 396.
59. Braidotti 2012.
60. Bear 2001, 77.
61. See Bukatman 1993, 268–272. Hayles 1999, 252–256.
62. Butler 1985.
63. Cadigan 2001, 309. Gibson's *Neuromancer* had introduced the idea of computer programs causing cerebral damage to people jacked into the matrix. While the virus programs were a form of attack software, ICE programs were antivirus viruses, designed to protect the data banks and resources of large institutions. These were visualized in the 1995 *Johnny Mnemonic* movie, written by William Gibson and directed by Robert Longo.
64. Stephenson 1993, 378. On postmodernism and Stephenson's *Snow Crash*, see Porush 1994. See also Hayles 1999, 251.
65. Harrasser 2002, 822.
66. See, e.g., Channell 1991. On bodies in cyberpunk literature of the 1980s, see McCarron 1996. On bodies and technology in contemporary culture, see Balsamo 1996.
67. Hayles 1999. Cf. Gere 2002, 47–74.
68. Blackmore 1999, 21. Cf. "The Guru Trap or What Computer Viruses Can Tell Us about Saddam Hussein." *Computer Underground Digest*, vol. 3, issue 31, August 23, 1991, <http://www.textfiles.com/magazines/CUD/>.
69. See Thacker 2005.
70. *Il était une fois … l'homme* (1978) focused on explaining the evolution of the human being to children.
71. Kruger 1996, 11. Cf. Sontag 2002.
72. Burroughs 1985, 48. Cf. Bukatman 1993, 76–77.
73. Kruger 1996, 17. This all quite easily implies that there is something called "healthy code" that is desirable, original, and legitimate. Healthy code makes healthy bodies. One commentator from 1989 went so far as to claim that computer viruses are an offspring of malicious thoughts: "The evolution of the computer is also yoked to our evolution as a species, and to our understanding of health, illness, and well-being. And one of the things we are discovering is that disease, as a life process, is profound, especially when we consider that we are now creating and releasing diseases designed to afflict our very own brainchild. With computer viruses, our thoughts, especially destructive ones, can easily be turned into action." Lundell 1989, xii.
74. Massumi 1992, 41.
75. See Deleuze & Guattari 1987, 80–81.
76. "Science fiction has gone through a whole evolution taking it from animal, vegetable, and mineral becomings to becomings of bacteria, viruses, molecules, and things imperceptible." Deleuze & Guattari 1987, 248.
77. Huhtamo 1995. Cf. Huhtamo 1997. Ernst Robert Curtius introduced the term "topos" in his *Europäische Literatur und lateinisches Mittelalter* (1948), which focused on topics in rhetoric.
78. McAfee & Haynes 1989, 1.

79. Ibid., 4.

80. Ibid., 14–15.

81. Ibid., 15. On quasi-objects, see Latour 1993, 51–55.

82. AIDS references such as this imply that there are similar key risk groups within computing to those in culture in general. If homosexuals, drug users, Haitians, and black people were defined as such groups in the 1980s, what were such groups within the computer virus discourse? Often these are not stated aloud—the power of the analogy is based on its vagueness. The risk groups, those unsuspected but therefore very dangerous sources, could be represented by anyone. Curiously, here computer viruses connect to the articulations of AIDS. As Cindy Patton notes, the tropes of bisexual men and heterosexuals who occasionally pass through homosexual vectors were seen during the mid-1980s as figures of terror, untrustworthy elements within the otherwise safe middle-class cities and suburbs—trespassing borders, like viruses. Patton 2002, 68–69.

83. "An Israeli Virus." *The Risks Digest Forum*, vol. 6, issue 6, January 7, 1988, <http://catless. ncl.ac.uk/Risks/>.

84. "Computer Viruses and RETROVIRUSES." *The Risks Digest Forum*, vol. 7, issue 27, July 23, 1988, <http://catless.ncl.ac.uk/Risks/>.

85. Sontag 2002, 155. Kruger 1996, 21.

86. "AIDS Computer Virus." *The Risks Digest*, vol. 13, issue 1, January 3, 1992. See also "The Trojan Horse Named 'AIDS.'" *The Risks Digest*, vol. 9, issue 55, December 16, 1989. "The Trojan Horse Named 'AIDS' Revisited." *The Risks Digest*, vol. 9, issue 65, February 2, 1990. Harley, Slade, & Gattiker 2001, 31.

87. Ross 1991, 76.

88. Ibid., 79.

89. "The media affect-fear-blur is the direct *collective* perception of the contemporary condition of possibility of being human: the capitalized accident-form. It is the direct collective apprehension of capitalism's powers of existence. It is vague by nature. It is nothing as sharp as panic. Not as localized as hysteria. It doesn't have a particular object, so it's not a phobia. But it's not exactly an anxiety either; it is even fuzzier than that. It is *low-level fear*. A kind of background radiation saturating existence (commodity consummation/ consumption)." Massumi 1993, 24.

90. Deleuze & Guattari 1987, 167–171.

91. Goodchild 1996, 107.

92. As Friedrich Kittler (1990, 369–370) emphasizes, technical media works on very different codes irreducible to anthropological bodies or the handwritten texts of hermeneutic meaning.

93. Järvinen 1990, 153.

94. See Joost Van Loon's analysis of the virtuality of the viral object: "The first step in the formation of the virus as a virtual object is that it has to be visualized—either iconically or indexically. Second, it has to be signified, that is, endowed with the specific meaning through which the objectification can be anchored into the symbolic order, and become a discursive object, engendering a discursive formation. Third, it has to be valorized; the virtual object must not only be endowed with meanings, this endowment must be attributed a particular value in terms of its significance within the wider emergent

discursive formation. Objectification, therefore, is nothing but the singular decoding and encoding of a territory, a re-organization of particles and forces, not simply in terms of 'knowledge,' for example as in the Foucauldean (1970) notion of 'episteme,' but first and foremost in practices and technologies of enpresenting." Van Loon 2002a, 117.

95. Sven Stillich & Dirk Liedtke: "Die Wurm von der Würme." *Stern*, June 16, 2004.
96. See Jon Katz, "Who Are These Kids?" *Time*, vol. 155, May 15, 2000.
97. See "Girl Power's Point of Virus Written in Microsoft's C#." Computeruser.com, March 4, 2002.
98. Jon A. Rochlis & Mark W. Eichin: "With Microscope and Tweezers: The Worm from MIT's Perspective." *Communications of the ACM*, vol. 32, issue 6, June 1989, 695.
99. Ibid., 694. Interestingly, in another context the very same Morris worm was described using themes familiar from classic horror and science fiction films, with the worm playing the role of the abhorred monster, a digital Godzilla. Hafner & Markoff 1991, 254.
100. Helmreich 2000a, 477. See, e.g., Parker 1976, 85–106, where computer intrusion is described as rape. A desperate e-mail message from the 1980s addressing the hacker incidents that the company Digital Equipment Corporation confronted testifies to a view in which computers are part of the *polis* to be guarded and uses rather explicit sexualized language to make its point: "We seem totally defenseless against these people. We have repeatedly rebuilt system after system and finally management has told the system support group to ignore the problem. As a good network citizen, I want to make sure someone at network security knows that we are being raped in broad daylight. These people freely walk into our systems and are taking restricted, confidential and proprietary information." Quoted in Hafner & Markoff 1991, 120. On diagrams and imaging of biological viruses, see Weingart 2004.
101. Theriault 1999. Cf. Chun 2006, 177.
102. Lundemo 2003, 15.
103. Deleuze 1998, 51.
104. Martin 1994, 245.
105. Ibid., 248. Deleuze 1990, 240–247.
106. Goffey 2003, 3.
107. See for example Brown 2015.
108. Boyer 1996, 37–38.
109. See Stephanie Forres, Steven A. Hofmeyr, & Anil Somayaji: "Computer Immunology." *Communications of the ACM*, vol. 40, issue 10, October 1997. *Virus Bulletin* 1993, 107.
110. See Deleuze & Guattari 1987, 502–505. Goodchild 1996, 68–69.
111. *Time* reported in 1985 on the threat of malicious software: "Programs called 'worms' are capable of altering a system's fundamental operations or shutting it down entirely. They delete specific portions of a computer's memory, thus creating a hole of missing information. Another type of software demon, called a 'virus,' instructs the host machine to summon its stored files. Each time the machine does so, the program copies itself onto the software. The computer's memory can soon turn into a mass of confusion." "A Threat from Malicious Software." *Time*, November 4, 1985.
112. Gerrold 1975, 175.
113. See, e.g., Longley 1994a and 1994b. See also Patrick Wood: "Safe and Secure?" *Byte*, May 1989, 254. Byte lists computer security concerns in four subtopics: preventing

unauthorized access, preventing data compromise, preventing service denial, and preserving system integrity.

114. Bryan Kocher: "A Hygiene Lesson." *Communications of the* ACM, vol. 32, issue 1, January 1989, 3.
115. James H. Morris: "Our Global City." *Communications of the* ACM, vol. 32, issue 6, June 1989, 661.
116. Helmreich 2000a, 477.
117. Martin 1994, 53.
118. Ibid., 62. See, e.g., Jeffrey Laurence: "The Immune System in AIDS." *Scientific American*, vol. 253, December 1985, 70. "How is it that by damaging a single link the AIDS virus causes the immune system as a whole to unravel? The answer lies in the complex web of interactions among the different classes of blood cells that take part in immunity. The immune system is a flexible but highly specific defense mechanism that kills microorganisms and the cells they infect, destroys malignant cells and removes debris. It distinguishes such threats from normal tissue by recognizing antigens, or foreign molecules, and mounting a response that varies with the nature of the antigen."
119. Kay 2000, 112.
120. Gibson 1984, 63.
121. See Wendy Chun's (2006, 37–76) apt critique of the spatialization of cyberspace in the wake of Gibson.
122. Paul Saffo: "Consensual Realities in Cyberspace." *Communications of the* ACM, vol. 32, issue 6, June 1989, 664–665. Published also in Denning 1991a, 416–420. See also Ferbrache 1992, 10–11. Cf. Harrasser 2002.
123. Vic Vissotsky, e-mail to author, June 2, 2005. Cf. Kittler 1999, 243. In addition, in another novel, *Softwar/La Guerre douce* (1985), the United States donates a Trojan-infested computer to the Russians, hoping to penetrate their defense networks.
124. Jon A. Rochlis & Mark W. Eichin: "With Microscope and Tweezers: The Worm from MIT's Perspective." *Communications of the* ACM, vol. 32, issue 6, June 1989, 692–694.
125. Hafner & Markoff 1991, 254.
126. Lundell 1989, 113.
127. These ideas connect to Friedrich Kittler's emphasis on the interconnections of war and media. See Kittler 1999, 243. See also Virilio & Kittler 1999.
128. Forbes 2004, 104.
129. Ibid., 105.
130. Stephanie Forrest, Steven A. Hofmeyr, & Anil Somayaji: "Computer Immunology." *Communications of the* ACM, vol. 40, issue 10, October 1997, 88. Immunology against computer viruses was discussed in 1987 in connection with the Christmas Tree worm. See "The Christmas Card Caper, (Hopefully) Concluded." *The Risks Digest*, vol. 5, issue 81, December 21, 1987, <http://catless.ncl.ac.uk/Risks/5.81.html#subj1.1>.
131. Stephanie Forrest, Steven A. Hofmeyr, & Anil Somayaji: "Computer Immunology." *Communications of the* ACM, vol. 40, issue 10, October 1997, 92.
132. See "A Database of Normal Patterns." *Communications of the* ACM, vol. 40, issue 10, October 1997, 95. See also "Computer Immune Systems." <http://www.cs.unm.edu/~immsec/>.

133. "The IBM Virus Antidote." *Computer Fraud & Security Bulletin*, October 1995, 6.

134. *Virus Bulletin* 1993, 107.

135. Lundell 1989, 114.

136. Ibid., 115. In 1988, a hard drive write-protect application was introduced as a form of immunology against viruses. See "Write-Protection for Hard Disks." *The Risks Digest*, vol. 61, issue 73, April 29, 1988, <http://catless.ncl.ac.uk/Risks/6.73.html#subj5.1>. Examples of sophisticated techniques of observation were checksums, designed to look for changes within programs. This way the program was in theory able to perceive whether a virus had changed the structure of a program. The problem was that checksums were effective only against known viral strains, not new ones. In essence, virus writers were also able to find out where the checksums were located in a program. They were then replaced with ones that simulated the normal routines of that checksum. On checksums, see, e.g., McAfee & Haynes 1989, 144. Heuristics was a widely discussed antivirus technique in the early 1990s, trying to find solutions to the problem of the constantly increasing number of new virus strains. See Frans Veldman's papers "Combating Viruses Heuristically." *Virus Bulletin Conference Proceedings* 1993, 67–76, and "Why Do We Need Heuristics?" *Virus Bulletin Conference Proceedings* 1995, xi–xvi. The "problems of virus detection" are also discussed in David J. Stang: "Computer Viruses and Artificial Intelligence." *Virus Bulletin Conference Proceedings* 1995, 235–246.

137. See Deleuze 1990, 240–247.

138. Lundell 1989, 118–119.

139. Ibid., 119.

140. Stephanie Forrest, Steven A. Hofmeyr, & Anil Somayaji: "Computer Immunology." *Communications of the ACM*, vol. 40, issue 10, October 1997, 90.

141. Cohen 1986, 5–8.

142. Fleck 1979, 59. See also Martin 1994, 108–110.

143. Maturana & Varela 1980, 9, 81.

144. Fleck 1979, 61. Actually, Francisco Varela wrote about the immune system, together with M. Anspach, in 1994. Mackenzie 1996, 23. Mackenzie draws much of his analysis from Haraway's "The Biopolitics of Postmodern Bodies: Constitutions of Self in Immune System Discourse" (1991, 203–230).

145. Stephanie Forrest, Steven A. Hofmeyr, & Anil Somayaji: "Computer Immunology." *Communications of the ACM*, vol. 40, issue 10, October 1997, 91.

146. See Haraway 1991, 204–208. Haraway rests on A. N. Whitehead's notions of a process ontology, which aims to think beyond the subject–predicate determination of Western thought. These ideas are also apt concerning immunology and interaction of bodies. On Whitehead, see Halewood 2005.

147. Mackenzie 1996, 22–26.

148. Cf. Goffey 2003.

149. Parisi 2004a, 141.

150. See Heidegger 1996, §16.

151. Winograd & Flores 1986, 77.

152. Ibid., 36–37.

153. Sampson 2005. See also Galloway 2004 for a protological view of network genealogy.

154. See "Museum's Hack Art Piece Pulled." *Wired*, May 15, 2002, <http://archive.wired.com/culture/lifestyle/news/2002/05/52546>.

155. Chun 2015.

156. Brothers 1991, 365. Cf. "Health Insurance for Computers." *Computerworld*, April 23, 1990.

157. Rod Parkin: "Is Anti-Virus Software Really Necessary?" *Virus Bulletin Conference Proceedings* 1993, 59.

158. For an analysis of knowledge work in network culture, see Terranova 2004.

159. Kittler 1990.

160. Alan Kay: "Computer Software." *Scientific American*, vol. 251, September 1984, 47.

161. Saarikoski 2004, 89, 145.

162. On the archaeology of interactivity, see Huhtamo 1996.

163. Leary 1992, 43. Originally published in 1984 in *Digital Deli*, edited by Steve Ditlea (1984). Of course, the computer "revolution" did not happen overnight and has been a much slower process than many commentators of the 1970s and 1980s assumed.

164. Turner 2006, 163.

165. Mark Drew: "Distributed Computing—Business Risk or Risking the Business." *EICAR Conference Proceedings* 1994, 93.

166. William Murray: "Good Security Practice for Personal Computers." *Symposium on Applied Computing Proceedings of the Northeast ACM Symposium on Personal Computer Security*, September 1986, 11. (my italics)

167. Licklider 1960.

168. Shain 1994, 4.

169. Foucault has analyzed these in relation to the antiquity in his *The History of Sexuality*, Vol. 2: *The Use of Pleasure*, and Vol. 3: *Care of the Self*. See Foucault 2000b.

170. Sennett 1994, 261.

171. Tomes 1998, 6–7.

172. Kittler 1990.

173. Parker 1991a, 552.

174. *Virus Bulletin* 1993, 72.

175. Dorothy E. Denning: "Secure Personal Computing in an Insecure Network." *Communications of the ACM*, vol. 22, issue 8, August 1979, 476–482.

176. See Mattelart 2003, 130–131.

177. Martin Kochanski: "How Safe Is It?" *Byte*, June 1989, 257.

178. "Just like with biologic viruses, subject behaviour has a significant effect on the probability of infection. By altering the habits of the users, and examining how most virus infections occur, it is possible to educate staff on the risk which their different actions carry, and thus minimise the risk of virus infection." *Virus Bulletin* 1993, 72.

179. Wayne Rash Jr.: "Be Secure, Not Sorry." *Byte*, October 1988. See also Peter Stephenson: "Personal and Private: How Much Security Is Enough?" *Byte*, June 1989. Stephenson emphasizes that in the end, the user is the one choosing the right measures to protect her data: "You can encrypt the data on your hard disk, prevent access to the data in the first place, and watch active files for viral contamination that could damage or compromise data. Which of these approaches (or combinations thereof) you select will depend on

how secure your data needs to be and how open your computer is to outside intrusion" (p. 285).

180. Gene B. Williams: "Keep Your PC Healthy." *Byte*, Fall 1988.

181. Deborah Lupton has offered a similar argument. Analyzing the computer virus phenomenon in 1994 she notes how the virus anxiety in part stems from our intimacy with computer technology. Drawing on cyborg theory, Lupton writes about the erotic nature of our interaction with digital machines. The figure of the cyborg can be seen as a cultural symbol of the late twentieth century: ideal, clean, seamless, invulnerable, and hygienic, as Lupton lists. This figure represents perhaps exactly those qualities that are under threat in the intimate computer technology and AIDS culture of recent decades. This *fin de millennium* is one of anxieties concerning bodies and sexualities, limits and borders. Just as biological bodies were dwelling in this ambiguous state of pleasure and terror, so the signs of computing and our relationships with computers were marked by a tension between the intimacy with our personal computers and the fears of what was lurking inside those machines. Thus, the user was in a constant state of paranoid self-surveillance: "Panic computing extends the boundaries of the erotic Self, requiring even greater vigilance, surveillance and personal control to protect against invasion from both biological and computer viruses. Furthermore, panic computing problematizes the capacity of cyberspace to offer liberating, guiltless, safe and infection-free erotic pleasure" (Lupton 1994, 564).

182. Jerry Pournelle: "Dr. Pournelle vs. The Virus." *Byte*, July 1988, 199.

183. See, e.g., Järvinen 1990, 74–77. Hyppönen & Turtiainen 1990, 39–40. Harley, Slade, & Gattiker 2001, 284–300. *Virus Bulletin* 1993, 91.

184. Harley, Slade, & Gattiker 2001, 297–299.

185. Fites, Johnston, & Kratz 1989, 124.

186. *Virus Bulletin* editorial, July 1989.

187. "A Virus-Free Corporate Culture." *Virus Bulletin Conference Proceedings*, September 1992, 30.

188. "It is safer to use only programs from reputable manufacturers. A reputable manufacturer will implement anti-virus security procedures on its development computers to ensure that no virus is embedded in a program at that stage. There have been cases of manufacturers distributing infected copies of software; these incidents have reinforced the need for strict QA (Quality Assurance) procedures." "Computer Viruses—A Management Overview." *Virus Bulletin Conference Proceedings*, September 1992, xi. The article mentions the idea of a "dirty PC" used to try new software, play games, etc. It is physically isolated from network connections to avoid company files from being smothered.

189. "A Virus-Free Corporate Culture." *Virus Bulletin Conference Proceedings*, September 1992, 32.

190. Paul Ducklin/Sophos: "Is Virus Writing Really That Bad?" *Anti-Virus Asia Researchers (AVAR) Conference*, 2001.

191. Martin 1994, 134–135. Sontag 2002, 23.

192. Sontag 2002, 47.

193. "The 'Itch Syndrome.'" *Virus Bulletin*, October 1989, 2. See also Parker 1976, 16. Sontag (2002, 10–26) describes the trope of cancer as something that one might consider keeping to herself.

194. Sarah Gordon: "Why Computer Viruses Are Not—and Never Were—a Problem." *EICAR Conference Proceedings* 1994, 173.

195. Alan Solomon: "A Brief History of Viruses." *EICAR Conference Proceedings* 1994, 129.

196. "Peter J. Denning on Terminology." *The Risks Digest*, vol. 7, issue 4, June 6, 1988, <http://catless.ncl.ac.uk/Risks/>

197. "Computer Viral Center for Disease Control?" *The Risks Digest*, vol. 6, issue 70, April 26, 1988, <http://catless.ncl.ac.uk/Risks/>. "Re: Computer Viral Center for Disease Control?" *The Risks Digest*, vol. 6, issue 72, April 27, 1988.

198. See, e.g., Fites, Johnston, & Kratz 1989, 87–93. Hyppönen & Turtiainen 1990, 40. Järvinen 1990, 91–93. *Virus Bulletin* 1993, 91.

199. On the NII (National Information Infrastructure), see <http://clinton1.nara.gov/White_House/EOP/OVP/html/nii1.html>.

200. See Douglas 1989, xxv.

201. See Foucault 1976.

202. Cf. Van Loon 2002a.

203. Jim Bates: "Catching the Virus Writer." *Virus Bulletin Conference Proceedings*, September 1995, 2–4. (my italics)

204. Fites, Johnston, & Kratz 1989, 17. Cf. Sontag 2002, 47. Cf. Van Loon 2002b, 162–163.

205. See the "Russian's official answer." In: "More on 'Little Black Book of Comp. Viruses.'" *Computer Underground Digest*, vol. 4, issue 55, November 4, 1992.

206. See Jacob Gaboury, "Interview with Zach Blas." Rhizome, Aug 18, 2010, <http://rhizome.org/editorial/2010/aug/18/interview-with-zach-blas/>. Blas 2012. See also Clough and Puar 2012.

207. Of course, not every antivirus researcher has been so one-eyed in her analyses; one example has been Sarah Gordon, active for years in the antivirus research community. To quote Gordon from the mid-1990s: "The virus writer has been characterized by some as bad, evil, depraved, maniac; terrorist, technopathic, genius gone mad, sociopath. This image has been heightened not only by the media, but by some of the actions of the virus writers themselves. Public communications from the writers, in the form of echo-mail messages, often seem to indicate they are intent on doing as much damage as humanly possible. Their electronic publications have in the past reinforced this, and the very fact that they release viruses may seem to confirm it: these people are bad." However, as Gordon continues: "this is a gross oversimplification of the situation, and (…) the virus writing aspect of these individuals is not sufficient to characterize them into one group simply labelled 'unethical people.'" Sarah Gordon: "The Generic Virus Writer." *Virus Bulletin Conference Proceedings* 1994, 122.

208. "Case History of a Virus Attack." *Computer Fraud & Security Bulletin*, vol. 10, issue 4, 1988, 6. In a different way, *Viruses Revealed* disparages virus writers, saying that their code is sloppy and most often their viruses do not work. See Harley, Slade, & Gattiker 2001, 62–63.

209. Fites, Johnston, & Kratz 1989, 77, 121.

210. McAfee & Haynes 1989, 188.

211. Alistair Kelman, quoted in Paul Ducklin/Sophos: "Is Virus Writing Really That Bad?" *Anti-Virus Asia Researchers (AVAR) Conference*, 2001 (orig. 1997), 3.

212. McAfee & Haynes 1989, 39.
213. Games were sources of new forms of addiction, habits, and patterns of culture, and hence also a threat to Western culture. As Jerry Bruckner and Gary Garcia's 1982 hit song "Pac-Man Fever" satirized: "I gotta pocket full of quarters, And I'm headed to the arcade. I don't have a lot of money, But I'm bringing everything I've made. I've gotta callus on my finger, And my shoulder's hurtin' too. I'm gonna eat 'em all up, Just as soon as they turn blue. 'Cause I've got Pac-Man Fever, Pac-Man Fever, It's driving me crazy, driving me crazy, I've got Pac-Man Fever, Pac-Man Fever, I'm going out of my mind, going out of my mind." See the Buckner and Garcia official site for "Pac-Man Fever" at <http://www.bucknergarcia. com/>. I am grateful to Jaakko Suominen for originally pointing me to this example.
214. Huhtamo 1996, 194.
215. Lupton 1994, 566.
216. Douglas 1989, 190.
217. Ibid., 207–215.
218. "Punish Virus Spreaders." *Byte*, July 1989, 40.
219. Turner 2006.
220. Levy 1985, 40–45.
221. Ibid., passim.
222. Ibid., 127. Cf. Parker 1976, 48. Sulonen, who studied at Brown University and worked with the Xerox Palo Alto labs in the 1970s, recalled similar types of examples of tactical systems crashing. Reijo Sulonen, phone interview with author, November 23, 2005.
223. According to some commentators, 1984 was when "hacker" was for the first time used as a pejorative term to refer to computer vandals. Nissenbaum 2004, 206. Cf. Hafner & Markoff 1991, 10–12. Yet, already in the mid-1970s, the term had been used for a teleoperating computer criminal. See Parker 1976, 107–117.
224. "Runme.org" website. <http://runme.org/project/+forkbombsh/>. See Kittler's article on protected mode (1993b).
225. "Irresponsible Computer 'Game.'" *The Risks Digest*, vol. 1, issue 23, November 18, 1985, <http://catless.ncl.ac.uk/Risks/1.23.html#subj4.1>.
226. Nissenbaum 2004, 201. See, e.g., the High-Performance Computing Act of 1991. <http:// assembler.law.cornell.edu/uscode/html/uscode15/usc_sec_15_00005501----000-notes. html>. See also, e.g., Negroponte 1995. For an enlightening discussion of the term "hacker" by hackers themselves, see The Computer Underground Digest discussions from the 1990s on, archived online at <http://www.computer-underground-digest.org/>.
227. Nissenbaum 2004, 199–200.
228. Ross 1991, 80.
229. Flichy 2001.
230. Campbell-Kelly 2004. Following Lazzarato (2004, 197–199), Microsoft's power resides not in exploiting its workers (as the traditional Marxian explanation would suggest) but in creating a clientele and organizing the social field of production in a linear fashion: producers versus consumers (where consumers represent the huge majority of people). It is on this social field that alternative modes of production are easily called "suspicious."
231. Clough & Mungo 1992, 223.
232. See Terranova 2004, 151, passim.

233. Harley, Slade, & Gattiker 2001, 35.

234. David S. Bennahum: "Heart of Darkness." *Wired*, vol. 5, issue 11, November 1997, <http://www.wired.com/1997/11/heartof/>. Cf. "Bulgarians Linked to Computer Virus." *New York Times*, December 21, 1990.

235. Bennahum: "Heart of Darkness." Cf. Dmitry O. Gryaznov: "Russia: A Computer Virus Jungle." *Virus Bulletin Conference Proceedings* 1993, 149–150.

236. Dmitry O. Gryaznov: "Russia: A Computer Virus Jungle." *Virus Bulletin Conference Proceedings* 1993.

237. Pavel Baudis: "Viruses behind the ex-Iron Curtain." *Virus Bulletin Conference Proceedings* 1994, 158. For example, the 17th November 1989 (Pojer) virus included the message: "Viruses against political extremes, for freedom and parliamentary democracy." This illustrates how viruses have been understood also as media tools, perfect for efficient distribution of messages. In the United States, the MacMag Peace virus functioned in the same way, promoting a message of peace across the globe. Such viruses in the Eastern bloc countries can perhaps be analyzed using the notion of tactical media. See Lovink 2003, 254–274.

238. Lampo 2002.

239. Scott Berinato: "Attack of the Bots." *Wired*, vol. 14, issue 11, November 2006, <http://www.wired.com/2006/11/botnet/>.

240. Chun 2015. Stone-Gross et al. 2009.

241. Terranova 2004. See also Lovink 2003.

242. "One of the most fascinating aspects of the entire software/medicine analogy is the amazing degree to which it holds. Modern computer systems and software are now complex enough to support a crude simulation of life-cycle processes." Steve Gibson: "Computer Viruses Express Themselves in Many Ways." *Infoworld*, April 18, 1988. See also Johnston 2009.

243. See Terranova 2004, 98–100; and Johnston 2008.

INTERMEZZO

Viral Philosophy

The viral expands into various contexts from cybernetics and computing to biology, literature, television, cinema, and media art. In addition, the term "viral" also slipped in as part of philosophical theory and cyber theory in the 1990s. As Ruth Mayer and Brigitte Weingart aptly note, the viral culture of the 1980s and its marginalization of AIDS carriers gave birth to a related buzz within philosophy and cultural theory where the liminality of the viral and its associations with subversion, novelty, and transversality were taken as motors of a certain brand of theory.[1] The resonance of the term "viral" with Derrida's *pharmakon* seemed suddenly obvious, and hence also the incorporation of the viral into theories of deconstruction and plays of difference.[2] In addition, in the chapter on "Rhizome" in their A *Thousand Plateaus*, Deleuze and Guattari highlight the philosophical underpinnings and promises of the idea of a "virus." This alignment is to be understood as a vector of becoming where two series (the host and the parasite) momentarily resonate together and form a novel circuit of entanglement. Thinking with Deleuze and Guattari, evolution does not have to rely on the arborescent models of hierarchy and descent. Instead, viral evolution is a transversal connection machine that jumps across species and smuggles renegade bits of DNA along with it. Not merely "biological fact," it amounts to an image of thought as well, jumping scales: "We form a rhizome with our viruses, or rather our viruses cause us to form a rhizome with other animals. (…) Transversal communications between different lines scramble the genealogical trees. Always look for the molecular, or even submolecular, particle with which we are allied."[3]

Hailing from such theoretical directions, virality as a subversive strategy infected media critique and net activism in the 1990s. During that decade, viruses were suddenly a common theme, from net art to viral marketing. Similarly, the viral was celebrated also in the cyberfeminism of the 1990s. This was well exemplified by the spirit of détournement by the VNS Matrix cyberfeminist manifesto:

> we are the virus of the new world disorder
> rupturing the symbolic from within
> saboteurs of big daddy mainframe
> the clitoris is a direct line to the matrix.[4]

Although it might be easy to deconstruct such concepts as the metaphorics of a certain era of media theory, I want to think through such figurations as potential vectors of critical thought. Even if these theories often feature in the same context as discussions about computer viruses and, for example, second-order cybernetics, this does not make using them less interesting. This is the cultural-historical part of understanding why viruses and related notions, including issues of complexity and metastable systems, featured at a certain time not only in biology but in computer science, cultural discourses, philosophy, and more. This contextualization does not remove the fact that the concepts can be used to gather and summon up forces to give a better understanding of the virality of late twentieth-century culture—a virality that is not a mere metaphor but a description of how various cultural platforms from technology to biological sciences and, for example, economics and aesthetics work. Furthermore, concepts do not merely describe "matters of fact" but act as creators of new circuits of concern and hence can be used to highlight previously neglected issues concerning digital culture.

My claim is that as contemporary power operates on increasingly abstract levels, such as the molecular interactions of the body (as in genome research) or at level of the program code (digital culture), we also need complex theories and insights into this field of new production of networked control. Viral philosophy can be offered as one way to think of the complex ontologies of this technological culture. The viral and parasitic have deterritorialized across a range of fields and theoretical discourses to describe, for example, the state of subjectivity in network society and the logic of global power. For Steven Shaviro, selfhood is increasingly depicted as an information pattern, where the "individual" becomes a host of parasitic invasion by information capitalist patterns of repetition.[5] On the other hand, Hardt and Negri regard the parasite as an apposite description of how the empire dips into the virtual powers of the multitude.[6]

Virality is not merely code but an environment of contagion. What needs to be underlined is the danger in code-centered thought, as Tony Sampson argues. According to Sampson, the thematics of the viral have tended to reduce the matter to an emphasis on the issue of viral *code* as in itself subversive instead of looking at the larger assemblages of media ecologies that enable virality.[7] Focusing on viral code risks making "virality" in itself an objectified piece of rebel code, a mode of critical resistance, a Luddite gesture. Instead, we need a more careful analysis of the historical forces of contagion and its multiple manners of distribution across technology and theory. Hence, in a similar manner, we might want to consider the parasite and the viral not merely as qualities of a specific piece of software but as assemblages of network culture, working both in concrete machines and in the abstract machine (diagram) of network capitalism.[8] Like Sampson, I underline the environmental dynamics of virus research, where there is a constant layering of territories (ecologies) of heterogeneous nature—that is, technical, conceptual, social, and historical.

If we take such arguments seriously, the need to elaborate a "viral politics" and a "viral ontology" is even more pronounced: power operates in the imperceptible networks of the digital code and molecular biology. As mapped above, information capitalism is increasingly tied to the viral and the autopoietic diagrams of flexibility, different from national, centripetal state capitalism.[9] Hence, as I have tried to stress, issues of software and cultural history of digitality should be approached from perspectives that take into account the corporeal materiality *and* the incorporeal order-words of power/knowledge. This is also where we can think through Guattari's three ecologies and the ethics of diversity. We are in need of concepts that can map transversal ideas. In this, I relate especially to certain themes of virality and molecular bodies elaborated by Braidotti and Ansell-Pearson.

Braidotti addresses the argument for a viral politics, a theme that follows from her emphasis on philosophical nomadism. Braidotti articulates what I have been approaching as an issue of ecology: to find concepts and approaches that rely on the constant foldings of the outside and the inside. For Braidotti, viral politics is "a form of micro-politics that is embedded in the human body. It is territorially-based and environmentally-bound, much like an animal-machine compound. It is also a relentlessly generative organism that aims at living on."[10] It is a form of agency that abandons anthropocentricity, being always directed toward the external, the outside—that is, such a politics avoids the creation of rigid segments of interiority with which we are so familiar: the ego, the family, the sex, and so forth. Even though Braidotti focuses on the imaginaries of the body–machine, her insights are valuable concerning other patterns of contagion as well. Braidotti's affirmative mission is to take the pathologized bodies of the Western cultural unconsciousness, the monsters and grotesque figures, and turn them into positive (con)figurations. This amounts to loving the monstrously new and different in hope of a future of *affirmative difference*. For us, of course, this connects to the possibility of affirming the virus, the anomalous, and with it a culture of complexity and difference. Is not the virus also a relative of these monstrous figures of the nineteenth century, a cousin of Frankenstein's creature and other human-made figures of horror?

One of the most interesting writers in this respect is Elizabeth Grosz, who engages with issues of life, duration, and becoming. To paraphrase Grosz, viruses are by definition agents of replication and evolution regardless of their material substance in carbon or silicon. The analogous symmetry between biological and computer viruses is, therefore, not to be neglected. For Grosz, this parable blurs "conceptual and definitional boundaries" concerning organisms, life, and inorganicity. In this, the question connects essentially to the tension between being and becoming: "How can any clear line be drawn in any case, such that material objects are characterized by inertia and by temporal self-containment (i.e., by being) that the organic world enlivens (through becoming)?"[11]

Grosz's question strikes at the core of the issue. Just as the problematics of life, biological lineage, and technological autopoiesis have been at the center of modernity, especially since the end of the nineteenth century, so the virus is an agent of deterritorialization that short-circuits key issues of philosophy of life and nature and technology. This blurring forces a reconsideration, or a Nietzschean reevaluation, of values, concepts, and practices of life and technology. In biology and biophilosophy, the viral has already been addressed by Ansell-Pearson. For Ansell-Pearson the issue connects to finding alternative, transversal ways to understand evolution, life, and technologies. One key biological context for this transversality is introduced by Lynn Margulis and her ideas on symbiosis in evolution. To paraphrase Ansell-Pearson, since the 1950s the biological disciplines have been so organized into discrete departments (virology, genetics, pathology, etc.) that synthetic views on evolution have been hard to establish. In other words, until then and the point at which genetics also addressed microorganisms, sex was seen as the only vehicle for transmitting genes. But Margulis's work from the 1970s on, in particular, sym- biotic bacteria challenged such an anthropocentric account. These ideas of bacterial symbiosis provided the hypothesis that evolution rested not only on mere slow accumulation of random changes, or mutations, but also on "intra- cellular symbiosis in which some cells incorporated into their own cell con- tents partner cells of another kind that [have] different metabolic activities."[12] A symbiotic view of evolution offered an alternative to accounts that focus on individuals and selection. Symbiotic perspectives see individuals (whether humans, cells, or software) as cooperative colonies that feed (and feed back) on their environments.[13] Instead of a reduced view of evolution as competi- tion, there are a number of coexisting ecological strategies. Life's a multiplic- ity, and so are its tactics and strategies.

Viroids had also, according to some researchers, acted as such "intra- cellular symbionts," transversal vectors of genetic material. These bio- logical-objects-turned-philosophical-vectors can also be read in terms of evolution. Drawing from Deleuze and Guattari, Ansell-Pearson argues the need to understand evolution as *creative involution*. The notion is critical of the more passive Darwinian model of adaptation, and it underlines the transversal communication between heterogeneous series that occasionally launch vectors of becoming. This is where the difference between rhizomes and trees as diagrams of thought and organization comes clear. Neither thinking nor evolution proceeds as a clean-cut filiation expressed in the evolutionary trees that have been part of the standard geological and bio- logical iconography of phylogeny since the 1840s. A more accurate descrip- tion is found in the simulation systems of artificial life or in the trackings of viral patterns in the global networks of information. Rhizomes interact transversally across predetermined lineages. As Ansell-Pearson writes:

> Like philosophy, the field of biology is full of born Platonists, but symbiosis shows that the delineation of "organic units," such as genes, plasmids, cells, organisms, and genomes, is a tool of a certain mode of investigation, not at all an absolute or ideal model. It challenges notions of pure autonomous entities and unities, since it func- tions through assemblages (multiplicities made up of heterogeneous terms) that oper- ate in terms of alliances and not filiations (that is, not successions or lines of descent). The only unity within an assemblage is that of a plural functioning, a symbiosis or "sympathy."[14]

Hence, the overall mission is to think through biology with new concepts and orientations, such as new materialist feminism expressed in Grosz's philosophy,

Parisi's writings, and the patterns of becoming described by Braidotti's viral politics.[15] This list is not exhaustive—far from it—but it indicates how issues of science entangle with the dynamic body of cultural theory, often feminist. Such perspectives address the need to rethink the ontologies of network culture, a techno-biology of sorts, which is not to be reduced to postmodern metaphorics. There is more at stake in new materialism that also detours around the linguistic-centered postmodern theory and grounds itself in a multilayered dynamic reality of actions and intra-actions, of distributed agencies and the posthuman.[16]

We can also speak of the ethology of bodies. Bodies and their environments are entangled as multiple milieus that resonate and infect each other. Drawing from the ethologist Jakob von Uexküll's works, Deleuze and Guattari focus on animal milieus as self-sustaining processual unities, an example of which is the bloodsucking tick, with its own restricted milieu, *Umwelt*. It is receptive only to specific phenomena: butyric acid found in mammals that attracts the tick, sunlight, the sense of mammalian heat, hair, skin, and the taste of blood. This is an affectual perspective on the world, a pragmatic viewpoint where the focus is on what bodies do, with what other bodies, with what types of relationships (affects).[17] Such are the coordinates, or the attractors, that define the tick's world. Of course, with more complex animals and milieus there are enormous numbers of coordinates and attractors, but still it is an option to approach such systems as consisting of movements and moments of rest. A plane of immanence where bodies interact, affect each other, and form together is *a life*—"the important thing is to understand life, each living individuality, not as a form, or a development of form, but as a complex relation between differential velocities, between deceleration and acceleration of particles."[18]

This moving transversally, on border zones, crossing them, zigzagging is what could be thought of as an ethological perspective on the world. Just as ethological views have provided important insights into nature and territoriality, these views can be extended to the technological nature of media assemblages that we are occupied with. In this sense, the Deleuzian–Spinozan approach to bodies and territories provides a key addition to the issue of media ecology that we will turn to next.

What attracts me in this perspective is that it renounces the linear and teleological notion of technology, just as these views have complexified the understanding of nature. This is a specific rhythmic view of the world where the world is seen as consisting of territorializing refrains, deterritorializing music, rhythms flowing between milieus, making them vibrate.[19] This means a focus on relations, movement, and rhythms as cosmological constituents, not predefined forms, terms, substances, subjects, or objects. Technological media culture can be followed along similar conceptualizations: not as hierarchical techno-scientific plans of modern control of nature or purely as postmodern self-organizing systems of fluidity, but as movements between different stages of rigidity, stratification, and opening up to the great outdoors of dynamics of life—a life that is not merely organic.[20]

Notes

1. See Mayer & Weingart 2004b.
2. Derrida 1972, 71–196. Cf. Bardini 2006.
3. Deleuze & Guattari 1987, 10–11.
4. Quoted in Plant 1996, 171.
5. "I may describe this process that subtends my consciousness in several ways: as embryonic infolding, as fractal self-similarity, or as viral, cancerous proliferation. But the difference between these alternatives is just a matter of degree. The crucial point is that the network induces mass replication on a miniaturized scale and that I myself am only an effect of this miniaturizing process." Shaviro 2003, 13.
6. "Imperial power is the negative residue, the fallback of the operation of the multitude; it is a parasite that draws its vitality from the multitude's capacity to create ever new sources of energy and value. A parasite that saps the strength of its host, however, can endanger its own existence." Hardt & Negri 2000, 361.
7. Sampson 2012.
8. Cf. Chun 2006, 17–18. On software, see also Fuller 2003. Mackenzie 2006.
9. Cf. Lash & Urry 1987.
10. Braidotti 2002, 266.
11. Grosz 1999, 23. See also Grosz 2004, 2005.
12. Ansell-Pearson 1997, 132. See Margulis & Sagan 1995.
13. Parisi 2004a, 56.
14. Ansell-Pearson 1997, 134.
15. Braidotti 2002. Grosz 2004, 2005. Parisi 2004a, 2004b.
16. See for example Braidotti 2012. Dolphjin and van der Tuin 2012.
17. Deleuze & Guattari 1987, 257. Bogue 2003, 58–59.
18. Deleuze 1988, 123.
19. For an overview, see Bogue 2003, 55–76.
20. See Fuller 2005. Hence, even in thinking through biology, one should not fall for easy analogies between biology and digital culture as with the rhizome boom of the 1990s, where the Internet was suddenly seen directly in terms of the Deleuzian–Guattarian concept. Instead, the Internet is something that connects hierarchies and heterogenesis. See Galloway 2004. Terranova 2004.

· I I I ·

LIFE

Viral Ecologies

This ability to reproduce is, of course, the most important and distinctive feature of viruses. For the first time in the history of technology, mankind has created an artificial device that is capable of reproducing itself and, without further human intervention, pursue a course of action than can cause harm, even if the original programmer had no such intention.[1]

—John McAfee and Colin Haynes (1989)

At the center of these problems one finds that of error. For, at the most basic level of life, the processes of coding and decoding give way to a chance occurrence that, before becoming a disease, a deficiency, or a monstrosity, is something like a disturbance in the informative system, something like a "mistake." In this sense, life—and this is its radical feature—is that which is capable of error. And perhaps it is this datum or rather this contingency which must be asked to account for the fact that the question of anomaly permeates the whole of biology. And it must also be asked to account for the mutations and evolutive processes to which they lead.[2]

—Michel Foucault (1985)

Prologue: The Life of Information

The media archaeological roots of self-reproducing technology and the fear of technological automata reach much further back in time than has been suggested earlier. The interesting thing is how certain themes come to dominate both the biological and the technological focus. As the epigraph from Foucault argues, anomaly rose to be a key theme in biology (but also in technology) during the cybernetic, late twentieth-century phase of life sciences. Self-reproduction, duration, and distributed processes had, however, already characterized both spheres in the nineteenth century. The end of the nineteenth century is especially interesting. Charles Darwin introduced radical ideas of time and development in the context of the animal kingdom, but evolution was perceived to be part of the technological sphere as well: near the end of the nineteenth century, not only animals were described as having evolved but also technology. Lt.-Gen. A. Lane-Fox Pitt-Rivers became famous for his collection of tools and his arguments concerning the evolution of such artificial organisms.[3] For Pitt-Rivers, material culture, such as weaponry, worked through similar patterns to those of organic evolution. Even more famous have been the views—marked by an astute sense of satire—of Samuel Butler and his novel *Erewhon*, a novel about "nowhere," yet read as "now-here"—a conception of time and history also as something else than linear.[4]

Although the narrative of *Erewhon*, first published in 1872, is loyal to the genre of utopia novels, it also presents themes that attach it to an epistemic field that is also pertinent to our digital perspective. Whereas Darwin opened up history both as an evolutionary past and as a potentially open future, Butler's fantasies map a certain event of technological evolution that presents keys to understanding the intertwining of technology and biology.

In the novel, a Western traveler stumbles upon an isolated tribe where all pieces of advanced technology are restricted to museums. As it turns out, the tribe has consciously rejected using technology owing to a fear of the evolution of machines. Even the protagonist's watch is confiscated and put into the museum next to other freaks of technological nature:

> It was filled with cases containing all manner of curiosities—such as skeletons, stuffed birds and animals, carvings in stone (whereof I saw several that were like those on the saddle, only smaller), but the greater part of the room was occupied by broken machinery of all descriptions. The larger specimens had a case to themselves, and tickets with writing on them in a character, which I could not understand. There were fragments of steam engines, all broken and rusted; among them I saw a cylinder and a piston, a broken fly-wheel, and part of a crank, which was laid on the ground by their side. Again, there was a very old carriage whose wheels in spite of rust and decay, I could see, had been designed originally for iron rails. Indeed, there were fragments of a great many of our own most advanced inventions; but they seemed all to be several hundred years old, and to be placed where

they were, not for instruction, but curiosity. As I said before, all were marred and broken.[5]

The sudden change in Erewhon's history was due to a book, *The Book of Machines*, that argued that machines were to be regarded as living and vital entities that evolve. *The Book of Machines* contains a thorough exposition of this peculiar stance toward technology. Written by a "hypothetic," a scholar of the College of Unreason, the treatise functions to demonstrate that machines are capable of reproduction and evolution. For this representative of the College, machines are cities or societies; that is, they are not to be understood as single entities but as complex organizations of parts that communicate. Machines are inherently interconnected, similar to nature, through complex structures of kinship, filiation, and symbiosis. Hence, we find the recurring theme of the late nineteenth century in interfacing nature and technology, perhaps the strongest outgrowth planted by the Romantic age. The knowledge of the evolutionary patterns of animal and plant life provides the necessary understanding to see where technological progress is headed. But thinking about evolution involves acknowledging reproduction:

> Surely if a machine is able to reproduce another machine systematically, we may say that it has a reproductive system. What is a reproductive system, if it be not a system for reproduction? And how few of the machines are there by other machines? But it is man that makes them do so. Yes; but is it not insects that make many of the plants reproductive, and would not whole families of plants die out if their fertilisation was not effected by a class of agents utterly foreign to themselves? Does any one say that the red clover has no reproductive system because the humble bee (and the humble bee only) must aid and abet it before it can reproduce? No one. The humble bee is a part of the reproductive system of the clover. Each one of ourselves has sprung from minute animalcules whose entity was entirely distinct from our own, and which acted after their kind with no thought or heed of what we might think about it. These little creatures are part of our own reproductive system; then why not we part of that of the machines?[6]

Butler's *Erewhon* introduces imaginary reproducing machines a hundred years before digitalized self-reproduction. In this sense *Erewhon* acts as a passage between the age of industrial machines and the era of viral ecologies. This early expression of fear of dynamic material and evolutionary science can be expressed in terms of a parable that connects to another form of figuration of artificial life in a contemporary media context. Produced during the early years of the artificial-life boom, the hit movie *Jurassic Park* (1993)—written by Michael Crichton, the writer of the first "virus novel," *The Andromeda*

Strain, and the writer and director of *Westworld*—shows a prefabricated arti-ficial ecology that runs out of control and demonstrates how dynamic living systems can be. The laboratory-grown dinosaurs exhibit out-of-bounds behav-ior in relation to the prefabricated amusement park ecology they are placed in. The life of such partially artificially created creatures overflows the closed ecologies, showing how unpredictable the organism–environment coupling can be. Actually, this theme of systems spreading outside their (designed) bor-ders is a one of recent decades that connects audiovisual expressions from *Blade Runner* (with replicants leaving their designated habitat) to *Tron* (with the malicious master program aiming to control the world outside it) and on to the various movies on biological contagions. Technology breaches bound-aries of the insides and outsides. Similar concerns to those articulated already in *Erewhon*'s world of metastable, distributed technological systems that over-flow their intended design contexts have been distributed across the wider field of genetics and computer artificial life.

Only during the course of the twentieth century did such ideas of evolv-ing technologies gain more consistency and start to form the diagram that characterizes the media ecology of network culture. Of course, automated self-perpetuating technologies of the clock and, for example, the cinematic image had already characterized the late nineteenth-century fear of automation, act-ing as a form of probing for contemporary technologies of self-reproduction. In the midst of new technological creatures, Butler's ideas expressed a field of reproduction that works as a machinic assemblage, as Luciana Parisi notes. Here, techno-cultural reproduction is not tied to the hierarchical principle of reproductive intelligence but proceeds as a complex field of connectivity: "There is no centre of reproduction, but only a continuously scattered con-nection of machines of reproduction, related and mixed with each other. For example, the egg of a butterfly becomes a caterpillar, which then becomes a chrysalis, which then produces a new butterfly. (…) The butterfly is a machine that affords the egg ways to make another egg: a machinic production."[7] It is important to note that this model of evolution is based on ideas of symbi-osis and affirmative parasitism. The neo-Darwinian model, which has been widely embraced both in biology and in computer culture, rests on seeing competition as the key force. But such views have not gone uncontested, and Lynn Margulis has been the key person in introducing alternative ideas into the biological field, and similar ideas need to be addressed in respect to dig-ital network culture. Of the research so far, John Johnston's magnificent *The Allure of Machinic Life* stands out, and much of this section should be read in parallel with his insightful cartography of entanglement of sciences of life and complexity with the new computational machine culture.[8]

Computers have become the general reference points—and catalyzers—for a whole range of cultural entities and activities, from intelligence to life. In this regard, it is not surprising that computers have also been figured as living entities, ecosystems of a sort. At least since the 1940s, information has been at the heart of the Western scientific understanding of life. For example, in his famous "What Is Life" (1944), Erwin Schrödinger depicted living systems as being born of a "code-script," information that guides the development of systems from birth to adulthood. Genetics adopted this idea of information as the key to hereditary traits, and James Watson and Francis Crick's discoveries concerning the structure of DNA rested on similar allusions to the informatics of life in general. Later, computers played a crucial part in the Human Genome Project, which in a way mapped the alphabet, or the information codes, of human life. Digital archives became the ultimate cultural memory banks of humanity, deposits of the very stuff we humans were made of.[9] Similarly, software tools were increasingly used to help "biologists understand how nature operates."[10]

The Universal Turing Machine of the late twentieth century acts in various contexts as the storage model for life. In the words of François Jacob, a Nobel Prize winner from 1965, who continued the project of the physico-chemical conceptualization of living organisms:

> Modern biology belongs to the new age of mechanism. The program is a model borrowed from electronic computers. It equates the genetic material of an egg with the magnetic tape of a computer. It evokes a series of operations to be carried out, the rigidity of their sequence and their underlying purpose.[11]

His colleague Jacques Monod proceeded along similar lines in this atmosphere of refocusing biology with the help of a surprising figure of the nineteenth century, namely, George Boole and his algebra. Cybernetically inspired biology of digital culture was recircuited through the nineteenth century.[12] From the 1950s on, life and information became entangled and understood through the negative entropy principle: life means resistance to the disordering force of entropy, a temporary organization against disorder.[13] Hence, life was not a specific substance but information and organization, which opened the way for designing technical patterns of organization that resisted entropy. This marked the first steps of artificial life (ALife) research. Thus, it should be noted up front that the fields of artificial life, computer science, and, for example, cybernetics, which seem to have conflated the biological and the technological during recent decades, were expressions of the historically specific understanding of life as information, a mode of organization. Here, the question of structure (understood as material substance) was deemed crucial, and it became a key cultural theme in various contexts throughout the latter part of the twentieth century.

The newly technologically emphasized biology also affected the nascent field of virology. As part of the techniques of vision and conceptualization, biological viruses had since the late nineteenth century also been seen as technological parasites, and technological models and tools were increasingly used to understand their patterns of reproduction and virality. Jacob and Monod's work included a constant feedback loop between concepts such as bacteria, phages, information, circuits, and switches that tied the spheres of biology and information science intimately together.[14] As cybernetics incorporated biology as an essential part of its self-understanding and practices, biology was cybernetized. The intimate cooperation between mathematicians, biologists, and researchers in physics and computer science worked toward finding convenient crossing-points between the disciplines.[15] This informationalization of life was already a part of the episteme of the nineteenth century, with Bertillon's system of criminal phrenology, Muybridge and the quantification of human movement, and similar systems of measuring and objectifying life into tables, paragraphs, and diagrams.[16] In this sense, the discourse network of 1900 analyzed by Kittler can be seen as a general diagram of abstraction and automation: instead of "hallucinating meaning" in writing, as in the discourse network of 1800, we have machines that write for us, Boolean algebra that thinks for us, and the media technologies of inscription that record life (with its noise). Cultural practices such as writing become separated from human subjects and automated as isolated (countable) functions, as in the psychophysics of Hermann Ebbinghaus.[17]

The previous section focused on something we intuitively think of as an essential part of life, that is, the body as a mode of organization, a cultural metaphor but also a concept mobilized as part of the security discourses. The concepts of body and virality provided the central focus for a cultural history of disease in the late twentieth century. In this sense, bodies and diseases were not just about biology but taken in their diagrammatic dimension spanning the whole social field. Moreover, the world of technology and digital culture connected with this sphere to develop an understanding of the contemporary culture of computers. This provided elements for a media ecology that essentially relies on a certain metaphoric and metamorphotic basis that reshifted the borders of biology and technology.

Paradoxically, there is nothing natural about nature, and similarly the digital culture of bodies and viruses is not to be understood as a deterministic system of laws of technological nature. Instead, as discussed, it has been a culture of bifurcations and contingencies, of potentialities as virtualities, of a constant struggle for meaning and articulation, and of a general battle to find stable states of order, healthiness, and control with which sickness and disease could be easily deciphered. AIDS as the central disease (syndrome) of the 1980s was the platform for the use such concepts as "safe hex," "responsibility in use," "digital hygienics," and "computer hygiene," which posited a certain ideal horizon of a natural, healthy culture of computing.

This positing worked through micropolitical acts and conditions. The conceptual elements were turned into recommendations for action for the users, analyzed above as a form of care for the digital self. Two central figures emerged: the idea of a responsible user, who practiced digital hygiene and safe hex, and the feared and loathed irresponsible virus-writing vandal, who was often understood as part of the genealogy of the hacker—in itself an ambiguous figure of digital culture. These discourses, in addition to elements from Section I such as viral capitalism, networking, and risk society, are, bit by bit, pieces of which the diagram or media ecology of viral digital culture consists.

This section deepens the understanding of "the biology of digital culture" by addressing the discussions of computer viruses as forms of artificial life. From the early 1990s, in particular, such articulations gained more visibility and institutional status, partly because the specific field of ALife (analysis of artificial processes of life) was established at the end of the 1980s—in 1987 in Los Alamos, New Mexico. Of course, viruses and the informationalization of life sciences were discussed not merely in scientific circles but also in various cultural products, such as the aspiring literary genre of late modernity called "killer virus novels."[18]

In fact, a whole bundle of practices and discourses of artificial life emerged at the end of the 1980s and the 1990s. Artificial life was not merely an academic endeavor; ideas of complexity, self-reproduction, evolution, and adaptability were widespread within the emerging media culture. The early models and ideas of ecology and self-organization stem from the end of the nineteenth century, when Eduard Suess coined the term, which Vladimir Vernadsky inserted into an ecological context in the 1920s. As Charlie Gere sums up the more recent history of the concept's variations, from the 1960s on the ecology movement took advantage of and also produced these new scientific and cultural ideas, and at the same time digital culture was stamped with the label of its own form of ecology. Maturana and Varela's idea of autopoiesis emphasized the interaction of an organism with its surroundings; Edward Lorenz used computers to model atmospheric events in the 1960s; John Conway's Game of Life from the 1970s used the idea of a cellular automaton to exhibit the potential for complexity to emerge from a simple set of states; Benoit Mandelbrot introduced the fractal ontology of the world, an idea made possible by the simulation power of computers.[19] These ideas, which are close to systems theory and second-order cybernetics, were also in use since the 1980s in a range of robot projects, installations, and software programs that combined engineering with artistic ambitions in an attempt to produce entwinings of nature and technology that challenged many traditional ideas concerning life.[20]

The paradigm of artificial life rested on techno-cultural assumptions, well summarized by N. Katherine Hayles. First, wetware research refers to the creation of artificial biological life in, for example, test tubes. Second, hardware artificial life means a focus on embodied life forms, such as robots. Third, software artificial life is focused on computer programs that exhibit "emergent or evolutionary processes." For Hayles, all share a "bottom-up" agenda of research:

> In the software branch, with which I am concerned here, the idea is to begin with a few simple local rules and then, through structures that are highly recursive, allow complexity to emerge spontaneously. Emergence implies that properties or programs appear on their own, often developing in ways not anticipated by the person who created the simulation. Structures that lead to emergence typically involve complex feedback loops in which the outputs of a system are repeatedly fed back as input. As the recursive looping continues, small deviations can quickly become magnified, leading to the complex interactions and unpredictable evolutions associated with emergence.[21]

Hayles convincingly argues that the gap between self-reproductive software and living organisms has remained wide, and has often been obscured by selected narrative strategies. Similarly, computer viruses have been, especially since the beginning of the 1990s, described in various contexts as forms of life. In addition to mapping these articulations, I present a genealogy of network virality and ALife, starting from the early phases of computer culture with John von Neumann and Norbert Wiener, and demonstrate that ideas of self-production and technological life were already present then. While pursuing such a cartography, I develop another, more implicit idea. Perhaps computer viruses are a symptom, a sign of the very basis of network culture, which in general has the same functional capabilities as viruses, namely, self-reproduction (copying), networking, and communication? Perhaps viruses and contagion are just what digital network culture is all about anyway?[22] I return to the question of media ecology with the aim not so much to draw analogies between technology and nature as to find and create concepts that help us understand the processes of digital culture. "Ecology" functions as a diagrammatic aid and a pilot.[23] Diagrams channel and create; they do not represent.

Section III, "Life: Viral Ecologies," offers, then, a counternarrative, a countermemory, to Section I, "Fear and Security." In a way I am writing here an alternative account of computer viruses that emphasizes the active and countermemorizing methodology of media archaeology. This amounts to finding cracks, openings, and anomalies within the usual narratives of computing and offering slightly more surprising aspects as to the impact of the viral. Just as the research on computer viruses as artificial life is connected to a certain experimental ethos of science, so media archaeology is an experimental way of questioning in terms of its methodology of problematizing the already known.[24] If the cultural history of computer worms and viruses can be mapped from the viewpoint of how they became malicious in the cultural contexts of the digital culture of the 1980s, their history can also be written from the viewpoint of experimentality and networking. In this, viruses and worms do not remain anomalous objects of malicious nature but stand at the center of our cultural condition of network societies. What follows is a genealogy of the incorporeal and corporeal forces that affirm the nonorganic life of reproductive, semiautonomous software. It's a story of life, computation, artificial life, and experimentation.

The Benevolent Viral Machine

During the early 1990s, viruses and worms became everyday occupants of the media ecology of network culture. After the 1988 Morris worm incident, viruses became a widely recognized and often overestimated danger. This led to a boom in the antivirus market, with new companies offering their security programs for safe computing. Of course, the recurring overkill statements of viral dangers did not guarantee safety, something that was then already widely criticized.[25] However, as discussed in the first section of this book, some virus writers organized themselves into clans and bulletin board systems to spread viruses. Sometimes viruses were even sold on special bulletin boards that acted as trading houses for the miniprograms.[26] At the same time, the research community turned from novel ideas in out-of-control (metastable) computing and distributed programs toward an emphasis on security. As the ideas spread from research laboratories to "the wild," the perception of self-reproductive code changed into a new form of malicious software.[27]

During the early 1990s, several researchers also participated in practices and discussions concerning ideas of computer viruses as a form of artificial life. Many turbulences were stirred up by researcher Mark Ludwig when he published his *Little Black Book of Computer Viruses* in 1991. Although merely a re-presentation of new media (computer viruses) in an older media form (the book), the event saw Ludwig and his publisher, American Eagle Publishing, labeled as vandals. All of that only because of the seemingly small detail that he had printed working viral code on the pages of a scientific book. According to some researchers, even if the virus code was "old and silly," the book was still harmful, and such actions could not be justified. Some suggested that most people within the antivirus community probably viewed the book "with considerable distaste." According to such views, *The Little Black Book of Computer Viruses* was making people's lives more difficult, something that was referred to as "digital suicide," poisoning oneself.[28] The book quickly joined the long genealogy of black books containing clandestine pieces of information. In contrast to a few years of more liberal discussion of ALife and benevolent viruses, the responses grew tougher throughout the 1990s. Several unorthodox views concerning viruses, among them those of Cohen and Ludwig, were quickly and acrimoniously attacked.[29]

Of course, Ludwig himself was quite aware of the possible stir the book would cause. In the foreword to the book he described his task as a commitment to *truth*. Consciously or not, Ludwig was using the basic hacker motto, "Information wants to free," which avers that no information should be kept secret. Publishing virus code was an attempt to help people fight malicious viruses:

> I am convinced that computer viruses are not evil and that programmers have a right to create them, posses them and experiment with them. That kind of a stand is going to offend a lot of people, no matter how it is presented. Even a purely technical treatment of viruses which simply discussed how to write them and provided some examples would be offensive. The mere thought of a million well armed hackers out there is enough to drive some bureaucrats mad. These books go beyond a technical treatment, though, to defend the idea that viruses can be useful, interesting, and just plain fun. That is bound to prove even more offensive. Still, the truth is the truth, and it needs to be spoken, even if it is offensive. Morals and ethics cannot be

determined by a majority vote, any more than they can be determined by the barrel
of a gun or a loud mouth. Might does not make right.[30]

Such ideas were part of the globally widespread hacker culture of the 1980s
already. As, for example, Bernd Fix recollects of his years with the Chaos
Computer Club in the mid-1980s, the aim was to explore what could be done
with computer technology. This amounted to a protective ethos that aimed to
write viruses in order to come up with efficient antivirus tools against potentially malicious virus writers. Hence the first antivirus tools were developed
by hackers and, in particular, the Chaos Computer Club, proving the practical side of experimenting with viral programming.[31] In addition, the mid-
1990s saw these issues of experimentality, artificial life, and computer viruses
discussed in, for example, the electronic magazine *Alive*, published online in
1994–1995 by Suzana Stojakovic-Celustka. The magazine set itself the task
of finding new methods of digital protection, but this task was complemented
with a keen interest in looking at rather bold fundamental questions: "What
can be 'alive' in a computer environment?"[32]

What interests me is this ethos of experimentality in this context of computer practices. Part of hacker ethics, it can be also connected to the work of
such experimenters as Ludwig who aimed to link programming with issues in
law and social institutions. One could even speak of an interest in the micropolitics of code where open source and anticommercialism connect with the
aim of finding new protocols or an "elaborate instruction list of how a given
technology should work, from the inside out, from the top to the bottom."[33]
The aspiration to evade the control of hierarchical institutions becomes a
novel model of soft control, or power, that turns to finding the internal limits
of an organizational platform, such as networked computers.

In the midst of all the talk about control—and even control societies,
as Gilles Deleuze suggested—it seems paradoxical that *out of control* became
such a key topic. The term refers of course to the title of the book by Kevin
Kelly,[34] but it also expresses a wider theme in viral capitalism. Out of control actually referred to a new form of subtle control over complex systems
modeled on the principles of living autopoietic systems. As discussed above,
software turned commercial during the 1980s, and network computing for
businesses was being increasingly touted as the next frontier, the new gold
rush. Of course, Ludwig was not alone in his views. The old hacker spirit
was being kept alive alongside—and as part of—the commercialization of the
Internet, as expressed in the "Declaration of Independence of Cyberspace" by
John Perry Barlow in the mid-1990s:

Governments of the Industrial World, you weary giants of flesh and steel, I come from Cyberspace, the new home of Mind. On behalf of the future, I ask you of the past to leave us alone. You are not welcome among us. You have no sovereignty where we gather. We have no elected government, nor are we likely to have one, so I address you with no greater authority than that with which liberty itself always speaks. I declare the global social space we are building to be naturally independent of the tyrannies you seek to impose on us. You have no moral right to rule us nor do you possess any methods of enforcement we have true reason to fear.[35]

The cyberspace of the mind was injected with a "virus of liberty" underlining the infectious logic of network computing: "In China, Germany, France, Russia, Singapore, Italy and the United States, you are trying to ward off the virus of liberty by erecting guard posts at the frontiers of Cyberspace. These may keep out the contagion for a small time, but they will not work in a world that will soon be blanketed in bit-bearing media."[36] The aspiration to create a new social space of liberty and freedom of expression and thought continued to characterize the cyberlibertarian American angle to the Internet. Indeed, what has to be underlined is the U.S.-influenced rhetorics of this new social contract, articulated both in Ludwig's book and in Barlow's declaration. Barlow's definitions and references fit in well with the rhetoric of the "original" American dream of freedom, corrupted by big politics and commercial corporations.[37] This combination of freedom and communitarian utopia was, however, logically connected to the utopia of frictionless capitalism, which also demanded decentralization, globalization, harmonization, and empowerment, to borrow key words proposed by Nicholas Negroponte.[38]

The *Little Black Book of Computer Viruses* was a black book about micropolitics of code. It lists different types of viruses from simple .com infectors to sophisticated boot-sector viruses, offering hex code and assembly language listings for five viruses. The point in the listings and Ludwig's message is that even though viruses and other programs can have malicious variations and can be used for destructive goals, as with military viruses, computer viruses are not destructive *per se*. In other words, it is not their destructiveness or any malicious payload that defines them as viruses. Instead, viruses are copy-machines that can use the machine to reproduce. This makes computer viruses actually "self-reproducing automata," underlining the genealogy of the idea and practices stemming from John von Neumann's cellular automaton theory.[39]

The notion of computer viruses as a form of artificial life was taken up again with Ludwig's sequel to *The Little Black Book of Computer Viruses*, called *Computer Viruses, Artificial Life and Evolution* (1993). Even though it was obvious that digital organisms were not the same as carbon-based life, it remained reasonable to ask whether other traits of life were present in computer viruses. In this, Ludwig proposed to follow the criteria put forth by artificial life researchers before him, looking for the basic characteristics of life in general:

1. The ability to reproduce and the method of reproduction.
2. The concept of emergent behavior.
3. The possession of metabolism.
4. The ability to function under perturbations of the environment and interact with the environment.
5. The ability to evolve.[40]

The virus as artificial life was a theme discussed during the early 1980s in Fred Cohen's pioneer work on computer viruses. In his 1986 doctoral thesis, in particular, Cohen articulated the view that viruses could be conceived as exhibiting formal characteristics of reproduction and evolution, both fundamental properties of life.[41] This aspect of Cohen's work was neglected, and such themes remained marginal until a special field of research into artificial life gained was consolidated in 1987 (yet it remained marginal within the field of science). The first workshop was organized by Christopher Langton in Los Alamos and more or less set the agenda for this the highly transdisciplinary field, which ranged from computer life to ecological dynamics, on to synthetic biology and theories of self-organization.[42] Curiously, Langton invited A. K. Dewdney to give a demonstration of the Core Wars game but did not extend the invitation to Fred Cohen, who was explicitly engaged in viral programming.[43] Despite this downplaying of the viral in early ALife contexts, a few years later, in 1990, the stage was set for such writers as Eugene Spafford to question whether computer viruses were a form of artificial life.

For several critics, the lesson from studying computer viruses was the realization of the danger inherent in such miniprograms. Systems that were somewhat alive were never totally controlled, which was also claimed to expose society to risks. In programming, this related to ideas of floating code and self-recurring programs in speculative software research. Such code experiments in genetic algorithms and programming were designed to incorporate variations, recombinations, and mutations into the modeled systems.[44] The problem with most accounts of evolution in computer culture discourse is that they rest on neo-Darwinian assumptions of what evolution is. These warlike models of competition and selfishness are not able to take into account the possibility that network culture and its software are fundamentally parasitic and symbiotic.[45] This is the problem with many of the accounts concerning viruses, even though Cohen can be seen as working toward ideas of symbiosis in software culture.

However, the idea of computer viruses as artificial life was not taken at face value. Even Mark Ludwig ended up being skeptical. Although viruses had gained some degree of autonomy in environments that were not explicitly designed to foster them, thus showing capabilities of adaptation and emergence behavior, they had in several senses failed the "test of life."[46] Ludwig designed his own version of the polymorph virus with a form of a genetic memory. This way the virus was equipped with potential evolutionary capacity as it could remember the useful variations it went through. It did not, however, work as an evolutionary unit, partly because the actual computer systems were (and still are) too unstable to allow radical mutations. Mutating code did not work in these carefully structured computer operating systems.

More interesting than strict analytical evaluations of whether computer viruses and worms are alive are the problematics of what life in computer discourse and ecology could mean. Why was there such an interest in new forms of out-of-control programs and environments? What did the forms of experimental programming imply? The question of living computer programs has not been a mere theoretical daydream; it connects with the interesting topic of benevolent viruses, which was picked up at the start of the 1990s and dropped some years later. It had a life span as short as the topic of artificial life in viral computing. Some might argue that despite the superficial resemblances of these ideas, the two discourses were not connected, but I suggest looking at the issue from another perspective and in another scale.[47] The idea of benevolent and useful viruses was very much part of the idea of viral life, and these ideas have a common, though neglected, history.

The connecting node can again be found in Fred Cohen's work. As stated above, Cohen had an early interest in artificial life, when he explicitly figured computer architecture as a form of ecology. Computer organisms, such as viruses, could not be understood outside the context of their natural habitat, which concretely meant the Universal Turing Machine architecture. This led to the important conceptualization of (artificial) life as coupling:

> The essence of a life form is not simply the environment that supports life, nor simply a form which, given the proper environment, will live. The essence of a living system

is the coupling of form with environment. The environment is the context, and the form is the content. If we consider them together, we consider the nature of life.[48]

The formality of the Turing machine presents itself as the ontological technical principle of contemporary digital culture. The idea of algorithmic coding and a machine that is able to process those algorithms forms the basis of this idea, formulated by Cohen in the early 1980s. This Universal Turing Machine is equivalent to digital computers, which are able to code heterogeneous units of information into discrete symbols and process them effectively in their logical circuits.[49] In this sense, the mathematicians of the early twentieth century (Church, Gödel, Turing) were in a key position to define the future of computing machines as *abstract machines* in the technical sense of the term. Logical sequences that controlled a machine's functions were not essentially part of its material form, but algorithmic and formal(ized). What mattered were the blueprints for how specific machines were organized; thus the emphasis was on the formal relationships of parts, not so much the specific material of the parts. This was already the key assumption of artificial life projects.[50]

What Cohen adds to this schema of computers is a viral twist: first, viruses share the formal characteristics of the Turing universe, but, second, viruses include a potential for new forms of evolutionary principles of computing, an evolved version of the Turing machine, which Cohen depicts as the Universal Viral Machine. In other words, this represents a turn to the *virulence* of virus programs, not their payloads. Given that viruses are bits of code that by definition function only to infect, self-reproduce, and activate from time to time, it is no wonder that several computer scientists have been unable to view them as passive material (crude technological components). Instead, they have been viewed as something acting, spreading, almost like living. Rather than just an articulation on the level of the cultural imaginary, this is also a description of the machinic processes of these programs and of digital culture in general.

So perhaps this is the most interesting idea: Cohen's most lasting legacy might actually be the realization that digital culture was on the verge of a paradigm shift from the culture of Universal Turing Machines to an ecology of Universal Viral Machines, which were no longer restricted to the noisy capabilities of the people designing the algorithms. Such evolutionary concepts of computing provided a model for a digital culture that increasingly relied on capabilities of self-reproductive, distributed, semiautonomous actors. To quote Cohen's all-too-neglected words encapsulating the media ecology of networking digital culture:

Since we have shown that an arbitrary machine can be embedded with a virus (The-orem 6), we will now choose a particular class of machines to embed to get a class of viruses with the property that the successive members of the viral set generated from any particular member of the set, contain subsequences which are (in Turing's notation) the successive iterations of the "Universal Computing Machine." The successive members are called "evolutions" of the previous members, and thus any number that can be "computed" by a TM [Turing Machine], can be "evolved" by a virus. We therefore conclude that "viruses" are at least as powerful class of computing machines as TMs, and that there is a "Universal Viral Machine" which can evolve any "computable" number.[51]

In other words, as with Ludwig, viruses were to be understood as powerful mechanisms of computing, not purely as malicious pieces of software, even though malicious subroutines could be part of a virus sequence. Security against malicious software (and the people using it to wage war) was only one component of computer viruses, expressed in the difference between the quasi-code of

```
        subroutine infect-executable:=
        {loop:file = get-random-executable-file;
        if first-line-of-file = 01234567 then goto loop;
        compress file;
        prepend compression-virus to file;
        }
and
        subroutine trigger-pulled:=
        {return true if some condition holds}
        main-program:=
        {infect-executable;
        if trigger-pulled then do-damage;
        goto next;}
```

In plain English, the activities of viruses are not reducible to the potential damage malicious software is capable of inflicting on national and inter-national bodies of organizational order. Even if Cohen's general aim was obviously to find models and procedures for secure computing—in order to maintain the flow of information in a society—this task was accompanied by something of a more fundamental nature. The viral routines were not con-fined to damage; they enabled the idea of benevolent viruses, too. For exam-ple, the "compression virus" could function as an autonomous maintenance unit to save disk space.[52] In 1994 Cohen introduced other such viral programs that for the sake of political correctness were called "live programs," or LPs: software distribution LPs could maintain and update network databases; other

LPs could be used to implement distributed databases because of their built-in parallel processing capabilities; and LPs could also, as noted before, perform such maintenance operations as "hunting down" and killing temporary files.[53]

Hence, the virus was not merely a problematic noisy infiltrator in the channels of communication; it was also a potentially benevolent power of viral computing and "friendly contagions." Tony Sampson has described this new phase of network ecology well:

> The *viral ecosystem* is an alternative to Turing–von Neumann capability. Key to this system is *a benevolent virus, which epitomises the ethic of open culture. Drawing upon a biological analogy, benevolent viral computing reproduces* in order to accomplish its goals; the computing environment *evolving rather than being "designed every step of the way."* (…) The *viral ecosystem demonstrates how the spread of viruses can purposely evolve* through the computational space using the shared processing power of all host machines. Information enters the host machine via infection and a translator program alerts the user. The *benevolent virus passes through the host machine with any additional modifications made by the infected user.*[54]

What Sampson underlines, and what I find a helpful emphasis, is that such ideas are basically grounding steps for a certain form of viral ecosystem of digital culture in which worms and viruses are to be regarded not as necessarily malicious but as potentially powerful processes of computing. Such ideas have been advanced more concretely in genetic algorithm applications that breed new processes and routines for computer systems.

This discussion raises questions: What if we do not take the warnings about and definitions of worms and viruses as malicious at their face value, but look for alternative definitions, such as Cohen's or Ludwig's, or practices such as genetic algorithms or cellular automata? What if we take these more or less marginal ideas as the starting point in the countermapping of an alternative, a supplementary, understanding of viruses and the cultural history of digital culture in general? Even if such ideas gained explicit consistency at the end of the 1980s and beginning of the 1990s, their lineages span back through the early experiments with network computing of the 1960s and 1970s all the way to the computing pioneers of the 1940s and 1950s.

Cellular Automata and Simulated Ecologies

If our digital culture starts with Turing and von Neumann, then so does the culture(ing) of digital viruses. The Turing machine also leads to Universal Virus Machines that are self-reproductive automatized calculating processes, not far from the idea of later genetic algorithms and other forms of evolutionary calculation. As Fred Cohen perhaps slightly ironically noted at one point, the Morris worm of 1988 was perhaps to be understood as the most powerful high-speed computation event ever![55] In an e-mail to me in 2005, Cohen stressed the same point about computation in distributed networks: "The point is that viruses are general purpose computing mechanisms and, as such, could be useful for reliable, high performance, resilient, distributed computing."[56] Parasitic power can, then, be understood as springing from an experiment in massive parallel computing that uses thousands of computers on the Internet to further its patterns, as with the Internet worm. Such viruses and worms "in the wild" have frequently been the focus of researchers, but one must notice that often worm and virus programs have been tested only in restricted conditions. In this sense, several worms and viruses discussed here are "laboratory viruses," or, as was the case with von Neumann's replicating programs, they were merely formal models, mathematical patterns.

As von Neumann thought in the aftermath of World War II, designing computers meant designing organs and organisms, that is, machines that could function independently as natural beings. The relationship between nature and technology was, however, complex:

> Natural organisms are, as a rule, much more complicated and subtle, and therefore much less well understood in detail, than are artificial automata. Nevertheless, some regularities which we observe in the organization of the former may be quite instructive in our thinking and planning of the latter; and conversely, a good deal of our experiences and difficulties with our artificial automata can be to some extent projected on our interpretations of natural organisms.[57]

Nature has been a regular imaginary reference point for digital culture ever since. Of course, the cybernetic and computer science and systems theory projects had very down-to-earth, pragmatic aims of developing efficient tools for simulating and controlling complex environments. Herbert Simon's ideas from the 1960s of how artificial systems reflect the complexity of their surroundings, just as ants couple as part of their environment, gives a good idea of how control management was conceptualized during the latter half of the twentieth century. Simon sees the artifact as interfacing the inner environment with its outside, the surroundings. Simon also gives a special place to digital computers as systems of imitation and simulation.[58] Computers catalyzed and channeled the complexity of the larger social field, and specific computer routines, such as virality, were also an interfacing with the complexity of the surrounding social field.

Yet, applications and systems are to be seen as events beyond their predefined goals, and as introducing interesting ideas in complexity, becoming, and virality. This is a point I want to open up from the perspective of media ecologies. As Elisabeth Grosz notes, we are obliged to think of such ecologies not in terms of holistic balance, of unity, but as a mutual production of partners that interact. To emphasize the *ecological* aspect, this should not be understood as a representation or a mirroring, nor even perhaps as the metaphorization of technology via nature, but as a connection where neither partner to the union precedes the other and both enter into a symbiotic emerging, a conjunction of flows. Hence, instead of ecological balance, we have a "disunified series of systems, a series of disparate flows, energies, events, or entities, bringing together or drawing apart their more or less temporary alignments."[59]

Technological and biological constellations of power and knowledge are continuously intertwined and connected via feedback loops. Such circuitry has, of course, happened on the level of language, and also in concrete design projects and plans. Such have touched not merely the specialized field of computing labs but also, through various intermediaries, the everyday life of computerized societies around the globe, laying a sort of digital ecology on top of the other ecologies (natural, societal, industrial, economical, psychical, etc.). Such an idea is close to Félix Guattari's three ecologies. In other words, computer ecology refers here to a need to include complexity as part of the designs of network culture, where "ecology" does not remain a linguistic metaphor but becomes a more fundamental concept to elaborate the topological nature of network culture. Such couplings have also been continuously used as economic strategies underlining the "naturalness" of certain trends of cybernetic media culture (an extrapolation of the past into the future).[60] If we recognize the politics and the economic value in this use of biological concepts, this coupling can be further discussed in terms of not merely ecology but ethology, as briefly addressed in the Intermezzo and with the help of Deleuze and Guattari.

What matter are the intensive movements that define how, for example, cybernetic systems work, how certain potentials are captured (domesticated) for capitalist profit-making, and how alternative models of coupling are restricted and labeled as dangerous and as an expression of vandalism. This ethological touch can be developed into a becoming-animal of computer culture, a mutual becoming—not imitating but codetermining diagramming, capturing affects and relations from another sphere and contracting them into a technological mode of composition.[61] In the history of computing, "learning" from biological intensities of life has been a continuous theme, and the work done in laboratories and computer science departments has not been only about metaphorics but also about capturing the potentials and affects living entities express.

In the history of computing, couplings of biology and technology have been articulated on various levels. As regularly pointed out, the contemporary culture of digital computers owes a lot to von Neumann's design of computer architecture. This von Neumann model is to be understood primarily as a general-purpose, stored-program machine that is also reprogrammable. The central processing unit is separated from the memory (and the input/output functions), and the presence of storage memory allows instructions to be handled as data. We can speak of an organism of sorts, understood as a hierarchical set of "organs" that function in collaboration, relating to processing, memory, control, and user interaction. This is something that also allows the basic functioning of viruses: after instructions were stored in the form of data, viruses also could "take over" the instruction routines handling the functions and operations of the computer. Whereas earlier computer programming meant mechanically altering the hardware—hardwiring the computer—with von Neumann came the idea that one could store these connections in the form of informational patterns. This made it possible for a computer program to interrupt and alter the data and processes of other programs.[62]

Von Neumann was also engaged with issues of parallel and evolutionary computing, distributed information processing, and neural nets, which became the central trends of digital culture only some years after his work. Although, particularly from the end of the 1940s, he was interested in mapping analogies between technology and the human neural system, von Neumann was not a naïve proponent of the analogy between the brain and the computer or of any other simple form of artificial intelligence. As George Dyson writes, von Neumann was actually preoccupied not so much with the question of thinking machines as with designing computers that could *learn to reproduce*.[63]

Von Neumann was deeply engaged with automaton theory, where automaton refers to "any system that processes information as part of a self-regulating mechanism."[64] Automata capable of reproduction included logical control mechanisms (modeled on the McCulloch–Pitts theory of neurons), the necessary channels for communication between the original automaton and the one under construction, and muscles to enable the creation. This kinetic model of automata was, however, soon discarded, as it proved to be too complex for actual construction: a physical automaton was dependent on its environment for a continuous supply of resources, and providing it with such an ecology proved to be too cumbersome. It would have had to be more like a whole factory of self-reproducing automata. Von Neumann turned to developing *cellular* automata, formal models of reproductive systems with "crystalline regularities."[65] One of the models for formal self-reproductive patterns was the very primitive living organism, the bacteriophage.[66] This is an amusing analogy when we remember that the early "bacteria" programs in mainframe computers have been listed as among the oldest forms of programmed threats.[67] Of course, these programs got their name because of their ability to clog the computer's memory and disk space via extensive reproduction (and, in fact, were an earlier form of the forkbomb routine).

Von Neumann was also very interested in virology. Just after World War II he turned to viruses as the minimal organisms that are interesting because of their ability for orientation, reproduction, and mutation. For von Neumann, such minuscule subcellular actors were links between information processing and life sciences, particularly because of their ability to reproduce.[68] In general, virus research had raised novel perspectives concerning the "informatics of life." These were of keen interest to researchers in molecular biology but also to the wider public, as a headline from the *New York Times* in 1955 demonstrates: "Reconstruction of a Virus in Laboratory Opens the Question: What Is Life?"[69] This research is interesting both as an archaeological trait of studies of artificial life and as part of the interconnection of living organisms and synthetic systems. Lily E. Kay notes how "viruses and genes were becoming agents of information storage and transfer"[70] during the 1950s, and the virus of biological research was itself becoming an informational entity already, before computer viruses per se were invented.

Von Neumann himself did not publish anything on the topic of cellular automata. He engaged with the topic around 1946 and discussed his ideas at Princeton and at the Hixon symposium in Pasadena, California, a couple of years later, under the title of "The Logic of Analogue Nets and Automata." In December 1949, von Neumann addressed the issue at the University of Illinois in five lectures entitled "The Theory and Organization of Complicated Automata." The theme of cellular automata was then continued in an incomplete manuscript, "The Theory of Automata: Construction, Reproduction, Homogeneity," originally from 1952–1953 but published posthumously in the 1960s.[71] Hence, it is clear that von Neumann did not achieve any clear results, and even fewer "products," from the research; rather, they remained sketches that resonate with issues especially established decades later. Such models were, however, influential in the field of molecular genetics, where in general cybernetic system theories they functioned as effective catalyzers of genetic research and, for instance, the discovery of the structure of DNA in Cambridge (UK) by Watson and Crick's team.[72]

Von Neumann's ideas of cellular automata were distributed by John Kemeny in *Scientific American* in the 1955 article "Man Viewed as a Machine." It was mutually arranged that he would write an article based on von Neumann's Vanuxem lectures at Princeton University in 1953.[73] Drawing a history from Turing's machines to von Neumann, Kemeny emphasized the idea of reproduction that von Neumann added to previous models of logic machines. Cellular automata are such reproduction machines that spread according to their internal logic and self-organizing movements. Of course, the model was basically quite simple: a space divided into cubical cells, occupied by "entities" or "actors" that interact according to the logic of the nervous system. The state of a cell is determined by its current state and its relationship with neighboring cells. The whole automaton changes in cycles: "The neurons and transmission cells are either quiescent or they can send out an impulse if properly stimulated. The muscle cells receive commands from the neurons through the transmission cells, and react either by 'killing' some undesired part (i.e., making it inert) or by transforming some inert cell in the environment to a machine part of a specified kind."[74]

A more extensive selection of von Neumann's work on automata was collected and edited by Arthur Burks in 1966 in his *Theory of Self-Reproducing Automata*. The work reveals that von Neumann was actually thinking of five different forms of self-reproductive behavior: kinematic, cellular, continuous, probabilistic, and one based on the excitation–threshold–fatigue model. In general, as he noted at the beginning of his 1949 lectures entitled "Theory and Organization of Complicated Automata," computing machines were a *variety* of artificial automata,[75] implying, of course, that whereas automata were a mathematical and formal problem, computers were more intimately tied to practical engineering work. What was evident was that even though von Neumann was working in the context of computers that were still more or less mere number crunchers, such ideas already went some way toward understanding computers as potential simulation machines that could function as a form of ecology and in some ways partially autonomously. Programming code and run-time are not reducible to each other; the machine contains more than what is being consciously inputted, and with the complexity of systems this fact becomes even more pronounced. This is underlined by the construction of visual aids to facilitate the understanding of the complex nature of such operations. Instead of a linear, one-dimensional calculation we have now a two-dimensional diagram of computing events that would be hard to grasp without visual tools to think with. What we have with such reproducing machines are "nerve cells," "muscle cells," and a tail that contains the instructions for producing offspring, as Kemeny explains.[76] It is as if the whole computing process had come alive with parts that refer to processes of the living world. Of course, the visual nature of such operations was emphasized in subsequent developments of cellular automata, to which I return shortly. At the center were the new diagrams of machinic life, successors of the circuit diagrams of Gottlob Frege's *Begriffsschrift*. Writing had turned into a two-dimensional coordinate system, a technological diagram.

Figure 6. The von Neumann universal constructor is one example of how automata are diagrammatized as two-dimensional figures.

Source: Burks 1970, 44. Image used with permission, © Arthur W. Burks.

Thus, what we have with such cellular automata is a model for parallel processing computing that, once put into action, could potentially go on uninterrupted. But how does such a checkerboard structure with organism-like creatures, or neurons, provide us with a precedent for computer viruses? Instead of seeing cellular automata as a direct ancestor of contemporary viruses, it forms a point of orientation within the history of digital culture that offers the backdrop to the material and incorporeal network structure of the contemporary media condition. In other words, even if the classic von Neumann computer architecture is often seen as the paradigmatic technological model of computer culture, we might further emphasize the role of this abstract model of parallel processing, of replicatory self-organizing systems. Von Neumann believed that the development of automaton theory would be in connection with developments in probability theory, thermodynamics, and information theory, suggesting that the field of inquiry into automata would have to deal also with new paradigms of thinking and logic for computing machinery. As Arthur Burks notes, von Neumann thought that there were "qualitatively new principles involved in systems of great complexity" and he searched "for these principles in the phenomenon of self-reproduction, which clearly depends on complexity."[77] Such aspirations found further resonance after some decades with theories of complexity, artificial life, and network cultures, which were increasingly understood as ecologies.

Other ideas of computational ecologies of complex nature emerged during the 1950s.[78] Among them, Nils Barricelli's 1953 experiments with ideas of symbiogenesis applied to computers stand out. The Princeton Institute of Advanced Studies again provided the playground facilities for such artificial ecologies and digital creatures, as it did for several other key computer projects of post–World War II America. Barricelli's project is important for being more than a mathematical formula, as it engaged in actual experimental work with the institute's computer, whereas von Neumann himself always refrained from practical engineering work with computers. Although he was interested in symbiogenesis as a biological phenomenon, Barricelli proceeded to deterritorialize it from its basis in plasmatic life. Konstantin Merezhkovsky had defined symbiogenesis at the beginning of the century, giving the original impetus for ideas that look at evolution as mergings of distinct entities into symbiotic forms. Competition as the basic form of evolution was thus challenged by cooperation, as Lynn Margulis emphasized later during the twentieth century.[79]

Barricelli approached the process of symbiogenetic evolution not as tied to a specific substance but also as a certain general pattern that could be tested in any phylum. The computer memory offered Barricelli a platform to engage in experiments with processes that could be speeded up. George Dyson describes Barricelli's computer program in the following manner:

> Working directly in binary machine instruction code, Barricelli constructed a cyclical universe of 512 cells, each cell occupied by a number (or the absence of a number) encoded by 8 bits. Simple rules that Barricelli referred to as "norms" governed the propagation of numbers (or "genes"), a new generation appearing as if by metamorphosis after the execution of a certain number of cycles by the central arithmetic unit of the machine.[80]

The reproduction of genes was tied to the other genes, which effectively made the cells into an interconnected whole. "Connectedness" and "interdependence" were the key terms in Barricelli's own ecology of computer symbiogenesis, which provided him with interesting results concerning the interactions and complexity of such a system. Of specific interest in the context of this book are the parasites. At first, the parasites threatened the balance of the system by reproducing too actively, and Barricelli inhibited this reproduction using a specific norm that allowed parasites to reproduce only once per generation. This led to the parasites becoming either harmless or even useful symbiotic genes.

Instead of seeing his tests focusing on biological phenomena as *representations* or second-order models of natural processes, they were something more dynamic: "They are not models, not any more than living organisms are models. They are a particular class of self-reproducing structures already defined."[81] What we have here is an affirmation of the computer as a simulation machine that is not merely a *tool* to research the real world outside it. Instead, the computer was in Barricelli's experiments enacted as an ecology on its own, not subordinate to any other transcendent reality. Whether the organisms within the computer were living according to a comprehensive definition of the term is irrelevant; what is important is that they were real in their own environment. It is unnecessary for our purposes to point out the possible problems with Barricelli's ideas from a biological viewpoint. Again, what is important is that he designed a system with organisms and parasites that would be able to reproduce and evolve within a computer environment—something that cannot be neglected when mapping the genealogy of computer worms and viruses.

Barricelli's ecosystem was supported by the logic circuits and vacuum tubes of the computer designed by von Neumann for scientific work. Von Neumann perhaps never got the chance to know about these practical implementations of computational ecology, as he left Princeton in 1954 and died just a few years later. Computer scientists and biologists neglected Barricelli's work, and only during the 1990s did Barricelli acquire the status he deserves as one of the pioneers in artificial life.[82]

What is, of course, noteworthy is that the IAS (Institute for Advanced Study) computer, like computers of that time in general, was designed for weapons research, in particular computations concerning atomic weapons. At the same time, it was used to interface nature and technology in novel ways, for instance, with calculations concerning weather phenomena, and in creating such artificial ecologies as Barricelli's experiments. Technologies of death could also be used to create new modes of life.

The 1950s saw the first artificial intelligence applications in the form of simulations and tests with human–machine interfaces. RAND Corporation, founded in 1946, was a think tank funded by the Defense Department and dedicated to interdisciplinary forecasting of social trends, and we owe to it several of the key innovations in networking. It received its own version of von Neumann's IAS computer in 1952 and an IBM 701 in 1953.[83]

RAND's two computers were used for simulation purposes. One of the chief architects was Allen Newell, the 1975 Turing award winner, who emphasized the potential of such simulation practices: computers were clearly more than large calculators and were capable of maintaining complex symbolic processes.[84] The future became a computational issue, but besides the Cold War politics, the computational epistemology was also an ecology. Computers were occasionally during the 1950s seen as self-organizing systems. Particularly interesting is the report from 1959 by Beatrice and Sydney Rome on the Leviathan system, developed at the System Development Corporation (a spin-off from the RAND think tank).[85] Leviathan was a system for organization analysis that simulated social events and flows of information. It was to be based on adaptability and not only on preprogrammed systems of sequential logical steps: "It appears reasonably certain that neither classical symbolic logic nor existing mathematical formulations of social processes are adequate at present to provide analytical predictive control over such multi-level processes."[86] The system is a good expression of the Cold War emphasis on analysis and simulation of social, economic, and military scenarios.

Leviathan was a self-organizing system that integrated humans in cybernetic fashion as part of the circuits. In my view, it presents an even more interesting scenario of human–computer interaction than Wiener's cybernetics in that the Leviathan model is directly conceived as a form of media ecology. In a way, the model was not planned as a computational enhancement of, for example, decision making but as a more thorough platform or an environment. Of course, its purpose was very functionally defined: to find efficient models of hierarchical organizational interaction. More interesting was the way this research was conducted and the presupposition expressed that organizations are multilayered and dynamic systems, built from the bottom up, "in analogy to the organization of molecules into cells, of cells into organs, of organs into animals."[87] The IBM 709 was in this regard analogous to the molecular and animal kingdom and also to "large social groups," which were analyzed in terms of their functions, coalitions, policies, and, importantly, flow of information, where the temporal dynamics of the system was emphasized. In the system, social actions were described in terms of interactive computer processes—computerized agents:

> Our program, then, begins with a design for an automaton that will be made to operate in a computer. Circuits will be so imposed on the computer that their performance will be analogous to the operations of human agents in real social groups. Next, we shall cut the computer free from its ordinarily employed ability to accomplish mathematical computations. (…) The patterns and entailments of the specific activations will be controlled so that they will be isomorphic with significant aspects of individual human actions. (…) The micro-processes in the computer resemble the microfunctioning of real agents under social constraints."[88]

As George Dyson notes, the project became "an extensive experiment in communication and information handling,"[89] introducing new ways to understand organizations. These were inherently learning systems, a concept that was later adapted as a key phrase of information capitalist culture in general, alongside "flexibility." We could reasonably argue that this has been an aspiration in systems design ever since these projects of cybernetics and systems theory. This reminds us of the fact that adaptive computer systems have been discussed at least since the end of the 1950s.[90] Illustrative in this context was Oliver Selfridge's Pandemonium project, which was modeled to receive and analyze Morse code. As Dyson notes, Selfridge's project from the end of the 1950s was based on Darwinian principles of information evolution. It was also modeled as a parallel processor, which Selfridge saw as a more "natural" manner of handling information. The Pandemonium platform was inhabited by a semiautonomous code of processing demons:

> At the bottom the data demons serve merely to store and pass on the data. At the next level the computational demons or sub-demons perform certain more or less

complicated computations on the data and pass the results of these up to the next
level, the cognitive demons who weigh all the evidence, as it were. Each cognitive
demon computes a shriek, and from all the shrieks the highest level demon of all, the
decision demon, merely selects the loudest.[91]

Pandemonium predated contemporary probabilistic choice tools by decades.
Even though it was too heavy or "wasteful" in its own time, Pandemonium
clearly exhibited system tendencies that actualized on a large scale only
decades later in the 1980s. Manuel DeLanda sees Pandemonium as an early
form of computational ecology that one can find in autonomous weapons systems and also in global computer networks. Intelligence is distributed to local
actors, which "barter, bid, and compete" for resources and consequently create
complex interactional patterns. Such interactions of computer demons can be
seen as societies reminiscent of natural ecologies, similar to insect societies.[92]
In Pandemonium, a special place was reserved for "natural selection," which
was supposed to allow the system to evolve in a self-organized manner, independent of its designers. The successful demons were fed back to the system for
evaluation so that the overall scheme for a specific task was kept optimal. The
idea was to create "organisms" and "processes" that survived and were thus fit
for replication: "Therefore, instead of having but one Pandemonium we might
have some crowd of them, all fairly similarly constructed, and employ natural
selection on the crowd of them. Eliminate the relatively poor and encourage
the rest to generate new machines in their own images."[93] It is obvious that
such projects were very keen on using Darwinian ideas and phrases.

In other words, we have already, since the 1950s, an important amount of
research on computer processes that are based on self-organization and replication, complexity, and a certain simulacrum of algorithmic nature. Cybernetic
research was in a key position with a keen interest in systems that displayed
traits of growth, learning, and self-reproduction. Patterns of differentiation
were planned for complex artificial systems, which were intended to be learning systems, open to their surroundings (instead of merely developing systems,
closed to information coming from outside).[94]

Norbert Wiener included a chapter with the title "On Learning and
Self-Reproducing Machines" in the second edition of his influential Cybernetics book. Wiener writes in 1961 about living systems as having the power to
learn and to reproduce:

These properties, different as they appear, are intimately related to one another.
An animal that learns is one which is capable of being transformed by its past

environment into a different being and is therefore adjustable to its environment within its individual lifetime. An animal that multiplies is able to create other animals in its own likeness at least approximately, although not so completely in its own likeness that they cannot vary in the course of time.[95]

The issues of learning and reproduction in machines were also central to his 1964 book *God and Golem, Inc.* Wiener saw that such weird creatures, of *machines* recreating themselves and even learning, provided a threat to the established (religious) worldview of man at the center of the universe. Taking as his cue religious metaphysical themes such as "man creates man in his own image," Wiener asked a key question of the late twentieth century: "What is the image of a machine? Can this image, as embodied in one machine, bring a machine of general sort, not yet committed to a particular specific identity, to reproduce the original machine, either absolutely or under some change that may be construed as a variation?"[96] This question addressed the very ontological premises of machines but also their connection with humans. The Turing machine seemed to offer such a platform for these thoughts, in a similar way to how novel biological theories of evolution increasingly addressed symbiosis and nonlinear evolution. Also, Wiener contributed words towards issues of molecular replication.[97] As Alex Galloway notes, Wiener's ideas of life saw it as resisting the second law of thermodynamics, which states that the world is governed by entropy. Life works through creating consistencies that (temporarily) resist entropy. Galloway emphasizes that Wiener's radical significance is in the way he includes machines in this diagram: technologically created "organisms," too, can resist entropy and hence are by this definition something akin to living beings.[98] Of course, cybernetics in general was occupied with such an agenda, as, for example, Michael J. Apter's study *Cybernetics and Development* from 1966 demonstrates.[99] In addition, various biological and ethological ideas were incorporated into experimental projects, an apt example being adaptation machines that learn, a project at MIT in the early 1970s.[100]

The projects and designs mapped the computer as a simulation platform or a cybernetic environment where artificial agents were promoted to be active participants in the self-organization of such ecological platforms. What Wiener engaged with was the production of the design blueprints, or at least ideas, for such agents. Repeating the *topos* of the digital culture design of interfacing nature with technology, Wiener studied animal behavior and characteristics to organize them into digital environments. Why were Wiener and so many other computer pioneers preoccupied with nature and animals?

The key explanation lies in the realization that they are the perfect examples and models for complex systems, adaptive behavior, collective functioning, ecological coupling, and self-reproduction, all themes that were incorporated into the third nature of the network culture.[101]

All in all, such perspectives reveal that seeing computers as merely calculating machines misses several points. This whole section revolves around the intertwining genealogy of computer worms and viruses, artificial life of complexity, and the network culture; such ideas did perhaps, on a wider scale, actualize during the 1980s, but they had a reality already in the 1950s. Interesting are the mediators—for example, computer projects, design blueprints, or other texts—that partly incorporate certain ideas of artificial life, worms and viruses, or network computing "before their time." This realization relates to the method of "accidentalization" or "eventualization" and producing a countermemory, a genealogy. We are not looking for origins and natural filiations. Instead, we are looking for events, perhaps even *lost* ones, that raise the issue of *Herkunft*, "descent." Following Foucault, genealogy does not mean deciphering continuities behind appearances, as the past is not present as any lived reality but only in fragments of the archive, as monuments. Genealogy as a method of cultural analysis activates the need for a rethinking of archaeological events as constituent of our present being, but also as a potential way to look for new modes of being. Genealogy becomes a way to underline the Nietzschean will-to-knowledge that underlies any apparently innocent truth or natural state of being. One must follow the deviations instead of the usual narratives in order to fulfill the full potential of the genealogical method.[102]

Organisms of Distributed Networks

Leibniz had already imagined a machine that allows numbers themselves to do the counting. Machines, but also numbering numbers, might actually have a life independent of the human fallacy of anthropocentrism. The automata illustrate a key theme of the twentieth century, earlier than computers. Automated machines had been a source of amazement since the eighteenth century, the early years of industrialization. The Vaucanson duck and other moving machines exhibited the idea of simulation of life, and hence the beginnings of artificial life, in their uncanny self-movement and coordination of systematic activities. In factory production, this was part of the normalized functioning of the institution.[103] Manuel DeLanda sees this automatization of tasks from the human to the machine as the crucial moment in the birth of software, locating the focal point in Jacquard's loom and subsequently Babbage's interests in analytical machines and the transformation of control from humans to machines. Jacquard's loom incorporated data (but not control) as part of its card program system. This idea was used for decades with tabulators and calculators, but the principle of the Turing machine included the idea that control structures, the instructions for handling data, could also be represented as data. As DeLanda notes in his genealogy of distributed system intelligence, Turing emphasized in the 1950s the movement of control from hardware to software with the idea that computer tasks can be distributed into subprograms (although still at that point subjugated to the master program). The ideas of computer science were closely related to, for example, Herbert Simon's theories of the design of complex artificial systems from the 1960s.[104]

In 1922, *Scientific American* prophesied how "strips of paper," that is, machines programmed with perforated punch cards, would be taking control: "The time is coming when workmen will be largely supplanted by such strips of paper; when a walk through a factory will disclose hundreds of machines in operation with a mere handful of attendants fussing about. *In some uncanny way, things will seem to be running themselves.*"[105] Years later, such uncanny technological quasi-objects seemed to be multiplying, and the latter half of the twentieth century was repeatedly characterized as an age of automation. In this light it is interesting to review the Darwin and Core Wars projects briefly analyzed in the first section of the book. As we learned, Darwin was an early game-like program designed at the AT&T Bell laboratories in the early 1960s. The game's digital organisms fought for the memory space of the computer, each trying to win the habitat for itself. Despite such "hostile" implications, the game can also be viewed as a digital world of sorts. The game was played inside the computer: whereas a conventional game might use its game board as a mere tool for human-to-human interaction, Darwin allowed the platform to take on a life of its own.[106]

Vic Vyssotsky was one of the programmers, and he recalls that the question driving their work was whether such self-reproducing organisms could be built: "I wasn't thinking in terms of 'viruses' or 'Trojan Horses' or 'worms' or whatever; I was just idly curious about what the most simple and effective ways would be of designing programs whose only function would be to make copies of themselves."[107] The patterns were, on a local level, simple: programs in Darwin tried (1) to replicate in unoccupied parts of the game arena (a restricted part of the memory) and (2) to destroy other species by attacking their memory locations. Vyssotsky, Doug McIllroy, and Robert Morris used a biologically loaded vocabulary of "species" and "organisms" to describe the game, which leads one to think of miniecologies of digital nature. The organisms were constrained by simple rules that kept the programs bounded within the arena but that also allowed cooperation and synergy in the game: "[An organism] may employ any desired computational procedures, may look at any cell in the arena, including cells occupied by members of other species. A player is entitled to make the members of his species communicate or cooperate in any desired fashion, or he may make them ignore each other."[108]

As mentioned earlier Darwin was picked up again after years of silence in the early 1980s. The Core Wars game of A. K. Dewdney used similar premises for its operations. Again, the emphasis was on the novel ecology of semiautonomous actors: "It is unlike almost all other computer games in that people do not play at all! The contending programs are written by people, of course, but once a battle is under way the creator of a program can do nothing but watch helplessly as the product of hours spent in design and implementation either lives or dies on the screen."[109]

In Core Wars and Darwin we see a culmination of the early interests in programs that exhibit autonomous behavior within a computer environment. Although computers had, of course, been designed from the beginning as sort of automation machines for extensive mathematical tasks, their automatism was limited as the operator had to control and interact with the processes of early mainframe computers. In this context, such autonomous processes were undoubtedly inspiring: computers and programs that act nearly autonomously, cooperate, and even reproduce. There was even the slight chance of an unplanned spread of these epidemics, as Vyssotsky recalls: "At that time there was of course nothing like the Internet, but the various computation centers of Bell Labs were networked together for load-balancing, and the Bell Labs operating system BE SYS was used by many other organizations, shipped out on mag[netic] tape, and the last thing we wanted was to have one of our beasties accidentally wind up on a distribution tape of BE SYS."[110]

Such ideas were not restricted to Darwin but followed from very simple realizations. The "Move(program counter) program counter+1" command made the computer follow a repetitious process to fill up its memory and was used as a cleanup utility in early core memory computers, such as the IBM 1620 (released in 1959).[111] Similar recursive processes were mobilized in the form of rabbit programs that turned the linear structure of batch processing computers into loop structures. The instructions were sent back to the beginning of the jobstream queue, which caused "constipation."[112] Of course, such commands could be perpetual motion machines only on a fictional Turing machine, where the tape would be imagined as infinite. Nevertheless, the idea of a computer recursively processing its own output seems fascinating: computer software parasiting its "host."

As a challenge to the traditional metaphysical view of inert material, these technological organisms seemed to have a potential life of their own—"beasties," as Vyssotsky called them. Technology was not anymore merely the massive machines of iron and steel, but now the subtle electronics that had a special relation to information. Referring to the computer culture of the 1960s, the 1983 Turing award winner, Ken Thompson, recalls a set of programs called "life":

> A computer program would have a set of species, they would interact with other species, they would live, die, reproduce, etc. based on these interactions. Species would eat species, species would kill species for no reason. Species would gang up and kill species. Species would compete for reproduction, etc. We thought of it as an aquarium full of things that tried to survive for a long time.[113]

According to Thompson, such self-reproducing programs were tested in computer departments and labs in the early 1960s. Thompson also recalls Darwin as a program based on similar ideas to "life": for the young programmers, it was "easy and straight forward."[114] Von Neumann's ideas of cellular automata of self-reproduction were also actively on the agenda of computer programmers during the 1960s and 1970s.[115] In particular, another program called Life has often been mentioned in connection with viruses.

Von Neumann's cellular automata were at one point even seen as the basis for a Cellular Automata Machine. Among the most important and famous proponents of research into cellular automata has been Stephen Wolfram, whose project, started in the 1980s, has been to show how the world in general is an ontological grid based on the logic of cellular automata. These have been used as calculatory principles "drawing" complex patterns that, according to Wolfram, are nature's own patterns, found, for example, in mussel shells.[116] Such projects are a good example of how complex simulation machines such as cellular automata have, since the 1960s and 1970s, been seen also as the essence of nature and the world. If genes have been informationalized, so has the cosmos at large too.

We will, however, take a more modest approach and focus on computer structures and simulations. As mentioned, another life program, or Game of Life as it has also been called, is seen as influential in this respect. John

Conway was working as a mathematician at the University of Cambridge in the late 1960s when he remodeled the von Neumann cellular automata into "a game" where the cells could have only two states: dead or alive, on or off. Game of Life was "played" on a checkerboard structure, where the aim was to inspect the possibilities of growing complex structures using basic building principles. Conway was also interested in the principles of universal computation, but we can focus on the more concretely defined implications of this work and the attention it has received. Hence, the two important aspects of this computer project include that it was "one of the earliest attempts to simulate something resembling life on a computer"[117] and its practical experience with interacting, complex computational structures.

Self-reproduction had a key role in the Game of Life and other early cellular automata. Such games were designed in the 1960s and 1970s to simulate patterns of proliferation and growth, and molecular biologists such as Manfred Eigen used similar ideas with a special emphasis on introducing errors, mutations, and randomness into the games.[118] Whereas Eigen was after evolution, Conway's aim, including that of others such as computer scientist Tommaso Toffoli's, was to show how such simple principles could extend to processes and phenomena that were self-reproducing and self-sustaining.[119] The interest was in automating certain computational processes: even if programmers were responsible for coding the basic behavior of the cells and the grid, the aim was to let the cells interact in a way that would make the structure emerge into a second-order phenomenon, able to sustain its own being without external help.

From von Neumann's cellular automata onwards, such ideas represented the goal to see nature as a computational process and to analyze (and synthesize) such phenomena of *global computation*. Relying on ideas of population thinking, global computation has meant modeling computational ecologies as a form of evolutionary phenomena. Evolution, however, has been viewed on the basis of populations not individuals, meaning that evolution and other Darwinist phenomena happen on the statistically approachable level of "global" populations. Cellular automata, as one form of such biological computation, are thought of as using such fundamental computational models of evolution in their systems. Local and simple rules governing relationships of cells produce widespread global results that span the whole of the (cellular automaton) system. Such ideas developed during the late twentieth century represent attempts to capture computational procedures of population biology, or as Terranova differentiates this from of cellular automaton computation from linearly biased models: "Biological computation envisages an abstract computational diagram able to simulate (and hence capture) the productive capacities of multitudes of discrete and interacting elements. The most productive challenge of (cellular automaton) systems to the sequential computer lies in the fact that they do not start with the easily controllable linearity of a tape, but with the multiplicity of a population."[120]

If we look at Conway's work from another perspective, his aim resided in creating a self-replicating machine.[121] The main focus was perhaps not on the cells but on the interactions between them that created the replication process. This emergent phenomenon implied that replication was something inherently part of the world, and part of the simulated computer environment. Such "recreational mathematics" were recognized also as part of the history of mathematical organisms and simulations: "Because of its analogies with the rise, fall, and alterations of a society of living organisms, it belongs to a growing class of what are called 'simulation games'—games that resemble real-life processes,"[122] as Martin Gardner described Conway's brainchild in his famous "Mathematical Games" column in 1970.

Whereas Conway focused on "cells" and their interaction as the basic pattern of automata, another experiment at the MIT Artificial Intelligence laboratory referred already in 1973 to "worms." Michael Beeler wrote a memo on his mathematical tests of a pattern called "Paterson's worm," which was named after Michael Paterson and John Conway's original ideas concerning the mathematical modeling of a prehistoric worm that follows innate rules regarding its movements and actions. Paleontologists had traced the fossils of such worms; mathematicians tried to bring them back to life as simulations:

> Early in 1971, Michael Paterson mentioned to me a mathematical idealization of the prehistoric worm. He and John Conway had been interested in a worm constrained to eat food only along the grid lines of graph paper. Take, for instance, quadrille paper, and let a "worm egg" hatch at an intersection in an arbitrarily large grid of food. The worms starts eating in some direction, say east (E). When it has traveled one unit of distance, it arrives at a new intersection. Its behavior at this (and every following) intersection is determined by a set of fixed, innate rules. Each rule is of the form, "if the intersection has distribution D of eaten and uneaten segments, then leave the node via (uneaten) grid segment G."[123]

Paleontological digital worms? It's difficult to avoid the lure of metaphorics, but there is more there in the lineage of computer processes based on models and also as simulations of life. There was von Neumann's idea of creating computational "organisms," and the same idea was used in Michael Apter's mid-1960s notions of simulating developing organisms on a computer. Apter used in his examples the sea urchin and the zygote, among others.[124] Nature in its complexity and efficiency also proved to be an ideal partner to be interfaced in these computer projects of the end of the twentieth century. As the organizational and processual requirements of society and thus communication networks grew more complex, solutions were sought from the highly intriguing organizational patterns of animals and their milieus. As Evelyn Fox Keller writes in discussing the entanglement of cybernetics and life sciences on the post–World War II agenda: "Can it be any surprise, then, that in the bootstrap process of modeling organisms and machines, each upon the other, not only do organisms and machines come increasingly to resemble each other but that, as they do, the meaning of both terms undergoes some rather critical changes?"[125]

In other words, these pilot projects of digital organisms and interaction paved the way for new informational milieus. Network projects and the creation of distributed interactions, in particular, can be seen as occupying the crucial position, especially from the viewpoint of contemporary globalized Internet culture.

Of course, John Conway's game was still based on such simplicity that he could use a single Digital PDP-7 computer for his experiments on life.[126] These processes were not network organisms, even though such experiments paved the way for the distributed programs to come. Yet, in general, the growing efficiency of computers that could process more complex simulations was a key requirement for such tests. Even though one should be careful not to put too much weight on the rhetoric of information revolutions, George Dyson's notes on the changing face of computing power during the 1960s and 1970s are interesting. Dyson writes how the microprocessor boom of the 1970s led to a huge number of new numerical symbio-organisms—that is, new programs and new code. Dyson's choice of words takes careful advantage of the ecological implications. Even though we are used to talking about the history of computers as focused on people making computers and code and using them (whether it is the focus on the inventors and geniuses behind the machines or the recent emphasis on users in cultural studies of technology), it is possible to take an even more complex view and look at the big picture as one formed of parasites, symbionts, and interdependency, just as in any ecology. To follow Dyson, most software can thus be seen as parasitic/symbiotic, because it depends on the "host metabolism" or the structuration to which it is coupled. Dyson refers to the new operating systems:

By the 1960s complex numerical symbioorganisms known as operating systems had evolved, bringing with them entire ecologies of symbionts, parasites, and coevolving hosts. The most successful operating systems, such as OS/360, MS-DOS, and UNIX, succeeded in transforming and expanding the digital universe to better propagate themselves. It took five thousand programmer-years of effort to write and debug the OS/360 code; the parasites and symbionts sprouted up overnight.[127]

But it needs to be underlined that Dyson problematically naturalizes operating systems and programs without taking into account the other side of the coin. Cybernetic systems are based on control, modulation, cultivation, and updating, instead of being straightforwardly emergent.[128] They emerge in a particular Cold War culture of computing and in relation to particular institutions and labs that form the backbone of the military-industrial-university system.[129] If we speak of emergence, it has to be in relation to the continuous efforts where technological systems are articulated as part of national and international politics, economic interests, and more: the work put into new computational systems and epistemologies, as well as simulations, and how those systems feed back to the world of the authors, collectives and institutions. Naturally, Dyson is not writing about computer worms and viruses as we understand them—but that is the core of the issue: to rethink what we mean by parasites and to see if our whole computer infrastructure is actually based on such patterns of symbiosis and interdependence. Whereas Dyson focuses on the operating systems, I want to stress the importance of networking and the techniques and processes related to it. Instead of automatically emerging, they were developed as part of national politics of the Cold War era. Although it is customary to start stories of network culture with the ARPANET (1969), it is equally important to contextualize it in general within the national (and later international) developments irreducible to this one network design. Ralph Smith used the rhetoric of information highways as early as 1970 in his article in The Nation, followed by his 1972 book The Wired Nation—Cable TV: The Electronic Communication Highway: "In the 1960s, the nation provided large federal subsidies for a new interstate highway system to facilitate and modernize the flow of automatic traffic in the United States. In the 1970s it should make a similar national commitment for an electronic highway system, to facilitate the exchange of information and ideas."[130] Indeed, there was more going on in terms of networks: highway system to cable as well as computers. As Alex Galloway notes, the building of the Dwight D. Eisenhower System of Interstate & Defense Highways, or the interstate highway system, begun in 1956, represented the first intentionally distributed network system and was probably a perfect model for informational networks.[131]

Such views concentrating on the communication sphere of "information and ideas" were not individual utopias but at the very core of discussions concerning post-Fordist society. Ralph Smith was channeling ideas that were actually from a 1969 report he produced with the Electronics Industry Association (EIA), which emphasized cable TV as the main infrastructure for the information society of the future. As Vincent Mosco paraphrases the report: "The EIA called for the development of a national cable system that, at the start, would provide electronic delivery of mail, access from the home to the world's libraries, comprehensive video surveillance to curtail crime ('within a community, streets and stores can be kept under surveillance from a central source'), and electronic shopping and banking. These are familiar themes in the forecasts about the Internet."[132] This highlights the fact that even though the emphasis has been put on computer networks, it was very unclear perhaps until the 1980s what types of technological solutions would actualize these aspirations toward networking. How would they relate to existing infrastructures and the new, emerging ones? What sort of management structures would be in place in relation to such networks? What are the issues that emerged from this hardware and infrastructure side that is still part of our Internet in terms of the rural—and often subaquatic—side of networking?[133]

ARPANET and other local networks since the 1970s saw a new batch of digital organisms and practices that form the genealogical framework for contemporary network software. It is no accident (except in Virilio's sense of the word) that the first viruses and worms were utility and test programs of the early network projects. Networking meant new paradigms for programming, and providing a fertile platform for novel ideas of digital ontology. Viruses and worms were a functional element within this new trend of computing, such as the Creeper virus in 1970, designed for the Tenex operating system. Creeper was able to use modem connections to infiltrate remote systems. It was, however, a utility program.[134] To quote a bunch of the key architects of the Internet and ARPANET, looking back at the early applications of the 1970s:

> In addition to email, file transfer, and remote login, other applications were proposed
> in the early days of the Internet, including packet-based voice communication (the
> precursor of Internet telephony), various models of file and disk sharing, and early
> "worm" programs illustrating the concept of agents (and viruses). The Internet was
> not designed for just one application but as a general infrastructure on which new
> applications could be conceived, exemplified later by the emergence of the Web.[135]

The principles of networking inherent in such computer projects promoted new ways of thinking about the design of computer organisms. Organizations were increasingly depicted as distributed systems. Even though the 1980s and 1990s, in particular, were labeled with such ideas of adaptability, evolution, and complexity in business, technological, and social organizations, this sort of "swarm intelligence" was already part of the socio-technological diagram of networking. A perfect example is the idea of packet switching, which was pioneered with ARPANET. It introduced local intelligence to communications: instead of being controlled from above from a centralized, hierarchical position, network communications distributed the control into small packets that found their own way from sender to recipient with the help of a set of nodes where they were routed. In a way, such packets, and the routing algorithms across geographically spread nodes, included the idea of autonomy and local intelligence of bottom-up systems, and the network in general was formed into a distributed communications system.[136] Nowadays, as Wendy Chun notes, your networked Mac or Windows machine actually wanders all the time in interaction with other networked machines despite the illusion that the user is in control of her machine.[137] This reflects how the actions, affects, and events of the Internet do not take place solely on the level of the human being but also between protocol, software, and hardware processes.

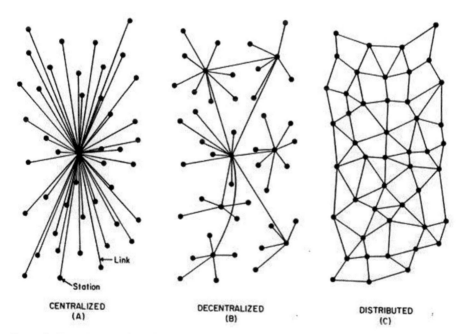

CENTRALIZED   DECENTRALIZED   DISTRIBUTED
(A)   (B)   (C)

Figure 7. Baran's network models. (© RAND Corporation. Used with permission.)

Manuel DeLanda describes as a formation of a novel type of a "mechano-sphere" of interconnected computational societies that are modeled as ecological systems. With packet switching we have, according to DeLanda, a novel class of actors, "independent software objects, or demons that roam across the networks." He sees these semiautonomous programs as catalysts for the networks' self-organization, a key component of adaptable and distributed networks.[138]

Packet-switching computer networks were not too common at first, the pioneers being ARPANET and the MERIT network, a research network in Michigan.[139] Models of networking were created by networked think tanks and university labs, especially MIT and UCLA. RAND Corporation, too, was active, and it produced in the early 1960s an important paper concerning the diagrams of networking: Paul Baran's "On Distributed Communications" (1964). Although the Internet is definitely not a development that originates only from Baran's paper, the paper addressed several key organizational and logistical traits of complex networking.[140] To quote Baran's paper:

> This simple simultaneous learning and forgetting mechanism implemented inde-pendently at each node causes the entire network to suggest the appearance of an adaptive system responding to gross changes of environment in several respects, with-out human intervention. For example, consider self-adaptation to station location. A station, Able, normally transmitted from one location in the network, as shown in Fig. 12(a). If Able moved to the location shown in Fig. 12(b), all he need do to announce his new location is to transmit a few seconds of dummy traffic. The net-work will quickly learn the new location and direct traffic toward Able at his new location. The links could also be cut and altered, yet the network would relearn. Each node sees its environment through myopic eyes by only having links and link status information to a few neighbors. There is no central control; only a simple local routing policy is performed at each node, yet the overall system adapts.[141]

Since a lot of the work in the 1960s and 1970s, the basic architecture of the Internet has been based on data that is "intelligent" in the sense that it contains its own instructions for moving, using networks to accomplish its operations. If the problems with computer security were intimately connected to this new form of connectionism and "intelligence" of using the address space and protocols of networking, so were the promises. It was not merely about the basics of packet switching—more specific cases were emerging. As with automation during the previous industrialization processes, the new autonomous network programs promised to automate several repetitious and dull procedures, for example, the updating of programs. John Walker's quiz program Animal, which was written in Univac assembly language, demanded updates because of its sudden popularity. Walker had to send magnetic tapes to people via ordinary mail before he realized how to change this. In January 1975, he wrote the Pervade addition to the Animal program, which was based on autonomous processes: "When called, it created an independent process which, while the host program was going about its business, would examine all the directories accessible to its caller. If a directory did not contain a copy of the program, or contained an older version, PERVADE would copy the version being executed into that directory."[142]

The program was installed in San Francisco on a business computer, and later it was added by Walker to company computers in Washington, D.C. Owing to a small operating system characteristic of the Univac computers, Pervade managed to send itself to "numerous installations of Univac computers." Apparently Walker wanted, in addition to the utility part, to use the program as a test of potential security problems in computers. Even though the computers were not connected via UNIX or worldwide networks, Pervade testified to the powers of self-spreading software. Although Animal was a "good citizen," as Walker describes it, in that it did not destroy data or programs, he was later very keen to underline the potential problems in having such distributed software: "A program which works exactly like ANIMAL with PERVADE is, in fact, much easier to implement under Unix today than on the Univac System in 1975. In fact, the technique will work on any system which allows multiple processes per user and shared directories. And with networks, things can happen much, much faster."[143]

To take another look at the tension between the corporeal elements and incorporeal effects of the Pervade, or Pervasive Animal as it has also been called: the corporeal coupling of distributed systems with semiautonomous virus-like and worm-like programs developed into an interesting theme during the 1970s—yet, it was not surrounded with the order-words of vandalism, criminality, and the disgust reactions that were frequently expressed after the mid-1980s (incidentally, Walker's memoirs of the Pervasive Animal are from 1985). Self-reproductive software was approached through wholly different layers and practices: such programs might have been amusing tests, programming challenges, mathematical puzzles, and also representatives of a new phase of digital culture, focused on distribution, adaptation, multiprocessing, and so forth.

The Palo Alto worm programs of the late 1970s and early 1980s resonate with Walker's miniprograms. Palo Alto was one of the highly esteemed institutes at the core of Cold War computer research in the United States. Along with other similar organizations, many of them mentioned above, the computer and cybernetics research and development scene at Palo Alto was dominated by military and defense projects. For example, the ARPANET project was heavily influenced by military funding and interests. Baran's famous 1964 paper was "sponsored by the United States Air Force under Project RAND-Contract No. AF 49(638)-700 monitored by the Directorate of Development Plans, Deputy Chief of Staff, Research and Development, Hq USAF." Hence, security interests have been at the core of cybernetics and computers since their inception: first, national defense interests, then increasingly also business and corporate interests.[144]

The Palo Alto worm tests probably cannot be reduced to merely part of the history of defense- and security-oriented computing. These programs of distributed computing—also called "vampire programs" in some contexts—spanned the more than 100 computers connected to the Palo Alto Ethernet local network and constituted, in fact, a "100-element multiprocessor in search of a program to run."[145] The worm programs were designed as connection makers, living on "the cooperation of many different machine users." Although, as discussed in Section I, the worm caused problems as a result of its semiautonomous nature, it cannot be labeled as malicious software. In addition, it promised interesting prospects in terms of the networking paradigm. The Billboard worm was designed as message automation mechanism, distributing images and texts across a network. The Alarm Clock worm was, self-evidently, a worm-based alarm clock programmed to signal users at a prescribed time. Among other applications, the Diagnostic worm was used to run diagnostics and maintenance on the Ethernet network.[146]

As noted by the Palo Alto experimenters, such ideas were already "suggested by the mechanisms used within the ARPANET or demonstrations build on top of that network."[147] The Creeper virus and an enhanced version by Ray Tomlinson, the person often remembered as the inventor of e-mail, were examples of even earlier self-replicators. And it was not only the programs but also the ARPANET structure itself that was seen as a giant routing algorithm, "multimachine distributed computation," used for organizations, simulations, and communications of complex systems such as airspace simulations.

Although Shoch and Hupp stress that these were among the trends of the 1970s and that many of the experiments in "distributed applications using the long-haul capabilities of the ARPANET"[148] had, if not waned, then remained as a mere promise, they do demonstrate several traits that connect with a whole new paradigm of computing, or science in general. In computer science, ideas of distributed programming and later, for example, neural network programming were gaining ground, becoming part and parcel of the new order of digital culture. This was due to the growing complexities of the new networks of computation and communication. Computers were no longer since the 1970s only calculation machines but "components in complex systems," where systems are built not from the top down. They were now built as part of a cluster of "subsystems" and "packages," and the basic idea of a programmer designing algorithms to carry out a task and achieve a goal had started to grow outdated. The systems were used by various people and in various locations, and the design included cooperation both on the human level and on the program level. The emphasis moved to programming as integration, modification, and explanation of already existing sets. One needed to write the key modules of computing, such as memory management, the user interface, and network communication, only once and then work with those preexisting components, which, of course, nowadays is a more than a familiar part of how design works as a collective modular set of principles. Designing distributed program environments for multiple users and programmers was a central requisite for the new organizational ideas.[149] Of course, contemporary Internet topology now is not a direct implementation of ideas expressed early on. As network theories have demonstrated, Baran's ideas of distributed networks do not resemble the nonscalar topology that defines most complex networks. The greatest difference lies in the paradoxical-sounding combination of distribution and hierarchy that such link structurations of nonscalar models exhibit. Instead of a democracy of nodes and connections, such systems are constituted of a few nodes that have a wide range of links and a majority with very few connections.[150] It's the long tail effect of the Internet topology. Interestingly, such a combination of hierarchy and distribution resonates well with the issue of viral capitalism as a machine of heterogenesis but subordinated to antiproduction (monopolies, the state).

Hierarchies took a new form across many fields. Besides computer science, also human sciences, brain research, and many other fields were for a long time enthusiastic about the possibilities of complex systems and emergence. Hierarchies seemed passé. In terms of the discussions concerning complexity, several positions in distributed artificial life shifted during the 1980s toward valuing systems that were designed not as central data banks for intelligence but as learning systems that would interact with their surroundings. Before that, the opposition to such ideas from proponents of "hard artificial intelligence" was severe. In a way, the turn participated in the longer geneal-ogy of moving data and control routines from the human first to the machine and then to the distributed interaction between computers and their environ-ments. Manuel DeLanda wrote of this as a paradigm shift from "conservative systems thinking" toward open systems. Instead of promoting models based on systems that are detached from their surroundings, DeLanda saw these novel systems theories underlining the dynamic aspects of flows of matter and energy, a reorientation that "allow[ed] us to discern phenomena that, a few decades ago, were, if they were noticed at all, dismissed as anomalies."[151]

This resonates with a shift of emphasis from top-down artificial intelli-gence paradigm in computing to seeing connectionism as a fruitful path to be followed. "Complexity" and "connectionism" became the key words of digital culture from the 1980s on. The nonlinear processes of computing expressed the "new ideas of nature as a computer and of the computer as part of nature"[152] functioning as an emergent whole irreducible to single constit-uent parts. Emergence is more than the sum of interacting individual parts. Relations matter. The general understanding (both in sciences and in human-ities) of the world sees nonequilibrium states not as mere disturbances but as increasingly central in describing, for instance, the network culture. As Prigogine and Stengers noted in their early best-seller *Order out of Chaos* from the late 1970s, matter near equilibrium and dynamic states far from equilib-rium were becoming useful in understanding how systems interact with their surroundings and envelop the potential for an open-ended becoming.[153]

Not restricted to a merely technical paradigm, the media ecology of net-working can be described as a social machine of organization, perhaps one of *swarm intelligence*. The term "swarm," as used in artificial intelligence research (and ALife research, we might add) connects with notions derived from analyz-ing the collective behavior of ants, bees, and termites: multi-agent distributed systems. Dumb as individuals, their forces lie in the continuous interaction on a systematic level of emergence. Applying the model to contemporary network societies suggests a complex sort of a political ecology:

> The swarm model suggested by animal societies and developed by these researchers assumes that each of the agents or particles in the swarm is effectively the same and on its own not very creative. The swarms that we see emerging in the new network political organizations, in contrast, are composed of a multitude of different creative agents. This adds several more layers of complexity to the model. (…) What we need to understand, then, is the collective intelligence that can emerge from the commu-nication and cooperation of such a varied multiplicity.[154]

In Hardt and Negri's take, swarm intelligence, which can be seen as one expression of the logic of networking and cooperative communication structures, becomes one key model through which to analyze management of contemporary culture, including the political resistance in the multitude. But it is a theme that permeates the field broadly—across technology, biology, politics, and even economics in some ways—and it suggests a becoming insect of digital culture that I analyze in my *Insect Media* in a historical and critical context.[155]

Ecologies of Complexity and Networking

The early experiments in networking capabilities express an interesting image of the computer scientist that does not adhere to the traditional view of a hierarchical systems engineer. When reading Shoch and Hupp's description of their work, one is led to think of these experiments as minor, or nomad, science in the sense the philosophers Deleuze and Guattari use the term. The issue is not one of imposing a form, a code, on the crude passive material of the computer. The programmer is not a demiurge who feels the obligation to conjure up the otherwise nonexistent life of matter. Instead, we follow here a metallurgical notion of programming and technology that diverges from the basic hylomorphic models of materiality (which presuppose material to be passive and waiting for a god or a social constructionist to blow form and meaning into it).[156] Furthermore, material and energetic flows are full of emergent activity and not only passively subject to the differences imposed by human-social categories.

As in metallurgy, the issue is one of following the flows of matter specific to the metal (or, in the case of programming and the computer architecture) at hand. Making tools of specific metal means adjusting oneself to the singularities and tendencies inherent in the metal and working *with* them, not *against* them. "Matter-flow can only be *followed*,"[157] write Deleuze and Guattari in a fashion that also fits well with more current applications in networking and network programming. Digital platforms can be approached as affects and affordances of active matter.

The flow of matter is a machinic phylum that the artisan follows. For Deleuze and Guattari, the artisan, the metallurgist, is an itinerant and ambulant following the flow, a nomad. Instead of breaking the material flow (*hylē*) by slicing or detaching, one aims to extract elements of residual energy.[158] The material is itself intensive and full of potential, and the metallurgist taps into this field of potential as a co-component. Similarly, we can think of the computer architecture (part of the more widespread and abstract media ecology) as a machinic phylum that has its own potential tendencies for flows, operations, logics, uses, and ways of functioning. These tendencies are virtual in that they are real yet not necessarily actual. They are not determined as in the model of a Platonic heaven where ideas lie waiting, but they are only in the mode of becoming actual, of potentially actualizing with the codetermining situations of concrete assemblages. Thus the programmer works on such a phylum too, and in the assemblages as one component, experimenting with what can be done. The programmers working with the new phylum of network computing have, since the 1960s and especially the 1970s, been experimenting with the flows proper to a network of connected computers and the flows, protocols, and so on that are part of it. And as a part of this experimentation, viruses and worms have been followed as patterns inherent in this machinic phylum.

Of course, much of the discussion is not merely about concrete programs but about abstract models and diagrams. Just as cellular automata were mainly abstract models of cooperative computation that attracted the interest of mathematicians, computer scientists, and also hackers at various laboratories, viral algorithms represented a field of interest that resonated with the work done in mathematical modeling, systems design, and software programming.

We can cite apt examples from the 1970s and later where certain publications—usually aimed at professional programmers but occasionally also for the hobbyist—acted as circulation channels. Such ideas of self-reproducing machines are probably to be interpreted as part of the enthusiasm surrounding cellular automata. Printed on the old media of paper publications, these ideas self-reproduced beyond the strict confines of media labs and computer science departments. Self-reproducing programs were addressed, for instance, by Paul Bratley and Jean Millo from the University of Montreal in the *Software— Practice and Experience* journal in 1972. Their aim of showing "that self-reproducing programs can be written in SNOBOL, LISP, FORTRAN and ALGOL 60"[159] programming languages was later taken up by *Byte* magazine in its program listing. Bratley and Millo's work was supported by the National Research Council of Canada, and neither it nor the *Byte* program included any hint of a malicious nature in its coverage of the topic. Instead, it contextualizes as part of the hobbyist circles interested in the topics of mathematical puzzles and computer "recreations" (with an explicit reference to a Pascal Users' Group newsletter from 1978). A program that duplicates itself without any help was conceived as a fascinating idea—here is an example of the version in the C program language:

```
Main () {
char q=042, n=012,
*a="main () {%cchar q=042, n=012,%c*a=%c%s%c;%cprintf(a,n,n,q,a,q,n,n);}%c";
printf (a,n,n,q,a,q,n,n);}[160]
```

Around the turn of the decade, we find other, similar examples. Of these, Douglas Hofstadter's patterns are among the most interesting. A key name in research in computer intelligence, Hofstadter won the 1980 Pulitzer Prize for his *Gödel, Escher, Bach: An Eternal Golden Braid*, which is an intriguing puzzle of mathematical logic and word games. The book, which covers a variety of mathematical word games and the like, also addressed self-reproducing sentences and programs.[161] Instead of a merely noncontextualized interest in programming, as in the case, for example, of the *Byte* program code, Hofstadter creates a fascinating problematics of self-reference and replication that does not actually reduce to being a function of any particular technological system, although computers seem to provide the perfect structure for these ideas of copying and reproduction.

The ideas and sentences are examples of a media ecology where the machines act on their own. The computer is no longer a determinate linear machine, but now a population processor with potentially indeterminate results. In a curious posthuman vein, the computer obtains some sort of partial agency. As Friedrich Kittler argues, technological subjects were born with the realization of conditional jump instructions, known also as the IF/THEN function.[162] This implies the possibility of the program autonomously changing its mode of operation in the course of its action. In Kittler's schema, where computers have autonomized their read/write capabilities from human assistance, it also means the entrance of a new form of subjectivity on the level of society. So, no more "Turings" and "von Neumanns" or any other male designers as demiurges of computer hardware and software, except as distant forefathers of a posthumanist digital culture of viral organisms? Through such ideas of autonomy and agency of computer programs, Cohen's abovementioned Universal Viral Machine fantasies, several artificial life projects of self-organization, and the above-analyzed programs of virus-like and worm-like quality find a common ground and participate in the same diagram. This is the important point to be noted: the ideas are not merely part of the digital network of computers or computer science, even though computers represent the perfect class of machines for this type of diagrammatic piloting.

The interest in reproduction is part of the *longue durée* of modernity and its media technologies; there is also a certain memetic tendency inherent especially in the media ecology that focuses on communications and copying. In this respect, it cannot be taken as a mere coincidence that the interest in memetics arose in the mid-1970s, as related ideas were part of the experimental repertoire in mathematics and computer science. Richard Dawkins introduced in 1976 the idea that memes can serve as the equivalents of genes in terms of cultural reality. Genes were to be understood as enduring through "survival machines" of repetition and reproduction, and memes transferred the same idea to cultural transmission: "Examples of memes are tunes, ideas, catch-phrases, clothes, fashions, ways of making pots or of building arches,"[163] that is, everything that reproduces and mediates itself. Dawkins's *The Selfish Gene* proposed, then, the ontologization of replicators; as Matthew Fuller notes, Dawkins's idea of replicators "can be understood as an abstract machine whose activity can be recognized across a range of material instantiations."[164] Tiziana Terranova makes an even stronger claim when underlining how the scientific knowledge and theories of genetic reproduction have been channeled and translated with the biological turn in computing "into actual working pieces of software, that are capable of producing their own emergent phenomena."[165] Dawkins is, then, essentially connected to the themes of biological compu-tation prevalent during recent decades and a new form of incorporation of scientific knowledge into computers and networks. Of course, there are varia-tions within biological computing between software meme processes and, for example, concrete biomemetic computing ("wet computing") experiments.[166]

As part of the genealogy of the informationalization of life and matter, the emphasis of memetics on patterns and mathematical models as primary in relation to the material actualizations deserves analysis. Whereas a move away from technologies, especially computer technologies, helps us to see the "big picture" in relation to the diagrammatic (abstract machine) piloting such ventures, we are at the same time with memetic studies led back into the world of media: as Susan Blackmore noted in 2000, media are the perfect meme machines. In Blackmore's take on the media history of the past 7,000 years, memes have tried to find the best vehicles for replication in terms of fidelity, fecundity, and longevity. Hence, the Sumerians in Mesopotamia with their techniques of writing are in this sense an important step, as are the monks of the Middle Ages with their industrious work of copying manuscripts, later overtaken by the printing press. Modern technical media are read in the same vein: the telegraph, the telephone, radio, and television, not forgetting the networks of roads, railroads, and shipping routes.[167]

Actually, Blackmore is focusing on modernization and the inherent capacity of modern media technologies for copying, reproduction, and communications. Her memetically inspired views of the media landscapes and histories are filtered through the copy machine of technical media that Walter Benjamin analyzed so well.[168] Yet, it is worth concerning ourselves with linking the Internet, in particular, to this picture. The Internet media technology is represented as a posthumanist copy machine par excellence, where it becomes obvious that the net does not necessarily need us. Of course, to paraphrase Blackmore, the Internet is still more or less made and maintained by us, but that is not a logical necessity with respect to the inherent workings of the network creatures:

> Already there are free-floating programs which move around in cyberspace, called bots (short for robotic programs). The way forward in artificial intelligence seems to be to build small and stupid units that together do clever things. We can imagine the Net becoming full of such autonomous stupid creatures that run about doing useful jobs. (…) At the moment, the only viruses or parasites are ones deliberately created by malicious (or just mischievous) human beings, but could bots mutate into viruses and start clogging up the system? Certainly, copying errors happen in any system and occasionally they lead to a product that proliferates. General evolutionary principles suggest that this may occur if the fantastic copying and storage system of the Net is maintained for long enough.[169]

So, the meme theory incorporates viruses as a logical part of the tendency for copying that becomes a way to see media history through that particular lens. Blackmore's take should be read in relation to Dawkins's ideas from the 1970s, and to the diagrammatic reference points of the network paradigm that surrounded those ideas. It is however important to realize that Blackmore's and Dawkins's ideas are highly problematic if they are viewed as cultural theories: the ontological status of the meme remains unclear, to say the least, and is in danger of being too close to an image of a Platonic ideal object without materiality. In addition, the universality of the meme theory is insensitive to a more precise analysis of, for example, media technologies and their history. We must continuously remember to analyze theories of the meme as situated expressions of the aspiring digital culture of the late twentieth century and to see the biased stance toward immateriality, vitality, and, for example, universal communication as part of the abstract machine, which tries to produce such cultural assemblages.

Interestingly, Hofstadter also discussed meme theory in relation to virus-like sentences and self-replicating structures. A "metamagical theme," as his famous column in *Scientific American* following in the wake of Martin Gardner was called, virality was a memetic, mathematical, and hence a computational pattern.[170] No matter how idealistic such ideas of memes might have been, the computer and the network seemed to provide the fertile ground required for such viral patterns. In connection with the early ecologies of the 1950s, analyzed above, the computer seemed to be just the right testing ground for mathematical organisms, abstract structures of self-reproduction, and formal models of evolution. Hence, the mathematical interest in such sentence structures was easily transformed into computational experiments with programming languages and digital code. Of course, as argued earlier, several accounts of and experiments with virus-like software (for example, Core Wars) unfortunately rested on neo-Darwinian models of evolution, proposed also by Dawkins, where the symbiotic nature of software culture and network ecology was easily neglected.

The mainframe computer played a crucial part in the formation of theories and practices of classical artificial intelligence from the 1950s to 1980s. The idea that the computer could also provide a fertile ground for more complex ecologies matured during the same period. Emergent and neural network artificial intelligence, and the computational experiments in biology, contributed to this linking of the digital and the organic, although the genealogical lineages extend further back, as has been argued at the beginning of this section. Computing has certainly inspired biology and the research on intelligence and trends in computer science, but computers have been similarly interlocked in the biological diagram, the abstract machine interfacing computers and the computerized post-Fordist society with biology. This intertwining can be seen developing in a threefold manner:

1. The manner how biological organisms are also information processors, computers;
2. How informational systems use biological materials (cells, enzymes, etc.) as part of their structure instead of silicon and/or are modeled on biological processes;
3. Using biology metaphorically, inspirationally or as a pathway for developing "in silico algorithms."[171]

Points 2 and 3, in particular, strike me as interesting and apt when discussing viral culture, and the field of artificial life that has formed especially in the wake of complexity theories, cellular automata, and the novel trends in computer science. Life was considered to be calculated, because "life in itself realizes forms of movement, forms of processing, that are computational in nature," as ALife scientist Claus Emmeche noted in 1991, continuing that "if life is a machine, the machine itself can become living. The computer can be a path to life."[172]

A path to life for the scientists perhaps, but also a fertile platform for the various sidekicks of life, such as viruses and parasites, computers proved their power outside the laboratories too. The advances in the processing power, memory capacity, and multifunctionality of computers were connected to their spread throughout Western societies from the beginning of the 1980s. This circulation was crucial in the interfacing of high-tech artificial life ideas and the everyday media ecology of Western computer culture. Just as self-reproducing programs had been part of early hobbyist experiments and high-profile computer lab tests, viruses and the exciting ideas that computers were somehow connected to life were increasingly pervading society.

On the scientific side, a look at the Santa Fe artificial life conferences provides a good sense of the range of ideas discussed in professional circles. In the first conference, in 1987, the topics spanned from nanotechnologies and Hofstadter-inspired typogenetics to behavior modeling, movement analysis, genetic algorithms, and on to several papers on the problem of artificial organisms in computational environments. Artificial bugs in artificial ecologies and adaptation and evolution seemed to be the ideal topics for such simulated organism–environment couplings, as in the presentation by Norman Packard.[173] Similar topics were addressed by Howard Pattee, who also warned of the dangers of overestimating the power of ALife research: ALife should be able to "evaluate its models by the strength of its theories of living systems, and by technological mimicry alone."[174] Simulated systems are not, according to the warning, realizations of the processes they follow, but mere tools for thought.

In the following conference, in 1990, also in Santa Fe, the connections to viruses were even more intimate. The fear of viruses was forgotten, and evolution and computations had become hot topics, with several papers on "learning and evolution," but also some directly addressing self-reproduction. Whereas Alvy Ray Smith focused on self-reproduction from the point of view of the classical cellular automata configurations, Eugene Spafford, well known in antivirus research, addressed the topic head on: Are computer viruses a form of artificial life?[175]

Viruses and worms were examined in a microscope-and-tweezers style. Such necropsies had been a frequent theme in the professional and popular publications since the end of the 1980s, so the interesting point is the context: the introduction to viral patterns of movement and spreading, logics of infection and structure were part of the research themes of the professional ALife researchers. Spafford was surprisingly positive about the affinities between viruses and ALife. According to Spafford, computer viruses do have a metabolism (they convert energy), they are functional parts of their environments, they exhibit growth, and they even seem to evolve through mutations—a fact that was disputed by Mark Ludwig, who argued, quite rightly, that contemporary computer systems were still too unstable to tolerate significant mutations. Yet, as noted above, Spafford declined to acknowledge the idea of viral ALife, partly for ethical reasons: they are often maliciously built and distributed—as part of unethical practices, poor science. In addition, Spafford voices a warning:

> More seriously, I would suggest that there is something to be learned from the study of computer viruses: the importance of the realization that experimentation with systems in some ways (almost) alive can be dangerous. Computer viruses have caused millions of dollars of damage and untold aggravation. Some of them have been written as harmless experiments, and others as malicious mischief. All have firmly rooted themselves in the pool of available computers and storage media, and they are likely to be frustrating users and harming systems for years to come.[176]

What we have here is actually a very tantalizingly implicit observation of the media ecology of the late twentieth century. Spafford's hesitation is telling: where for some such programs are risks and errors (and hence connect to business interests), for others this "noise" is an index of emergence. Mark Ludwig's ethos of hackerism, then, is in line with the efforts during the 1990s to bypass economic interests in the design of digital culture and commit oneself to a hacker ethos of experimentality. In a way, contrary to Spafford and some others, such virus-like ideas and the hacker ethos of free information and experimentality were not adversarial to the principles of digital network computing. As Galloway aptly argues, hackerism and viruses are actually part and parcel of the protocological way of functioning of the networks of subtle smooth control.[177] For example, viruses as a specific logic of action use the bridges protocols build over heterogeneous machines, but they also "reveal" homogeneous platforms via high infection rates. Indeed, since the end of the 1980s, viruses have also been a part of "hacker art," especially in Italy with

Tommaso Tozzi's pioneering Rebel! virus (1989) and the net art viruses of recent years by groups such as 0100101110101101.ORG and epidemiC.[178] In fact, it is very possible that Tozzi's work was the first bit of net and software art in Italy and among the early wave in Europe in general.

Such pieces of self-reproductive software can be seen as part of the tacit knowledge of an average hacker and of a well-informed computer user, in general. As Sherry Turkle has argued in her influential studies, computers have been changing our fundamental perceptions of intelligence and life at least since the early 1980s. The platforms of complexity theories, evolution, genetic algorithms, and other experiments with artificial organisms were themselves also creating novel environments and thus perceptions of nonhuman actors and subjectivities. Although the psychoanalytically trained Turkle underlines the linguistic constructionism inherent in these perceptions—and I want to emphasize the more complex affects, intertwinings, and interfacings of things considered living and computers—I find her point useful in so far as it catches the basic tenet that ALife forces in its wake a redefinition of "what it means to call something alive."[179] ALife produces such uncanny objects that force new self-reflection concerning our concepts of life, technology, and culture.

Chris Langton is a perfect example of this interconnection of popular computer culture and high-tech artificial life theory. Langton was inspired by Conway's Game of Life in the late 1960s and was later piloted by a computer of his own, an Apple II (the computer with the friendly face and the one with the early viruses),[180] toward his own experiments. This serves as one of the key founding myths, as Turkle notes:

> A first element is that A-Life mobilizes people at the margins of established institutions who are empowered by personal computers. When he began his research, Langton was, after all, a college dropout with an Apple II. A second element is that A-Life is fueled by moments of epiphany. One night, when working alone in the Massachusetts General laboratory, Langton said that he felt a "presence." He believed it to be the Game of Life running unattended on a computer near his own. "You had the feeling that there was something very deep here in this artificial universe and its evolution through time," said Langton. "(In the lab) we had a lot of discussion about whether the program could be open ended—could you have a universe in which life could evolve?"[181]

Myth or not, such perceptions are characteristic of the post-Fordist computer culture of the late twentieth century, either in the form of software agents roaming the networks and computers, communicating in interaction with human and nonhuman partners, or in the form of popular narratives of "the nature of the computer" and "life in the gray box."[182] Around the late 1980s to early 1990s, the popular press took up the issue in newspaper articles,[183] and I have already mentioned that the theme was part of the cyberpunk science fiction genre, which offered the narratives for a wider popular cultural articulations.[184] In this framework of mythically lifelike computers, the conceptualization of the viral as alive was easy in newspaper articles and books, as several examples above have already testified.[185] Such translations of events into meanings, significations, and valorizations positioned the issue in a grid of societal concern[186] and also acted as a vehicle for domestication of the issue.

Of course, the complex structures of network computing were particularly easily incorporated into figures of nature and ecology. Since the 1990s, the complex structurations of the Internet have been depicted in terms of "grass roots," "branching structures," "growing," and "evolution." As Douglas Rushkoff noted in the mid-1990s, "biological imagery is often more appropriate to describe the way cyberculture changes. In terms of the way the whole system is propagating and evolving, think of cyberspace as a social petri dish, the Net as the agar-medium, and virtual communities, in all their diversity, as the colonies of microorganisms that grow in petri dishes."[187] Such articulations were supplemented with statements underlining the complexity of the novel systems of networking. In this complexity, the organisms of such systems, for example viruses, were seen as potential aids in revealing the potentialities of the net, as *Wired* wrote in 1995: "'We're just going to have to live with them,' artificial life researcher Chris Langton says of computer viruses. 'Our global web of digital systems,' he predicts, 'is fast unfolding towards a degree of complexity rich enough to support a staggering diversity of autonomously evolving programs.'"[188]

As I showed earlier in this book, the ecological understanding of network technologies was quickly turned into part of the capitalist abstract machine. Capitalism was now seen as a complexity theory–inspired system, a self-organizing platform that tolerates multiplicities and diversities in contrast to the old Fordist capitalism of mass production, state intervention, and stable controlled currencies and flows of capital. The serialism of Fordist production system was supplemented with a reflexive touch that spread across the whole biopolitical creation of digital culture and expressed itself in the new "viral quality" of network actors. This, of course, was not restricted to the nonorganic life of network programs; shifts in organizational structures and labor relations can also be seen moving toward such themes of distributed systems,

flexible units, and adaptation. A certain type of complexity theoretical naturalization was used as a tactic of capitalist interest; this is what I keep referring
to as the apparatus of capture of viral capitalism.

In addition to the Clinton administration, and the Al Gore–influenced
information superhighway plans in particular, the neoliberal digerati were
active in proposing a more decentralized ecology as the utopia of the Internet era. These ideas continued the neoliberalist wave of the 1980s that
struck the field of telecommunications. Alvin Toffler, George Gilder, Newt
Gingrich, and Esther Dyson connected the rhetoric of ecosystems with
information capitalist tendencies for free flow of information: "'Cyberspaces'
is a wonderful pluralistic word to open more minds to the Third Wave's civilizing potential. Rather than being a centrifugal force helping to tear society
apart, cyberspace can be one of the main forms of glue holding together an
increasingly free and diverse society."[189] This quotation expresses well the
double movement of the neoliberal agenda of the simultaneous desire to
cultivate diversity and glue it together so that it does not get out of control.
Despite the rhetoric of freedom, the cybernetic systems were primarily about
how to control the unknown future, that is, management.

For the Progress and Freedom Foundation (http://www.pff.org), cyberspace was "more ecosystem than machine," "a bioelectronic environment"
that "exists everywhere there are telephone wires, coaxial cables, fiber-op-
tic lines or electromagnetic waves."[190] Inhabited by organisms of knowledge
(including incorrect ideas), this world of electronic form was meant as the
next frontier after the space race: cyberspace as the next gold rush, as the
writers painted the promising future.

Such emphases can be seen as part of the "Californian Ideology" of information capitalism, a term proposed by Richard Barbrook and Andy Cameron.
This specific brand of high-tech liberalism springs from the conjoining of the
"cultural bohemianism of San Francisco" with its countercultural roots in the
hippy movement and from the success story of the post-Fordist industries of
Silicon Valley: "Promoted in magazines, books, TV programmes, Web sites,
newsgroups and Net conferences, the Californian Ideology promiscuously combines the free-wheeling spirit of the hippies and the entrepreneurial zeal of the
yuppies."[191] More specifically, we can pinpoint such publications as *Wired* and
Mondo 2000,[192] the Progress and Freedom Foundation, and the cybercultural
theories of Timothy Leary and Kevin Kelly (a founder of *Wired* in 1993)[193] as
keen proponents of the media ecologies of complex, diverse information capitalism. It is not a long stretch to see how this sort of rhetoric gets carried over to

the current social media corporate California, so well articulated and parodied in Dave Eggers's novel *The Circle* (2013).

There are, of course, different methodological ways to approach cultures of computing than an analysis of rhetorics. An apt example is Stefan Helmreich's meticulous ethnographically based analysis of the culture of artificial life as it is practiced in the famous Santa Fe Institute. The institute was founded in 1984 as a nonprofit institution. Yet, the funding of complexity research was intimately tied to capitalist interests, and the Santa Fe Institute was itself funded by Citibank "with the expectation that its research might contribute to the bank's capacity to understand and manage the complexities of globalized capital,"[194] as Charlie Gere outlines. The Santa Fe Institute offered an institutional setting and the possibility to develop tools for a novel view of complex network capitalism.

Analyzing John Holland's Echo system in particular, "a computational platform for simulating evolutionary processes in a variety of 'complex adaptive systems,'"[195] Helmreich pinpoints the proximity complexity theories, adaptive organisms, and evolutionary patterns display between the supposedly distinct fields of artificial life experiments in computers and economics and capitalism. By following the institutional practices of Santa Fe researchers, Helmreich tracks the path from the "International Finance as a Complex System" workshop in 1986 to a similar one called "Evolutionary Paths of the Global Economy" in 1987 and on to the fascination expressed in interviews with economists. Via the connection of information, information economies and biology (also an information science) find the common ground that so reminiscently of the previous fin-de-siècle discussions of evolution and capitalism approaches post-Fordism as a flexible mode of production of ways of life that "evolves." Of course, evolution is now nonlinear, adaptive, and flexible. It is remarkable how smoothly the talk of ecological niches in artificial life and, for example, evolutionary algorithms finds itself recontextualized in viral, parasitic capitalism. "Through the medium of the complex adaptive system, envisioned finally as a kind of computer or information-processing system, the economy becomes a kind of ecology and vice versa,"[196] Helmreich writes.

Moreover, accepted virus-like programs entered the arena. Cohen's utility programs from the 1990s were touted as benevolent as they could be tied to business interests (for example, his virus-like PayBack virus program that collects unpaid bills).[197] Similarly, the programs introduced by *Wired* in 1995 were exemplary of viral code transformed into financial profit. General Magic Corporation, working with handheld communications devices, came up with an idea of how to really turn viral code into accepted form. Designing intelligent agents that exhibit on some level contagious behavior might just be the way to get the full benefits out of the Internet. Although they were not called viruses, the link to such forms of action was underlined:

> Still, despite rather severe restrictions on the agents' ability to replicate, it's hard to deny certain broad similarities between intelligent agents and the offerings of your typical Vx board. Both wild viruses and Telescript agents routinely copy themselves from one computer to another. Both viruses and Telescript agents can run themselves on the computers they travel to, and, for those same reasons, raise differing degrees of concern about their security.[198]

Such intelligent agents seemed to form the ontology of the new digital culture that eases the pressures put on the (in)dividual by the facilitating filtering of information.[199] Intelligent agents that take care of the ordinary tasks on your computer or run such errands as reserving tickets, arranging meetings, and finding suitable information from the (Inter)net are, according to J. Macgregor Wise, describing changes in the understanding of agency in the age of digital culture,[200] and we might emphasize further that such programs are actually the culmination of key potentials within the ontology of digital network culture. They also feed to new business models and relations concerning labor, and represent a new class of capitalist actors and functions that roam across technological networks. Although the fear that crept in from the 1980s had banned the use of the term "virus" in such contexts, the basic principles lived on and prospered in the assemblages of informational capitalism and its new network platforms, among them the Internet. This is why, for example, Cohen preferred to use terms such as "Living Programs" or "Tiny Experts" in these contexts.[201]

Coupling and Media Ecology

I want to add another twist to the analyses above, which might otherwise end up with a rather overly hegemonic picture of capitalism, media ecologies, and viruses. Hence, complementing Barbrook and Cameron's otherwise apt remarks on the Californian Ideology of the Internet ecology, we might want to follow Franco (Bifo) Berardi's objections that the net and the culture of globalizing capitalism must not be taken as a unitary territory of one Hegelian movement toward capitalism but as a co-symbiotic proliferation of differences.[202] Although capitalism does serve as a decoding parasitic machine of actualization of the virtual tendencies inherent in software culture and net-working, there remains a residue of something else too. This is where the stance toward thinking media *ecologies* might help.

We have to also recognize the various more affirmative takes on artificial life, too, and consider how they play a role in the context of digital culture and cultural theory of 1980s, 1990s, and our current era. To consider an influ-ential name, the philosopher Isabelle Stengers, originally in the context of a 1995 European meeting of artificial life scientists, argued for a method that jumps aboard the dreams of artificial life and follows the visions as one sort of an experiment in speculative thinking. Recognizing that there is a very strong tendency that takes artificial life along the fixed tracks of modern sci-ence and its myths of control and conquest, she also sees the positive aspects in the aspirations of this specific field invested in connectionism. Although the image of creating autonomous creatures that break free from prescribed laboratory frames is one of the founding myths of the field, Stengers seems to hope that this idea of breaking loose, of open-ended systems, would feed back into the scientific ideals and practitioners themselves, who are always connected to these machinations. When material is no longer considered as passive, Stengers hopes that such creations might lure the parties involved "towards new feelings, new possibilities, new ways of becoming."[203] Stengers is not giving a holistic view of the field of artificial life research in its various expressions; seeing the whole of ALife as one of revolutionary science would be to overestimate the field. Instead, her pointers can be seen as extracting certain crucial tendencies that pop up in various fields of digital culture, from ALife to other machinic formations that resist seeing matter, energy, or their informational expressions as passive.

ALife becomes a wider issue than just technology, or, perhaps, to put it like this: technology's relation to Western philosophy and ontology of mat-ter. Ansell-Pearson noted the binarized role machines and organisms have traditionally played in philosophy. Organisms are thought of as self-organized unities that (according to Kant) "display finality (purposiveness)."[204] Technol-ogies are, in contrast, subjected to their designers and remain mere artifices of humans without the ability to "self-produce, reproduce, and self-organize."[205] Most often, computers are thought of as determined machines, bound by the original linear instructions inserted into them (another idea of hylomorphic nature). This, of course, is exactly contested by the creation of self-reproductive software or, more fundamentally, the principles of the Turing machine and von Neumann automata, ideas that are taken one step further in the speculative projects of ALife. The projects also perhaps provide a new stance toward speculative, new materialism.

Nurturing new tendencies of the material can be seen as an ethos of experimentality and cultivation of hybrids. In addition, this etho-ecology of practices can be connected to issues of media ecology. To follow Stengers's line of thought, the ethos of media ecology could also lie in the need to create new assemblages of enunciation, "which will undo the molar socio-professional strata and their order-words."[206] Such assemblages might just act as temporary passwords that open up new spheres of ideas and action.

We need tools to understand the complexity, the connectionism, and the flexibilities that function at the core of the contemporary media condition, which justifies the use of "ecology" as a central concept here. In a way, this also accentuates the need to ground a theory of digital culture in cybernetics (Wiener, von Neumann) and in second-order cybernetics (Maturana, Varela, Simon, also Bateson), which might provide an even more subtle and complex understanding of the connectionist technologies and assemblages of contemporary culture. As discussed earlier, such projects and orientations took as their leading preoccupation the *couplings* of systems and environments and the self-organization of complexity. Hence, approaching the issue of ecology with Gregory Bateson means apprehending ecology as the "study of the interaction and survival of ideas and programs (i.e., differences, complexes of differences, etc.) in circuits,"[207] implying that primary importance should be given to the *coupling* of organisms and their environment as the basic unit of a system. Such ideas were built into the cybernetic agenda with the ecology movement of the 1960s.[208] The issue resonates also with Maturana and Varela's influential theories of autopoiesis: "Living systems are units of interaction; they exists in an ambience. From a purely biological point of view they cannot be understood independently of that part of the ambience with which they interact: the niche; nor can the niche be defined independently of the living system that specifies it."[209] Maturana and Varela insisted that "autopoiesis" is a term reserved for living systems, using the term "allopoiesis" to refer to social systems and technology. In allopoiesis the product is something else from the producer.[210] Here I stick, however, to Guattari's use of the term "autopoiesis" as applicable also to other than biological systems. To be exact, technological systems as machinic can be seen as incorporating both autopoietic and allopoietic elements. For example, the media ecology of network culture is at the same time self-referential and self-recreative as well as designed, engineered, and planned in various assemblages of enunciation.[211]

Herbert A. Simon had actually articulated a similar issue in 1969 in his *The Sciences of the Artificial*, and he viewed ants as creatures whose collective complex behavior is to be understood as the reflection of the *environment* in which they live. For Simon, complex systems were constituted both of emerging and hierarchical parts, and he saw no contradiction in such an assemblage.[212] Living and affective systems are in this regard not restricted to their personal boundaries but constitute larger collectivities, or assemblages, with their surroundings.

In this vein, the perspective of ecologies should be seen as self-referential systems, or processes, where in order to understand and observe the functioning of the system, one cannot detach single elements from its synthetic consistency (and label some elements as purely anomalous). Instead, one should focus on Maturana's question: "How does it happen that the organism has the structure that permits it to operate adequately in the medium in which it exists?"[213] In other words, a focus on such a systems approach allows one to think also of digital culture as couplings where "organisms" or "components" participate in the autopoiesis of the general system, which in our case is the digital culture of networking. This is also the abstract sense in which the *life* of digital culture could be understood: as a machine (in the Deleuzian–Guattarian sense) of coupling and connecting, of linking between and across assemblages and abstract machines— the continuous movement that keeps such machines recursively renewing themselves. Incidentally, Deleuze and Guattari were also keen on drawing from second-order cybernetics and from Maturana and Varela. Hence, the focus on autopoietic systems seems to be justified; the autopoietic system is a reproductive system, aiming to maintain its unity in organizational form:

> This circular organization constitutes a homeostatic system whose function is to produce and maintain this very same circular organization by determining that the *components* that specify it be those whose synthesis or maintenance it secures. Furthermore, this circular organization defines a living system as a unit of interactions and is essential for its maintenance as a unit; that which is not in it is external to it or does not exist.[214]

Yet, such a reproductive system should be seen as consisting of both actual and virtual parts in order to allow dynamism and to short-circuit the often too conservative focus on homeostasis found in some strands of systems theories. Systems do not merely aim at minimizing energy and restraining change.

This is where the abovementioned ethos of experimentality and novelty steps in and connects with media ecological interests. Especially pertinent

is Matthew Fuller's way of twisting the status of the standard object and seeing media ecological experimentality as a method of immanent engagement
through permutations and metamorphosis:

> Accumulate information, techniques, spread them about, stay with a situation long
> enough to understand its permutations. Find a conjunction of forces, behaviors, tech-
> nologies, information systems, stretch it, make it open up and swell so that each of
> the means by which it senses and acts in the world become a landscape that can be
> explored and built in. Speed it up and slow it down so that its characteristic move-
> ments can be recognized at a glance. Lead it through a hall of mirrors until it loses a
> sense of its own proper border, begins to leak or creates a new zone.[215]

Here experimentality connects as a method to mapping, or an experimentality *as* cartography of potentials of computational assemblages—not mere
writing of representations or reacting to a preexisting solidified reality but a
simultaneous testing of the limits of an operational field, an assemblage, and,
a phylum. Media objects are always multiplicities in the sense that they can
be mobilized into new connections and assemblages. Similarly, systems can be
seen as occupying a potential for such twistings, becomings.

As technological objects, viruses and worms are programs, but they
are also *tendencies* within this machinic ecology of digital culture of recent
decades. They are part of a machinic phylum of network culture, which can
be understood as the level of potential interactions and connections. It is a
plane of *virtuality* where specific actualizations, or individuations, are able to
occur. Thus there is always the perspective of (nonlinear) evolution in such
a grasping of virtuality. The virtual as a plane of potentiality is something
that does not exactly actually exist (although it is real), for it is in a constant
process of becoming. Just as nature cannot be grasped as something "given,"
media ecologies should be seen as planes of giving, an iterative reserve. Brian
Massumi writes about nature as virtuality and as a becoming, which "injects
potential into habitual contexts," where "nature is not really the 'given,'" but
in fact "the giving—of potential."[216] As Massumi continues, this is Spinoza's
"naturing nature," which cannot be reduced to an actual substance, an extensive and exhaustible state of being. This stance of active creation can underline for us the fact that media ecologies cannot be seen as static, hylomorphic
structures of autonomous technologies but as active processes of creation, or a
useful orientation, a horizon, on which to think the media condition of digital
culture. The future of a media ecological system is open-ended, making radical
changes possible. The system is not a determined *natura naturata* but has a

constant potential for change; viruses are a good example here in their unstable interaction with their environments. Yet, fundamentally, nature works via parasitism and contagion. Nature is "unnatural" in its constant machinic striving and adaptation.

From the point of view of a plane of immanence, nature is not constituted around a lack or a transcendental principle of naturalness; instead it constantly operates as a self-creating process of life: "That is the only way Nature operates—against itself."[217] Spinozan understanding of life sees it as an affect: movements, rests, and intensities on a plane of nature (whether media ecological or otherwise). Life is, then, not a form, but movement and coupling, as Deleuze's reading of Spinoza affirms: "The important thing is to understand life, each living individuality, not as a form, or a development of form, but as a complex relation between differential velocities, between deceleration and acceleration of particles."[218] This perspective does not, then, rely on formal characteristics of life, but it is a tracing of the lineages of the machinic phylum and also a tracing of the paths of organisms that move on this plane. Nature as a potential becoming connects to Guattari's project of virtual ecology, *ecosophy*: "Beyond the relations of actualized forces, virtual ecology will not simply attempt to preserve the endangered species of cultural life but equally to engender conditions for the creation and development of unprecedented formations of subjectivity that have never been seen and never felt."[219] This experimental ethos amounts to a project of ecosophy cultivates "new systems of valorization, a new taste for life."[220] This justifies the turn toward assemblages of artificial life where the notions of self-reproducing digital organism and simulations of digital ecologies have been addressed as positive potentialities of the new. Chris Langton called the science of artificial life digging into not merely what life is but into "life-as-it-could-be."[221] This interestingly works in productive tension with the other way of approaching the same task: of looking at computing through "natural computation-as-it-is."[266] Here computer scientists are mapping new territories also for cultural theorists to excavate, acting as probeheads of potential modes of digital culture. Such simulations of life might put the very basic categories and dualisms of biology into question as a form of scientific drag show or transvestitism, as Stefan Helmreich proposes, calling ALife a *playful* science.[222]

In short, on a plane of media ecology as a self-referential system it becomes irrelevant to label some elements as "anomalous," as not part of the system, for every element is *given* by the virtual system (which in itself and in its virtuality cannot be taken as given, as a preformed Platonist idea). Anomaly can be identified only in a predefined grid of identities (self versus other, inside versus outside). Instead, "anomalies," if defined alternatively as figures of potentiality, are particular trackings of certain lineages, of potentials on that plane, not necessarily disruptions of a system. "Desiring-machines work only when they break down, and by continually breaking down,"[223] as Deleuze and Guattari note.

The late 1980s saw a new exchange between computer viruses and artificial life research that affected the incorporeal articulations of self-reproductive processes and also sparked new attention to the material tendencies inherent in platforms of artificial populations. As a concrete example, Thomas S. Ray's Tierra project relates directly to the emerging the Internet infrastructure, computer viruses and parasites in general, and artificial life and the experimental ethos of digital creation. Ray's Tierra has been frequently cited as one of the most exciting examples of early 1990s ALife projects, although it has its historical affinities with the digital ecologies of the 1950s, for instance, Nils Barricelli's work and the Leviathan project. Ray, originally an evolutionary biologist occupied with fieldwork in rainforests in Central America, designed the first version of the program, or simulated ecology, at the beginning of 1990. His idea was to model the Cambrian era of Earth's natural history (approximately 600 million years ago) on a computer platform and hence "relive" the physico-chemical events that took place. An evolution machine of sorts, Tierra was a virtual computer running on top of the computer infrastructure, but isolated for the sake of security. This method was adopted because of the control problem encountered so many times with dynamic software, from the early ARPANET programs to the Shoch–Hupp worm programs. The Tierra computer system allocated memory space and computing time to each organism, and it controlled their life cycles and deleted the older programs. In addition, the operating system also allocated mutations to organisms, which caused "some organisms to self-replicate imperfectly."[224]

The idea originated from way back, actually from Ray's time as a graduate student at Harvard in 1979. Stumbling across a Go game club, he started to observe the play and ask about the basics of the game. Ray got into a conversation with a professor from the MIT Artificial Intelligence lab, and the conversation strayed quickly to self-replicating software and how easy it would be to create such programs. As Ray remembers it:

> I imagined: start with self-replication, then add mutation, and get evolution. A very simple formula for life: self-replication with errors should generate evolution, the essence of life. I was intimately familiar with the beautiful complexity and diversity that evolution had generated in the tropical rain forests. I imagined an independent

evolution generating a digital jungle in a computational universe, teeming with unimaginably alien evolving digital life forms.[225]

Computers proved to be the useful platform for such projects. Ray got his first computer at the end of the 1980s and equipped it with Borland's Turbo C compiler and its Turbo Debugger. Educating himself into thinking of the computer as an ecology "that could be inhabited by life (self-replicating computer programs),"[226] Ray started with computer architectures, operating systems, programming, and all the computer theoretical theory that seemed to open up new worlds to an evolutionary biologist. As he recalls, finding the research community of Santa Fe in 1989 was a groundbreaking event: there were people already doing this sort of work on computers, not merely thinking about it! Steen Rasmussen's work struck Ray as exemplary in its occupation with computer ecologies and self-reproduction (although it also differed from Ray's interests).[227]

Developing his ideas, Ray's next step was the 1995 proposal for an Internet-spanning virtual ecology of organisms. To bypass the problems with the von Neumann architecture that processes things serially, Ray needed a parallel processing machine, or a network, and the Internet seemed to provide just this. The idea was something that Danny Hillis was thinking of already in the mid-1980s with his diagrams and designs of parallel connection machines.[228] Ray's step also marked a move toward emphasizing the machinic phylum of networking, instead of the mere processing power of solitary computers.

Ray's "A Proposal to Create Two Biodiversity Reserves: One Digital and One Organic" leads us straight to Guattarian thematics of ecological "cultivation." The organic reserve plan was designed to conserve the existence and diversity of large areas of rainforests in northern Costa Rica, and it was paralleled with a digital ecology project:

> The proposed project will create a very large, complex and inter-connected region of cyberspace that will be inoculated with digital organisms which will be allowed to evolve freely through natural selection. The objective is to set off a digital analog to the Cambrian explosion of diversity, in which multi-cellular digital organisms (parallel MIMD processes) will spontaneously increase in diversity and complexity. If successful, this evolutionary process will allow us to find the natural form of parallel processes, and will generate extremely complex digital information processes that fully utilize the capacities inherent in our parallel and networked hardware. The project will be funded through the donation of spare CPU cycles from thousands of machines connected to the net, by running the reserve as a low priority background process on participating nodes.[229]

The 1990s saw several projects that attempted to capture the idle powers in network processes, such as SETI, which looked for extraterrestrial life, and ideas of "parasite computing," which tapped into the protocols of the Internet to extract computing power. Even though Tierra experiments were reduced to cooperation and interaction between research facility computers via local area networks in the latter half of the 1990s,[230] the proposal has not lost any of its vital nature. Were these, in a way, the prehistory of the more malicious bot-networks that emerged in the 2000s? Speculative questions aside, in any case the issue was and continues to be about processing power of distributed network of computers. Demonstrating that connected organisms can be employed also in beneficial, even perhaps etho-aesthetic processes, is key in terms of understanding the multiplicity of the phenomena at hand. A curious form of remediation of the Cambrian era several million years ago, Ray's project is a curious type of media archaeological excavation into the segments and flows of life. An experimentation (a creative stuttering) with the media ecology of networking and with virus-like programs, it serves as the perfect example of the virtual potentialities inherent in the diagrams of media ecologies. In this, it perhaps also can be made to infect people, practices, and principles in the digital culture of networking in the manner Stengers was thinking of.

Notes

1. McAfee & Haynes 1989, 36.
2. Foucault 2000d, 476.
3. Channell 1991, 83–84. See also Marvin 1988, 141–143.
4. Deleuze 1994, xx–xxi.
5. Butler 1918, 64–65. See also Dyson 1997, 15–34.
6. Butler 1918, 253.
7. Parisi 2004a, 186–187.
8. Johnston 2008.
9. Gere 2002, 53–54. Fox Keller 1995, 79–118.
10. Peter Friedland & Laurence H. Kedes: "Discovering the Secrets of DNA." *Communications of the ACM*, vol. 28, issue 11, November 1985, 1164.
11. Quoted in Channell 1991, 131.
12. Monod 1970, 102. For a critical view, see Lafontaine 2004, 199–206.
13. For a wonderful cultural history of the genetic code, see Kay 2000.
14. Borck 2004, 52. Kay 2000, 221.
15. See Mayer & Weingart 2004b, 16.
16. Galloway 2004, 111.
17. Kittler 1999, 1–19. Kittler 1990, 214.

18. See Dougherty 2001.

19. Gere 2002, 121–124.

20. See Whitelaw 2004.

21. Hayles 1999, 225.

22. Lupton 1994, 56. See also Sampson 2012.

23. See Massumi's note concerning diagrammatics: "The important thing is that any theoretical analysis or 'diagram' of a phenomenon is an incomplete abstraction designed to grasp from a restricted point of view an infinitely abstract monster fractal attractor that is alone adequate to the complexities of life. (…) No presentation envelops a complete knowledge of even the simplest system." Massumi 1992, 68. Hence, "ecology" offers us *a* view of the functioning of network culture, channeling our thoughts and perceptions toward thinking this interfacing of nature and technology.

24. See Siegfried Zielinski's (2006) "an-archaeological" research. Huhtamo and Parikka 2011.

25. See Ilkka Keso: "View from Large Corporation: Anti-Virus Tests" and "Cloaked Business." *EICAR Conference Proceedings* 1994, supplementary papers. Kari Laine: "The Cult of Anti-Virus Testing." *EICAR Conference Proceedings* 1994, 65–87. See also, in general, the discussions in the Computer Underground Digest in the early 1990s. <http://www.soci.niu.edu/~cudigest/>.

26. Such bulletin board systems were probably globally quite common, with, for instance, Finland having its own fair share of them, often run by teenagers. See F-Prot, Data Fellows, *Päivitystiedote*, vol. 2, issue 4, June 1992. Such trading posts were, in addition, backed up by the novel virus construction kits, such as the Virus Construction Set (1990), the Virus Creation Laboratory (1992), the Instant Virus Producer, and GenVir, which was probably a completely commercial program tool fabricated in the Netherlands. See F-Prot, Data Fellows, *Päivitystiedote*, vol. 2, issue 7, January 1993.

27. See Sampson 2005, 2007.

28. "More on 'Little Black Book of Comp. Viruses.'" *Computer Underground Digest*, vol. 4, issue 55, November 4, 1992. The online version of the book is at <http://vx.netlux.org/lib/vml00.html>.

29. As Cohen recollected in 1994: "By now, I have published almost everything that has come up. The only real disappointments relate to my inability to find any paying work related to computer viruses. Lots of people have offered me work if I will say things that aren't true, or endorse a product that I think is not very good. People want the use of my name, but not the results of my effort and analysis. A good example is the controversy surrounding benevolent viruses. I have been black balled by many members of computer security community because I refuse to renounce what I feel to be the truth. Among the leaders of the black balling are academics who I think should be fighting for academic freedom and the proliferation of new ideas, but it turns out they can get more research grants by speaking out against new ideas than by giving them a fair airing. It should be no big surprise—after all, as recently as 1988, I had an NSF grant proposal rejected by poor reviews from academics who claimed that there was no such thing as a computer virus and that viruses could not work in systems with memory protection. Obviously, they never bothered to read any of the 50 or so papers I have written on the subject." "The

Legend—Fred Cohen." *Alive* (electronic magazine), vol. 1, issue 1, 1994. Archived at http://vxheaven.org/vx.php?fid=1060.

30. Ludwig 1996, 1.

31. Bernd Fix, e-mail to author, November 7, 2005. On hacker subculture, see Ross 1990.

32. See the editor's introduction in *Alive*, vol. 1, issue 0, March 1994. The magazine is archived at http://vxheaven.org/vx.php?fid=1060.

33. Galloway 2004, 171.

34. Kelly 1995.

35. Barlow 1996.

36. Ibid.

37. See Ludwig 1996, 7.

38. Mattelart 2003, 139.

39. Ludwig 1996, 12–14.

40. Ludwig 1993, 22.

41. Cohen 1986, 219–220. Cohen and, for instance, Thomas Ray also attracted popular attention. See "Is There a Case for Viruses?" *Newsweek*, vol. 125, issue 9, February 27, 1995, 65. See also "The Virtuous Virus." *Economist*, vol. 325, issue 7781, October 17, 1992.

42. See Langton 1989a.

43. Johnston 2009.

44. See Trogemann 2005, 124–125.

45. See Speidel 2000. Parisi 2004a.

46. Ludwig 1993, 305.

47. Fred Cohen has been careful not to make any hasty statements, and the hacker Bernd Fix, for instance, did not see an allegory of viruses as artificial life as especially fruitful: "Artificial life? With the development of better anti-virus tools some viruses that can change appearance popped up (polymorphic viruses), but I (personally) don't think that this is sufficient to be called AL. Viruses don't evolve—they simply spread. No genetics at all." Bernd Fix, e-mail to author, November 7, 2005.

48. Cohen 1986, 222. At the same time, in the early 1980s, David Jefferson, an artificial life researcher, was active at the University of Southern California, providing Cohen with his support. Levy 1992, 254, 315.

49. See Kittler 1999, 243–263. Turing's original paper can be found at the Turing Digital Archive. <http://www.turingarchive.org/browse.php/B/12>. Cf. John E. Hopcroft: "Turing Machines." *Scientific American*, vol. 250, May 1984.

50. See Langton 1989b.

51. Cohen 1986, 52–53.

52. Ibid., 13–14.

53. See Cohen 1994, 65–87.

54. Sampson 2004, 6. See Cohen 1991b.

55. Levy 1993, 324.

56. Fred Cohen, e-mail to author, March 3, 2005.

57. Quoted in Aspray 1990, 190.

58. Simon 1969, 6–7, 14.

59. Giusz 1995, 108–110.

60. Munster & Lovink 2005.
61. Massumi 1992, 93. Deleuze & Parnet 1996, 62.
62. Bürger 1988, 255.
63. Dyson 1997, 108. On von Neumann and artificial life, see Langton 1989b, 12–15.
64. Aspray 1990, 189.
65. Von Neumann 1966, 94. Aspray 1990, 202–203.
66. Heims 1980, 204–205, 212.
67. Thomas R. Peltier: "The Virus Threat." *Computer Fraud & Security Bulletin*, June 1993
68. Kay 2000, 108.
69. "Reconstruction of a Virus in Laboratory Opens the Question: What Is Life?" *New York Times*, October 30, 1955. See also "Mutation Agent Held Clue to Life." *New York Times*, January 26, 1960.
70. Kay 2000, 185.
71. Aspray 1990, 189–202.
72. Mayer & Weingart 2004b, 16.
73. Von Neumann 1966, 95.
74. John G. Kemeny: "Man Viewed as a Machine." *Scientific American*, vol. 159, April 1955, 65.
75. Von Neumann 1966, 32.
76. John G. Kemeny: "Man Viewed ss a Machine." *Scientific American*, vol. 159, April 1955, 66.
77. Von Neumann 1966, 20.
78. Dyson 1997, 125.
79. See Dyson 1997, 111–113. Cf. Margulis & Sagan 1995. Interestingly, the anarchist thinker Pjotr Kropotkin also introduced ideas of "mutual aid" and coevolution in the early twentieth century (1902). Armand Mattelart (2003, 43–44) links Kropotkin to early ideas of decentralization that stem from Joseph Proudhon's mid-nineteenth-century views on decentralized organization of community to Kropotkin's thoughts from the 1880s on, when he started to emphasize decentralization as pertinent to the neotechnical era. This was a form of evolutionary stance toward mutual support, symbiosis, which also represented a form of anarchist organization.
80. Dyson 1997, 114.
81. Quoted in ibid., 117.
82. Dyson 1999, 78–79.
83. See Mattelart 2003, 50–53.
84. Dyson 1997, 178–179. Gere 2002, 66–74. The U.S. Air Force's need for computers was pushing the requirements for complex systems. The huge SAGE early warning system was a pioneering project. When it was finished in 1961, it was already technologically obsolete, but several ideas and components from SAGE were useful for in the development of simulations. According to Charlie Gere (2002, 63), such inspirational spin-off technologies and techniques included magnetic memory, video displays, effective computer languages, graphic display techniques, simulation techniques, analog-to-digital and digital-to-analog conversion techniques, multiprocessing, and networking.
85. "Leviathan: A Simulation of Behavioral Systems, to Operate Dynamically on a Digital Computer." System Development Corporation report no. SP-50, November 6, 1959.

Dyson 1997, 178. See information on the corporation's archives at Burroughs Corporation Records System Development Corporation Records. <http://www.cbi.umn.edu/collections/inv/burros/cbi00090-098.html>.

86. "Leviathan Studies." *Communications of the* ACM, vol. 4, issue 4, April 1961, 194.
87. Ibid.
88. Quoted in Dyson 1997, 182.
89. Ibid., 183. Later Beatrice and Sydney Rome moved to analyze issues of organization and decision making in the use of computers. See Rome & Rome 1971.
90. See John H. Holland: "Outline for a Logical Theory of Adaptive Systems." *Journal of the* ACM, vol. 9, issue 3, July 1962, 297–314. Daniel J. Cavicchio Jr.: "Reproductive Adaptive Plans." *Proceedings of the Annual* ACM *Conference*, vol. 1, 1972, 60–70. See also the report on MIT's program on self-learning software: "Computers: Machines That Learn from Mistakes." *The Times*, August 10, 1974, 14.
91. Selfridge 1989, 118. Cf. Dyson 1997, 185.
92. DeLanda 1991, 177–178.
93. Selfridge 1989, 121.
94. Apter 1966, 71.
95. Wiener 1961, 169.
96. Wiener 1964, 29.
97. Ibid. "Nevertheless, behind all this fantastically complex concatenation of processes lies one very simple fact: that in the presence of a suitable nutritive medium of nucleic acids and amino acids, a molecule of a gene, consisting itself of a highly specific combination of amino acids and nucleic acids, can cause the medium to lay itself down into other molecules which either are molecules of the same gene or of other genes differing from it by relatively slight variations. It has been thought indeed that this process is strictly analogous to that by which a molecule of a virus, a sort of molecular parasite of a host, can draw together from the tissues of the host, which act as a nutrient medium, other molecules of the same virus. It is this act of molecular multiplication, whether of gene or of virus, which seems to represent a late stage of the analysis of the vast and complicated process of reproduction."
98. Galloway 2004, 105–106.
99. Apter 1966.
100. "Computers: Machines That Learn from Mistakes." *The Times*, August 10, 1974, 14. The project included a curious-sounding "Hacker" program that was designed as a self-learning program for debugging, for instance.
101. On third nature, see Wark 1994. See also Simon 1969.
102. To quote Foucault (2000e, 374): "to follow the complex course of descent is to maintain passing events in their proper dispersion; it is to identify the accidents, the minute deviations—or conversely, the complete reversals—the errors, the false appraisals, and the faulty calculations that gave birth to those things that continue to exist and have value for us; it is to discover that truth or being do not lie at the root of what we know and what we are, but the exteriority of accidents."
103. Riskin 2003. Bagrit 1965.
104 DeLanda 1991, 167–173. DeLanda 1998. Simon 1969, 84–118.

105. "When Perforated Paper Goes to Work: How Strips of Paper Can Endow Inanimate Machines with Brains of Their Own." *Scientific American*, vol. 141, December 1922, 394. (my italics)

106. See "Darwin, A Game of Survival of the Fittest among Programs." A Letter by V. Vissotsky et al. to C. A. Land, 1971, transcribed and online at <http://www.cs.dartmouth.edu/~doug/darwin.pdf>.

107. Vic Vyssotsky, e-mail to author, June 2, 2005. Doug McIllroy recalls similarly: "Darwin was sui generis, except perhaps for the old puzzle that every programmer has attacked: write a program whose sole output is the program source. We were also familiar with the work of our colleague C. Y. Lee, who described a universal Turing machine that began its computation by outputting a description of itself. Nothing further was inspired by Darwin until Dewdeney's article in the *Scientific American*." Doug McIllroy, e-mail to author, April 25, 2005.

108. "Darwin, A Game of Survival of the Fittest among Programs." <http://www.cs.dartmouth.edu/~doug/darwin.pdf>.

109. A. K. Dewdney: "In the Game Called Core War Hostile Programs Engage in a Battle of Bits." *Scientific American*, vol. 250, May 1984, 15.

110. Vic Vyssotsky, e-mail to author, June 2, 2005.

111. See "Early Viruses (RE: RISKS-6.48)." *The Risks Digest*, March 24, 1988, <http://catless.ncl.ac.uk/Risks/>.

112. "Two Old Viruses." *The Risks Digest*, March 29, 1988, <http://catless.ncl.ac.uk/Risks/>.

113. Ken Thompson, e-mail to author, April 27, 2005.

114. Ibid.

115. Richard Stallman, e-mails to author, June 3 and 4, 2005.

116. Emmeche 1994, 81–83. Forbes 2004, 34.

117. Ibid., 33.

118. Kay 2000, 321.

119. Forbes 2004, 33. There are various versions of the Game of Life on the Internet; see, e.g., <http://www.bitstorm.org/gameoflife/>.

120. Terranova 2004, 111.

121. See Ward 2000, 70.

122. Martin Gardner: "The Fantastic Combinations of John Conway's New Solitaire Game 'Life.'" *Scientific American*, vol. 223, October 1970, 120.

123. Beeler 1973, 1.

124. Apter 1966. On the connetions of biology and technology, see Channell 1991. Cf. Fox Keller 2002, 247–248, 265–294.

125. Fox Keller 1995, 108.

126. Ward 2000, 72.

127. Dyson 1997, 121–122.

128. Munster & Lovink 2005.

129. Bishop 2006.

130. Quoted in Mosco 2004, 137. See also Ralph Lee Smith: "The Wired Nation." *Nation*, vol. 210, May 18, 1970.

131. Galloway 2004, 35. The plan had been accepted by Congress after World War II, yet it was implemented only years later.

132. Mosco 2004, 138.
133. Starosielski 2015.
134. Hafner & Markoff 1991, 280. Lundell 1989, 21.
135. Barry M. Leiner et al.: "The Past and Future History of the Internet." *Communications of the ACM*, vol. 40, issue 2, February 1997, 104.
136. Robert E. Kahn: "Networks for Advanced Computing." *Scientific American*, vol. 257, October 1987. Of course, packet-switching networks represented merely one model of networking. See Stephen R. Kimbleton & G. Michael Schneider: "Computer Communication Networks: Approaches, Objectives, and Performance Considerations." *Computing Surveys*, vol. 7, issue 3, September 1975. On the history of packet switching, see Abbate 2000, 27–41. Matthew Fuller (2005, 128–129) makes a very important point when underlining the controlled nature of the packet-switching technique: even though it connotes self-organization, it is at the same time controlled by protocols and other socio-technical dimensions. On the politics of packets and microdecisions, and the contemporary Internet, see Sprenger 2015.
137. Chun 2006, 3–4.
138. DeLanda 1991, 120–121.
139. Stephen R. Kimbleton & G. Michael Schneider: "Computer Communication Networks: Approaches, Objectives, and Performance Considerations." *Computing Surveys*, vol. 7, issue 3, September 1975, 139.
140. Gere 2002, 67. Barabási makes an important argument when writing how the contemporary Internet is actually not modeled on the Baran diagram of distributed networks. Instead, argues Barabási (2003, 143–159), the Internet is to be seen as a scale-free topological formation where not every node is democratic but certain nodes act as key hubs that have more contacts than others. This means that such a topology contains distributed and hierarchic elements. See also Sampson 2007. In another context, Barabási sketches an interesting idea of "parasitic computing" as part of the Internet infrastructure, a mode of operation that blurs "the distinction between computing and communication" and takes advantage of the Internet protocols. Albert-László Barabási, Vincent W. Freeh, Hawoong Jeong, & Jay B. Brockman: "Parasitic Computing." *Nature*, vol. 412, August 30, 2001, 894–897.
141. Baran 1964, ch. 4.
142. John Walker: "The Animal Episode." 1985. <http://www.fourmilab.ch/documents/univac/animal.html>.
143. Ibid.
144. As Paul N. Edwards (1996, 15) has argued, in the United States during the Cold War, computers were discussed together with international and domestic political practices. What Edwards calls "closed-world discourse" refers to a set of mathematical techniques, computer technologies, and computer simulations as well as different political and ideological fictions and fantasies and linguistic articulations of global mastery, nuclear strategies, and centralized automated command-and-control structures.
145. John F. Shoch & Jon A. Hupp: "The 'Worm' Programs—Early Experience with a Distributed Computation." *Communications of the ACM*, vol. 25, issue 3, March 1982, 173.
146. Ibid., 177–179.
147. Ibid., 179.

148. Ibid.
149. See Terry Winograd: "Beyond Programming Languages." *Communications of the ACM*, vol. 22, July 1979, 391–401. Jerome A. Feldman: "High Level Programming for Distributed Computing." *Communications of the ACM*, vol. 22, June 1979, 353–368. Cf. Halbach 1998. For similar examples in programming and databases, see, e.g., J. B. Gunn: "Use of Virus Functions to Provide a Virtual Interpreter under User Control." *Proceedings of the International Conference on APL Programming Language*, vol. 14, Issue 4, 1984, 163–168. Alan Demers et al.: "Epidemic Algorithms for Replicated Database Maintenance." ACM *SIGOPS Operating Systems Review*, vol. 22, issue 1, January 1988, 8–32.
150. Barabási 2003, 144–145.
151. DeLanda 1992, 129. DeLanda 1998.
152. Turkle 1996, 136.
153. Prigogine & Stengers 1984, 12–14.
154. Hardt & Negri 2004, 92.
155. Parikka 2010. Cf. Terranova 2004, 98–130. As also Thacker (2004) importantly notes, networks and swarms do not automatically translate as radical politics of multitude.
156. See DeLanda 1999, 32. Cf. Fuller 2005, 17–24.
157. Deleuze & Guattari 1987, 409.
158. Ibid., 408–413. I am grateful to Jukka Sihvonen for helping with the formulation of the idea.
159. Paul Bratley & Jean Millo: "Self-Reproducing Programs." *Software—Practice and Experience*, vol. 2, 1972, 397.
160. John Bürger, David Brill, & Filip Machi: "Self-Reproducing Programs." *Byte*, August 1980, 74.
161. Hofstadter 1979, 498–504.
162. Kittler 1999, 258. The IF/THEN pair functions also at the heart of the viral principle: first, in the infection mechanism that looks for infectable objects, then in the trigger part, and finally in the potential payload part. IF the condition for date accords with, for example, Friday 13, THEN set the trigger status to yes. See Harley, Slade, & Gattiker 2001, 87–88.
163. Dawkins 1977, 206. See also Richard Dawkins: "Is God a Computer Virus?" *New Statesman & Society*, December 18, 1992. Symbiotic theories of evolution provide an alternative account concerning population thinking and evolution. They proceed in terms of transversal connections across populations (instead of a genealogical lineage) and heterogeneous assemblages (bacteria, animals, plants, humans, technology). See Parisi 2004a, 141.
164. Fuller 2005, 111.
165. Terranova 2004, 125.
166. Hayles 1999, 225.
167. Blackmore 2000, 204–213. Cf. Dawkins 1977, 203–215.
168. See, e.g., Benjamin's "The Work of Art in the Age of Mechanical Reproduction" (1969, 217–251). Cf. Gere 2002, 32–35.
169. Blackmore 2000, 217.
170. Douglas R. Hofstadter: "Virus-Like Sentences and Self-Replicating Structures." *Scientific American*, vol. 248, January 1983, 14–19.
171. Forbes 2004, xiii.
172. Emmeche 1994, x.

173. Packard 1989.

174. Pattee 1989, 74.

175. Smith 1992. Spafford 1992. Of course, viruses and artificial life had been discussed in the same breath in the 1980s. See, e.g., Bürger 1988, 269–274. See also the *Alive* e-magazine archived on the site http://vxheaven.org/. A quote from the first "Beta" issue from 1994: "This magazine is one more try to find answers to some questions. The search for the best definition of computer virus will be continued. It is a general opinion that computer viruses are inherently malicious software. The possibility of viruses to be beneficial will be (hopefully) discussed here. However, protection against malicious viruses will not be neglected. This magazine will try to introduce new ways of protection, e.g. 'immune systems.' The question 'What can be "alive" in a computer environment?' will be repeated in all possible variations as long as wish to find answers exists. The examples or descriptions of 'liveware' will be presented here as soon as they appear. Probably some new topics will arise as 'Alive' progresses. And, of course, I expect a lot of fun for both readers and contributors."

176. Spafford 1992, 744.

177. Galloway 2004, 147–186.

178. See Tozzi 1991. There is also a wiki-page of Tozzi's art: http://www.tommasotozzi.it/.

179. Turkle 1996, 157.

180. Ceruzzi 1998, 264.

181. Turkle 1996, 157.

182. See Huhtamo 2011.

183. John Markoff: "Beyond Artificial Intelligence, a Search for Artificial Life." *New York Times*, February 25, 1990. Richard Marton: "Real Artificial Life." *Byte*, January 1991, and "Is There Life in Your Computer?" *Boston Globe*, October 5, 1992. Cf. James Daly: "Can a 'Good' Virus Be a Bad Idea?" *Computerworld*, vol. 26, October 5, 1992. Julian Dibbell: "Viruses Are Good for You." *Wired*, vol. 3, issue 2, February 1995, <http://www.wired.com/>. See also Pattie Maes: "Intelligent Software." *Scientific American*, vol. 273, September 1995.

184. Cf. Harrasser 2002.

185. See, e.g., Hafner & Markoff 1991, 254.

186. See here Van Loon 2002b.

187. Rushkoff 1996, 247.

188. Julian Dibbell: "Viruses Are Good for You." *Wired*, vol. 3, issue 2, February 1995, <http://www.wired.com/wired/archive/3.02/>.

189. Dyson et al. 1994. Terranova 2004, 120.

190. Dyson et al. 1994.

191. Barbrook & Cameron 1996. See also Helmreich 2000b, 94.

192. See Rucker, Sirius & Mu 1993.

193. See Leary 1992. Kelly 1995.

194. Gere 2002, 143.

195. Helmreich 2000b, 162.

196. Ibid., 174.

197. "The Virtuous Virus." *Economist*, vol. 325, October 17, 1992. See also "Is There a Case for a Virus?" *Newsweek*, vol. 125, February 27, 1995.

198. Julian Dibbell: "Viruses Are Good for You." *Wired*, vol. 3, issue 2, February 1995, <http://www.wired.com/>.

199. Negroponte 1995, 149–159.
200. Wise 1997, 150–157.
201. "The Virtuous Virus." *Economist*, vol. 325, October 17, 1992. Cohen 1994.
202. Berardi, n.d.
203. Stengers 2000, 118.
204. Ansell-Pearson 1997, 136.
205. Ibid., 137
206. Stengers 2000, 90.
207. Bateson 1972, 483.
208. See Gere 2002, 121–122.
209. Maturana & Varela 1980, 9.
210. See Parisi 2004a, 142.
211. Guattari (1995, 37) writes in *Chaosmosis* how autopoietic machines differ from structures. Instead of a "desire for eternity," there is a movement of difference (of abolition) at the heart of the self-recreation of autopoietic machinic systems. Such machines are always characterized by disequilibria, which implies an alterity—a radical, material potential of the new that does not just stem from a creative human factor but from a machine's relation to other virtual or actual machines (nonhuman).
212. Simon 1969, 24.
213. Maturana & Varela 1980, xvi.
214. Ibid., 9.
215. Fuller 2005, 106.
216. Massumi 2002, 237.
217. Deleuze & Guattari 1987, 241–242.
218. Deleuze 1988, 123. Cf. the discussions concerning the "body" in the previous section.
219. Guattari 1995, 91.
220. Ibid., 92. Guattari places special emphasis on the aesthetic machines in such a cultivation of a virtual ecology.
221. Langton 1989b, 2.
266. Deleuze 1988, 123.
222. Helmreich 2000b, 246.
223. Deleuze & Guattari 1983, 8.
224. Forbes 2004, 46. See also Dyson 1997, 125–127. Emmeche 1994, 39–44. Ward 2000, 195–212. Home page for Tierra: http://life.ou.edu/tierra/.
225. Ray 1993. Cf. Ward 2000, 195–197.
226. Ray 1993.
227. On Rasmussen's work, see Rasmussen 1989. Rasmussen, Knudsen, & Feldberg 1992.
228. See Hillis 1989. Ward 2000, 207–208. Relevant are also Hillis's later research interests, for instance, his paper at the second Artificial Life conference in 1990, where he discussed coevolving parasites and simulated evolution. Hillis 1992. In addition, his Thinking Machines Inc. company was already looking into evolutionary software in the early 1990s. See "A Darwinian Creation of Software." *New York Times*, February 28, 1990.
229. Ray 1995.
230. Ward 2000, 209–212.

AFTERWORD

An Accident Hard, Soft, Institutionalized

Instead of a summarizing "Conclusion" that would attempt to close down the discussion, the function of this short "Afterword" is to show some new themes that have emerged in discussions concerning viruses and digital security. This is to very briefly complement some of the historical discussion in the book, and demonstrate both continuities and discontinuities in how security folds as part of digital culture. In many ways, one can speak of the persisting theme of how accidents fold as part of digital service economy, platforms, and the generalized zigzagging of security and insecurity from the personal to the corporate transactions. Security itself has become a contagion—a generalized affect, business themes, product, and political tool. And it has happened at the same time as the massive popularity of social media platforms, issues of data leaks, surveillance, and the generalized issues of trust all permeate our interactions.

So what's even an accident in this situation? What's there in an accident? Clearly, a lot more than first meets the eye. Accidents are rich events: they suddenly reveal much more than the actual accident taking place, and they unfold into a new sort of a time, situation: we see things differently after an accident. The burst tire opens up a whole different assemblage for the afternoon than what was planned: a 100-kilometer road trip turns into an acute awareness of location, mobile signal reach, delays and rescheduling, insurance issues, and more—a trail of other technological, administrative, and social issues in which the road trip was secretly nested. "As planned" is always a tricky thing anyway; some accidents are planned, or included in plans, and calculated as risks. There's money in accidents, as researchers in cybercrime keep on pointing out: according to one estimate, antivirus software industry is worth $94 billion per year.[1] By the time this text is published, the figures will have changed, and most likely grown dramatically. One man's accident is another one's business opportunity: not merely an online form of transaction, malware meant for specific forms of crime becomes part of local service economies too. For example, in some favelas in Rio de Janeiro the malware disc comes with proper service provided for the purchases: the stolen credit card numbers work or you get your money back; use of Customer Relationship Management software to maintain customer relations, etc.[2] Software crime and the associated accidents it produces are managed as a service, like any other digital service, intimately entangled as part of the corporate culture. Ransomware is another example of this trend. Characterized as "a strange hybrid of digital mugging and commercial-grade coding and 'customer service,'" it uses encryption to deny a user access to one's own files.[3] They are partly exploits of system faults, partly social engineering and encryption attacks that can infect one's computer, and represent one recent discussion in the odd world of digital crime and/or business. The mushrooming of different forms of malware and crime is tightly linked with the lucrative-sounding nature of the security business with both representing major parts of digital economy in the twenty-first century. One could almost speak of a pervasiveness of malware and cybercrime as part of the contemporary business landscape: as targeting the corporations[4] and as the product sold (whether for criminal purposes or as the promised security).

Early on in software development and research it was warned that there would never be full security. Fred Cohen and others voiced that if you want communication, it is always in the context of possible insecurities, leaks. The leak is not, perhaps, so directly an accident as we usually think of accidents: demanding instant attention, coming out in more or less visible ways, abrupt interruption of the everyday. Leaks can be slow. Perhaps they are a form of a slow accident that are not spectacular but insistent as sort of dark underbellies of the system. More recently, Wendy Chun has demonstrated that the leak is the *modus operandi* of networks: the constant interference and possibility of information moving outside the channels where it was supposed to be contained.[5] The leak is found both in the politics of whistleblowing and in the infrastructural leakiness of information that moves between machines before it talks to people. It's here that we also find issues relevant for the politics of software viruses, worms, and other related programs. In other words, while the emergence of software forms as seemingly out of control becomes integrated as part of everyday communications and risk calculation, it means issues of security are also out of control—or, at best, are on the level of *just about in control.* Complex systems and artificial life are one way to tell this story of just-about-in-control culture that feeds on both metaphors of nature and ecology and also on design plans that build according to an understanding of interdependencies, interactions, and relationality. Now with the reemergence of robotics in popular culture and in science-corporate plans, it is good to be reminded of the link between physical robotics and the software formations, such as artificial life, that define it as complex, autonomous, and part of the longer genealogy of cybernetics.[6] In other words, the interesting side to a lot of these discussions is not only the hardware, but also how it connects to emergent forms of intelligence, and the longer legacy of software "life."

So if the complex software systems that structure everyday life today are vulnerable to hacks—power plants, cars, and "smart" fridges are all seen at risk with the emergent "Internet of Things," a connected world of data relations that define both physical infrastructures and object-behaviors—then this surely expands software security again back into the world of everyday, mundane reality. The accident scales with the various connections the network establishes; not merely between users and systems, but now also across devices and physical platforms. This is visible in the emergence of specific malware targeting, for example, the energy sector (such as the Stuxnet worm was designed to do as part of geopolitics executed by way of software), but it is also seen in the possibilities of other sorts of accidents that design culture has to start thinking about with automated, networked physical systems in urban settings, such as driverless cars as part of transport infrastructures. Much of the history of computer virus discourse was associated with malware—malicious software that intentionally or unintentionally was made to do things deemed against the law and social order. However, looking at contemporary software culture that extends to the corporate platforms of everyday life management (which is perhaps how we should define social media), one starts to understand how leaky this definition itself is. Sometimes it is difficult even with antivirus software to recognize what malware is; this is because of the problem of false positives and normalized operating system or program processes recognize as malway by some antivirus software. And now there is also the issue about how many of the services and platforms adopt technologies and techniques that are bordering on being harmful to users. There's a bigger philosophical question having to do with the nature of data harvesting, but let's first examine some more contained examples.

An investigation into Uber's app led at least some tech journalists to the conclusion that it's "literally malware." The app is a portal to the company servers, feeding back data about a range of circumstances of which the user of the service is unaware, including personal communications (SMS logs and call histories) and Wi-Fi information (including information about neighboring Wi-Fi routers), GPS location, and so on. These requests for data by the Uber app—some of which occur without specific user permission—are justified by the company because of the increased functionality the app then offers, and by this interesting detail the company says it operates under: "The blanket access is actually a requirement from Google, which forces Android developers to ask for privacy permissions up front."[7] The revelation spread quickly, but TheNextWeb was quick to argue against the scandal and to demonstrate that there was nothing out of the ordinary in the way the app works: there's a list of permissions Uber needs (from location to Device ID) that all falls within the normal operational routine. Demonstrating that nothing extraordinary had taken place, it also brought to the fore what *is* then normalized as part of the operations of services. Hence the general feelings of insecurity—and security paranoia—become themselves the contagious objects that relate to the complex ways in which technical and legal issues entangle in user relations of digital culture.

In the culture of leaky data, it's not only malicious software that is the cause of leaks but the more general tendency of platforms, services, and devices. Indeed, such a vulnerability is normalized to the service situation that defines both mobile app culture and also the big data culture of social media. The wider sense in which the "terms and conditions" sort of arrangement makes users and their devices part of data gathering and circulation is only the proverbial tip of the iceberg; more widely, and for those of us concerned with issues of security and the software accidents of digital culture, it becomes an interesting insight into how such platforms operate. It has also forced some changes in the focus of antivirus and security software companies. In short, and as one passage from the main historical themes of the book to contemporary social media platforms, perhaps the legacy of malware and insecurity is not only an issue that is contained in the specific examples of types of software. Perhaps it is, more strongly than ever, an issue that now is entrenched as part of the foundations of current platforms as part of the aforementioned leakiness of data and the contagious nature of insecurity as a default affect. Looking at issues of security, it has meant a broadening of the scope of discussions again to user relations and agreements but also to the ecology of surveillance.

For example, one of the several things revealed in the aftermath of the Edward Snowden leaks concerning NSA and GCHQ operations was that F-Secure (and its frontman Mikko Hyppönen) became a very articulate proponent of issues of privacy and an opponent of such security agency intrusions. Security became understood in rather broad terms across the private-public-criminal organizations spectrum. Experts in the antivirus community made public statements in support of Snowden. Hyppönen called out the revelations about PRISM and data gathering from service providers as a threshold to a new awareness not only of issues of insecurity, but also of educating about the other programs run by the NSA, including Xkeyscore, Cybertrans, DoubleArrow, and Skywriter. Presenting some of these views in a TED talk from 2013, Hyppönen invoked an earlier example of Flame malware that, he argued, was likely to have been designed by the U.S. as a way to hack into the Windows network. He also cited further examples of state-sponsored malware and *Der Spiegel* leaks about "elite hacker units operating inside … intelligence agencies"[8] such as the NSA unit TAO (Tailored Access Operations) and GCHQ's British version, called NAC (Network Analysis Centre). Of course, the high-profile case of the Stuxnet worm, a cyberattack against an Iranian nuclear plant construction, was revealed in 2010 as an early example of attack malware designed by intelligence agencies. Kaspersky Lab reported about a malware program that was claimed to be an NSA creation, along with a suite of other software tools named as if they were creations of a 1980s and 1990s cyberpunk hacker group made of teenagers: STRAIGHTACID, STRAITSHOOTER, and GROK.[9]

Hence, it is no wonder that intelligence services targeted antivirus companies in their operations. Breaking encryption had become such an important task for different government agencies, and this emphasis became visible in how a post–9/11 fight against terror extended also to software companies. Besides the operating systems and service providers who may or may not have cooperated, companies in the security business such as Kaspersky and F-Secure were reported to have been targeted.[10] The operations were executed in order to better understand the vulnerabilities of antivirus and security software as well as learn about the range of new viruses and malware, potentially repurposing some for use by intelligence services. In one of the many high-profile stories revealed in the wake of the Snowden leaks, *The Intercept* offered details and possible reasons why this targeting happened.

Their interview with the information security consultant Joxean Koret suggests, as one insight, that the intelligence gathering and reverse engineering served to find possible inroads to systems:

> If you write an exploit for an anti-virus product you're likely going to get the highest privileges (root, system or even kernel) with just one shot (…) Anti-virus products, with only a few exceptions, are years behind security-conscious client-side applications like browsers or document readers. It means that Acrobat Reader, Microsoft Word or Google Chrome are harder to exploit than 90 percent of the anti-virus products out there.[11]

Reverse engineering became one key software technique to expose the possibilities and affordances of already existing software for later repurposing. NSA's understanding of the Kaspersky software was claimed to expose how to use "'User-Agent' strings included in the headers of Hypertext Transfer Protocol, or HTTP, requests"[12] as a sort of addressing toolbox that helped to identify machines and to tap into the traffic between customer computer requests from Kaspersky servers.

It is clear that the past 10 to 15 years have seen an intensified field of digital network security. It is normal to speak of the "arms race" in cybersecurity while, at the same time, national organisations are justifying massive investments in cyberwar centers of various kinds. It would be an exaggeration to call this a nonhuman landscape of autonomous software attacks, as they are tied to massive institutional operations, but it is clear that the software programs started to play even a more crucial role as part of the SIGINT (signal intelligence) landscape. As Friedrich Kittler points out, the NSA's history extends both to the invisibility of its role and existence ("No Such Agency") and its aggressive entry into the field of cryptology. Technological warfare revolves around operationalized mathematics, where encryption, claims Kittler, has an especially central role.[13]

One can easily see this theme running through the topics and discussions in this book, too; security, the emergence of "battle programs," and the Cold War contexts in which computer viruses and related programs emerge. They are mathematical puzzles of self-reproducing programs that feature in publications and other contexts, but they are also embedded in emerging networks in different ways since the 1960s. Part of this book maps this history—the links between institutions in which the interest in viruses, malware, and computer security emerges, as well as the ways in which the antivirus industry and the broader security industry connected to national interests tackle problems related to software. The body politic of digital organisms and their territories is where these issues move across discourses and practices of embodiment in the most political of ways—software is never merely a technological execution of a sequence but a wider social event, which also gathers around it different articulations, collectives, and a long trail of other sorts of actions and consequences.

Of course, it should never be mistaken that issues of networks and security were restricted entirely to software. Far from it. One could justifiably claim that computer security has a history that runs much deeper, at even submarine depths, as Nicole Starosielski demonstrates in her book *The Undersea Network*. The Cold War computing culture's reliance on encryption was not merely an issue of mathematics but also of infrastructures, including discussions about security of wireless communications against what were perceived as more stable, reliable, secret coaxial cables. Security was a key driver in many of the considerations, from phone communication to cable and then to electronic information networks.[14] As Starosielski narrates, the geographies of communication that form that backdrop of our contemporary networked culture were always laid according to the politically charged geographies and issues that often had to do with security and the various ways of insulating data traffic.

What's more, the issues addressed here are not restricted to security in the narrow sense. Indeed, we are not only dealing with a malicious set of programs but also an area that connects to the emergence of artificial life as a scientific project. Besides theoretical excavations that examine how life functions beyond carbon-based biological forms and simulated ecologies of life, the practical operationalization of life becomes key. Many of the projects looking at viruses and other software forms that investigate parallel processing, symbiosis, and so on, are interesting as practice-based excavations both for computers and for questions of life. The new ecologies of agency are in the memories and networks of a computer culture that emerged out of various contexts from Cold War computing to other sorts of research projects, including projects that dealt directly with the following question: Can computer viruses and worms be considered forms of artificial life?

One has to recognize how the discussions concerning ecologies of computing were not merely about an enthusiasm for new forms of life. Despite the stated goals, the wider context against which they emerged was a different planetary situation, itself produced by industrial, technological culture. The massive environmental problems that had surfaced, both in climate research and in public awareness, had been discussed since the 1970s, at least, with new environmental disasters heightening the debate about the impact of scientific and technological culture on the planet. Work on software ecologies resonated in multiple ways with the surfacing of environmental problems, with new sorts of technological life emerging at the conjunction of media and

Figure 8. The Perpetual Self Dis/Infecting Machine, a custom-made computer infected with Biennale.py. During the past twenty years, various software and art projects have addressed the computer virus as a curious aesthetic and media cultural phenomenon. One such example was the Biennale.py net art virus from 2001, which was distributed on T-shirts and sold on CD-ROMs ($1,500 each. It was also installed in this physical form, illustrating that there's more to computer viruses than the screen—a whole hardware assemblage, infrastructure, a contagious environment. (Image reproduced with permission, image credits: Eva and Franco Mattes, Biennale.py, 2001, Computer virus.)

ecology. As Nigel Clark notes in his article "Panic Ecology," the ALife viruses of the early 1990s can be understood also as hybrids of scientific and aesthetic concerns in the midst of our polluted cultures of late modernity.[15] Set in the context of post-Chernobyl (1986) global culture, such projects might, then, be understood as experimentations with new articulations of nature and "out-of-control biology" in computational platforms. The loss of control over the environment enacted by different sorts of political and political-economic conditions concerning energy, for instance, was a driver for some sort of different variation on the theme; an investigation of life on software platforms, while life in its biological form was increasingly threatened in so many ways, in so many catastrophes that we now also witness on a weekly basis, from mud slides of toxic sludge from mining waste (in the U.S., in Brazil) to nuclear accidents (Fukushima) to the general planetary catastrophes of global warming, melting of ice caps, rising sea levels, and other sort of things that often feed apocalyptic narratives. Panic ecologies produce an anxiety that spreads both as a metaphor and as an affect full of impact.

From this perspective, and others presented in this book, viruses do not merely represent an example of malicious viral code but are part of a cultural-historical assemblage of digital culture. They become understood as part of wider contexts of culture, technology, and even art. From a focus on what contagious code does, we have managed to move to discussions about contagion itself as a technological reality and a narrative trope in contemporary culture. This refers to the media ecologies of network culture in which viruses function and become part of a broader body of discussions about art, politics, and, obviously, political economies and insecurities of digital culture. This is immediately a more fruitful way of investigating the issue than a kneejerk reaction narrating the dangers of such viral forms of digital culture. This other sort of a story is broader, and less easily contained with regard to the history of security issues, but it is also a much more interesting one in addressing the forms of generalized accidents we are dealing with. I hope this book has offered at least a glimpse of such complexity, and that it has provided an insight to computer viruses, worms, and the security of digital culture and also further ideas about how to continue writing on the same issues, as seen both in current culture and in a media archaeological perspective.

Notes

1. Marshall Honorof: "Cybercrime Gets Much Worse, Expert Says." Tom's Guide, March 15, 2015, <http://www.tomsguide.com/us/future-cybercrime-worse,news-20639.html>.

2. Goodman 2015, 184–185.
3. Sean Gallagher: "Inside CryptoWall 2.0: Ransomware, professional edition." Ars-Technica, January 9, 2015, <http://arstechnica.com/information-technology/2015/01/inside-cryptowall-2-0-ransomware-professional-edition/>.
4. As Mikko Hyppönen, CRO of F-Secure, puts it: "How many Fortune 500 companies are hacked right now? Answer, 500." Mikko Hyppönen talk at Slush 2015-event in Helsinki, November 12, 2015. Quote via @slushHQ-Twitter account.
5. Chun 2015.
6. Johnston 2008.
7. Buster Hein: "Uber's Data Sucking App Is Dangerously Close to Malware." Cult of Mac, November 26, 2015, <http://www.cultofmac.com/304401/ubers-android-app-literally-malware/>.
8. Mikko Hyppönen: "How the NSA Betrayed the World's Trust—Time to Act." Ted.com, November 2013, <https://www.ted.com/talks/mikko_hypponen_how_the_nsa_betrayed_the_world_s_trust_time_to_act/transcript>.
9. Ryan Gallagher: "Researchers Find 'Astonishing' Malware Linked to NSA Spying." The Intercept, February 17, 2015, <https://theintercept.com/2015/02/17/nsa-kaspersky-equation-group-malware/>.
10. Thomas Fox-Brewster: "NSA Spied on Non-American Anti-Virus Companies." *Forbes*, June 22, 2015, <http://www.forbes.com/sites/thomasbrewster/2015/06/22/foreign-av-companies-targeted-by-nsa/>.
11. Andrew Fishman and Morgan Marquis-Boire: "Popular Security Software Came under Relentless NSA and GCHQ Attacks." The Intercept, June 22, 2015, <https://theintercept.com/2015/06/22/nsa-gchq-targeted-kaspersky/>.
12. Ibid.
13. Kittler 2014.
14. Starosielski 2015, 39.
15. Clark 1997.

APPENDIX

A Timeline of Computer Viruses and the Viral Assemblage

This timeline is intended as a heuristic tool-for-thought that places various events and contexts together in order. It is not an exhaustive archive of all the important dates, but it does give an overview of the development of viruses and related phenomena. The information has been gathered from a number of sources mentioned in the Bibliography. The estimated numbers of PC viruses are from F-Secure statistics.

For a more detailed list of virus and worm incidents, see the Wikipedia-page at https://en.wikipedia.org/wiki/Timeline_of_computer_viruses_and_worms.

1872	Samuel Butler discusses the fear of technology becoming self-reproductive in his novel *Erewhon*.
1936	Alan Turing develops his ideas of a so-called Turing machine that is able to simulate any other machine.
1948	C. E. Shannon formulates his mathematical theory of communication, where he includes noise as part of the communicative act.
1949	John von Neumann lectures on "The Theory and Organization of Complicated Automata."
1950s	Biological virology is established as a key research area.

1953	Nils Barricelli's experiments with ideas of symbiogenesis are applied to computers at the Princeton Institute of Advanced Studies.
1958	The principles of the modem for computer communication are established.
1959	Beatrice and Sydney Rome's experiment on a "Leviathan-computer system" based on adaptability.
1961	Darwin, a game where digital organisms fight for memory space, is developed at the Bell Labs (a precursor of Core Wars, see year 1984).
	The second edition of Wiener's *Cybernetics* (orig. 1948) is published, where he discusses self-reproducing machines.
1964	Paul Baran's key paper "On Distributed Communications" is published.
1966	Michael Apter discusses self-reproductive organisms in his *Cybernetics and Development*.
	Von Neumann's *Theory of Self-Reproducing Automata* is edited and posthumously published by Arthur W. Burks.
	Students program rabbit programs that self-reproduce without limits.
1969	ARPANET is put online in the United States.
Early 1970s	The Creeper and Reaper worms spread through the ARPANET.
	Ralph Smith uses the rhetoric of information highways.
1970	Martin Gardner introduces John Conway's Game of Life in *Scientific American*.
1971	Paterson's informational worm is created at the MIT Artificial Intelligence lab.
	The e-mail application is designed by Ray Tomlinson.
1972	David Gerrold's novel *When HARLIE Was One* introduces the idea of a VIRUS program that spreads through the telephone network.
	Self-reproducing programs are discussed in the *Software—Practice and Experience* journal.
1973	The "flu virus" hits the University of Oulu, Finland.
	The principles of Ethernet local networking are established.
1975	John Brunner's *The Shockwave Rider* plays with the idea of a tapeworm that lives inside a computer. These worms have the ability to spread to other computers.

Pervasive Animal (or Pervade), a viral-like update program, is developed by John Walker.

1976   Richard Dawkins introduces his viral theory of cultural reproduction: memes.

1977   Thomas J. Ryan's *The Adolescence of P-1* explores themes similar to those of David Gerrold's novel. The novel was made into the PBS TV movie *Hide and Seek* in 1984.

Apple II, the computer system with a friendly face and with one of the earliest viruses, is released.

1980   A thesis on self-reproduction is submitted at the University of Dortmund, Germany: "Selbstreproduktion bei Programmen auf dem Apple II-Rechner."

1981   The MS-DOS operating system for PC-compatible computers is released.

1981–1983   Several Apple II viruses recorded, including Elk Cloner by Rich Skrenta and another virus programmed by Joe Dellinger that spread itself via the game Congo.

1982   *Time* magazine names the computer as the machine of the year.

Researchers Shoch and Hupp report the Xerox Palo Alto Lab worm program tests from the end of the 1970s.

The information security company Symantec is founded in the United States.

1983   The first computer virus is born—at least officially. On November 3, Fred Cohen participates in an experiment that demonstrates the virus to a security seminar. The name "virus" was conceived by Len Adleman.

The *War Games* movie features a young computer enthusiast breaking into military computers.

HIV is argued to be the cause of AIDS.

1984   Dewdney's article in *Scientific American* describes the basics of the Core Wars game. In Core Wars, programs "fight" for memory space.

Fred Cohen gives a scientific definition of a computer virus.

William Gibson's novel *Neuromancer* presents computer viruses as part of the population of the cyberspace—along with artificial intelligences, ROM-constructs, cyber cowboys, etc.

1985	Computer viruses are discussed in *Time* magazine.
1986	Fred Cohen's PhD thesis "Computer Viruses" is published. Cohen develops the idea of a "universal viral machine" as a special version of a Turing machine.
	Perhaps the first PC virus, Brain originates from Pakistan and infects 360-kb floppy disks.
	Ralf Bürger's VIRDEM is demonstrated, a virus distributed at the Chaos Computer Club conference in December.
	The Computer Fraud and Abuse Act is approved by the U.S. Senate.
1987	The Los Alamos conference on artificial life is held.
	The destructive Lehigh file virus and the most widespread PC virus Stoned are recorded. The Christmas Tree worm spreads through the IBM network.
	The Computer Fraud and Abuse Task Force is founded in the US.
	Amiga's SCA virus, Atari's Pirate Trap virus, and Macintosh's nVIR virus are recorded.
1988	Dr. Solomon's Anti-Virus Toolkit is released, as are many other antivirus detection and removal programs.
	The Jerusalem virus breaks out at a large financial institution. The MacMag virus declares peace. The Scores, Ping Pong, and Cascade viruses are released into the wild.
	Computer viruses make it to the cover of *Time* magazine.
	Antivirus company Data-Fellows (which later becomes F-Secure) is founded in Finland.
	The Computer Emergency Response Team (CERT) is founded in the United States to battle threats to computers and computer networks.
	The Virus Epidemic Center is founded in Hamburg.
1989	Approximately 90 PC viruses are estimated to exist.
	The Friday 13th virus causes virus hysteria.
	The Datacrime virus is found, causing much overreaction. The Dutch police sell Datacrime detector programs at police stations for $1.
	The AIDS Trojan incident takes place.
	The Computer Virus Crisis by Fites, Johnston, and Kratz is published.

Computer Viruses, Worms, Data Diddlers, Killer Programs & Other Threats to Your System by McAfee and Haynes is published.

Lundell's *Virus! The Secret World of Computer Invaders That Breed and Destroy* is published.

IBM releases its first antivirus product.

Virus Bulletin is founded.

1990   Viruses written by The Dark Avenger (Bulgaria) introduce the idea of subtle and slow damage. The viruses also infected backup disks.

The Microsoft Windows 3.0 operating system is released. It is the first commercial success in the Windows series.

Robert T. Morris Jr. receives his sentence for the Internet worm. Morris receives three years' probation, a fine, and community service.

In the United Kingdom, the Computer Misuse Act is passed.

The European Institute for Computer Antivirus Research is founded.

Symantec releases the Norton Antivirus program.

1991   Approximately 360 PC viruses are estimated to exist.

The Tequila mutating virus is recorded.

The High Performance Computing Act is passed in the United States.

The first Virus Bulletin Conference takes place.

Computer viruses also infect humans in Pat Cadigan's novel *Synners*.

Computers under Attack: Intruders, Worms, and Viruses, edited by Peter Denning, is published.

Little Black Book of Computer Viruses by Mark Ludwig causes a stir in the antivirus community.

1992   The Michelangelo virus causes a media panic. It did not cause great damage, but the scare was advantageous for the antivirus companies: sales boomed.

The Dark Avenger releases the Mutating Engine virus design kit.

Neal Stephenson's novel *Snow Crash* includes a virus as a key part of its plot.

The Iraqi virus is recorded.

David Ferbrache's A *Pathology of Computer Viruses* is published.

1993   Approximately 2,450 PC viruses are estimated to exist.

A new virus construction kit from the Trident group (Holland), called the Trident Polymorphic Engine, is distributed.

The National Information Infrastructure program is established in the United States.

Computer Viruses, Artificial Life and Evolution is published by Ludwig.

1995   Approximately 5,500 PC viruses are estimated to exist.

The Word Concept virus infects Microsoft Word documents.

The human world is saved by a computer virus in the science fiction film *Independence Day*.

Thomas S. Ray's proposes an Internet-spanning virtual ecology of organisms.

The Black Baron is found guilty of spreading viruses in the United Kingdom.

1996   "Declaration of Independence of Cyberspace" by John Perry Barlow is published.

1997   Approximately 10,350 PC viruses are estimated to exist.

1999   Approximately 33,500 PC viruses are estimated to exist.

The Melissa e-mail worm is recorded.

2000   The I Love You virus makes the headlines.

2001   Approximately 55,000 PC viruses are estimated to exist.

The Nimda virus and the Sircam, CodeRed, and BadTrans worms are recorded.

The Biennale.py-media art virus is released at the Venice art Biennale.

2002   The author of Melissa is sentenced to prison.

The Klez worm acts as a malicious overwriting malware.

The Bugbear worm and the Shakira, Britney Spears, and Jennifer Lopez viruses are recorded.

The I Love You exhibition is held in Frankfurt on the culture of computer viruses.

2003   Approximately 80,000 PC viruses are estimated to exist.

The Slammer worm breaks the record as the fastest-spreading worm.

2004   The MyDoom and Sasser worms are recorded.

2006   Approximately 185,000 PC viruses are estimated to exist.

	According to *Wired*, malicious botnets represent a graver threat than viruses.
2008	Anonymous organizes its operation Chanalogy targeting Church of Scientology and starts receiving wider global attention.
2010	Stuxnet worm discovered. It was targeted against specific Iranian organizations involved in their nuclear power infrastructure.
2012	Shamoon virus, specifically designed for cyber operations in the energy sector, is discovered.
2013	A significant growth in ransomware type of programs.
2013	Edward Snowden's leaks reveal the extent of NSA and GCHQ operations that extend to global surveillance of individuals, parties, and governmental and intergovernmental organizations.
2016	The Malware Museum is opened at archive.org.

BIBLIOGRAPHY

A Note on Sources

Digital Contagions is formed of the various articulations of viruses in computer science, media representations (newspapers, magazines, television reports), and other products of media culture, such as films and science fiction litera-ture. A number of the sources are written from a more or less "official" point of view. Professionals in computer science are often guided by technical inter-ests, and much of the virus literature since the mid-1980s has underlined their maliciousness. The popular press was often found following such articulations, even though I have tried also to find opposing expressions on the topic. To find the alternatives within these discourse networks I have followed fiction literature, underground sources, such as the Computer underground Digest, and, for example, some computer art projects and activist groups.

The corpus of these sources was formed by a systematic excavation of written materials, such as *Communications of the* ACM (Association for Computing Machinery), one of the leading publications within computer science. In addition, such professional publications as *Scientific American, Computer Fraud & Security Bulletin, Virus Bulletin, Computers & Security*, and *Computer Law & Security Report* have provided me with valuable sources toward a scientific understanding of viruses and worms and similar computer programs. In addition, I have used conference proceedings from the antivirus business from the beginning of the 1990s on and invaluable Web resources archiving key discussions in computer security and the underground, for example, the Computer underground Digest and the Risks Digest Forum Archives.

These sources have been complemented with books, manuals, and guides from the late 1980s and early 1990s that acted as mediators between the public perception and scientific understanding of viruses. In that role, Ralf Bürger's *Computer Viruses: A High-Tech Disease* (1987), Peter J. Denning's *Computers under Attack: Intruders, Worms, and Viruses* (1991), David Ferbrache's *A Pathology of Computer Viruses* (1992), Philip Fites, Peter Johnston, and Martin Kratz's *The Computer Virus Crisis* (1989), and Bryan Clough and Paul Mungo's *Approaching Zero: Data Crime and the Computer underworld* (1992) are good examples. These discussions are supplemented with sources such as *Time*, *Wall Street Journal*, *Wired*, and *Byte*. In general, it is substantially easier to find sources from the security community and mainstream articulations, or technical diagrams and plans. In this sense, many of the antivirus protection sources contribute well to the first section of the book; similarly, the popular media articulations are emphasized to a certain extent in the second section. The third section draws from computer science texts, but also, for example, from the discussion in the early 1990s of living computer software, often within artificial life scientists' discourse but occasionally in popular media.

Fiction

Bear, Greg (2001) *Blood Music* (Orig. 1985). London: Gollancz.

Breton, Thierry and Beneich, Denis (1984). *Softwar—La Guerre Douce*. Paris: Robert Laffont.

Brunner, John (1976) *The Shockwave Rider* (Orig. 1975). New York: Ballantine Books.

Burroughs, William S. (1985). *The Adding Machine*. Collected Essays. London: John Calder.

Butler, Octavia (1985). *Clay's Ark*. New York: St. Martin's Press.

Butler, Samuel (1918). *Erewhon, or Over the Range* (Orig. 1872). London: William Brendon and Son.

Cadigan, Pat (2001). *Synners* (Orig. 1991). New York: Four Walls Eight Windows.

Crichton, Michael (1998). *Andromeda Strain* (Orig. 1969). London: Arrow Books.

Gerrold, David (1975). *When HARLIE Was One* (Orig. 1972). New York: Ballantine Books.

Gibson, William (1984). *Neuromancer*. New York: Ace Books.

Ryan, Thomas J. (1985). *The Adolescence of P-1* (Orig. 1977). New York: Baen Books.

Stephenson, Neal (1993). *Snow Crash* (Orig. 1992). London: Roc.

Movies and TV Series

Alien (1979). UK. Director: Ridley Scott. Writers: Dan O'Bannon and Ronald Shusett.

Alphaville (1965). France. Director and writer: Jean-Luc Godard.

The Andromeda Strain (1971). USA. Director: Robert Wise. Writers: Michael Crichton (novel) and Nelson Gidding (screenplay).

The Crazies (1973). USA. Director: George A. Romero. Writers: Paul McCullough and George A. Romero.

Hackers (1995). USA. Director: Iain Softley. Writer: Rafael Moreau.

Il était une fois la vie (1986). France. Director and Writer: Albert Barillé.

Independence Day (1996). USA. Director: Roland Emmerich. Writers: Dean Devlin and Roland Emmerich.

Johnny Mnemonic (1995). Canada/USA. Director: Robert Longo. Writer: William Gibson.

Jurassic Park (1993). USA. Director: Steven Spielberg. Writer: Michael Crichton.

The Matrix (1999). USA. Directors and writers: Andy and Larry Wachowski.

Outbreak (1995). USA. Director: Wolfgang Petersen. Writers: Laurence Dworet and Robert Roy Pool.

Scanners (1981). Canada. Director and writer: David Cronenberg.

Species (1995). USA. Director: Roger Donaldson; Writer: Dennis Feldman.

Tron (1982). USA/Taiwan. Director: Steven Lisberger. Writers: Steven Lisberger and Bonnie MacBird.

Videodrome (1983). Canada/USA. Director and Writer: David Cronenberg.

Wargames (1983). USA. Director: John Badham. Writers: Lawrence Lasker and Walter F. Parkes.

Westworld (1973). USA. Director and writer: Michael Crichton.

Magazines, Journals, Review Publications

ACM SIGCOMM Computer Communication Review 1981

ACM SIGOPS Operating Systems Review 1978, 1988

Bankers Monthly 1988

Boston Globe 1992

Byte 1980, 1985, 1989, 1991

C=lehti 1989

Communications of the ACM 1960–1961, 1967, 1979, 1982–1989

Computer Fraud & Security Bulletin 1983, 1985, 1988, 1989, 1993, 1995

Computer Law & Security Report 1990–1992

Computers & Security 1987

Computerworld 1990–1992

Computing Surveys 1969, 1975, 1979

Economist 1992

IEEE Computer 1989

Infosystems 1985
InfoWorld 1988, 1992
Journal of the ACM 1962
Mikrobitti 1987, 1988, 1991
Nation 1970
Nature 2001
Network World 1991
New Statesman & Society 1992
Newsweek 1995
New York Times 1955, 1960, 1989, 1990, 1992
Scientific American 1922, 1955, 1970, 1980–1989, 1995
The Times 1972, 1974, 1983, 1985
Time 1983–1988, 1992, 2000
Virus Bulletin 1989–1995
Wall Street Journal 1989–1992
Wired 1993, 1995, 1997, 2002, 2006
World Press Review 1993

Conference Proceedings

Anti-Virus Asia Researchers (AVAR) Conference 2001
EICAR Conference Proceedings 1994–1995
National Computer Security Association (NCSA) Conference Proceedings 1995
Proceedings of the Annual ACM Conference 1972
Proceedings of the International Conference on APL Programming Language 1984
Proceedings of the Northeast ACM Symposium on Personal Computer Security 1986
SIGPLAN Proceedings of the 1973 Meeting on Programming Languages and Information Retrieval 1974
Virus Bulletin Proceedings 1992–1995, 1997

Other Primary Material

Anderson, Alison, & Shain, Michael (1994). "Risk management." In: *Information Security Handbook*, edited by William Caelli, Dennis Longley, & Michael Shain. New York: Macmillan, 75–127.

Apter, Michael J. (1966). *Cybernetics and Development*. Oxford: Pergamon Press.

Bagrit, Leon (1965). *The Age of Automation*: The Reith Lectures 1964. Harmondsworth: Penguin Books.

Baran, Paul (1964). "On Distributed Communications." RAND Memorandum, August 1964. <http://www.rand.org/pubs/research_memoranda/2006/RM3420.pdf>. Accessed January 27, 2007.

Bateson, Gregory (1972). *Steps to an Ecology of Mind*. New York: Ballantine Books.

Beeler, Michael (1973). "Paterson's Worm." *Massachusetts Institute of Technology, A. I. Laboratory, Artificial Intelligence, memo 290*, June 1973. <ftp://publications.ai.mit.edu/ai-publications/pdf/AIM-290.pdf>. Accessed June 8, 2006.

Bell, D. E., & La Padula, L. J. (1976). "Secure Computer System: Unified Exposition and Multics Interpretation." MITRE Corporation report, March 1976.

Blackmore, Susan (2000). *The Meme Machine*. Oxford: Oxford University Press.

Brothers, M. H. (1991). "Computer Virus Protection Procedures." In: *Computers under Attack: Intruders, Worms, and Viruses*, edited by Peter J. Denning (pp. 357–380). New York: ACM Press.

Bürger, Ralf (1988). *Computer Viruses: A High-Tech Disease*. Grand Rapids, MI: Abacus/Data Becker.

Burks, Arthur W. (1970). *Essays on Cellular Automata*. Urbana: University of Illinois Press.

Caelli, William, & Tickle, Alan (1994). "Communications Security." In: *Information Security Handbook*, edited by William Caelli, Dennis Longley, & Michael Shain (pp. 649–746). New York: Macmillan.

Clough, Bryan, and Mungo, Paul (1992). *Approaching Zero: Data Crime and the Computer Underworld*. London: Faber and Faber.

Cohen, Fred (1984). "Computer Viruses—Theory and Experiments." DOD/NBS 7th Conference on Computer Security, originally appearing in IFIP-sec 84, also appearing as invited paper in IFIP-TC11, "Computers and Security, V6#1 (January 1987), 22–35. <http://www.all.net/books/virus/index.html>. Accessed March 6, 2007.

Cohen, Fred (1991a). "Implications of Computer Viruses and Current Methods of Defense." In: Cohen, Fred (1991b), "Friendly Contagion: Harnessing the Subtle Power of Computer Viruses." *The Sciences*, Sep/Oct 1991, vol. 31, issue 5, 22–29.

Cohen, Fred (1994). *It's Alive! The New Breed of Living Computer Programs*. New York: John Wiley & Sons.

Cohen, Frederick B. (1986). "Computer Viruses." Dissertation presented at the University of Southern California, December 1986.

Dawkins, Richard (1977). *The Selfish Gene*. Oxford: Oxford University Press.

Denning, Peter J. (ed.) (1991a). *Computers under Attack: Intruders, Worms, and Viruses*. New York: Addison-Wesley.

Denning, Peter J. (1991b). "Computer Viruses." In: *Computers under Attack: Intruders, Worms, and Viruses*, edited by Peter J. Denning (pp. 285–292). New York: Addison-Wesley. *Dictionary of Computing*. 2nd ed. (1986). Oxford: Oxford Science Publications.

Ferbrache, David (1992). *A Pathology of Computer Viruses*. Berlin: Springer-Verlag.

Fites, Philip, Peter Johnston, & Martin Kratz (1989). *The Computer Virus Crisis*. New York: Van Nostrand Reinhold.

Fleck, Ludwig (1979). *Genesis and Development of a Scientific Fact* (Translation of *Entstehung und Entwicklung einer wissenschaftlichen Tatsache: Einführung in die Lehre vom Denkstil und Denkkollektiv*, 1935). Chicago: University of Chicago Press.

F-Prot anti-virus software brochure, ca., beginning of the 1990s.

F-Prot Päivitystiedotteet (update memos) 2.01–2.24 (1992–1996).

F-Secure White Paper, 2001.

F-Secure, The Number of PC Viruses 1986–2006 Chart, 2006.

Gates, Bill (1996). *The Road Ahead.* London: Penguin Books.

Gravenreuth, Günter Frhr. von (1995). *Computerviren und ähnliche Softwareanomalien – Überlick und rechtliche Einordnung.* 2. Überarbeitete Auflage. München: Computer Verlag.

Hafner, Katie, & Markoff, John (1991). *Cyberpunk: Outlaws and Hackers on the Computer Frontier.* London: Fourth Estate.

Harley, David, Robert Slade, & Urs E. Gattiker (2001). *Viruses Revealed! Understand and Counter Malicious Software.* New York: Osborne/McGraw-Hill.

Highland, Harold Joseph (1991a). "The BRAIN Virus: Fact and Fantasy" (Orig. 1988). In: *Computers under Attack: Intruders, Worms, and Viruses,* edited by Peter J. Denning (pp. 293–298). New York: Addison-Wesley.

Highland, Harold Joseph (1991b). "Computer Viruses—A Post Mortem." In: *Computers Under Attack: Intruders, Worms, and Viruses,* edited by Peter J. Denning (299–315). New York: Addison-Wesley.

Hillis, Daniel (1989). *The Connection Machine.* Cambridge, MA: MIT Press.

Hillis, Daniel (1992) "Co-Evolving Parasites Improve Simulated Evolution as on Optimization Procedure." In: *Artificial Life II: SFI Studies in the Sciences of Complexity,* vol. 10, edited by C. D. Langton, C. Taylor, J. D. Farmer, & S. Rasmussen (pp. 313–324). Redwood City, CA: Addison-Wesley.

Hofstadter, Douglas (1979). *Gödel, Escher, Bach: An Eternal Golden Braid.* Stanford Terrace, Hassocks: Harvester Press.

Hyppönen, Ari, & Turtiainen, Esa (1990). *Virus—Tietokone sairastaa.* Espoo: Suomen ATK-kustannus.

Kelly, Kevin (1995). *Out of Control: The New Biology of Machines, Social Systems, and the Economic World.* Reading, MA: Perseus.

Järvinen, Petteri (1990). *Tietokonevirukset.* Helsinki: WSOY.

Järvinen, Petteri (1991). *Uusi pc-käyttäjän käsikirja.* Helsinki: WSOY.

Langton, Christopher (ed.) (1989a). *Artificial Life: A Proceedings Volume in the Santa Fe Institute in the Sciences of Complexity.* Redwood City, CA: Addison-Wesley.

Langton, Christopher (1989b). "Artificial Life." In: *Artificial Life: A Proceedings Volume in the Santa Fe Institute in the Sciences of Complexity,* edited by Christopher Langton (pp. 1–47). Redwood City, CA: Addison-Wesley.

Leary, Timothy (1992). *Chaos & Cyberculture.* Edited by Michael Horowitz. Berkeley, CA: Ronin.

Levy, Steven (1985). *Hackers: Heroes of the Computer Revolution* (Orig. 1984). New York: Dell Books.

Levy, Steven (1992). *Artificial Life: A Report from the Frontier Where Computers Meet Biology.* New York: Vintage Books.

Licklider, J. C. R. (1960). "Man-Computer Symbiosis." Originally in IRE Transactions on Human Factors in Electronics, Volume HFE-1, March 1960, pp. 4–11. Reprinted digitally at <http://memex.org/licklider.pdf>. Accessed March 8, 2007.

Longley, Dennis (1994a). "Access Control." In: *Information Security Handbook,* edited by William Caelli, Dennis Longley, & Michael Shain (pp. 455–544). Basingstoke: Macmillan.

Longley, Dennis (1994b). "Security of Stored Data and Programs." In: *Information Security Handbook*, edited by William Caelli, Dennis Longley, & Michael Shain (pp. 545–648). Basingstoke: Macmillan.

Ludwig, Mark A. (1993). *Computer Viruses, Artificial Life and Evolution*. Tucson, AZ: American Eagle.

Ludwig, Mark A. (1996). *The Little Black Book of Computer Viruses*. E-version. Tucson, AZ: American Eagle.

Lundell, Allan (1989). *Virus! The Secret World of Computer Invaders That Breed and Destroy*. Chicago: Contemporary Books.

Margulis, Lynn, & Sagan, Dorion (1995). *What Is Life?* New York: Simon & Schuster.

Maturana, Humberto, & Varela, Francisco (1980). *Autopoiesis and Cognition*. Dordrecht: D. Reidel.

McAfee, John, & Haynes, Colin (1989). *Computer Viruses, Worms, Data Diddlers, Killer Programs & Other Threats to Your System*. New York: St. Martin's Press.

Monod, Jacques (1970). *Le hasard at la nécessité: Essai sur la philosophie naturelle de la biologie moderne*. Paris: Seuil.

Negroponte, Nicholas (1995). *Being Digital*. London: Hodder & Stoughton.

Neumann, John von (1966). *Theory of Self-Reproducing Automata*. Edited and compiled by Arthur W. Burks. Urbana: University of Illinois Press.

Neumann, Peter (1991). "A Perspective from the RISKS Forum." In: *Computers under Attack: Intruders, Worms, and Viruses*, edited by Peter J. Denning (pp. 535–543). New York: Addison-Wesley.

Nori, Franziska (2002). "I Love You." In: The I Love You Exhibition Catalogue.<http://www.digitalcraft.org/index.php?artikel_id=284>. Accessed June 7, 2006.

Ornstein, Severo M. (1991). "Beyond Worms." In: *Computers under Attack: Intruders, Worms, and Viruses*, edited by Peter J. Denning (pp. 518–521). New York: Addison-Wesley.

Packard, Norman (1989). "Evolving Bugs in a Simulated Ecosystem." In: *Artificial Life: A Proceedings Volume in the Santa Fe Institute in the Sciences of Complexity*, edited by Christopher Langton (pp. 141–155). Redwood City, CA: Addison-Wesley.

Parker, Donn B. (1976). *Crime by Computer*. New York: Charles Scribner's Sons.

Parker, Donn B. (1991a). "The Trojan Horse Virus and Other Crimoids." In: *Computers under Attack: Intruders, Worms, and Viruses*, edited by Peter J. Denning (pp. 544–554). New York: Addison-Wesley.

Parker, Donn B. (1991b). "Take a Strong Stand." In: *Computers under Attack: Intruders, Worms, and Viruses*, edited by Peter J. Denning (pp. 521–522). New York: Addison-Wesley.

Pattee, H. H. (1989). "Simulations, Realizations, and Theories of Life." In: *Artificial Life: A Proceedings Volume in the Santa Fe Institute in the Sciences of Complexity*, edited by Christopher Langton (pp. 63–77). Redwood City, CA: Addison-Wesley.

Prigogine, Ilya, & Stengers, Isabelle (1984). *Order out of Chaos: Man's New Dialogue with Nature*. Toronto: Bantam Books.

Rasmussen, Steen (1989) "Towards a Quantitative Theory of the Origin of Life." In: *Artificial Life: A Proceedings Volume in the Santa Fe Institute in the Sciences of Complexity*, edited by Christopher Langton (pp. 79–104). Redwood City, CA: Addison-Wesley.

Rasmussen, Steen, Carsten Knudsen, & Rasmus Feldberg (1992). "Dynamics of Programmable Matter." In: *Artificial Life II: SFI Studies in the Sciences of Complexity*, vol. 10, edited by C. D. Langton, C. Taylor, J. D. Farmer, & S. Rasmussen (pp. 211–254). Redwood City, CA: Addison-Wesley.

Rome, Beatrice K., & Rome, Sydney C. (1971). *Organizational Growth through Decisionmaking: A Computer-Based Experiment in Eductive Method*. New York: American Elsevier.

Rucker, Rudy, R. U. Sirius, & Queen Mu (eds.) (1993). *Mondo 2000: A User's Guide to the New Edge*. London: Thames and Hudson.

Rushkoff, Douglas (1996). *Media Virus! Hidden Agendas in Popular Culture*. New York: Ballantine Books.

Samuelson, Pamela (1991). "Computer Viruses and Worms: Wrong, Crime, or Both?" In: *Computers under Attack: Intruders, Worms, and Viruses*, edited by Peter J. Denning (pp. 479–485). New York: Addison-Wesley.

Scherlis, William, Stephen Squires, & Richard Pethia (1991). "Computer Emergency Response." In: *Computers under Attack: Intruders, Worms, and Viruses*, edited by Peter J. Denning (pp. 495–504). New York: Addison-Wesley.

Selfridge, Oliver G. (1989). "Pandemonium: A Paradigm for Learning." In: *Neurocomputing. Foundations of Research*, edited by James A. Anderson and Edward Rosenfeld (pp. 117–122). Cambridge MA: MIT Press.

Shain, Michael (1994). "An Overview of Security." In: *Information Security Handbook*, edited by William Caelli, Dennis Longley, & Michael Shain. Basingstoke: Macmillan.

Shannon, Claude E., & Weaver, Warren (1949). *The Mathematical Theory of Communication*. Urbana: University of Illinois Press.

Simon, Herbert A. (1969). *The Sciences of the Artificial*. Cambridge, MA: MIT Press.

Smith, Alvy Ray (1992). "Simple Nontrivial Self-Reproducing Machines." In: *Artificial Life II: SFI Studies in the Sciences of Complexity*, vol. 10, edited by C. D. Langton, C. Taylor, J. D. Farmer, & S. Rasmussen (pp. 709–726). Redwood City, CA: Addison-Wesley.

Spafford, Eugene H. (1992). "Computer Viruses—A Form of Artificial Life?" In: *Artificial Life II: SFI Studies in the Sciences of Complexity*, vol. 10, edited by C. D. Langton, C. Taylor, J. D. Farmer, & S. Rasmussen (pp. 727–745). Redwood City, CA: Addison-Wesley.

Spafford, Eugene H. (1997). "Computer Viruses as Artificial Life." In: *Artificial Life: An Overview*, edited by Christopher G. Langton. Cambridge, MA: MIT Press.

Spafford, Eugene, Kathleen Heaphy, & David Ferbrache (1991). "A Computer Virus Primer." In: *Computers under Attack: Intruders, Worms, and Viruses*, edited by Peter J. Denning (pp. 316–355). Peter J. New York: Addison-Wesley.

Sterling, Bruce (1994). *The Hacker Crackdown: Law and Disorder on the Electronic Frontier*. London: Penguin Books.

Toffler, Alvin (1971). *Future Shock*. New York: Bantam Books.

Tozzi, Tommaso (1991). "Rebel! Virus.asm." In: *Oppositions '80'*, edited by T. Tozzi. Milan: Amen Editions.

Virus Bulletin (1993). *Survivor's Guide to Computer Viruses*. Abingdon: Virus Bulletin.

Tuomi, Ilkka (1987). *Ei ainoastaan hakkerin käsikirja*. Juva: WSOY.

Ward, Mark (2000). *Virtual Organisms: The Startling World of Artificial Life.* New York: St Martin's Press.

Wiener, Norbert (1961). *Cybernetics, or Control and Communication in the Animal and the Machine.* 2nd ed. New York & London: MIT Press and John Wiley & Sons.

Wiener, Norbert (1964). *God and Golem, Inc.* Cambridge, MA: MIT Press.

Winograd, Terry, & Flores, Fernando (1986). *Understanding Computers and Cognition: A New Foundation for Design.* Norwood, NJ: Ablex Publishing.

Interviews

Cohen, Fred (2003). E-mail to Jussi Parikka, November 4, 2003.

Fix, Bernd (2005). E-mail to Jussi Parikka, November 7, 2005.

Kleinrock, Leonard (2005). E-mail to Jussi Parikka, October 14, 2005.

Latva, Risto (2004). E-mail to Jussi Parikka, November 29, 2004.

McIlroy, Doug (2005). E-mail to Jussi Parikka, April 25, 2005.

Slade, Rob (2004). E-mail to Jussi Parikka, October 8, 2004.

Stallman, Richard (2005). E-mails to Jussi Parikka, June 3 & 4, 2005.

Sulonen, Reijo (2005). Phone Interview with Jussi Parikka, November 23, 2005.

Thompson, Ken (2005). E-mail to Jussi Parikka, April 27, 2005.

Vyssotsky, Victor (2005a). E-mail to Jussi Parikka, June 2, 2005.

Vyssotsky, Victor (2005b). E-mail to Jussi Parikka, June 11, 2005.

Web Pages and Resources

2600 web site. <Http://www.2600.com/>. Accessed November 9, 2006.

Alive. Electronic Magazine. Volumes I–III (1994–1995). Archived at http://vxheaven.org/. Accessed October 15, 2015.

Bangeman-Report (1994). Europe and the Global Information Society. <http://ec.europa.eu/archives/ISPO/infosoc/backg/bangeman.html>. Accessed October 16, 2015.

Barbrook, Richard & Cameron, Andy (1996). "The Californian Ideology." <http://www.hrc.wmin.ac.uk/theory-californianideology.html>. Accessed March 8, 2007.

Barlow, John Perry (1996). "A Declaration of Independence of Cyberspace." <http://homes.eff.org/~barlow/Declaration-Final.html>. Accessed March 9, 2007.

Barr, Lukas (s.a.). "Long Live the New Flesh. An Interview with David Cronenberg." <http://industrycentral.net/director_interviews/DC01.HTM>. Accessed March 6, 2007.

Berardi, Franco (Bifo) (s.a.). "Responses to the Californian-Ideology." <http://www.hrc.wmin.ac.uk/theory-californianideology-responses2.html>. Accessed March 8, 2007.

Buckner and Garcia Official Pacman Fever Site. <http://www.bucknergarcia.com/>. Accessed March 8, 2007.

Burroughs Corporation Records. System Development Corporation Records, 1946–1982. <http://www.chi.umn.edu/collections/inv/burros/cbi00090-098.html>. Accessed March 5, 2007.

Computer Immune Systems. <http://www.cs.unm.edu/~immsec/>. Accessed March 8, 2007.

Computer Underground Digest, volumes 1–7 (1990–1995). <http://www.textfiles.com/magazines/CUD/>. Accessed October 22, 2015.

Computer Virus Timeline. <http://www.infoplease.com/ipa/A0872842.html>. Accessed March 8, 2007.

"Darwin, A Game of Survival of the Fittest among Programs." A Letter by V. Vissotsky et al. to C. A. Land, 1971, transcribed and on-line at <http://www.cs.dartmouth.edu/~doug/darwin.pdf>. Accessed March 8, 2007.

Dictionary of the History of Ideas: Studies of Selected Pivotal Ideas, edited by Philip P. Wiener. <http://etext.virginia.edu/DicHist/dict.html>. Accessed December 14, 2006.

Dyson, Esther, George Gilder, George Keyworth, & Alvin Toffler (1994). "Cyberspace and the American Dream. A Magna Charta for the Knowledge Age." Published by Progress and Freedom Foundation, Release 1.2, August 22, 1994. <http://www.hartford-hwp.com/archives/45/062.html>. Accessed March 8, 2007.

EICAR Homepage. <http://www.eicar.org/>. Accessed December 14, 2006.

Hack-Tic magazine, 1989–1994. <http://www.hacktic.nl/>. Accessed December 14, 2006.

History of Computer Security, Early Computer Security Resources. <http://csrc.nist.gov/publications/history/index.html>. Accessed November 11, 2006.

Institute for Computational Engineering and Sciences, University of Texas at Austin. <http://www.ticam.utexas.edu/~organism/bug.html>. Accessed March 8, 2007.

Kevin, Kelly, Out of Control. <http://www.kk.org/outofcontrol/>. Accessed March 4, 2007.

Lampo, Luca (2002). "When The Virus Becomes Epidemic." An Interview with Luca Lampo by Snafu and Vanni Brusadin, April 18, 2002. <http://bbs.thing.net/c>. Accessed January 24, 2007.

Library of Congress. <http://thomas.loc.gov/>. Accessed August 24, 2006.

National Information Infrastructure (1994). <http://clinton1.nara.gov/White_House/EOP/OVP/html/nii1.html>. Accessed March 13, 2007.

Naval Historical Center, "The First Computer Bug." <http://www.history.navy.mil/photos/images/h96000/h96566kc.htm>. Accessed March 8, 2007.

Oxford English Dictionary. <http://www.oed.com/>. Accessed August 24, 2006.

Perry, John (1992) "Core Wars Genetics: The Evolution of Predation." <http://corewar.co.uk/perry.htm>. Accessed March 8, 2007.

Progress and Freedom Foundation. <http://www.pff.org/>. Accessed August 24, 2006.

Ray, Thomas S. (1993) "How I Created Life in a Virtual Universe." <http://www.his.atr.jp/~ray/pubs/nathist/>. Accessed March 8, 2007.

Ray, Thomas S. (1995) "A Proposal to Create Two Biodiversity Reserves: One Digital and One Organic." <http://www.his.atr.jp/~ray/pubs/reserves/>. Accessed March 8, 2007.

Risks Digest Forum Archives. Volumes 1–16 (1985–1995). <http://catless.ncl.ac.uk/Risks>. Accessed March 5, 2007.

Runme.org. "Say it with Software Art." <http://www.runme.org/>. Accessed March 13, 2007.

Sarah Gordon's web page. <http://www.badguys.org/>. Accessed March 13, 2007.

Slade, Robert (1992). "History of Computer Viruses." <http://members.tripod.com/thermopyle/sladehis.htm#C01>. Accessed March 8, 2007.

Stewart, D. J. (2000). "An Essay on the Origins of Cybernetics" (Orig. 1959). <http://www.hfr.org.uk/cybernetics-pages/origins.htm>. Accessed March 8, 2007.

Theriault, Carole (1999) "Computer Viruses Demystified." <http://www.securitytechnet.com/resource/rsc-center/vendor-wp/sopho/demy_wen.pdf>. Accessed March 13, 2007.

Tierra Web Page (Thomas S. Ray). <http://life.ou.edu/tierra/>. Accessed October 16, 2015.

Turing Digital Archive. <http://www.turingarchive.org/>. Accessed December 14, 2006.

U.S. Code Collection <Http://www4.law.cornell.edu/uscode/>. Accessed 2007.

Vanderbilt News Archive. <http://tvnews.vanderbilt.edu/>. Accessed March 13, 2007.

Virus Bulletin journal. <http://www.virusbtn.com/>. Accessed August 24, 2006.

Walker, John (1996). "The Animal Episode." <http://www.fourmilab.to/documents/univac/animal.html>. Accessed December 14, 2006.

Webdeleuze. <http://www.webdeleuze.com>. Accessed March 15, 2007.

Wikipedia. <http://en.wikipedia.org/wiki/Main_Page>. Accessed March 8, 2007.

Sales Brochures

All s.a., early 1990s:
F-Secure anti-virus program
Information Security-brochure from Computer Security Engineers (CSE)
ThunderBYTE PC Immunizer
VIREX anti-virus program brochure

Research Literature

Abbate, Janet (2000). *Inventing the Internet.* Cambridge, MA: MIT Press.

Agamben, Giorgio (1998). *Homo Sacer: Sovereign Power and Bare Life.* Translated by Daniel Heller-Roazen. Stanford, CA: Stanford University Press.

Ahonen, Kimmo (1999) "Palkoihmisten ongelma historiantutkimuksessa—Don Siegelin tieteiselokuva *Varastetut ihmiset* (1956) oman aikakautensa pelkojen tulkkina." In: *Pitkät jäljet. Historioita kahdelta mantereelta,* edited by Eero Kuparinen (pp. 14–43). Turku: Turun yliopisto, yleinen historia.

Ansell-Pearson, Keith (1997) *Viroid Life: Perspectives on Nietzsche and the Transhuman Condition.* London: Routledge.

Ansell-Pearson, Keith (1999). *Germinal Life: The Difference and Repetition of Deleuze and Guattari.* London: Routledge.

Armstrong, Tim (1998). *Modernism, Technology and the Body: A Cultural History.* Cambridge: Cambridge University Press.

Aspray, William (1990). *John von Neumann and the Origins of Modern Computing.* Cambridge, MA: MIT Press.

Bal, Mieke (1999). "Introduction." In: *The Practice of Cultural Analysis: Exposing Interdisciplinary Interpretation,* edited by Mieke Bal, with the assistance of Bryan Gonzales (pp. 1–14). Stanford, CA: Stanford University Press.

Balsamo, Anne (1996). "Forms of Technological Embodiment: Reading the Body in Contemporary Culture." In: *Cyberspace/Cyberbodies/Cyberpunk: Cultures of Technological Embodiment*, edited by Mike Featherstone and Roger Burrows (pp. 215–237). London: Sage.

Barabási, Albert-László (2003). *Linked: How Everything Is Connected to Everything Else and What It Means for Business, Science, and Everyday Life*. New York: Plume.

Bardini, Thierry (2006). "Hypervirus: A Clinical Report." *CTheory–An International Journal of Theory, Technology, and Culture*, February 2, 2006, <http://www.ctheory.net/articles.aspx?id=504>. Accessed March 13, 2007.

Bauman, Zygmunt (1993). *Postmodern Ethics*. Oxford & Cambridge: Blackwell.

Bauman, Zygmunt (1995). *Modernity and Ambivalence* (Orig. 1991). Cambridge: Polity Press.

Beck, Ulrich (1986). *Risikogesellchaft. Auf dem Weg in eine andere Moderne*. Frankfurt am Main: Suhrkamp.

Beck, Ulrich (1988). *Gegengifte. Die Organisierte Unverantwortlichkeit*. Frankfurt am Main: Suhrkamp.

Beck, Ulrich (2000). "Risk Society Revisited: Theory, Politics and Research Programmes." In: *The Risk Society and Beyond: Critical Issues for Social Theory*, edited by Barbara Adam, Ulrich Beck, & Joost Van Loon (pp. 211–229). London, Thousand Oaks, CA, & New Delhi: Sage.

Beck, Ulrich (2002). "The Cosmopolitan Society and its Enemies." *Theory, Culture & Society*, vol. 19, issue 1–2, 17–44.

Beniger, James R. (1997). *The Control Revolution: Technological and Economic Origins of the Information Society* (Orig. 1986). Cambridge, MA: Harvard University Press.

Benjamin, Walter (1969). *Illuminations*. Edited with an introduction by Hannah Arendt. New York: Shocken Books.

Bishop, Ryan (2006). "The Global University" *Theory, Culture & Society*, vol. 23, issue 2–3, 563–566.

Blas, Zach (2012). "Viral, Viral." *Women Studies Quarterly*, vol. 40, issue 1 & 2, 29–39.

Bogue, Ronald (2003). *Deleuze on Music, Painting and the Arts*. New York: Routledge.

Bolter, Jay David, and Grusin, Richard (1999). *Remediation: Understanding New Media*. Cambridge, MA: MIT Press.

Bolz, Norbert (1998) "The user-illusion of the world." *Mediamatic*, vol. 9, issue 2–3. <http://www.mediamatic.net/article-5672-en.html>. Accessed January 26, 2007.

Borck, Cornelius (2004). "Vivarium des Wissens. Kleine Ontologie des Schupfens." In *Virus! Mutationen einer Metapher*, edited by Ruth Mayer & Brigitte Weingart (pp. 43–60). Bielefeld: Transcript.

Boyer, Christine M. (1996). *Cybercities: Visual Perception in the Age of Electronic Communications*. New York: Princeton Architectural Press.

Braidotti, Rosi (2001). "How to Endure Intensity: Towards a Sustainable Nomadic Subject." In: *Micropolitics of Media Culture*, edited by Patricia Pisters (pp. 177–201). Amsterdam: Amsterdam University Press.

Braidotti, Rosi (2002). *Metamorphoses: Towards a Materialist Theory of Becoming*. Cambridge: Polity Press.

Braidotti, Rosi (2006). *Transpositions: On Nomadic Ethics*. Cambridge: Polity Press.

Braidotti, Rosi (2012). *The Posthuman*. Cambridge: Polity Press.

Braudel, Fernand (1997). *Les Ambitions de l'Histoire*. Paris: Éditions de Fallois.

Briggs, Asa, & Burke, Peter (2002) *A Social History of the Media: From Gutenberg to the Internet*. Cambridge: Polity Press.

Brown, Steven D. (2002). "Michel Serres: Science, Translation and the Logic of the Parasite." *Theory, Culture & Society*, vol. 19, issue 3, 1–27.

Brown, Wendy (2015). *Undoing the Demos. Neoliberalism's Stealth Revolution*. New York: Zone Books.

Brunton, Finn (2013). *Spam: A Shadow History of the Internet*. Cambridge, MA: MIT Press.

Buck-Morss, Susan (1991). *The Dialectics of Seeing: Walter Benjamin and the Arcades Project*. Cambridge, MA: MIT Press.

Bukatman, Scott (1993). *Terminal Identity: The Virtual Subject in Post-modern Science Fiction*. Durham, NC: Duke University Press.

Burke, Peter (2004). *What Is Cultural History?* Cambridge: Polity Press.

Campbell-Kelly, Martin (2004). *From Airline Reservations to Sonic the Hedgehog: A History of the Software Industry*. Cambridge, MA: MIT Press.

Campbell-Kelly, Martin, & Aspray, William (1996). *Computer: A History of the Information Machine*. New York: Basic Books.

Castells, Manuel (1996). *The Rise of the Network Society*. Cambridge, MA: Blackwell.

Castells, Manuel (2001). "Informationalism and the Network Society." In: *The Hacker Ethic and the Spirit of Capitalism*, edited by Pekka Himanen (pp. 157–178). New York: Random House.

Caygill, Howard (2004). "Walter Benjamin's Concept of Cultural History." In: *The Cambridge Companion to Walter Benjamin*, edited by David S. Ferris (pp. 73–96). Cambridge: Cambridge University Press.

Ceruzzi, Paul E. (1998). *A History of Modern Computing*. Cambridge, MA: MIT Press.

Channell, David F. (1991). *The Vital Machine: A Study of Technology and Organic Life*. New York: Oxford University Press.

Chartier, Roger (1997). *On the Edge of the Cliff: History, Language, and Practices*. Translated by Lydia G. Cochrane. Baltimore: Johns Hopkins University Press.

Chun, Wendy Hui Kyong (2006). *Control and Freedom: Power and Paranoia in the Age of Fiber Optics*. Cambridge, MA: MIT Press.

Chun, Wendy Hui Kyong (2015). "Open Life of Objects." A talk at the Secret Life of Objects conference, August 2015, Rio de Janeiro, Brazil.

Clark, Nigel (1997). "Panic Ecology: Nature in the Age of Superconductivity." *Theory, Culture & Society*, vol. 14, issue 1, 77–96.

Clough, Patricia, & Puar, Jasbir (eds.) (2012). Viral-special issue. *Women Studies Quarterly*, vol. 40, issue 1 & 2.

Colebrook, Claire (2002). *Understanding Deleuze*. Crows Nest: Allen & Unwin.

Colwell, C. (1996). "Deleuze, Sense and the Event of AIDS." *Postmodern Culture*, vol. 6, issue 2. <http://www3.iath.virginia.edu/pmc/text-only/issue.196/colwell.196>. Accessed March 13, 2007.

Davis, Martin (2000). *The Universal Computer: The Road From Leibniz to Turing*. London: W. W. Norton & Company.

Debray, Régis (1996). *Media Manifesto: On the Technological Transmission of Cultural Forms* (Orig. 1994). Translated by Eric Rauth. London: Verso.

Debray, Régis (2001). *Cours de médiologie générale*. Paris: Gallimard.

DeLanda, Manuel (1991). *War in the Age of Intelligent Machines*. New York: Zone Books.

DeLanda, Manuel (1992). "Nonorganic Life." In: *Incorporations*, edited by Jonathan Crary and Sanford Kwinter (pp. 129–167). New York: Zone Books.

DeLanda, Manuel (1998). "Meshworks, Hierarchies, and Interfaces." In: *The Virtual Dimension*, edited by John Beckman (pp. 275–285). New York: Princeton Architectural Press.

DeLanda, Manuel (1999). "Deleuze, Diagrams, and the Open-Ended Becoming of the World." In: *Becomings: Explorations in Time, Memory, and Futures*, edited by Elisabeth Grosz (pp. 29–42). Ithaca, NY: Cornell University Press.

DeLanda, Manuel (2002). *Intensive Science and Virtual Philosophy*. London: Continuum.

DeLanda, Manuel (2003). *A Thousand Years of Nonlinear History* (Orig. 1997). New York: Zone Books.

Deleuze, Gilles (1986). *Nietzsche & Philosophy* (Orig. 1962). Translated by Hugh Tomlinson. London: The Athlone Press.

Deleuze, Gilles (1988). *Spinoza: Practical Philosophy* (Orig. 1970). Translated by Robert Hurley. San Francisco: City Lights Books.

Deleuze, Gilles (1990). *Pourparlers 1972–1990*. Paris: Les éditions de minuit.

Deleuze, Gilles (1992). "What Is a Dispositif?" In: *Michel Foucault Philosopher*, essays translated from the French and German by Timothy J. Armstrong (pp. 159–168). New York: Harvester Wheatsheaf.

Deleuze, Gilles (1994). *Difference & Repetition* (Orig. 1968). Translated by Paul Patton. New York: Columbia University Press.

Deleuze, Gilles (1997a). "Immanence: A Life" (translated by Nick Millett). *Theory, Culture & Society*, vol. 14, issue 2, 3–7.

Deleuze, Gilles (1997b). "Desire and Pleasure." In: *Foucault and His Interlocutors*, edited by Arnold I. Davidson (pp. 183–192). Chicago & London: Chicago University Press.

Deleuze, Gilles (1998). *Foucault* (Orig. 1986). Translated by Seán Hand. Minneapolis: University of Minnesota Press.

Deleuze, Gilles, & Guattari, Félix (1983). *Anti-Oedipus: Capitalism and Schizophrenia* (Orig. 1972). Translated by Robert Hurley, Mark Seem, & Helen R. Lane. Minneapolis: University of Minnesota Press.

Deleuze, Gilles, & Guattari, Félix (1987). *A Thousand Plateaus: Capitalism and Schizophrenia* (Orig. 1980). Translated by Brian Massumi. Minneapolis: University of Minnesota Press.

Deleuze, Gilles, & Guattari, Félix (1994). *What Is Philosophy?* (Orig. 1991). Translated by Hugh Tomlinson & Graham Burchell. New York: Columbia University Press.

Deleuze, Gilles, & Parnet, Claire (1996). *Dialogues*. Nouvelle edition. Paris: Champs Flammarion.

Derrida, Jacques (1972). *La Dissémination*. Paris: Seuil.

Doane, Mary Ann (2006). "Information, Crisis, Catastrophe." In: *New Media, Old Media: A History and Theory Reader*, edited by Wendy Hui Kyong Chun & Thomas Keenan. New York & London: Routledge.

Dolphijn, Rich, & van der Tuin, Iris (eds.) (2012). *New Materialism: Interviews & Cartographies*. Ann Arbor, MI: Open Humanities Press.

Dougherty, Stephen (2001). "The Biopolitics of the Killer Virus Novel." *Cultural Critique*, vol. 48, Spring, 1–29.

Douglas, Susan J. (1989). *Inventing American Broadcasting 1899–1922*. Baltimore: Johns Hopkins University Press.

Dyson, Freeman (1999). *Origins of Life*. Cambridge: Cambridge University Press.

Dyson, George B. (1997) *Darwin among the Machines: The Evolution of Global Intelligence*. Reading, MA: Helix Books.

Edwards, Paul E. (1996). *The Closed World: Computers and the Politics of Discourse in Cold War America*. Cambridge, MA: MIT Press.

Elsaesser, Thomas (2004). "The New Film History as Media Archaeology." *Cinémas*, vol. 14, issue 2–3, Printemps. <http://www.erudit.org/revue/cine/>. Accessed August 24, 2006.

Emmeche, Claus (1994). *The Garden in the Machine: The Emerging Science of Artificial Life*. Princeton, NJ: Princeton University Press.

Erickson, Christa (2002). "Networked Interventions: Debugging the Electronic Frontier." *NMEDIAC*, vol. 1, issue 2. <http://www.ibiblio.org/nmediac/summer2002/networked.html>. Accessed March 8, 2007.

Ernst, Wolfgang (2002). *Das Rumoren der Archive. Ordnung aus Unordnung*. Berlin: Merve.

Ernst, Wolfgang (2006). "Dis/continuities. Does the Archive Become Metaphorical in Multi-Media Space?" In: *New Media, Old Media: A History and Theory Reader*, edited by Wendy Hui Kyong Chun & Thomas Keenan (pp. 105–123). New York: Routledge.

Flichy, Patrice (2001). *L'imaginaire d'Internet*. Paris: La Découverte.

Flieger, Jerry Aline (2003). "Is Oedipus On-Line?" In: *Jacques Lacan Critical Evaluations in Cultural Theory*, Vol. 3: *Society, Politics, Ideology*, edited by Slavoj Žižek (pp. 394–410). London: Routledge.

Forbes, Nancy (2004). *Imitation of Life: How Biology Is Inspiring Computing*. Cambridge, MA: MIT Press.

Foucault, Michel (1976). *Histoire de la sexualité. La volonté de savoir*. Paris: Gallimard.

Foucault, Michel (2000a). "The Birth of Biopolitics." In: *Ethics: Subjectivity and Truth: Essential Works of Foucault 1954–1984*, Vol. 1, edited by Paul Rabinow, translated by Robert Hurley et al. (pp. 73–79). London: Penguin Books.

Foucault, Michel (2000b). "Introduction to 'The Use of Pleasure'" (Orig. 1984). Translated by Robert Hurley. In: *Identity: A Reader*, edited by Paul Du Gay, Jessica Evans, & Peter Redman (pp. 360–370). London: Sage.

Foucault, Michel (2000c) "Questions of Method." In: *Power: Essential Works of Foucault 1954–1984*, Vol. 3, edited by Paul Rabinow (pp. 223–238). London: Penguin Books.

Foucault, Michel (2000d). "Life Experience and Science" (Orig. 1985). In: *Aesthetics: Essential Works of Foucault 1954–1984*, Vol. 2, edited by James D. Faubion, translated by Robert Hurley et al. (pp. 465–478). London: Penguin Books.

Foucault, Michel (2000e). "Nietzsche, Genealogy, History" (Orig. 1971). In: *Aesthetic:. Essential Works of Foucault 1954–1984*, Vol. 2, edited by James D. Faubion, translated by Robert Hurley et al. (pp. 369–391). London: Penguin Books.

Foucault, Michel (2002). *The Archaeology of Knowledge* (Orig. 1969). Translated by A. M. Sheridan Smith. London & New York: Routledge.

Foucault, Michel (2007). *Security, Territory, Population: Lectures at the College de France, 1977–1978.* Edited by Michel Senellart. Basingstoke: Palgrave.

Fox Keller, Evelyn (1995). *Refiguring Life: Metaphors of Twentieth-Century Biology.* New York: Columbia University Press.

Fox Keller, Evelyn (2002). *Making Sense of Life: Explaining Biological Development with Models, Metaphors, and Machines.* Cambridge, MA: Harvard University Press.

Franklin, Seb (2015). *Control: Digitality as Cultural Logic.* Cambridge, MA: MIT Press.

Freud, Sigmund (1995). "Civilization and Its Discontents" (Orig. 1930). In: *The Freud Reader,* edited by Peter Gay (pp. 722–772). London: Vintage.

Fuller, Matthew (2003). *Behind the Blip: Essays on the Culture of Software.* New York: Autonomedia.

Fuller, Matthew (2005). *Media Ecologies: Materialist Energies in Art and Technoculture.* Cambridge, MA: MIT Press.

Galloway, Alexander R. (2004). *Protocol: How Control Exists after Decentralization.* Cambridge, MA: MIT Press.

Gane, Nicholas (2005). "Radical Post-Humanism: Friedrich Kittler and the Primacy of Technology." *Theory, Culture & Society,* vol. 22, issue 3, 25–41.

Gere, Charlie (2002). *Digital Culture.* London: Reaktion Books.

Goddard, Michael (2011). "Towards an Archaeology of Media Ecologies: 'Media Ecology,' Political Subjectivation and Free Radios." *Fibreculture,* issue 17. <http://seventeen.fibreculturejournal.org/>.

Goffey, Andrew (2003). "Idiotypic Networks, Normative Networks." *M/C: A Journal of Media and Culture,* vol. 6, issue 4. <http://journal.media-culture.org.au/0308/07-idiotypic.php>. Accessed January 24, 2007.

Goodchild, Philip (1996). *Deleuze & Guattari: An Introduction to the Politics of Desire.* London: Sage.

Goodman, Marc (2015). *Future Crimes.* New York: Doubleday.

Grossberg, Lawrence (2000). "Contexts of Cultural Studies." In: *Inescapable Horizon: Culture and Context,* edited by Sirpa Leppänen & Joel Kuortti (pp. 27–49). Jyäskylä: Publications of the Research Unit for Contemporary Culture.

Grosz, Elizabeth (1995). *Space, Time, and Perversion: Essays on the Politics of Bodies.* New York: Routledge.

Grosz, Elizabeth (1999). "Thinking the New: Of Futures Yet Unthought." In: *Becomings: Explorations in Time, Memory, and Futures,* edited by Elisabeth Grosz (pp. 15–28). Ithaca NY: Cornell University Press.

Grosz, Elizabeth (2001). "Deleuze's Bergson: Duration, the Virtual and a Politics of the Future." In: *Deleuze and Feminist Theory,* edited by Ian Buchanan & Claire Colebrook (pp. 214–234). Edinburgh: Edinburgh University Press.

Grosz, Elizabeth (2004). *Nick of Time: Politics, Evolution, and the Untimely.* Durham, NY: Duke University Press.

Grosz, Elizabeth (2005). *Time Travels: Feminism, Nature, Power*. Durham, NC: Duke University Press.

Grusin, Richard (2010). *Premediation: Affect and Mediality after 9/11*. Basingstoke: Palgrave Macmillan.

Guattari, Félix (1992). "Regimes, Pathways, Subjects." Translated by Brian Massumi. In: *Incorporations*, edited by Jonathan Crary & Sanford Kwinter (pp. 16–37). New York: Zone Books.

Guattari, Félix (1995). *Chaosmosis: An Ethico-Aesthetic Paradigm* (Orig. 1992). Translated by Paul Bains & Julian Pefanis. Sydney: Power Publications.

Guattari, Félix (2000). *The Three Ecologies* (Orig. 1989). Translated by Ian Pindar & Paul Sutton. London: Athlone Press.

Guattari, Félix (2001). "Machinic Heterogenesis." In: *Reading Digital Culture*, edited by David Trend (pp. 38–51). Malden, MA: Blackwell.

Guillaume, Marc (1987). "The Metamorphoses of Epidemia." In: *Zone ½: The Contemporary City*, edited by Michel Feher & Sanford Kwinter (pp. 59–69). New York: Zone Books.

Gutting, Gary (1989). *Michel Foucault's Archaeology of Scientific Reason*. Cambridge: Cambridge University Press.

Haddon, Leslie (1993). "Interactive Games." In *Future Visions: New Technologies of the Screen*, edited by Philip Hayward & Tana Wollen (pp. 123–147). London: BFI.

Halbach, Wulf R. (1998) "Netzwerke." In: *Geschichte der Medien*, edited by Manfred Faßler & Wulf Halbach (pp. 269–307). München: Wilhelm Fink.

Halewood, Michael (2005). "A. N. Whitehead, Information and Social Theory." *Theory, Culture & Society*, vol. 22, issue 6, 73–94.

Hallward, Peter (2006). *Out of This World: Deleuze and the Philosophy of Creation*. London: Verso.

Haraway, Donna J. (1991). *Simians, Cyborgs and Women: The Reinvention of Nature*. New York: Routledge.

Hård, Mikael, & Jamison, Andrew (2005). *Hubris and Hybrids: A Cultural History of Technology and Science*. New York: Routledge.

Hardin, Michael (1997). "Mapping Post-War Anxieties onto Space: *Invasion of the Body Snatchers* and *Invaders from Mars*." *Enculturation*, vol. 1, issue 1. <http://enculturation.gmu.edu/1_1/hardin.html>. Accessed March 13, 2007.

Hardt, Michael, & Negri, Antonio (2000). *Empire*. Cambridge, MA: Harvard University Press.

Hardt, Michael, & Negri, Antonio (2004). *Multitude: War and Democracy in the Age of Empire*. New York: Penguin Press.

Harrasser, Karin (2002). "Transforming Discourse into Practice: Computerhystories and Digital Cultures around 1984." *Cultural Studies*, vol. 16, issue 6, 820–832.

Hayles, Katherine N. (1999). *How We Became Posthuman: Virtual Bodies in Cybernetics, Literature, and Informatics*. Chicago: University of Chicago Press.

Hebdige, Dick (1985). *Subculture: The Meaning of Style*. London: Methuen.

Heidegger, Martin (1993). *Basic Writings: From Being and Time (1927) to The Task of Thinking (1964)*. Edited by David Farrell Krell. San Francisco: Harper.

Heidegger, Martin (1996). *Being and Time* (Orig. 1927). Translated by Joan Stambaugh. Albany: SUNY Press.

Heims, Joshua (1980). *John Von Neumann and Norbert Wiener: From Mathematics to the Technologies of Life and Death*. Cambridge, MA: MIT Press.

Helmreich, Stefan (2000a). "Flexible Infections: Computer Viruses, Human Bodies, Nation-States, Evolutionary Capitalism." *Science, Technology, & Human Values*, vol. 25, issue 4, 472–491.

Helmreich, Stefan (2000b). *Silicon Second Nature: Culturing Artificial Life in a Digital World*. Updated edition with a new preface. Berkeley: University of California Press.

Heylighen, Francis, & Joslyn, Cliff (2001). "Cybernetics and Second-Order Cybernetics." In: *Encyclopedia of Physical Science & Technology*, 3rd. ed., edited by R. A. Meyers. New York: Academic Press.

Hiltzik, Michal (1999). *Dealers of Lightning: Xerox PARC and the Dawn of the Computer Age*. New York: HarperBusiness.

Hughes, Thomas P. (1989). *American Genesis: A Century of Invention and Technological Enthusiasm 1870–1970*. New York: Viking.

Huhtamo, Erkki (1995). "Armchair Traveller on the Ford of Jordan: The Home, the Stereoscope and the Virtual Voyager." *Mediamatic*, vol. 8, issue 2, 3. <http://www.mediamatic.net/article-5910-en.html>. Accessed January 24, 2007.

Huhtamo, Erkki (1996). "From Cybernation to Interaction: Ein Beitrag zu einer Archäologie der Interaktivität." In: *Wunschmaschine Welterfindung. Eine Geschichte der Technikvisionen seit dem 18. Jahrhundert* (pp. 192–207). New York: Springer.

Huhtamo, Erkki (1997). "From Kaleidoscomaniac to Cybernerd: Notes Toward an Archaeology of the Media." *Leonardo*, vol. 30, issue 3, 221–224.

Huhtamo, Erkki (2011). "Dismantling the Fairy Engine: Media Archaeology as Topos Study." In: *Media Archaeology: Approaches, Applications and Implications*, edited by Erkki Huhtamo & Jussi Parikka (pp. 24–47). Berkeley: University of California Press.

Johnston, John (1997). "Friedrich Kittler: Media Theory after Poststructuralism." In: *Literature, Media, Information Systems: Essays by Friedrich A. Kittler*, edited and introduced by John Johnston (pp. 2–26). Amsterdam: G+B Arts International.

Johnston, John (2008). *The Allure of Machinic Life: Cybernetics, Artificial Life, and the New AI*. Cambridge, MA: MIT Press.

Johnston, John (2009). "Mutant and Viral: Artificial Evolution and Software Ecology." In: *The Spam Book: On Porn, Viruses and Other Anomalies from the Dark Side of Digital Culture*, edited by Jussi Parikka and Tony Sampson (pp. 23–38). Cresskill, NJ: Hampton Press.

Kay, Lily E. (2000). *Who Wrote the Book of Life? A History of the Genetic Code*. Stanford, CA: Stanford University Press.

Kittler, Friedrich (1990). *Discourse Networks 1800/1900* (Orig. 1985). Translated by Michael Metteer, with Chris Cullens. Stanford, CA: Stanford University Press.

Kittler, Friedrich (1993a). "Es gibt keine Software." In: *Draculas Vermächtnis. Technische Schriften* (pp. 225–242). Leipzig: Reclam Leipzig. English version: "There Is No Software." published in *CTheory* (1996). <http://www.ctheory.net/articles.aspx?id=74>. Accessed March 13, 2007.

Kittler, Friedrich (1993b). "Protected Mode." In: *Draculas Vermächtnis. Technische Schriften* (pp. 208–224). Leipzig: Reclam.

Kittler, Friedrich (1996). "The History of Communication Media." *Ctheory*, July 30, 1996. <http://www.ctheory.net/text_file.asp?pick=45>. Accessed March 13, 2007.

Kittler, Friedrich (1997). "Dracula's Legacy." In: *Literature, Media, Information Systems*, edited by John Johnston (pp. 50–84). Amsterdam: G+B Arts.

Kittler, Friedrich (1999). *Gramophone, Film, Typewriter* (Orig. 1986). Translated by Geoffrey-Winthrop-Young & Michael Wutz. Stanford, CA: Stanford University Press.

Kittler, Friedrich (2001). *Eine Kulturgeschichte der Kulturwissenschaft*. 2, verbesserte Auflage. München: Wilhelm Fink.

Kittler, Friedrich (2014). "No Such Agency" (trans. Paul Feigelfeld). *Theory, Culture & Society*, February 12, 2014. <http://theoryculturesociety.org/kittler-on-the-nsa/>.

Kruger, Steven F. (1996). *Aids Narratives: Gender and Sexuality, Fiction and Science*. New York & London: Garland Publishing.

Künzel, Werner, & Bexte, Peter (1993). *Allwissen un Absturz. Der Ursprung des Computers*. Frankfurt am Main: Insel.

Lafontaine, Céline (2004). *L'empire cybernétique. Des machines à penser à la pensée machine*. Paris: Èditions du Seuil.

Lampert, Jay (2006). *Deleuze and Guattari's Philosophy of History*. London: Continuum.

Lash, Scott, & Urry, John (1987). *The End Of Organized Capitalism*. Cambridge: Polity Press.

Latour, Bruno (1993). *We Have Never Been Modern* (Orig. 1991). Translated by Catherine Porter. New York: Harvester Wheatsheaf.

Latour, Bruno (2004). *Politics of Nature: How to Bring the Sciences into Democracy* (Orig. 1999). Translated by Catherine Porter. Cambridge, MA: Harvard University Press.

Latour, Bruno (2005). *Reassembling the Social: An Introduction to Actor-Network-Theory*. Oxford: Oxford University Press.

Lazzarato, Maurizio (2004). "From Capital-Labour to Capital-Life." *Ephemera: Theory and Politics in Organization*, vol.4, issue 3. <http://www.ephemeraweb.org/journal/4-3/4-3index. htm>. Accessed March 13, 2007.

Lister, Martin et al. (2003). *New Media: A Critical Introduction*. London: Routledge.

Lovink, Geert (2003). *Dark Fiber: Tracking Critical Internet Culture*. Cambridge, MA: MIT Press.

Lundemo, Trond (2003). "Why Things Don't Work: Imagining New Technologies from *The Electric Life* to the Digital." In: *Experiencing the Media: Assemblages and Cross-overs*, edited by Tanja Sihvonen & Pasi Väliaho (pp. 13–28). Turku: University of Turku.

Lupton, Deborah (1994). "Panic Computing: The Viral Metaphor and Computer Technology." *Cultural Studies*, vol. 8, issue 3, 556–568.

Mackenzie, Adrian (1996). "'God Has No Allergies': Immanent Ethics and the Simulacra of the Immune System." *Postmodern Culture*, vol. 6, issue 2. <http://www3.iath.virginia.edu/ pmc/text-only/issue.196/mackenzie.196>. Accessed March 8, 2007.

Mackenzie, Adrian (2006). *Cutting Code: Software and Sociality*. New York: Peter Lang.

Magner, Lois N. (2002). *History of the Life Sciences*. 3rd ed. New York: Marcel Dekker.

Manovich, Lev (2001). *The Language of New Media*. Cambridge, MA: MIT Press.

Marshall, Jon (2003). "Internet Politics in an Information Economy." *Fibreculture Journal*, issue 1. <http://journal.fibreculture.org/issue1/issue1_marshall.html>. Accessed January 22, 2007.

Martin, Emily (1994). *Flexible Bodies: The Role of Immunity in American Culture from the Days of Polio to the Age of AIDS*. Boston: Beacon Press.

Marvin, Carolyn (1988). *When Old Technologies Were New: Thinking about Electric Communication in the Late Nineteenth Century*. New York: Oxford University Press.

Massumi, Brian (1992). *A User's Guide to Capitalism and Schizophrenia: Deviations from Deleuze and Guattari*. Cambridge MA: MIT Press.

Massumi, Brian (1993). "Everywhere You Want to Be: Introduction to Fear." In: *The Politics of Everyday Fear*, edited by Brian Massumi (pp. 3–37). Minneapolis: University of Minnesota Press.

Massumi, Brian (2002). *Parables for the Virtual: Movement, Affect, Sensation*. Durham, NC: Duke University Press.

Massumi, Brian (2005). "The Future Birth of the Affective Fact." In: *Conference Proceedings of Genealogies of Biopolitics*, October 2005. <http://www.radicalempiricism.org/biotextes/textes/massumi.pdf>. Accessed January 12, 2007.

Mattelart, Armand (2003). *The Information Society: An Introduction* (Orig. 2001). Translated by Susan G. Taponier & James A. Cohen. London: SAGE.

Mayer, Ruth, & Weingart, Brigitte (eds.) (2004a). *Virus! Mutationen einer Metapher*. Bielefeld: Transcript.

Mayer, Ruth, & Weingart, Brigitte (2004b). "Viren zirkulieren. Eine Einleitung." In *Virus! Mutationen einer Metapher*, edited by Ruth Mayer & Brigitte Weingart (pp. 7–41). Bielefeld: Transcript.

McCarron, Kevin (1996). "Corpses, Animals, Machines and Mannequins: The Body and Cyberpunk." In: *Cyberspace/Cyberbodies/Cyberpunk: Cultures of Technological Embodiment*, edited by Mike Featherstone & Roger Burrows (pp. 261–273). London: Sage.

McLuhan, Marshall (1962). *The Gutenberg Galaxy*. Toronto: Toronto University Press.

McNeill, William (1998). *Plagues and People*. New York: Anchor Books.

Mitchell, Peta (2012). *Contagious Metaphor*. London: Bloomsbury.

Mosco, Vincent (2004). *The Digital Sublime: Myth, Power, and Cyberspace*. Cambridge, MA: MIT Press.

Munster, Anna, & Lovink, Geert (2005). "Theses on Distributed Aesthetics. Or, What a Network Is Not." *Fibreculture Journal*, issue 7. <http://journal.fibreculture.org/issue7/issue7_munster_lovink.html>. Accessed January 12, 2007.

Murphie, Andrew, & Potts, Jon (2003). *Culture & Technology*. New York: Palgrave Macmillan.

Nissenbaum, Helen (2004). "Hackers and the Contested Ontology of Cyberspace." *New Media & Society*, vol. 6, issue 2, 195–217.

Nixon, Rob (2011). *Slow Violence and the Environmentalism of the Poor*. Cambridge, MA: Harvard University Press.

Nunes, Mark (ed.) (2010). *Error: Glitch, Noise, and Jam in New Media Cultures*. London: Bloomsbury.

Olkowski, Dorothea (1999). *Gilles Deleuze and the Ruin of Representation*. Berkeley: University of California Press.

O'Neill, Mathieu (2006). "Rebels for the System: Virus Writers, General Intellect, Cyberpunk and Criminal Capitalism." *Continuum: Journal of Media & Culture Studies*, vol. 20, issue 2, 225–241.

Otis, Laura (1999). *Membranes: Metaphors of Invasion in Nineteenth-Century Literature, Science and Politics*. Baltimore: Johns Hopkins University Press.

Parikka, Jussi (2005a). "Digital Monsters, Binary Aliens-Computer Viruses, Capitalism and the Flow of Information." *Fibreculture Journal*, issue 4, "Contagion and the Diseases of Information," edited by Andrew Goffey. <http://journal.fibreculture.org/issue4/issue4_parikka.html>. Accessed March 6, 2007.

Parikka, Jussi (2005b). "Viral Noise and the (Dis)Order of the Digital Culture." *M/C Journal*, vol. 7, issue 6, May 19, 2005. <http://journal.media-culture.org.au/0501/05-parikka.php>. Accessed March 8, 2007.

Parikka, Jussi (2005c). "The Universal Viral Machine: Bits, Parasites and the Media Ecology of Network Culture." *CTheory*, December 15, 2005. <http://www.ctheory.net/articles.aspx?id=500>. Accessed March 7, 2007.

Parikka, Jussi (2007). "Fictitious Contagions: Computer Viruses in the Science Fiction of the 1970s." In: *SciFi in the Mind's Eye: Reading Science through Science Fiction*, edited by Margret Grebowicz. Chicago: Open Court.

Parikka, Jussi (2010). *Insect Media: An Archaeology of Animals and Technology*. Minneapolis: University of Minnesota Press.

Parikka, Jussi, & Sampson, Tony (eds.) (2009). *The Spam Book: On Porn, Viruses and Other Anomalous Objects from the Dark Side of Digital Culture*. Cresskill, NJ: Hampton Press.

Parikka, Jussi, & Tiainen, Milla (2006). "Kohti materiaalisen ja uuden kulttuurianalyysia-tai representaation hyödystä ja haitasta elämälle." *Kulttuurintutkimus*, vol. 23, issue 2, 3–20.

Parisi, Luciana (2004a). *Abstract Sex: Philosophy, Bio-Technology and the Mutations of Desire*. London: Continuum.

Parisi, Luciana (2004b). "For a Schizogenesis of Sexual Difference." *Identities: Journal for Politics, Gender and Culture*, vol. 3, issue 1, 67–93.

Patton, Cindy (2002). *Globalizing AIDS*. Minneapolis: University of Minnesota Press.

Pisters, Patricia (2001). "Glamour and Glycerine: Surplus and Residual of the Network Society: From Glamorama to Fight Club." In: *Micropolitics of Media Culture: Reading the Rhizomes of Deleuze and Guattari*, edited by Patricia Pisters, with the assistance of Catherine M. Lord (pp. 125–141). Amsterdam: Amsterdam University Press.

Pividal, Rafaël (1999). "Leibniz ou le rationalisme poussé jusqu'au paradoxe" (Orig. 1972). In: *La philosophie du monde nouveau du XVI et XVII siècle. Histoire de la Philosophie III*, edited by Francois Châtelet. Paris: Hachette.

Plant, Sadie (1996). "On the Matrix: Cyberfeminist Simulations." In: *Cultures of the Internet: Virtual Spaces, Real Histories, Living Bodies*, edited by Rob Shields (pp. 170–183). London: Sage.

Porush, David (1994). "Hacking the Brainstem: Postmodern Metaphysics and Stephenson's *Snow Crash*." *Configurations*, vol. 2, issue 3, 537–571.

Protevi, John (2001). *Political Physics: Deleuze, Derrida and the Body Politic.* London: Athlone Press.

Redhead, Steve (2004). *Paul Virilio: Theorist for an Accelerated Culture.* Toronto: University of Toronto Press.

Reith, Gerda (2004). "Uncertain Times: The Notion of 'Risk' and the Development of Modernity." *Time & Society,* vol. 13, issue 2/3, 383–402.

Riskin, Jessica (2003). "The Defecating Duck, or, The Ambiguous Origins of Artificial Life." *Critical Inquiry,* vol. 20, issue 4, 599–633.

Rodowick, D. N. (2001). *Reading the Figural, or, Philosophy After the New Media.* Durham, NC: Duke University Press.

Ross, Andrew (1990). "Hacking Away at the Counterculture." *Postmodern Culture,* vol. 1, issue 1. <http://www3.iath.virginia.edu/pmc/text-only/issue.990/ross-1.990>. Accessed March 13, 2007.

Ross, Andrew (1991). *Strange Weather: Culture, Science and Technology in the Age of Limits.* London: Verso.

Saarikoski, Petri (2004). *Koneen lumo.Mikrotietokoneharrastus Suomessa 1970-luvulta 1990-luvun puoliväliin.* Jyväskylä: Nykykulttuurin tutkimuskeskuksen julkaisuja 83.

Salmi, Hannu (1995). "Elämän tragedia. Katastrofin pelon historiaa." *Historiallinen Aikakauskirja,* vol. 3, 195–203.

Salmi, Hannu (1996). "*Atoomipommilla kuuhun!*" *Tekniikan mentaalihistoriaa.* Helsinki: Edita.

Salmi, Hannu (2006). "Televisio, tietokone ja tietämisen politiikka." In: *Välimuistiin kirjoitetut. Lukuja Suomen tietoteknistymisen kulttuurihistoriaan,* edited by Hannu Salmi et al. (pp. 55–79). Turku: K&H.

Sampson, Tony (2004) "A Virus in Info-Space: The Open Network and Its Enemies." *M/C: A Journal of Media and Culture.* <http://journal.media-culture.org.au/0406/07_Sampson.php>. Accessed March 8, 2007.

Sampson, Tony (2005). "Dr Aycock's Bad Idea: Is the Good Use of Computer Viruses Still a Bad Idea?" *M/C Journal,* vol. 8, issue 1. <http://journal.media-culture.org.au/0502/02-sampson.php>. Accessed March 8, 2007.

Sampson, Tony (2009). "How Networks Become Viral." In *The Spam Book: On Porn, Viruses and Other Anomalies from the Dark Side of Digital Culture,* edited by Jussi Parikka & Tony Sampson. Cresskill, NJ: Hampton Press.

Sampson, Tony (2012). *Virality: Contagion Theory in Network Culture.* Minneapolis: University of Minnesota Press.

Sasso, Robert, & Villani, Arnaud (eds.) (2003). *Le Vocabulaire de Gilles Deleuze.* Nice: Les Cahiers de Noesis. Centre de Recherches d'Histoire des Idées, l'Université de Nice-Sophia Antipolis.

Schivelbusch, Wolfgang (1977). *Geschichte der Eisenbahnreise. Zur Industrialisierung von Raum und Zeit im 19. Jahrhundert.* München and Wien: Hanser.

Sconce, Jeffrey (2000). *Haunted Media: Electronic Presence from Telegraphy to Television.* Durham, NC: Duke University Press.

Seltzer, Mark (1992). *Bodies and Machines.* New York: Routledge.

Sennett, Richard (1994). *Flesh and Stone: The Body and the City in Western Civilization*. London: W. W. Norton & Company.

Serres, Michel (1982). *The Parasite*. Translated by Lawrence R. Schehr. Baltimore: Johns Hopkins University Press.

Shaviro, Steven (2003). *Connected, or What It Means to Live in the Network Society*. Minneapolis: University of Minnesota Press.

Siegert, Bernhard (2015). *Cultural Techniques: Grids, Filters, Doors, and Other Articulations of the Real*. Translated by Geoffrey Winthrop-Young. New York: Fordham University Press.

Slack, Jennifer Daryl, & Wise, J. Macgregor (2002). "Cultural Studies & Technology." In: *Handbook of New Media: Social Shaping and Consequences of ICTs*, edited by Leah A. Lievrouw & Sonia Livingstone (pp. 485–501). London: Sage.

Sontag, Susan (2002). *Illness as Metaphor and AIDS and Its Metaphors* (Orig. 1979 and 1989). London: Penguin Books.

Speidel, Michelle (2000). "The Parasitic Host: Symbiosis *contra* Neo-Darwinism." *Pli*, vol. 9, 119–138.

Spinoza, Benedict (2001). *Ethics*. Translated by W. H. White and A. H. Stirling. Hertfordshire: Wordsworth Editions.

Sprenger, Florian (2015). *Politics of Microdecisions*. Luneburg: Meson Press.

Starosielski, Nicole (2015). *The Undersea Network*. Durham, NC: Duke University Press.

Stengers, Isabelle (2000). "God's Heart and the Stuff of Life." *Pli*, vol. 9, 86–118.

Stone-Gross, Brett et al. (2009). "Your Botnet Is My Botnet: An Analysis of a Botnet Takeover." CCS '09, paper. <https://seclab.cs.ucsb.edu/media/uploads/papers/torpig.pdf>.

Suominen, Jaakko (2003). *Koneen kokemus. Tietoteknistyvä kulttuuri modernisoituvassa Suomessa 1920-luvulta 1970-luvulle*. Tampere: Vastapaino.

Terranova, Tiziana (2004). *Network Culture: Politics for the Information Age*. London: Pluto Press.

Thacker, Eugene (2004). "Networks, Swarms, Multitudes. Part One." *CTheory*, May 18, 2004. <http://www.ctheory.net/articles.aspx?id=422>. Accessed December 28, 2006.

Thacker, Eugene (2005). "Living Dead Networks." *Fibreculture Journal*, issue 4, "Contagion and the Diseases of Information," edited by Andrew Goffey. <http://journal.fibreculture.org/issue4/issue4_thacker.html>. Accessed March 6, 2007.

Tomes, Nancy (1998). *The Gospel of Germs: Men, Women, and the Microbe in American Life*. Cambridge, MA: Harvard University Press.

Trogemann, Georg (2005). "Experimentelle und spekulative Informatik." In: *Zukünfte des Computers*, edited by Heausgegeben von Claus Pias(pp. 109–132). Zürich-Berlin: Diaphanes.

Turkle, Sherry (1996). *Life on the Screen: Identity in the Age of the Internet*. London: Weidenfeld & Nicolson.

Turner, Bryan S. (2003). "Social Fluids: Metaphors and Meanings of Society." *Body & Society*, vol. 9, issue 1, 1–10.

Turner, Fred (2006). *From Counterculture to Cyberculture: Stewart Brand, the Whole Earth Network, and the Rise of Digital Utopianism*. Chicago: University of Chicago Press.

Urry, John (2003). *Global Complexity*. Cambridge: Polity Press.

Van Helvoort, Ton (1996). "When Did Virology Start?" *ASM News*, vol. 62, issue 3, 142–145.

Van Loon, Joost (2000). "Virtual Risks in an Age of Cybernetic Reproduction." In: *The Risk Society and Beyond: Critical Issues for Social Theory*, edited by Barbara Adam, Ulrich Beck, & Joost Van Loon (pp. 165–181). London: SAGE.

Van Loon, Joost (2002a). "A Contagious Living Fluid: Objectification and Assemblage in the History of Virology." *Theory, Culture & Society*, vol. 19, issue 5/6, 107–124.

Van Loon, Joost (2002b). *Risk and Technological Culture: Towards a Sociology of Virulence.* London: Routledge.

Virilio, Paul (1993). "The Primal Accident" (translated by Brian Massumi). In: *The Politics of Everyday Fear*, edited by Brian Massumi (pp. 210–218). Minneapolis: University of Minnesota Press.

Virilio, Paul, & Kittler, Friedrich (1999). "The Information Bomb: A Conversation." Edited and introduced by John Armitage. In: Special issue, *Machinic Modulations: New Cultural Theory & Technopolitics* of *Angelaki: Journal of the Theoretical Humanities*, vol. 4, issue 2, 81–90.

Vuorinen, Heikki S. (2002). *Tautinen historia.* Tampere: Vastapaino.

Väliaho, Pasi (2003). "From Mediasphere to Mediasophy—Nature, Machine, Media." In: *Experiencing the Media: Assemblages and Cross-overs*, edited by Tanja Sihvonen & Pasi Väliaho (pp. 281–299). Turku: Media Studies, University of Turku.

Wark, McKenzie (1994). "Third Nature." *Cultural Studies*, vol. 8, issue 1, 115–132.

Weingart, Brigitte (2004). "Viren visualisieren: Bildgebung und Popularisierung." In: *Virus! Mutationen einer Metapher*, edited by Ruth Mayer & Brigitte Weingart (pp. 97–130). Bielefeld: Transcript.

Weinstock, Jeffrey A. (1997). "Virus Culture." *Studies in Popular Culture*, vol. 20, issue 1, 83–97. <http://www.pcasacas.org/SPC/spcissues/20.1/weinstock.htm>. Accessed March 8, 2007.

Whitelaw, Mitchell (2004). *Metacreation: Art and Artificial Life.* Cambridge, MA: MIT Press.

Wiley, Stephen B. Crofts (2005). "Spatial Materialism: Grossberg's Deleuzean Cultural Studies." *Cultural Studies*, vol. 19, issue 1, 63–99.

Winthrop-Young, Geoffrey, Jussi Parikka, & Ilinca Iurascu (eds.) (2013). Cultural Techniques special issue. *Theory, Culture & Society*, vol. 30, issue 6.

Wise, J. Macgregor (1997). *Exploring Technology and Social Space.* London: Sage.

Zielinski, Siegfried (1999). *Audiovisions: Cinema and Television as Entr'actes in History.* Translated by Gloria Custance. Amsterdam: Amsterdam University Press.

Zielinski, Siegfried (2006). *Deep Time of the Media: Toward an Archaeology of Hearing and Seeing by Technical Means* (Orig. 2002). Translated by Gloria Custance. Cambridge, MA: MIT Press.

Žižek, Slavoj (2004). *Organs without Bodies: On Deleuze and Consequences.* New York: Routledge.

INDEX

General Editor: **Steve Jones**

Digital Formations is the best source for critical, well-written books about digital technologies and modern life. Books in the series break new ground by emphasizing multiple methodological and theoretical approaches to deeply probe the formation and reformation of lived experience as it is refracted through digital interaction. Each volume in **Digital Formations** pushes forward our understanding of the intersections, and corresponding implications, between digital technologies and everyday life. The series examines broad issues in realms such as digital culture, electronic commerce, law, politics and governance, gender, the Internet, race, art, health and medicine, and education. The series emphasizes critical studies in the context of emergent and existing digital technologies.

Other recent titles include:

Felicia Wu Song
  Virtual Communities: Bowling Alone, Online Together

Edited by Sharon Kleinman
  The Culture of Efficiency: Technology in Everyday Life

Edward Lee Lamoureux, Steven L. Baron, & Claire Stewart
  Intellectual Property Law and Interactive Media: Free for a Fee

Edited by Adrienne Russell & Nabil Echchaibi
  International Blogging: Identity, Politics and Networked Publics

Edited by Don Heider
  Living Virtually: Researching New Worlds

Edited by Judith Burnett, Peter Senker & Kathy Walker
  The Myths of Technology: Innovation and Inequality

Edited by Knut Lundby
  Digital Storytelling, Mediatized Stories: Self-representations in New Media

Theresa M. Senft
  Camgirls: Celebrity and Community in the Age of Social Networks

Edited by Chris Paterson & David Domingo
  Making Online News: The Ethnography of New Media Production

To order other books in this series please contact our Customer Service Department:
  (800) 770-LANG (within the US)
  (212) 647-7706 (outside the US)
  (212) 647-7707 FAX

To find out more about the series or browse a full list of titles, please visit our website:
  WWW.PETERLANG.COM